Shojo Beat

BE EDGE

Vol. 5

Story & Art by
Io Sakisaka

STROBE EDGE

Volume 5
CONTENTS

Story Thus Far

Ninako is a down-to-earth high school girl who's in love for the first time—with Ren, the most popular boy in her grade. Even though she knows he has a girlfriend, she can't deny her feelings for him and tells him. She's not surprised when he turns her down and asks if they can still be friends.

During the new school year, Ninako meets Takumi Ando, a guy who doesn't seem to take anything seriously. But as they get to know each other, Ando falls for Ninako. After Ninako, Ren and Ando start working part-time at a café together, Ando tells Ninako how he feels about her, but her feelings for Ren remain unchanged.

Meanwhile, friends begin to notice subtle changes in Ren's behavior toward Ninako, but he keeps his feelings in check. While his girlfriend, Mayuka, is devastated by the fact that her father is getting remarried, Ren is determined to stay by her side. He begins to distance himself from Ninako...

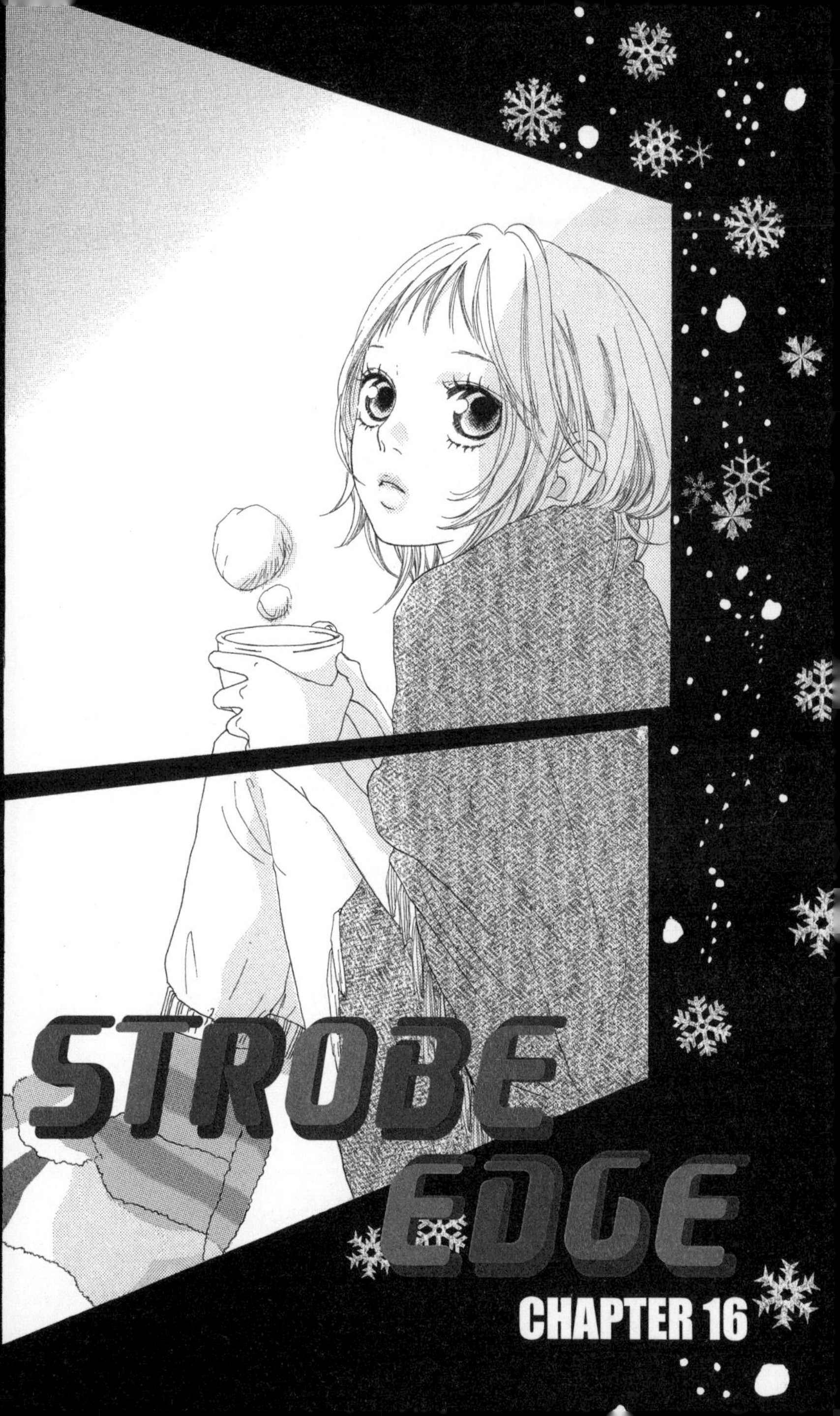
STROBE EDGE
CHAPTER 16

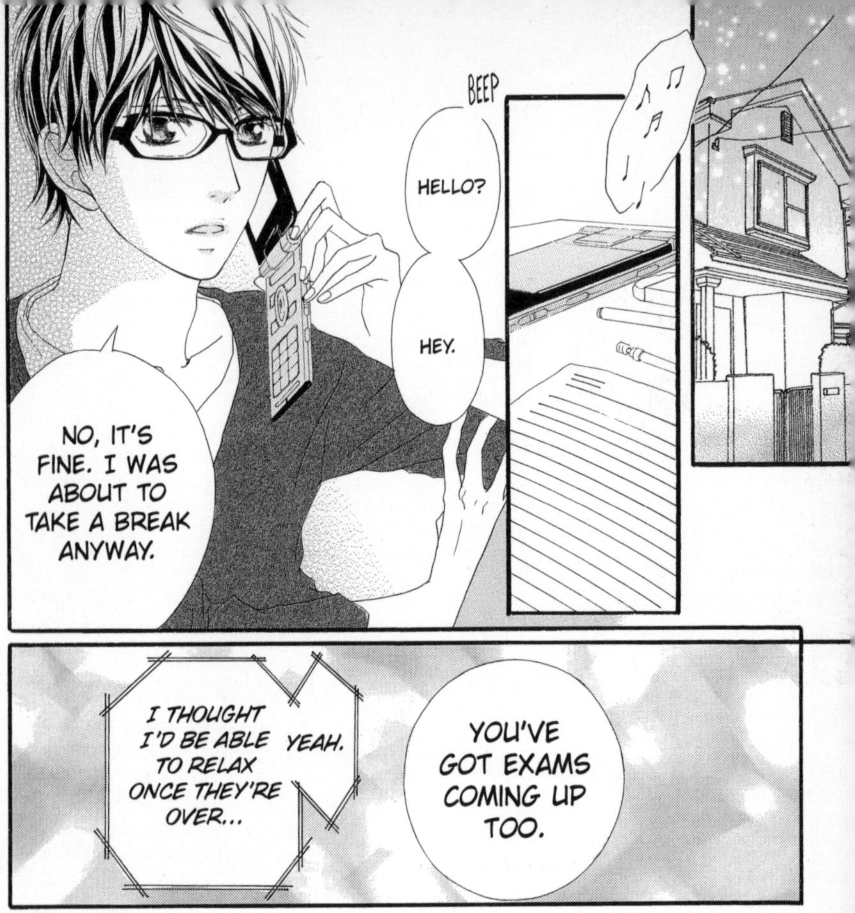
BEEP
HELLO?
HEY.
NO, IT'S FINE. I WAS ABOUT TO TAKE A BREAK ANYWAY.
YOU'VE GOT EXAMS COMING UP TOO.
YEAH.
I THOUGHT I'D BE ABLE TO RELAX ONCE THEY'RE OVER...

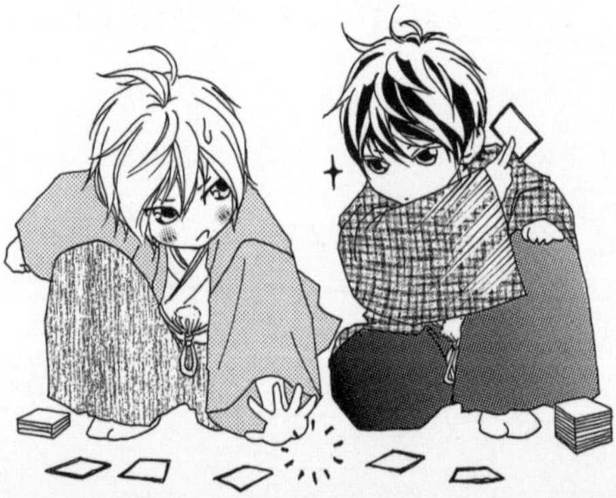

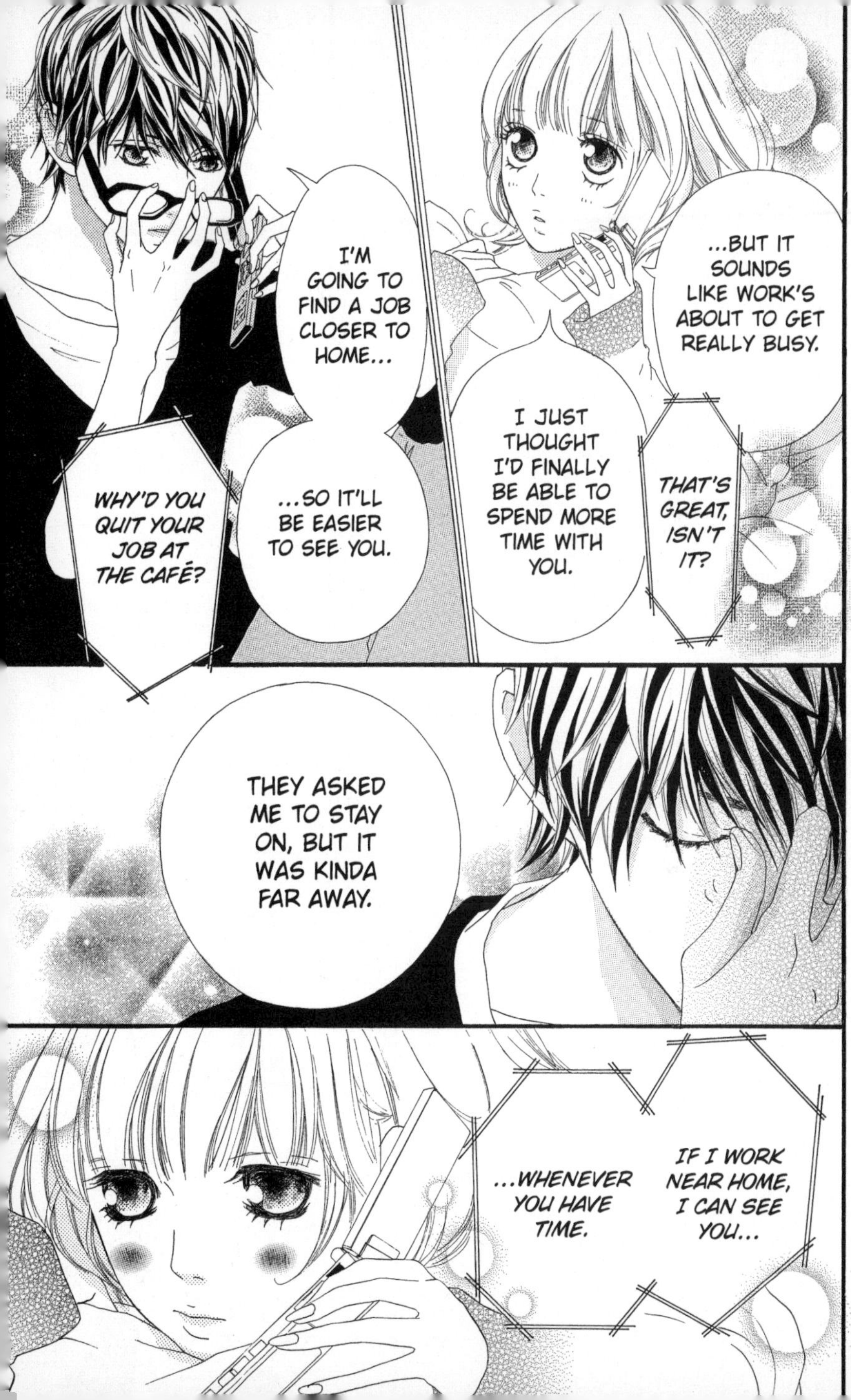
...BUT IT SOUNDS LIKE WORK'S ABOUT TO GET REALLY BUSY.
THAT'S GREAT, ISN'T IT?
I JUST THOUGHT I'D FINALLY BE ABLE TO SPEND MORE TIME WITH YOU.
I'M GOING TO FIND A JOB CLOSER TO HOME...
...SO IT'LL BE EASIER TO SEE YOU.
WHY'D YOU QUIT YOUR JOB AT THE CAFÉ?
THEY ASKED ME TO STAY ON, BUT IT WAS KINDA FAR AWAY.
IF I WORK NEAR HOME, I CAN SEE YOU...
...WHENEVER YOU HAVE TIME.

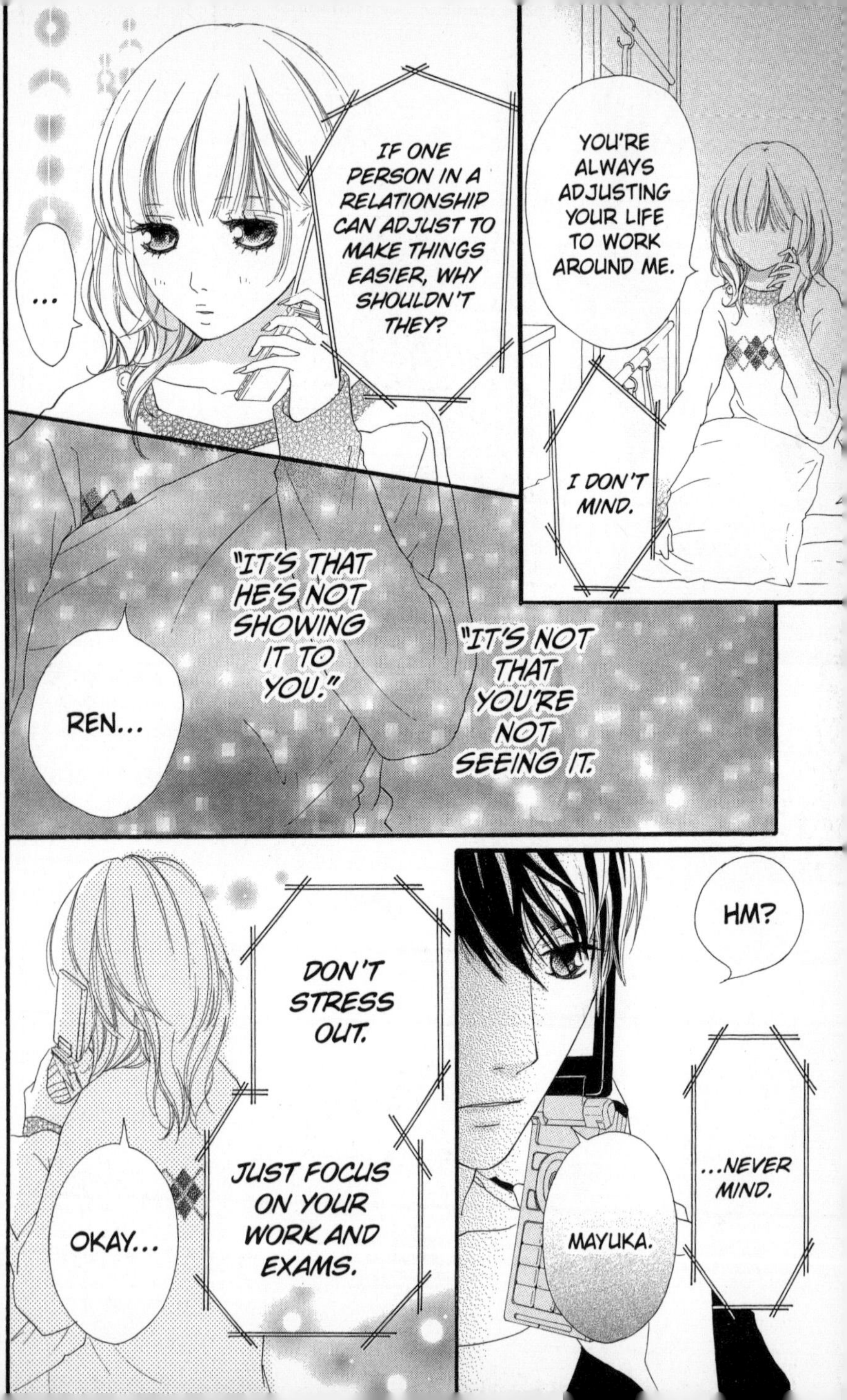
YOU'RE ALWAYS ADJUSTING YOUR LIFE TO WORK AROUND ME.
I DON'T MIND.
IF ONE PERSON IN A RELATIONSHIP CAN ADJUST TO MAKE THINGS EASIER, WHY SHOULDN'T THEY?
...
"IT'S NOT THAT YOU'RE NOT SEEING IT.
"IT'S THAT HE'S NOT SHOWING IT TO YOU."
REN...
HM?
...NEVER MIND.
MAYUKA.
DON'T STRESS OUT.
JUST FOCUS ON YOUR WORK AND EXAMS.
OKAY...

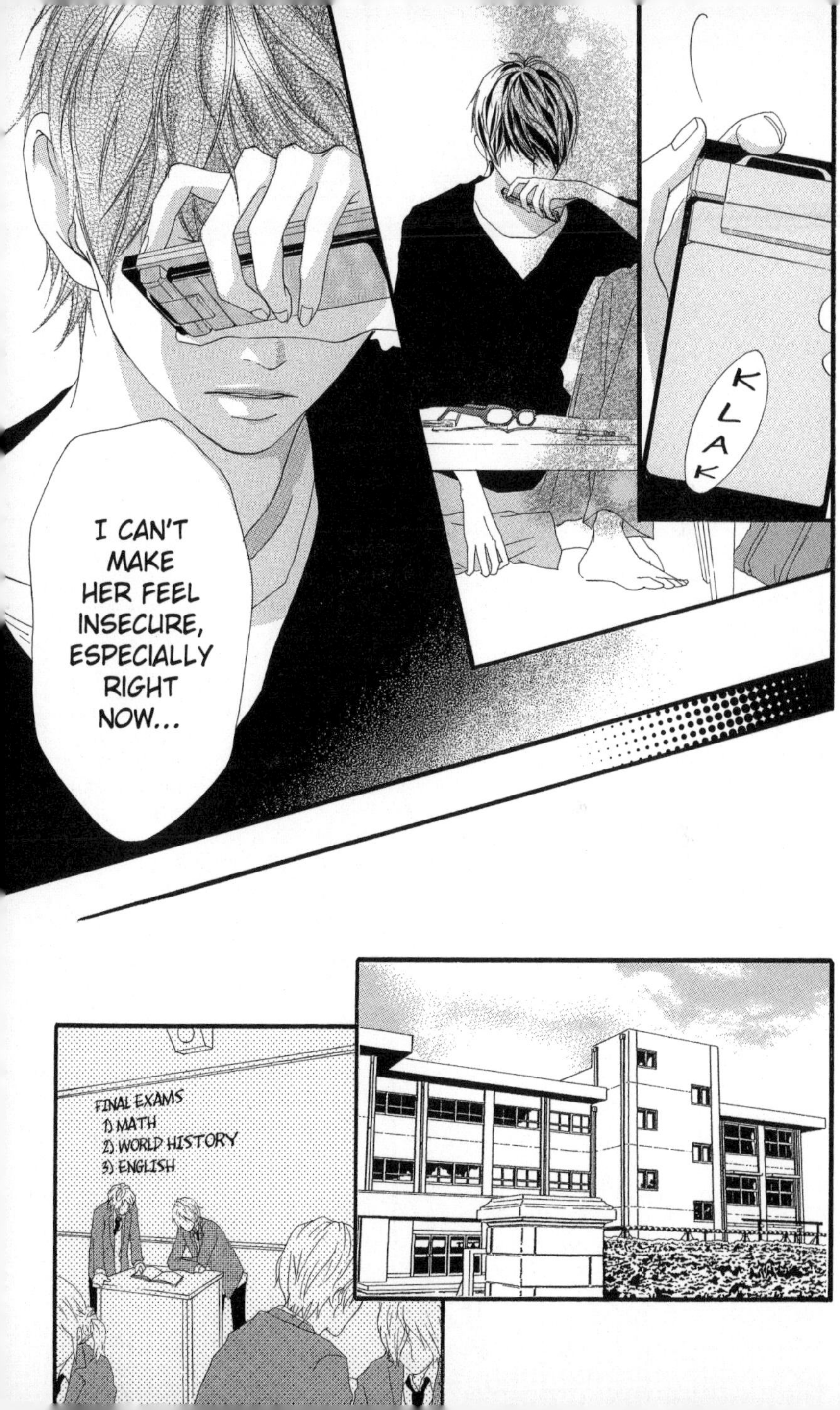
KLAK
I CAN'T MAKE HER FEEL INSECURE, ESPECIALLY RIGHT NOW...
FINAL EXAMS
1) MATH
2) WORLD HISTORY
3) ENGLISH

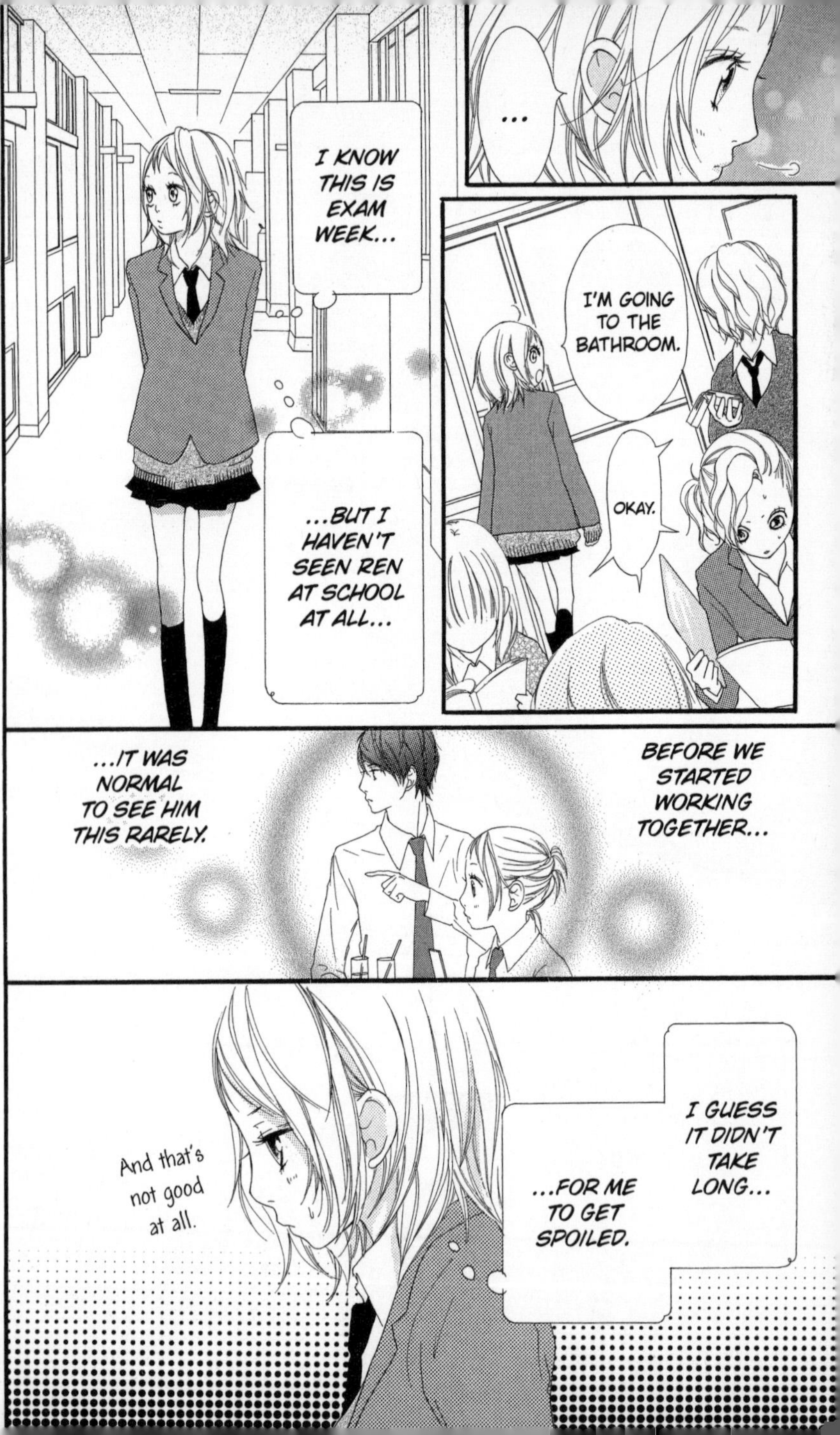
...
I'M GOING TO THE BATHROOM.
OKAY.
I KNOW THIS IS EXAM WEEK...
...BUT I HAVEN'T SEEN REN AT SCHOOL AT ALL...
BEFORE WE STARTED WORKING TOGETHER...
...IT WAS NORMAL TO SEE HIM THIS RARELY.
I GUESS IT DIDN'T TAKE LONG...
...FOR ME TO GET SPOILED.
And that's not good at all.

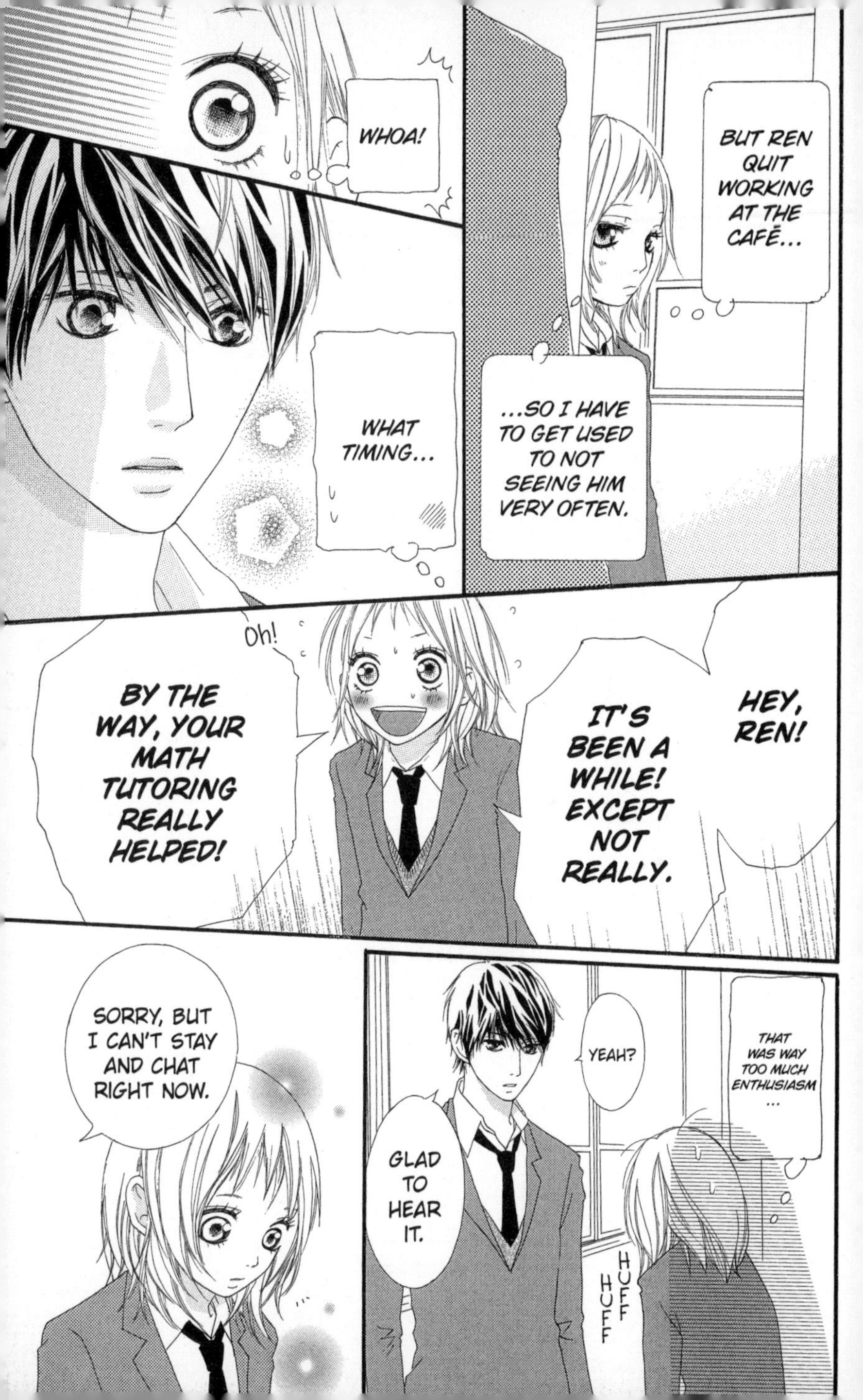
BUT REN QUIT WORKING AT THE CAFÉ...
...SO I HAVE TO GET USED TO NOT SEEING HIM VERY OFTEN.
WHOA!
WHAT TIMING...
HEY, REN!
IT'S BEEN A WHILE! EXCEPT NOT REALLY.
Oh!
BY THE WAY, YOUR MATH TUTORING REALLY HELPED!
THAT WAS WAY TOO MUCH ENTHUSIASM ...
YEAH?
GLAD TO HEAR IT.
HUFF HUFF
SORRY, BUT I CAN'T STAY AND CHAT RIGHT NOW.

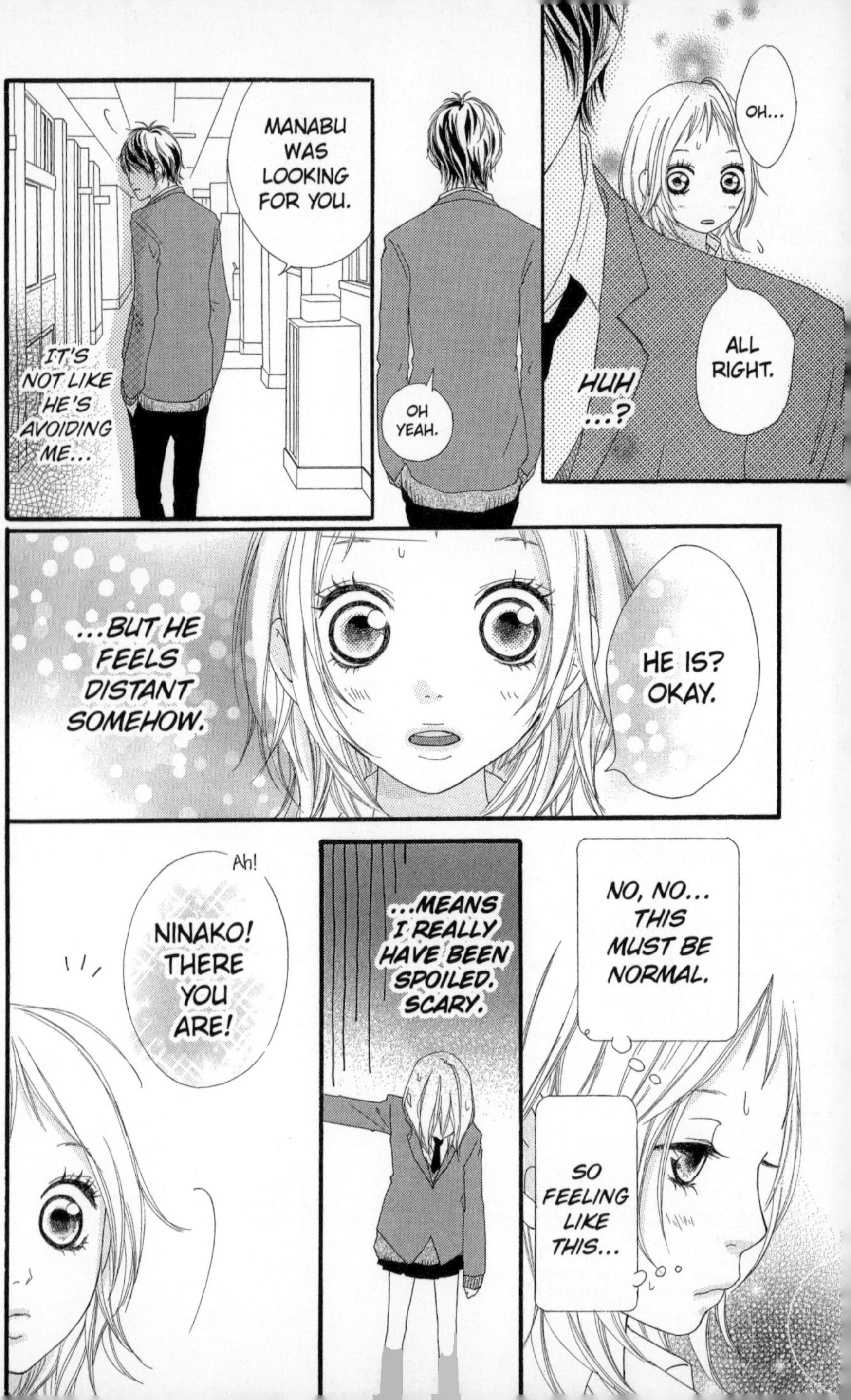
OH...
ALL RIGHT.
HUH ...?
OH YEAH.
MANABU WAS LOOKING FOR YOU.
IT'S NOT LIKE HE'S AVOIDING ME...
HE IS? OKAY.
...BUT HE FEELS DISTANT SOMEHOW.
NO, NO... THIS MUST BE NORMAL.
SO FEELING LIKE THIS...
...MEANS I REALLY HAVE BEEN SPOILED. SCARY.
Ah!
NINAKO! THERE YOU ARE!

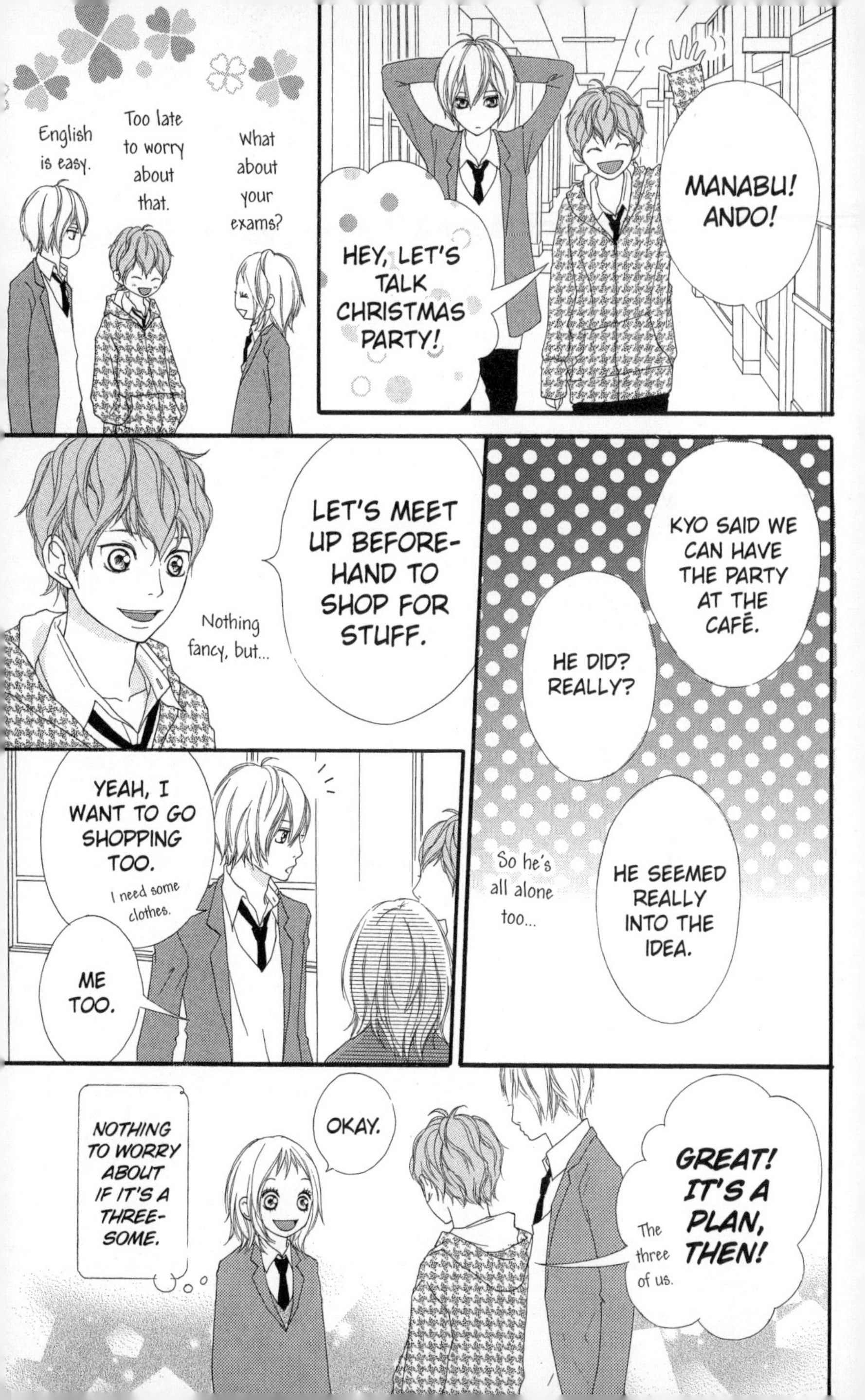
MANABU! ANDO!
HEY, LET'S TALK CHRISTMAS PARTY!
What about your exams?
Too late to worry about that.
English is easy.
KYO SAID WE CAN HAVE THE PARTY AT THE CAFÉ.
HE DID? REALLY?
HE SEEMED REALLY INTO THE IDEA.
So he's all alone too...
LET'S MEET UP BEFORE-HAND TO SHOP FOR STUFF.
Nothing fancy, but...
YEAH, I WANT TO GO SHOPPING TOO.
I need some clothes.
ME TOO.
GREAT! IT'S A PLAN, THEN!
The three of us.
OKAY.
NOTHING TO WORRY ABOUT IF IT'S A THREE-SOME.

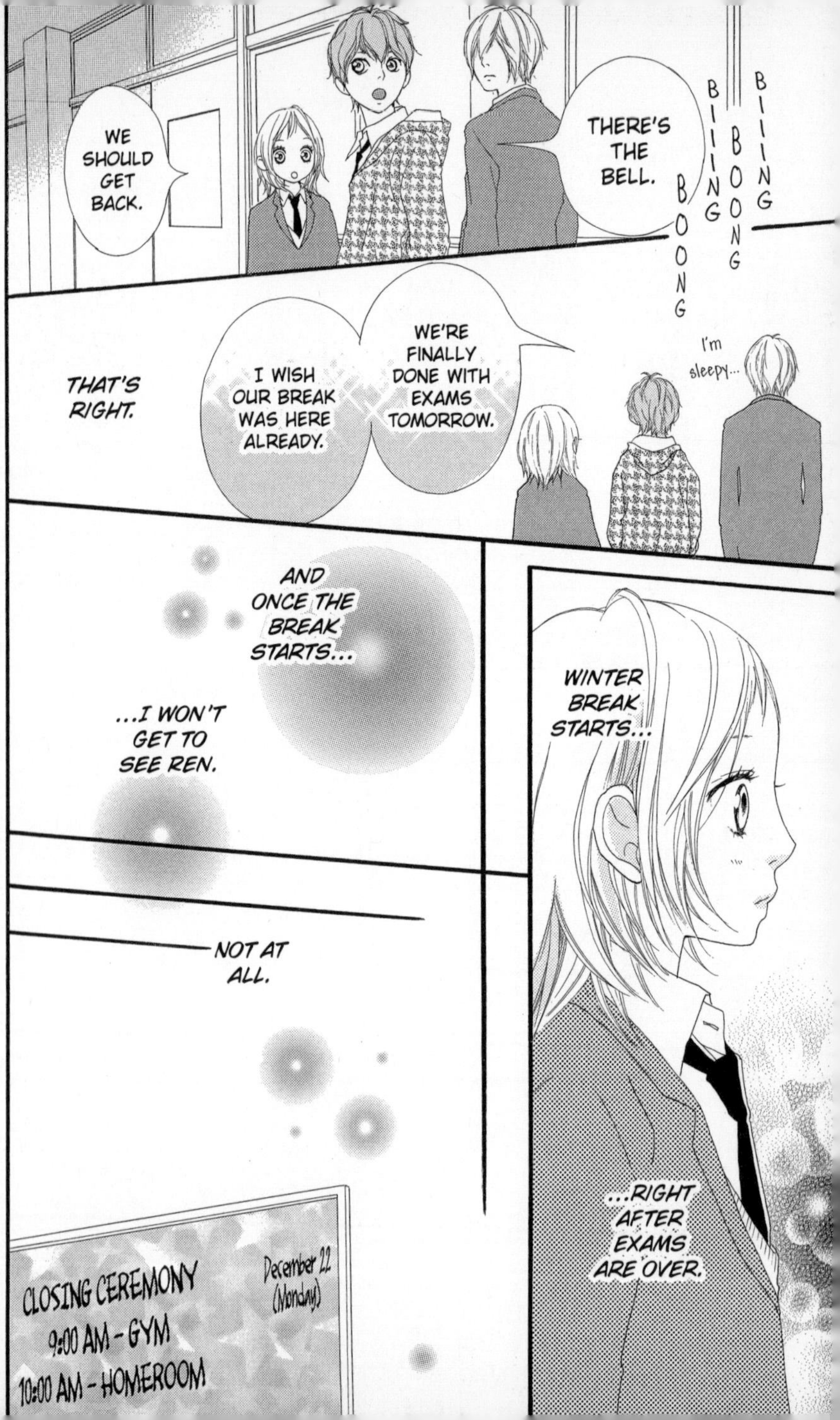
BIIING
BOONG
BIIING
BOONG
THERE'S THE BELL.
WE SHOULD GET BACK.
I'm sleepy...
WE'RE FINALLY DONE WITH EXAMS TOMORROW.
I WISH OUR BREAK WAS HERE ALREADY.
THAT'S RIGHT.
WINTER BREAK STARTS...
...RIGHT AFTER EXAMS ARE OVER.
AND ONCE THE BREAK STARTS...
...I WON'T GET TO SEE REN.
NOT AT ALL.
December 22 (Monday)
CLOSING CEREMONY
9:00 AM - GYM
10:00 AM - HOMEROOM

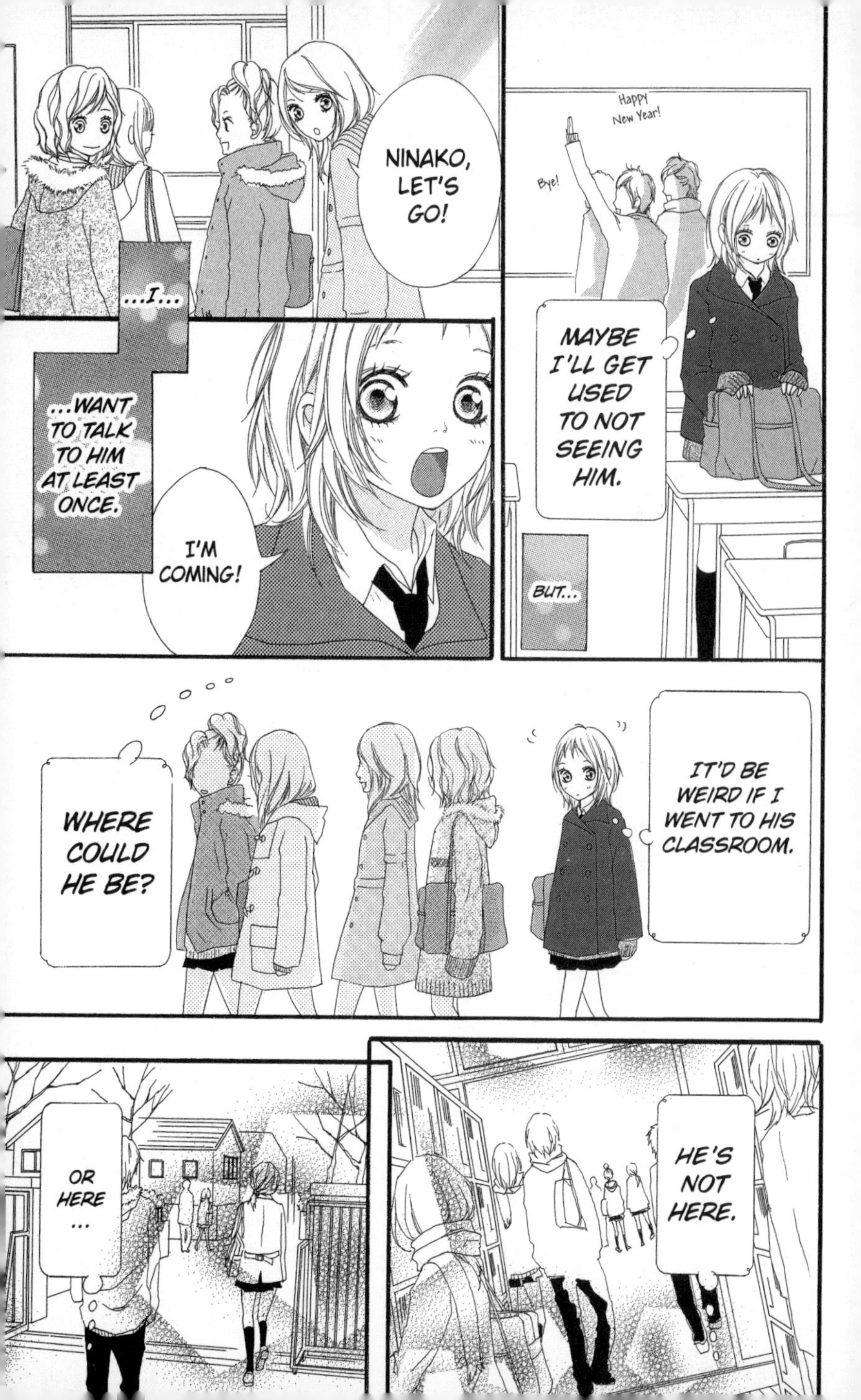
Happy New Year!
Bye!
MAYBE I'LL GET USED TO NOT SEEING HIM.
BUT...
NINAKO, LET'S GO!
...I...
...WANT TO TALK TO HIM AT LEAST ONCE.
I'M COMING!
IT'D BE WEIRD IF I WENT TO HIS CLASSROOM.
WHERE COULD HE BE?
HE'S NOT HERE.
OR HERE ...

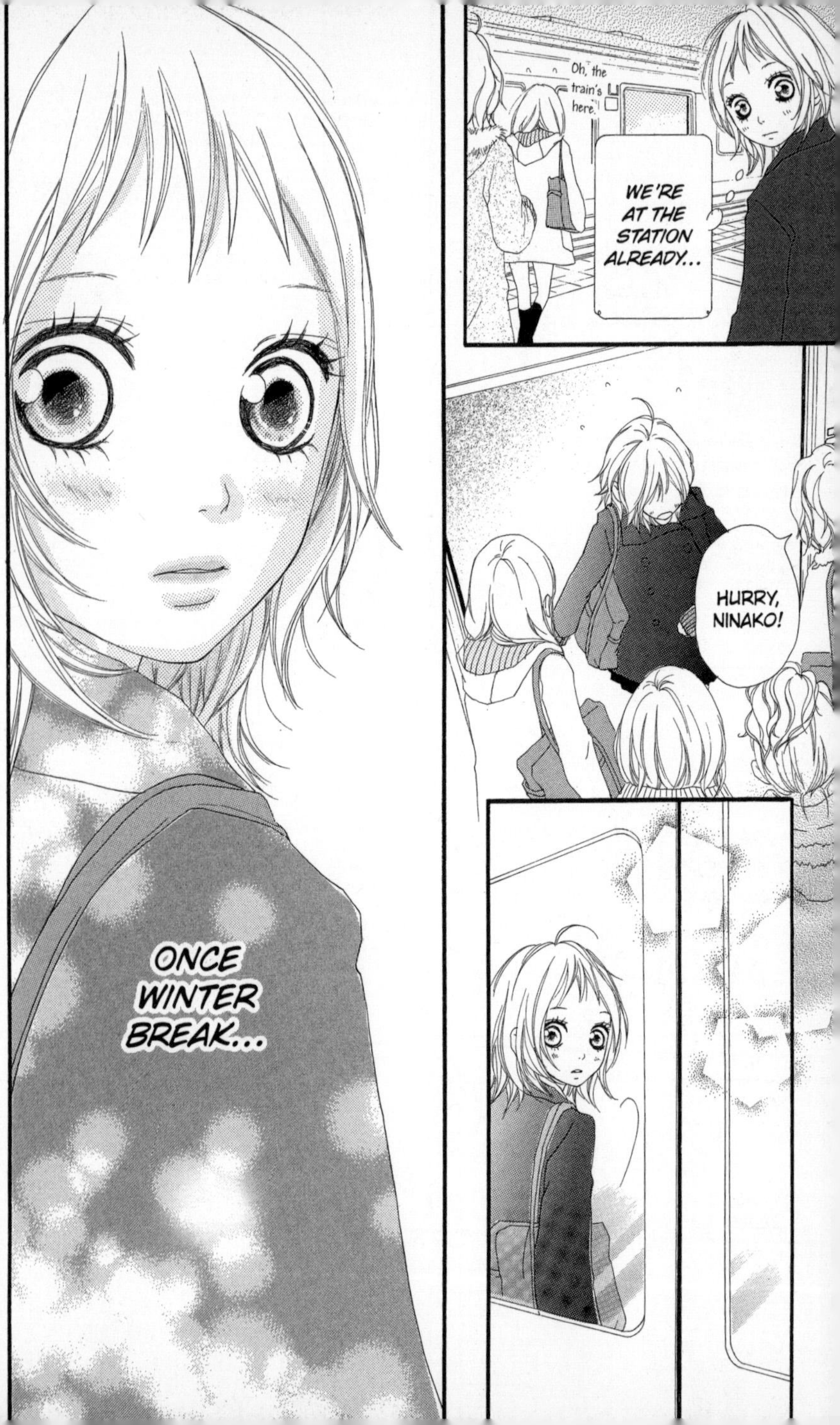

Oh, the train's here.
WE'RE AT THE STATION ALREADY...
HURRY, NINAKO!
ONCE WINTER BREAK...

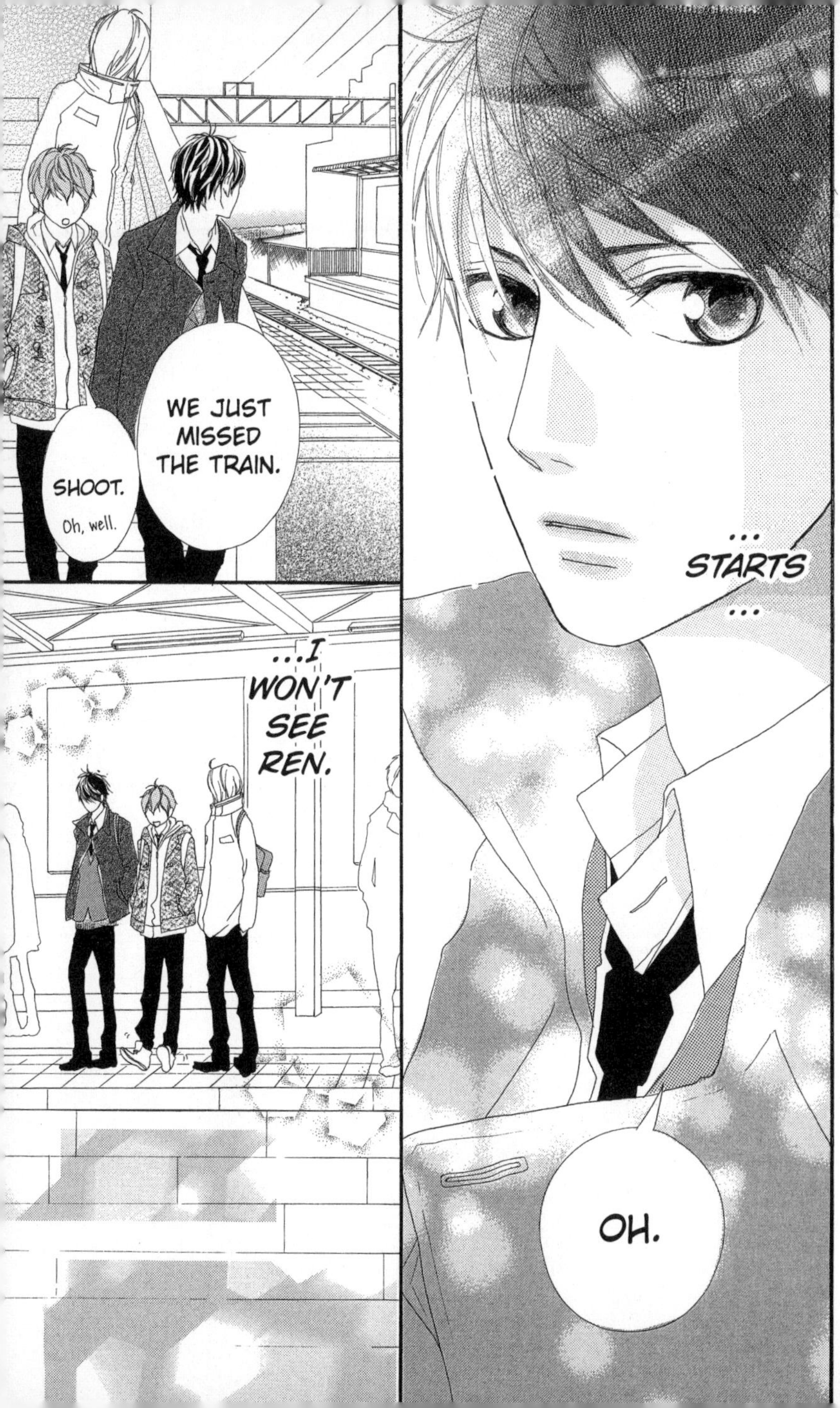
... STARTS ...
OH.
WE JUST MISSED THE TRAIN.
SHOOT.
Oh, well.
...I WON'T SEE REN.

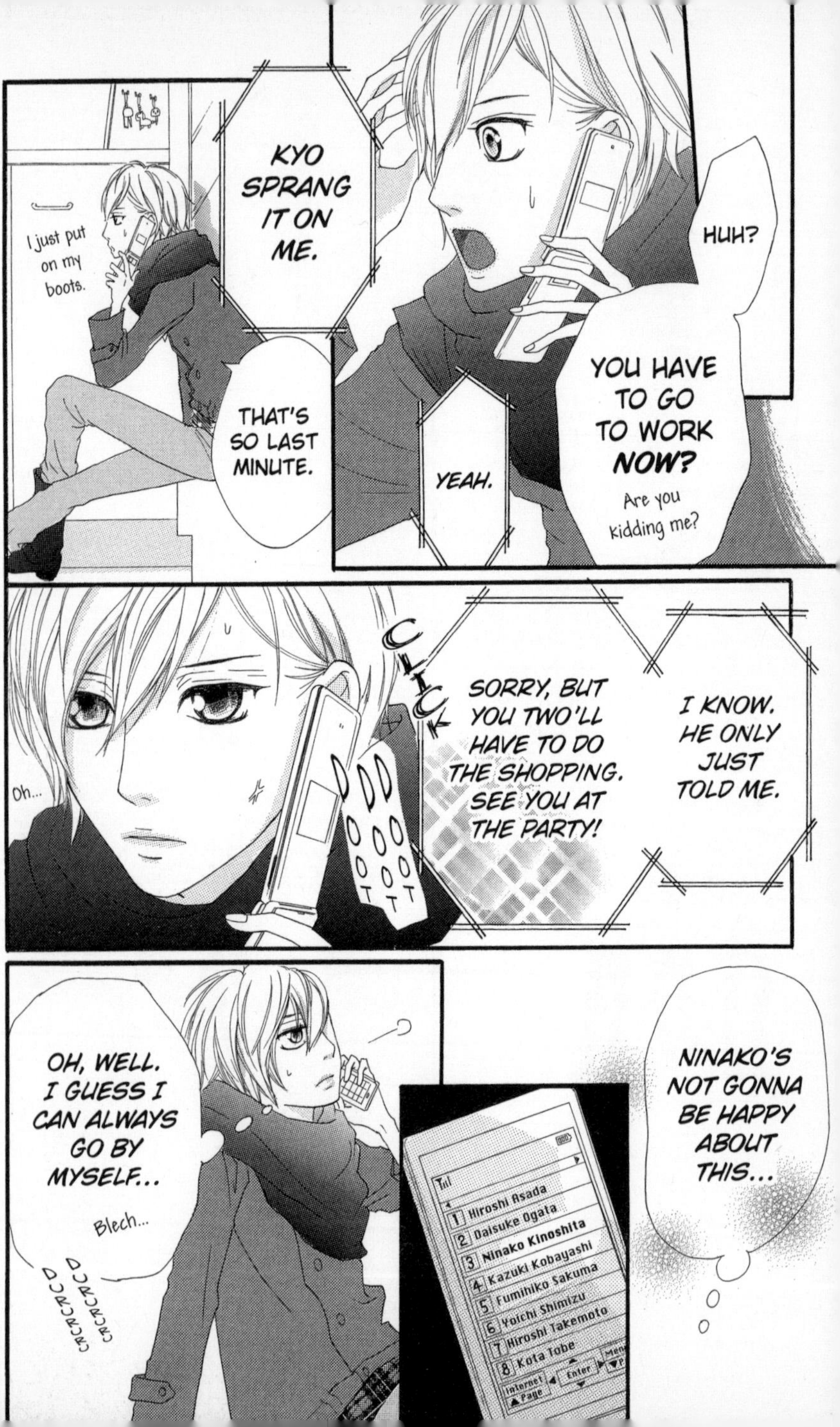
HUH?
YOU HAVE TO GO TO WORK NOW?
Are you kidding me?
YEAH.
KYO SPRANG IT ON ME.
THAT'S SO LAST MINUTE.
I just put on my boots.
I KNOW. HE ONLY JUST TOLD ME.
SORRY, BUT YOU TWO'LL HAVE TO DO THE SHOPPING. SEE YOU AT THE PARTY!
CLICK
DOOT DOOT DOOT
Oh...
NINAKO'S NOT GONNA BE HAPPY ABOUT THIS...
1 Hiroshi Asada
2 Daisuke Ogata
3 Ninako Kinoshita
4 Kazuki Kobayashi
5 Fumihiko Sakuma
6 Yoichi Shimizu
7 Hiroshi Takemoto
8 Kota Tobe
Internet Page
Enter
Menu
OH, WELL. I GUESS I CAN ALWAYS GO BY MYSELF...
Blech...

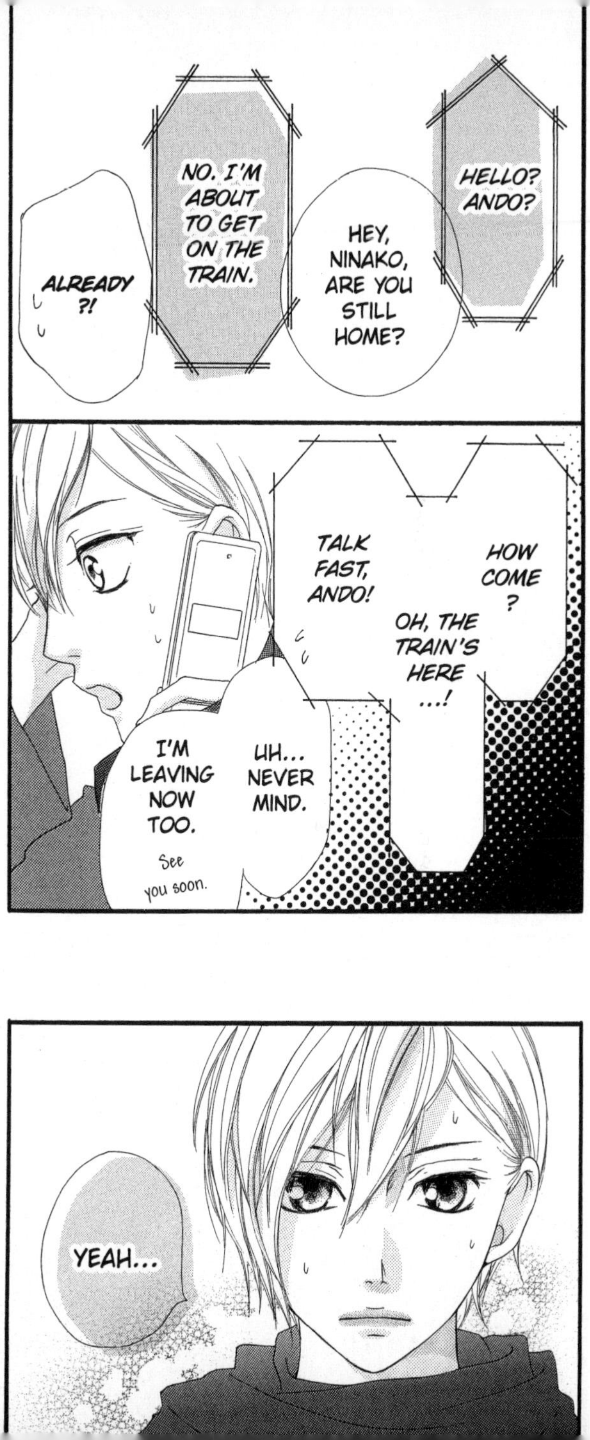
HELLO? ANDO?
HEY, NINAKO, ARE YOU STILL HOME?
NO. I'M ABOUT TO GET ON THE TRAIN.
ALREADY?!
HOW COME?
TALK FAST, ANDO!
OH, THE TRAIN'S HERE...!
UH... NEVER MIND.
I'M LEAVING NOW TOO.
See you soon.
YEAH...

Have you ever eaten a mint? Like Frisk or Mintia? Doesn't the first one just make you want to sneeze? Mints always make me sneeze, so I guess they probably stimulate my sinuses. It means I have to be careful...

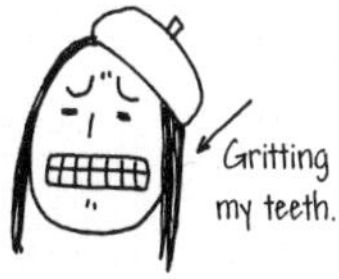
Gritting my teeth.

...or else the mint will torpedo out of my mouth when I sneeze. (It's not a deadly weapon, though.) Watch out, people!

No one around me understands, so I'm very sad...

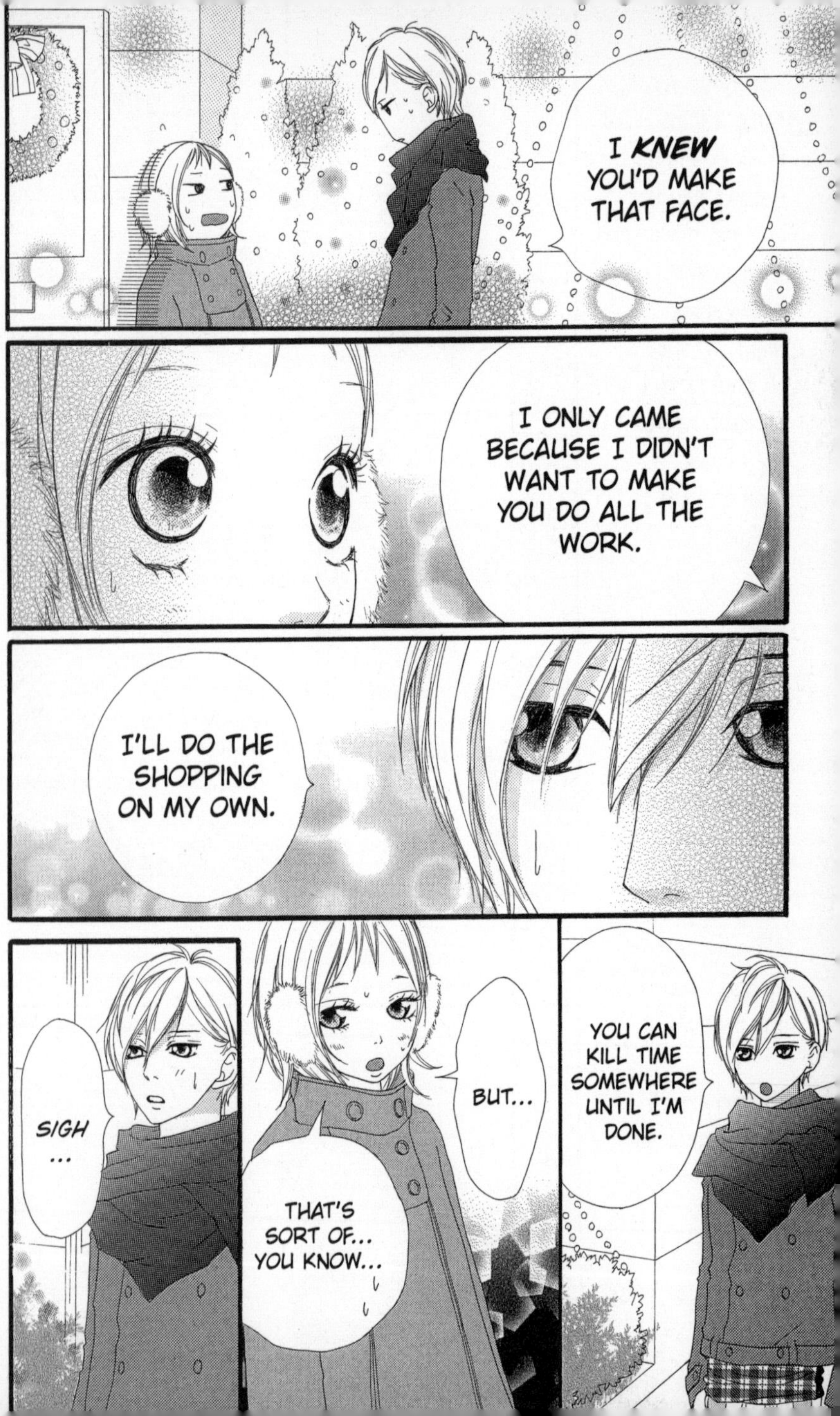
I *KNEW* YOU'D MAKE THAT FACE.
I ONLY CAME BECAUSE I DIDN'T WANT TO MAKE YOU DO ALL THE WORK.
I'LL DO THE SHOPPING ON MY OWN.
YOU CAN KILL TIME SOMEWHERE UNTIL I'M DONE.
BUT...
THAT'S SORT OF... YOU KNOW...
SIGH...

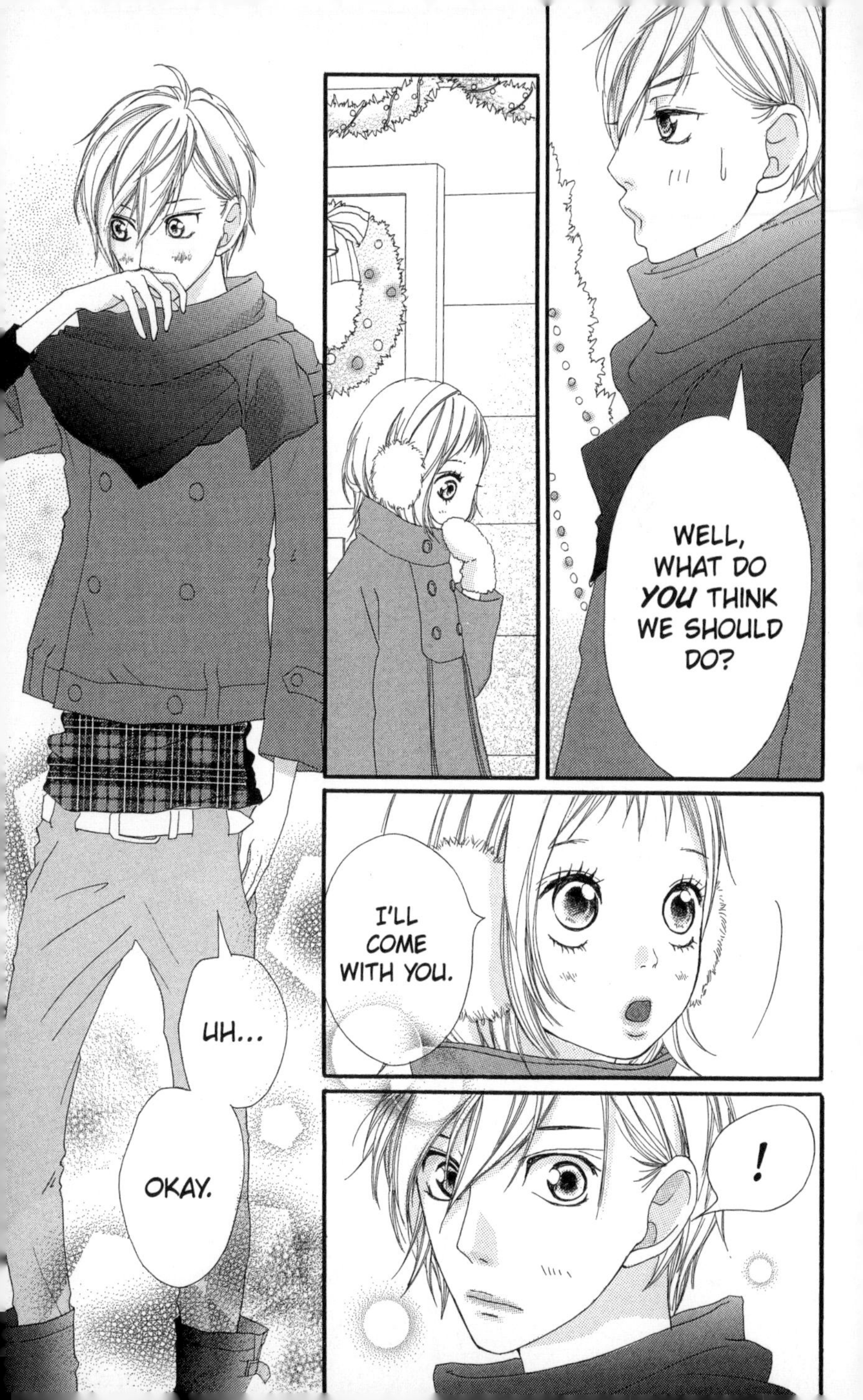
WELL, WHAT DO *YOU* THINK WE SHOULD DO?
I'LL COME WITH YOU.
!
UH...
OKAY.

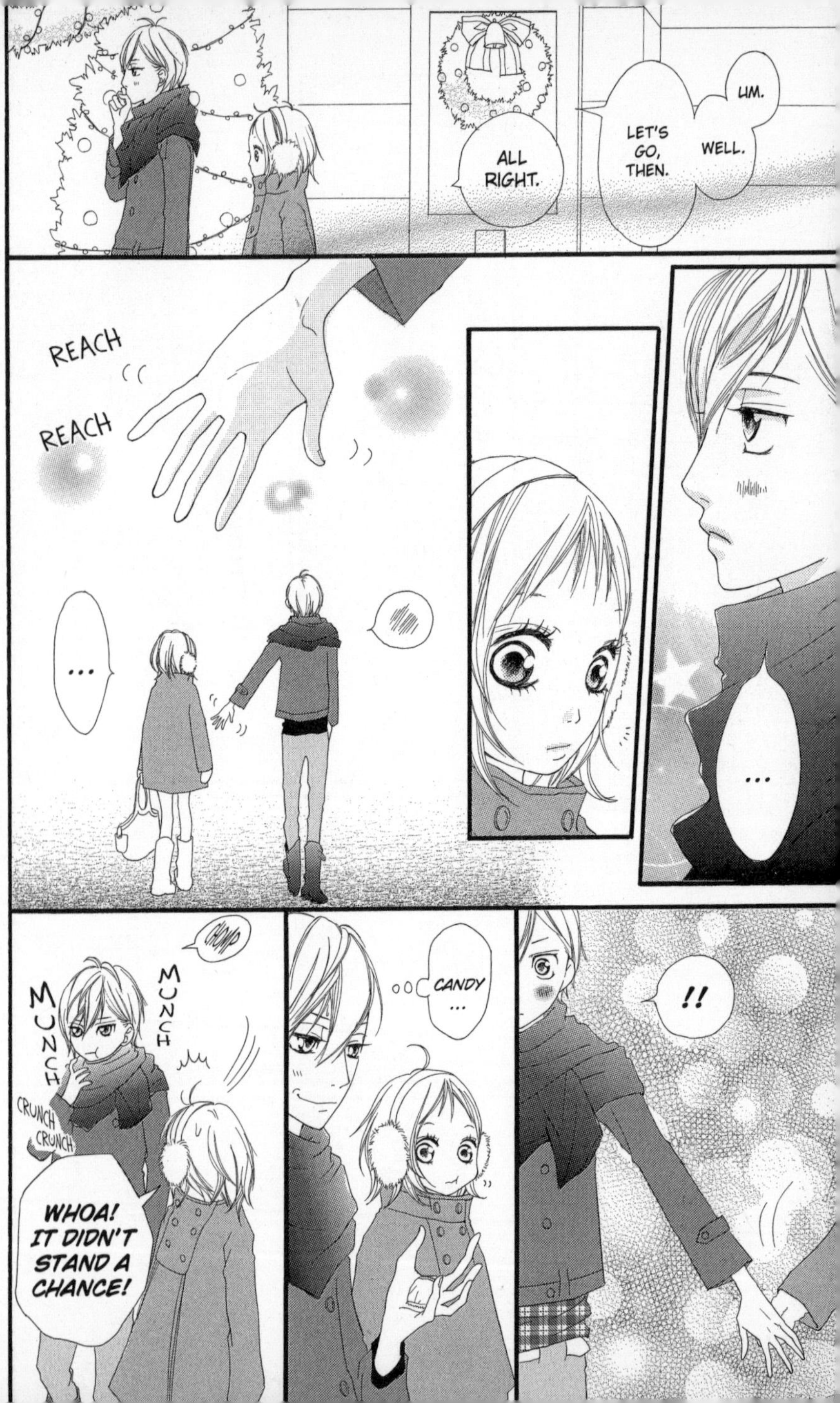

UM.
WELL.
LET'S GO, THEN.
ALL RIGHT.
...
REACH
REACH
...
!!
CANDY ...
CHOMP
MUNCH
MUNCH
CRUNCH CRUNCH
WHOA! IT DIDN'T STAND A CHANCE!

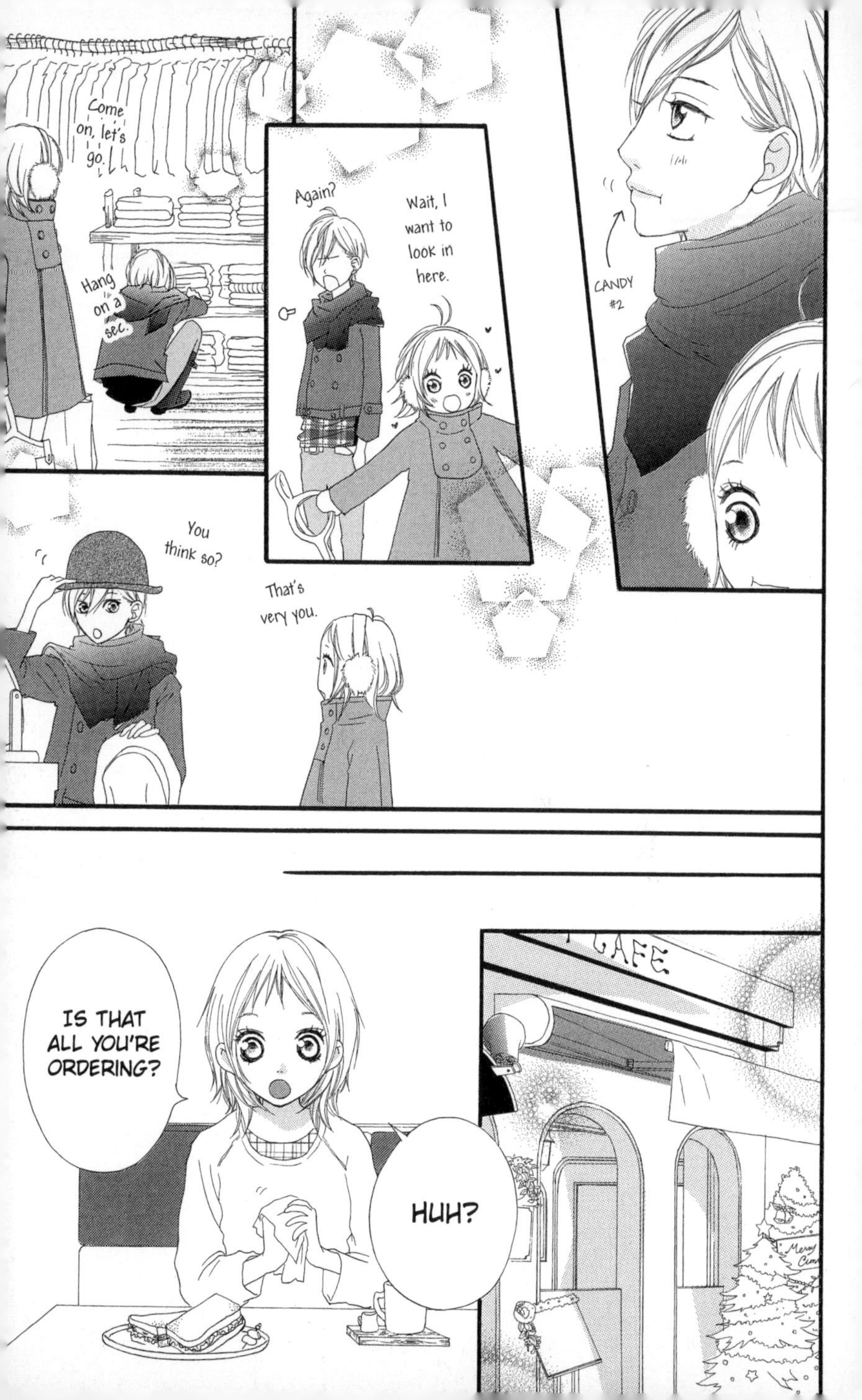
CANDY #2
Wait, I want to look in here.
Again?
Come on, let's go.
Hang on a sec.
That's very you.
You think so?
CAFE
IS THAT ALL YOU'RE ORDERING?
HUH?

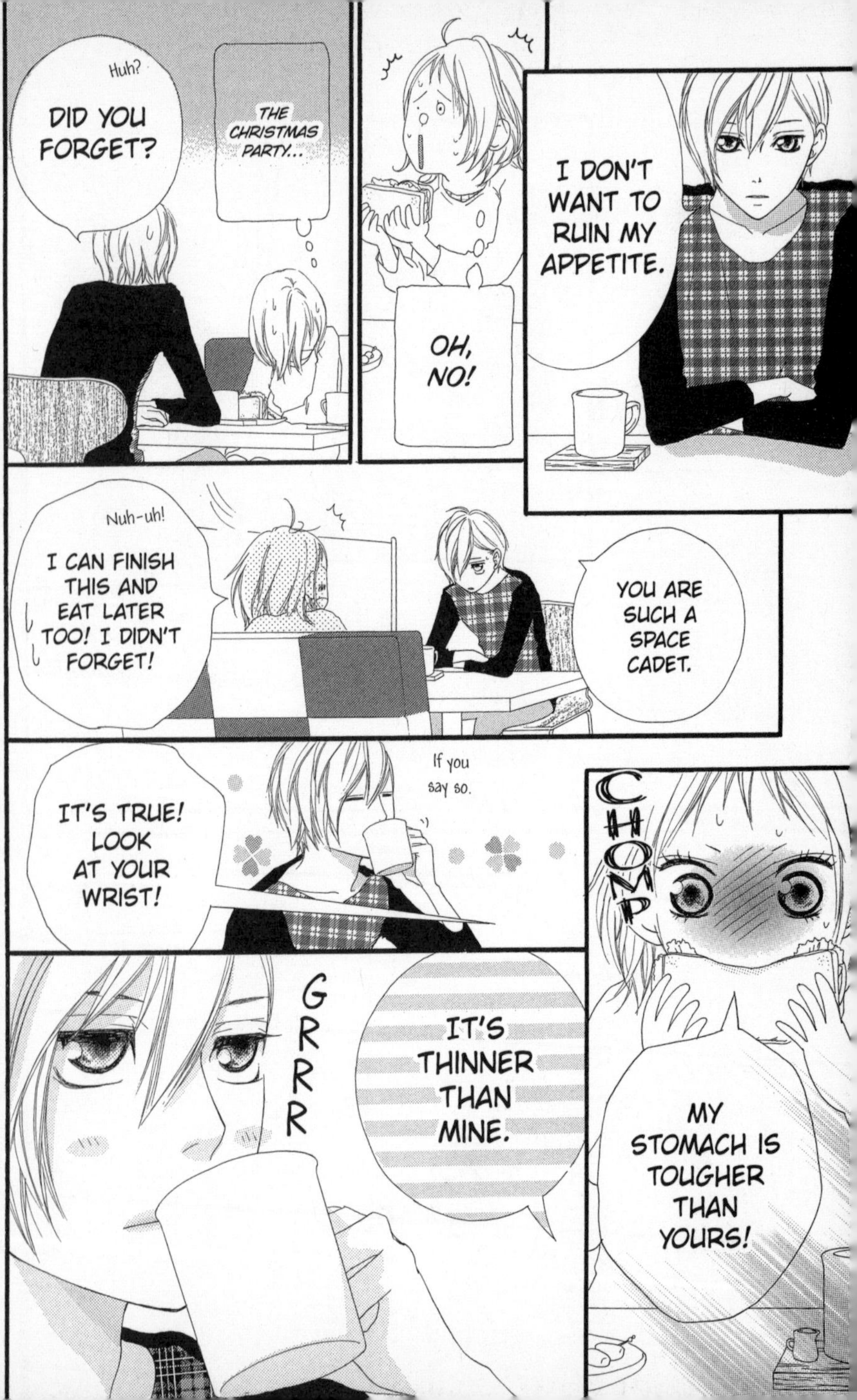
I DON'T WANT TO RUIN MY APPETITE.
OH, NO!
Huh?
DID YOU FORGET?
THE CHRISTMAS PARTY...
YOU ARE SUCH A SPACE CADET.
Nuh-uh!
I CAN FINISH THIS AND EAT LATER TOO! I DIDN'T FORGET!
CHOMP
MY STOMACH IS TOUGHER THAN YOURS!
If you say so.
IT'S TRUE! LOOK AT YOUR WRIST!
GRRR
IT'S THINNER THAN MINE.

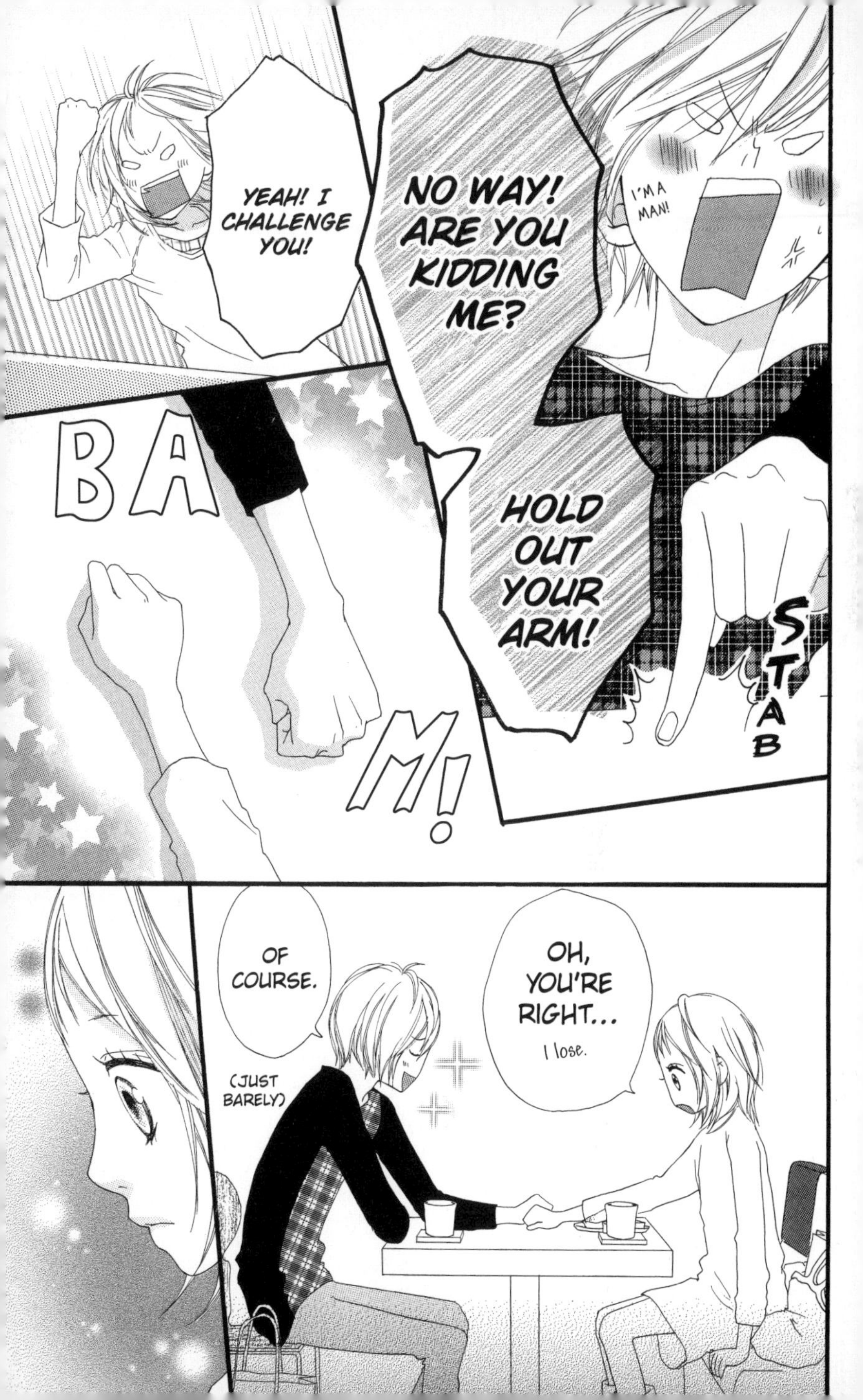
NO WAY! ARE YOU KIDDING ME?
I'M A MAN!
HOLD OUT YOUR ARM!
STAB
YEAH! I CHALLENGE YOU!
BAM!
OH, YOU'RE RIGHT...
I lose.
OF COURSE.
(JUST BARELY)

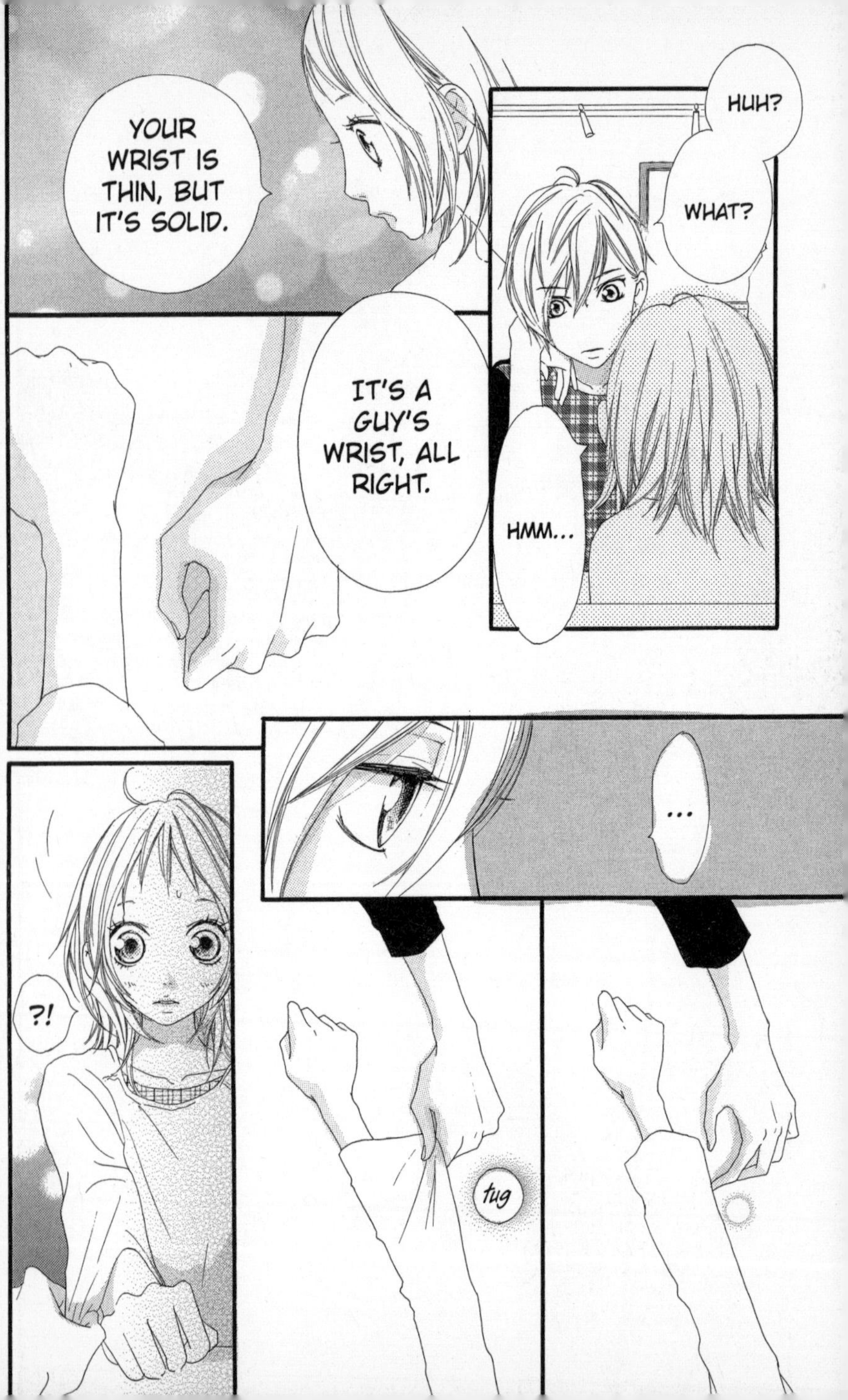
HUH?
WHAT?
HMM...
YOUR WRIST IS THIN, BUT IT'S SOLID.
IT'S A GUY'S WRIST, ALL RIGHT.
...
tug
?!

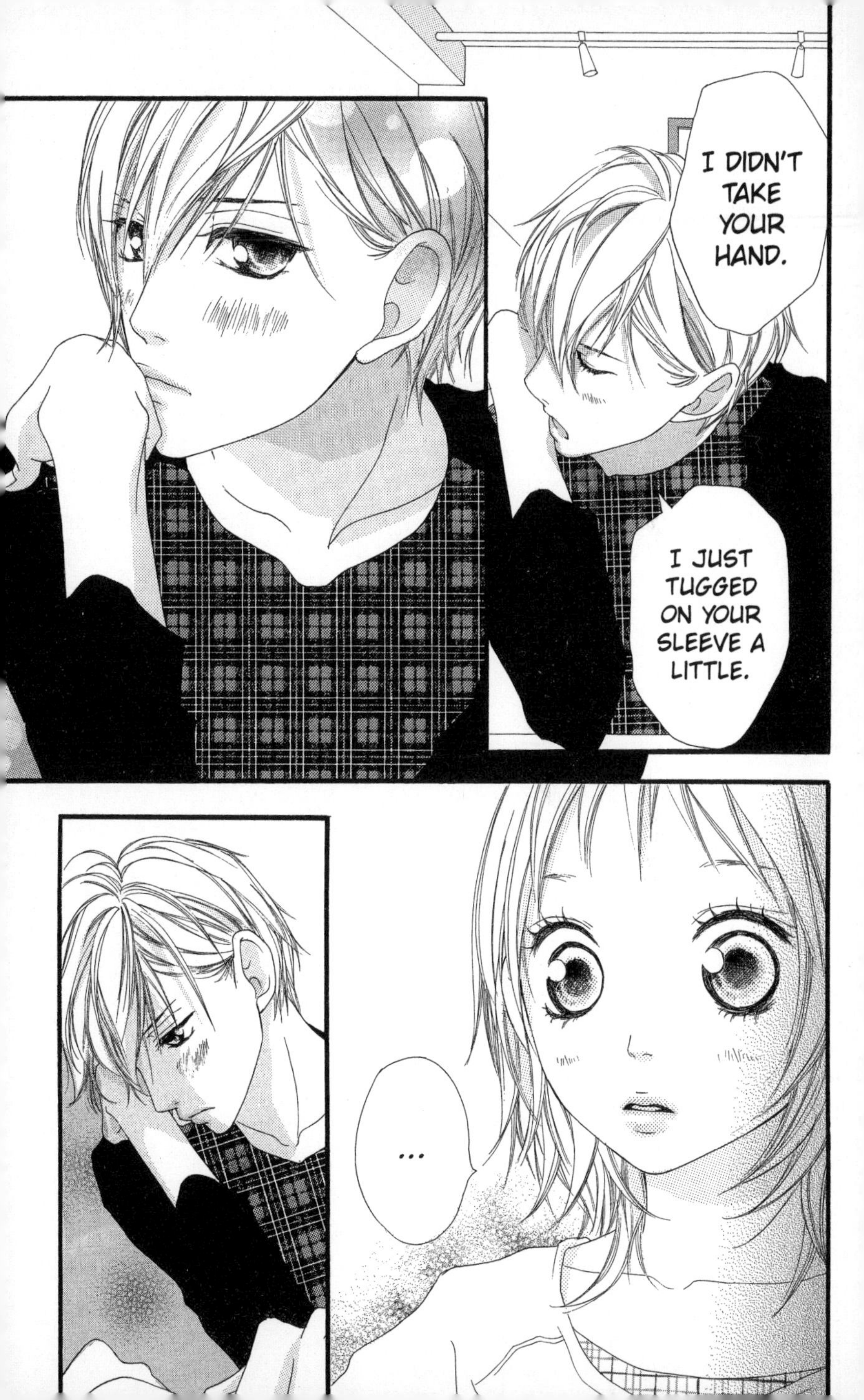
I DIDN'T TAKE YOUR HAND.
I JUST TUGGED ON YOUR SLEEVE A LITTLE.
...

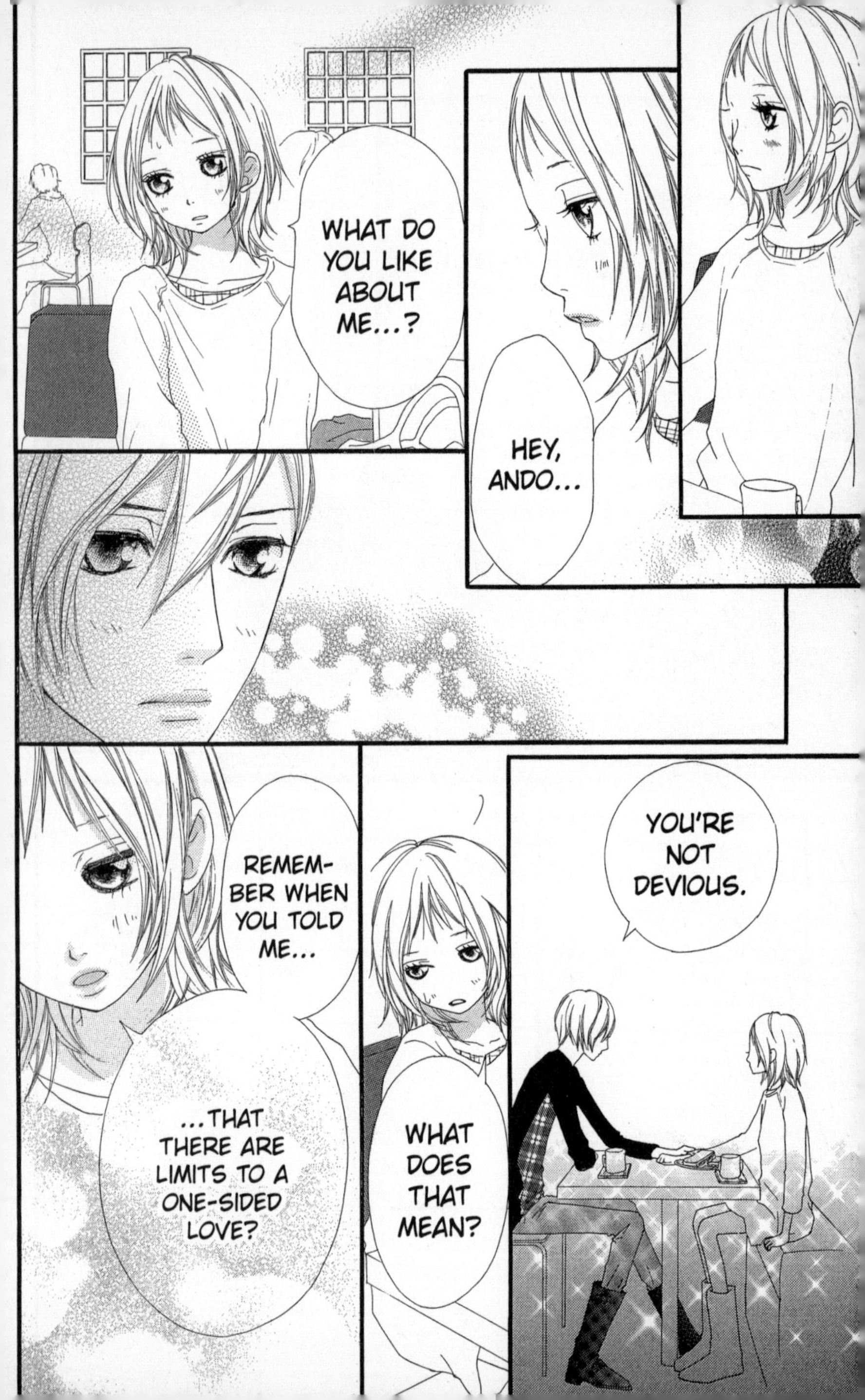
HEY, ANDO...
WHAT DO YOU LIKE ABOUT ME...?
YOU'RE NOT DEVIOUS.
WHAT DOES THAT MEAN?
REMEM-BER WHEN YOU TOLD ME...
...THAT THERE ARE LIMITS TO A ONE-SIDED LOVE?

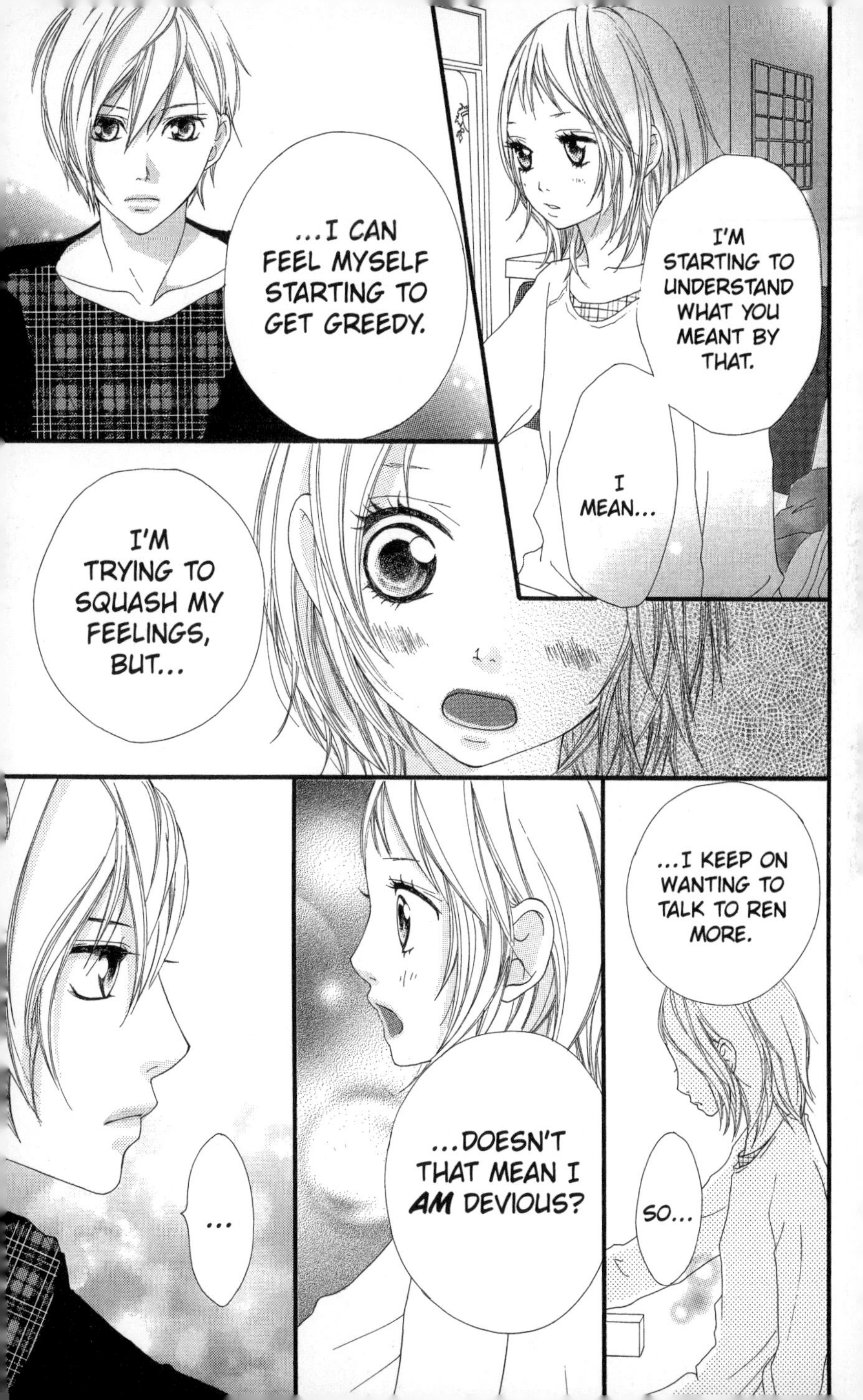
I'M STARTING TO UNDERSTAND WHAT YOU MEANT BY THAT.
I MEAN...
...I CAN FEEL MYSELF STARTING TO GET GREEDY.
I'M TRYING TO SQUASH MY FEELINGS, BUT...
...I KEEP ON WANTING TO TALK TO REN MORE.
SO...
...DOESN'T THAT MEAN I **AM** DEVIOUS?
...

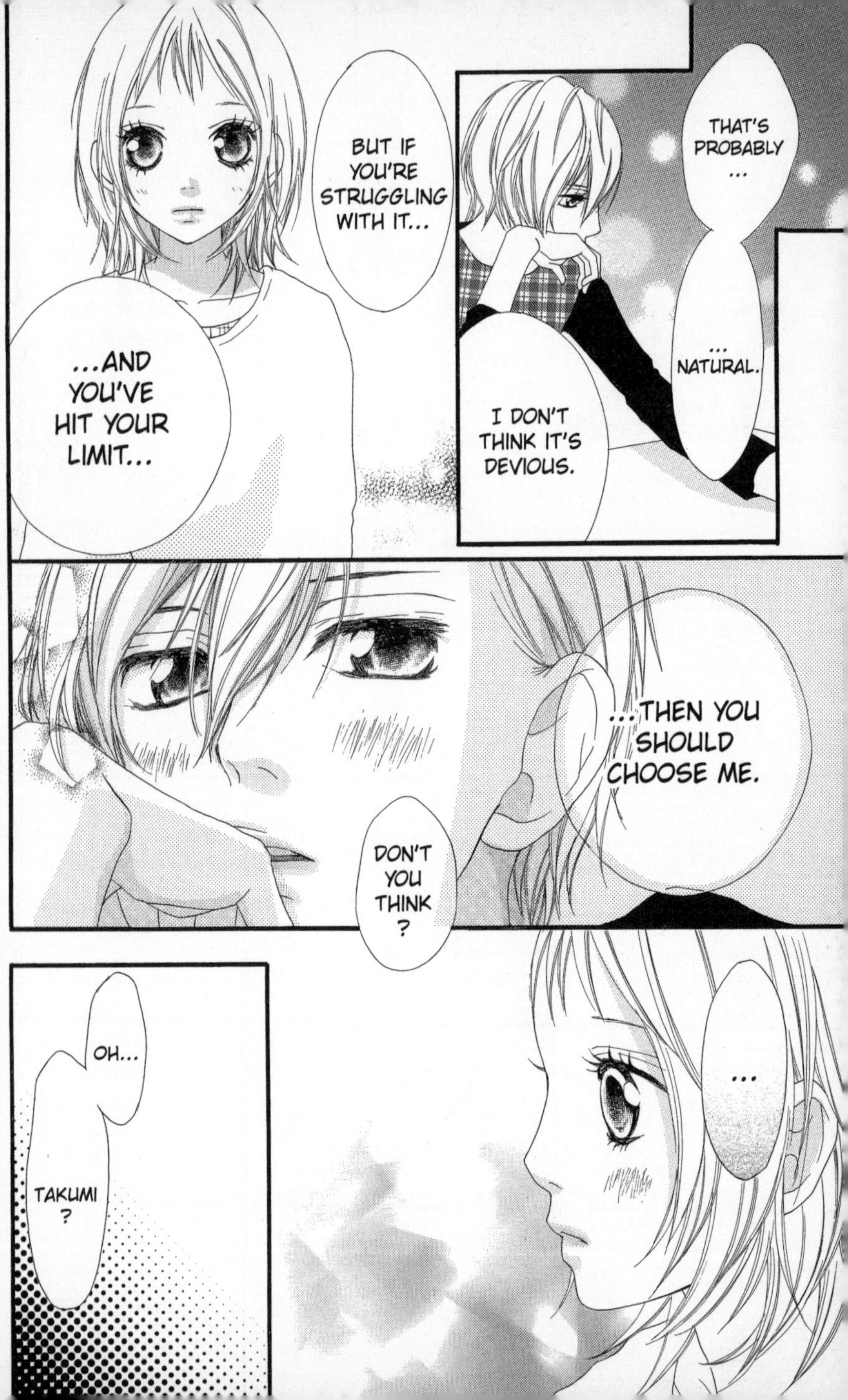
THAT'S PROBABLY ...
... NATURAL.
I DON'T THINK IT'S DEVIOUS.
BUT IF YOU'RE STRUGGLING WITH IT...
...AND YOU'VE HIT YOUR LIMIT...
...THEN YOU SHOULD CHOOSE ME.
DON'T YOU THINK ?
...
OH...
TAKUMI ?

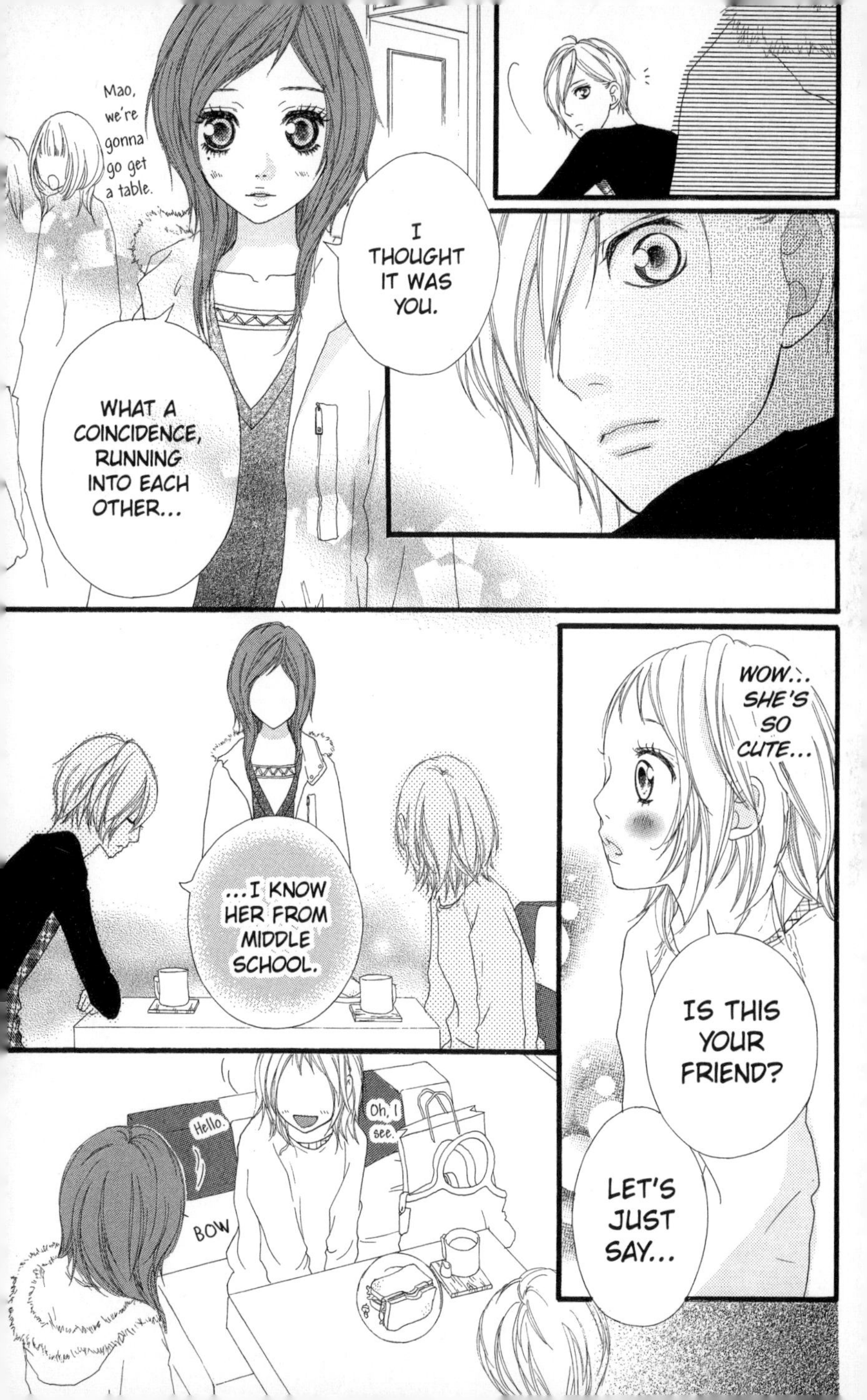
I THOUGHT IT WAS YOU.
Mao, we're gonna go get a table.
WHAT A COINCIDENCE, RUNNING INTO EACH OTHER...
WOW... SHE'S SO CUTE...
IS THIS YOUR FRIEND?
LET'S JUST SAY...
...I KNOW HER FROM MIDDLE SCHOOL.
Oh, I see.
Hello.
BOW

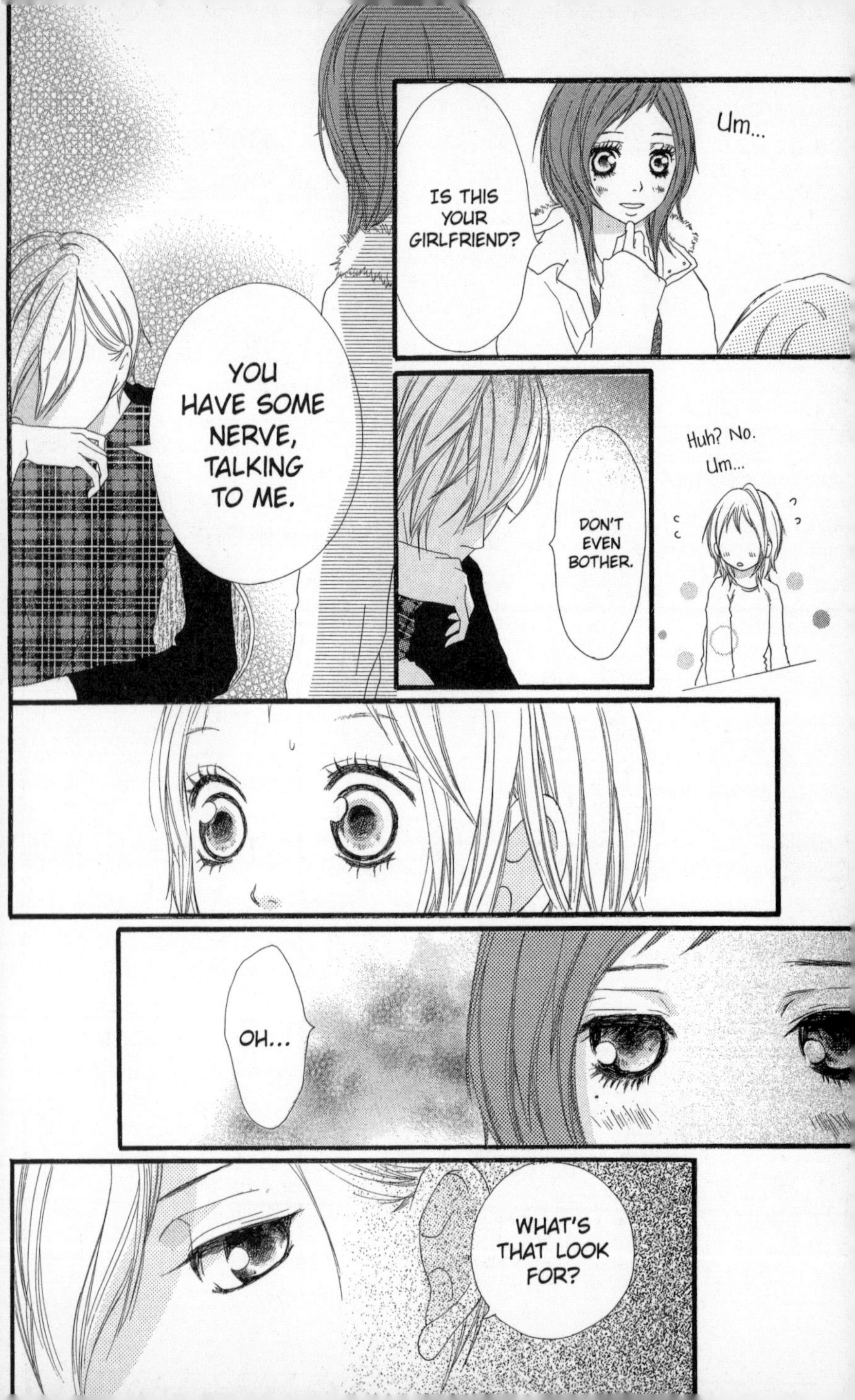
Um...
IS THIS YOUR GIRLFRIEND?
Huh? No. Um...
DON'T EVEN BOTHER.
YOU HAVE SOME NERVE, TALKING TO ME.
OH...
WHAT'S THAT LOOK FOR?

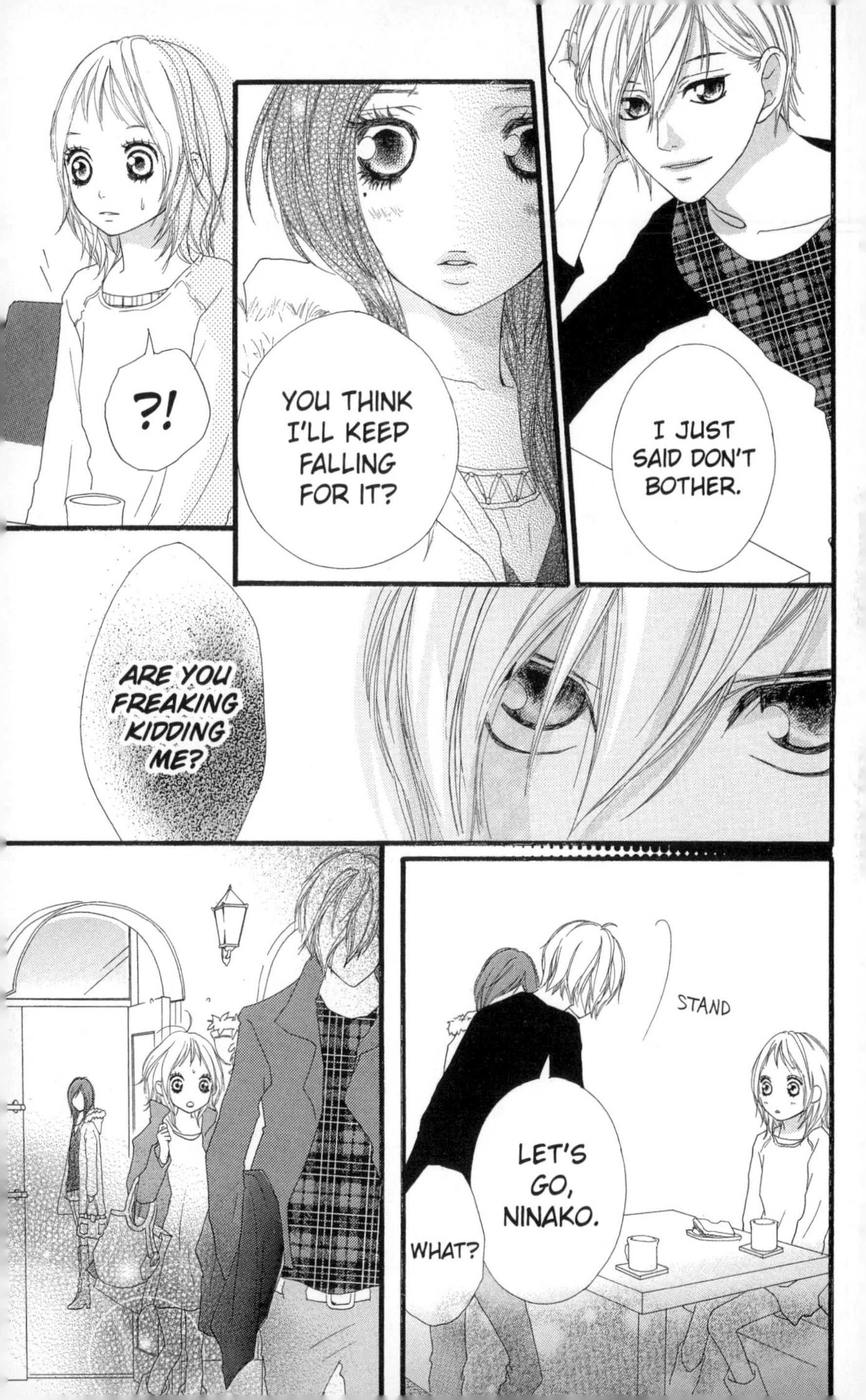
I JUST SAID DON'T BOTHER.
YOU THINK I'LL KEEP FALLING FOR IT?
?!
ARE YOU FREAKING KIDDING ME?
STAND
LET'S GO, NINAKO.
WHAT?

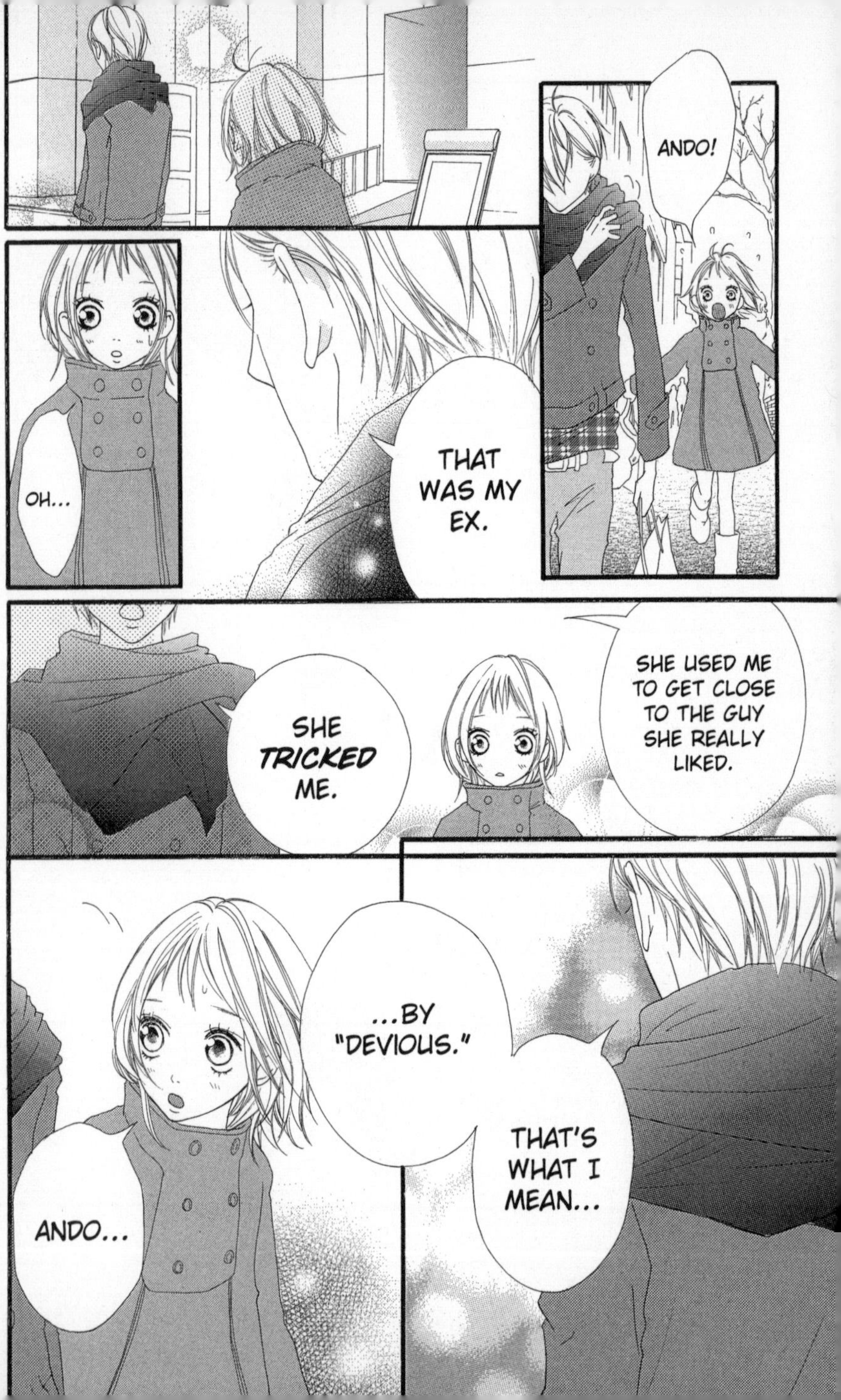
ANDO!
THAT WAS MY EX.
OH...
SHE USED ME TO GET CLOSE TO THE GUY SHE REALLY LIKED.
SHE *TRICKED* ME.
THAT'S WHAT I MEAN...
...BY "DEVIOUS."
ANDO...

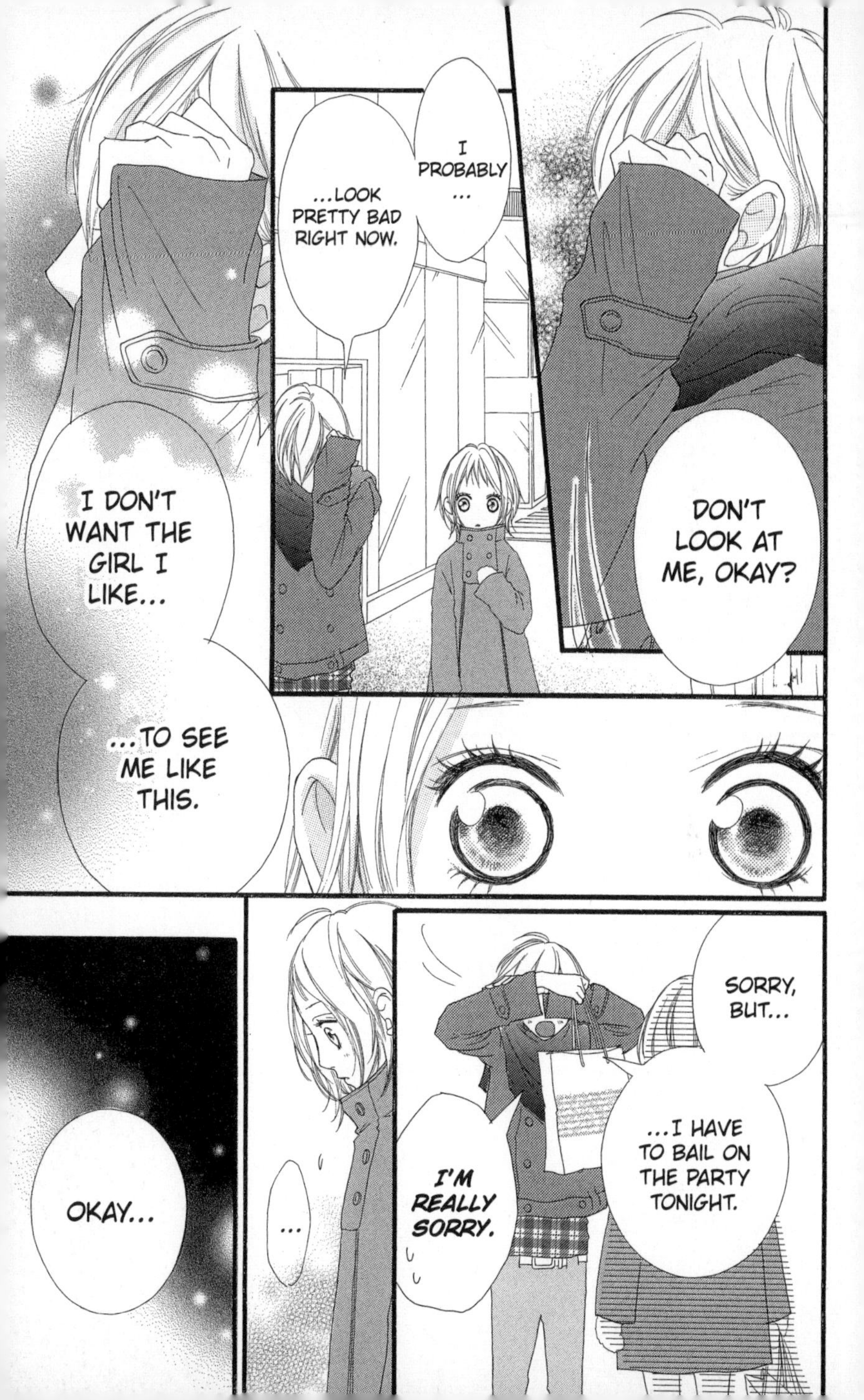
DON'T LOOK AT ME, OKAY?
I PROBABLY...
...LOOK PRETTY BAD RIGHT NOW.
I DON'T WANT THE GIRL I LIKE...
...TO SEE ME LIKE THIS.
SORRY, BUT...
...I HAVE TO BAIL ON THE PARTY TONIGHT.
I'M REALLY SORRY.
...
OKAY...

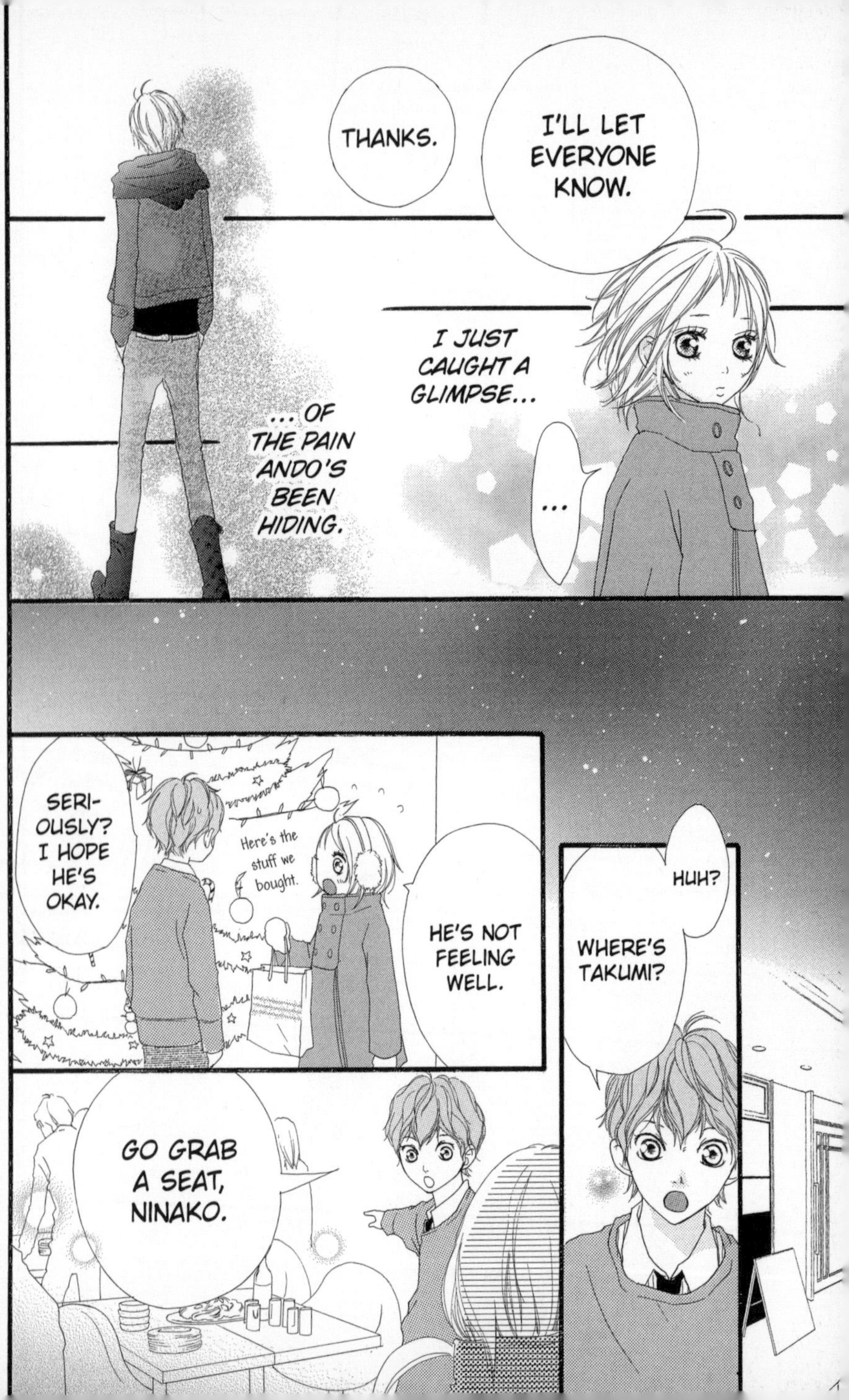
I'LL LET EVERYONE KNOW.
THANKS.
...
I JUST CAUGHT A GLIMPSE...
... OF THE PAIN ANDO'S BEEN HIDING.
HUH?
WHERE'S TAKUMI?
HE'S NOT FEELING WELL.
Here's the stuff we bought.
SERI-OUSLY? I HOPE HE'S OKAY.
GO GRAB A SEAT, NINAKO.

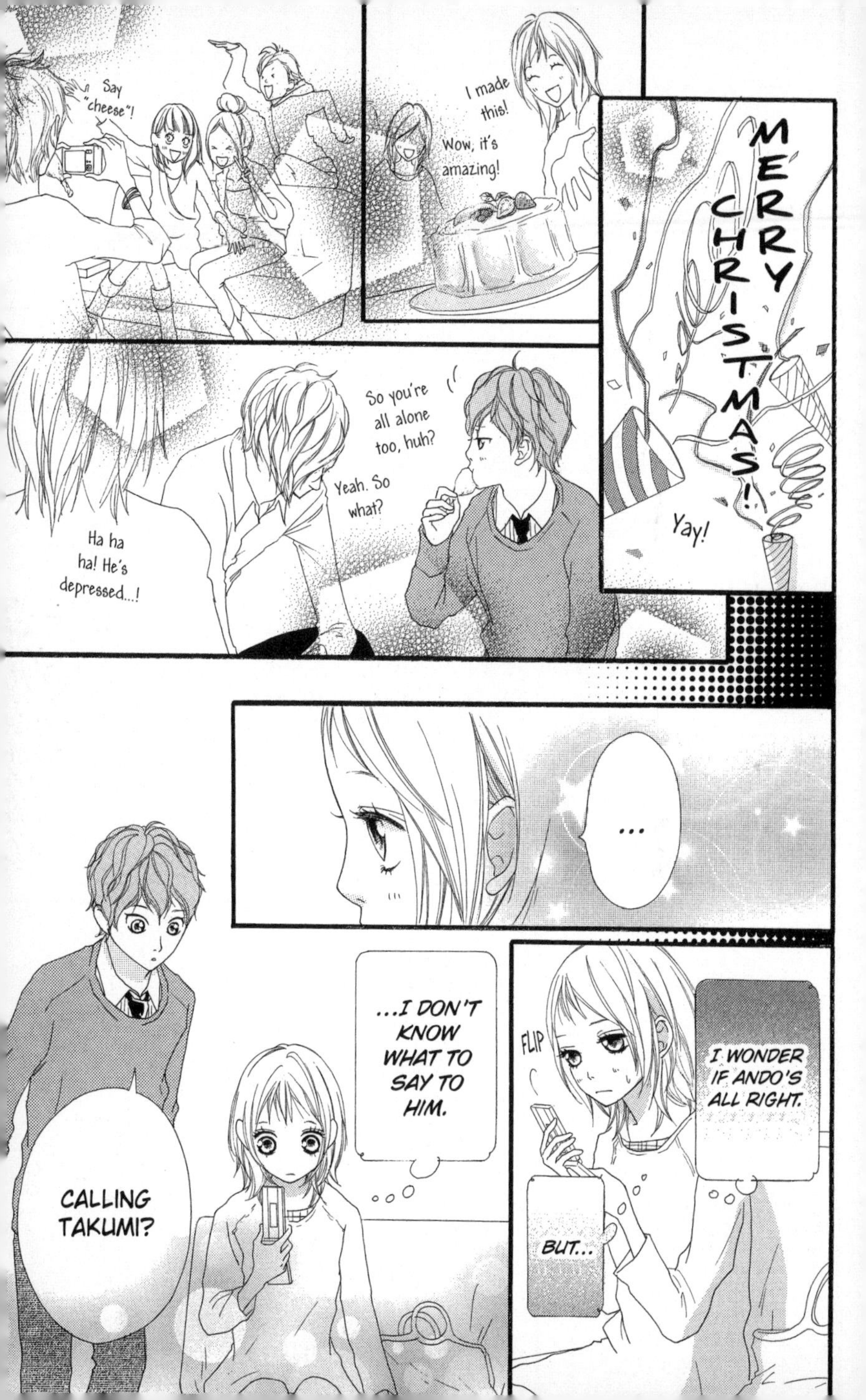
MERRY CHRISTMAS!
Yay!
I made this!
Wow, it's amazing!
Say "cheese"!
So you're all alone too, huh?
Yeah. So what?
Ha ha ha! He's depressed...!
...
FLIP
I WONDER IF ANDO'S ALL RIGHT.
BUT...
...I DON'T KNOW WHAT TO SAY TO HIM.
CALLING TAKUMI?

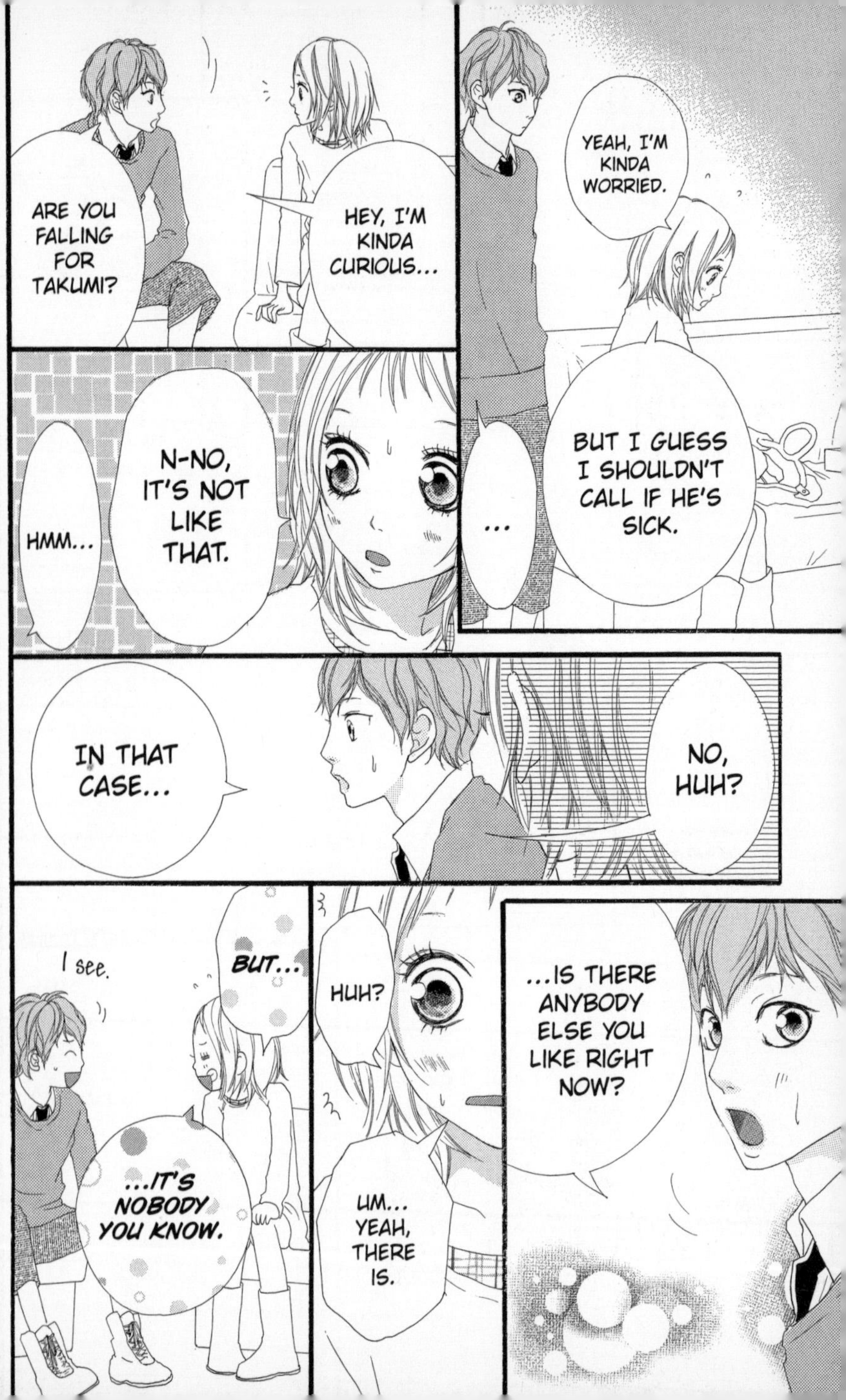
YEAH, I'M KINDA WORRIED.
BUT I GUESS I SHOULDN'T CALL IF HE'S SICK.
...
HEY, I'M KINDA CURIOUS...
ARE YOU FALLING FOR TAKUMI?
N-NO, IT'S NOT LIKE THAT.
HMM...
NO, HUH?
IN THAT CASE...
...IS THERE ANYBODY ELSE YOU LIKE RIGHT NOW?
HUH?
UM... YEAH, THERE IS.
BUT...
I see.
...IT'S NOBODY YOU KNOW.

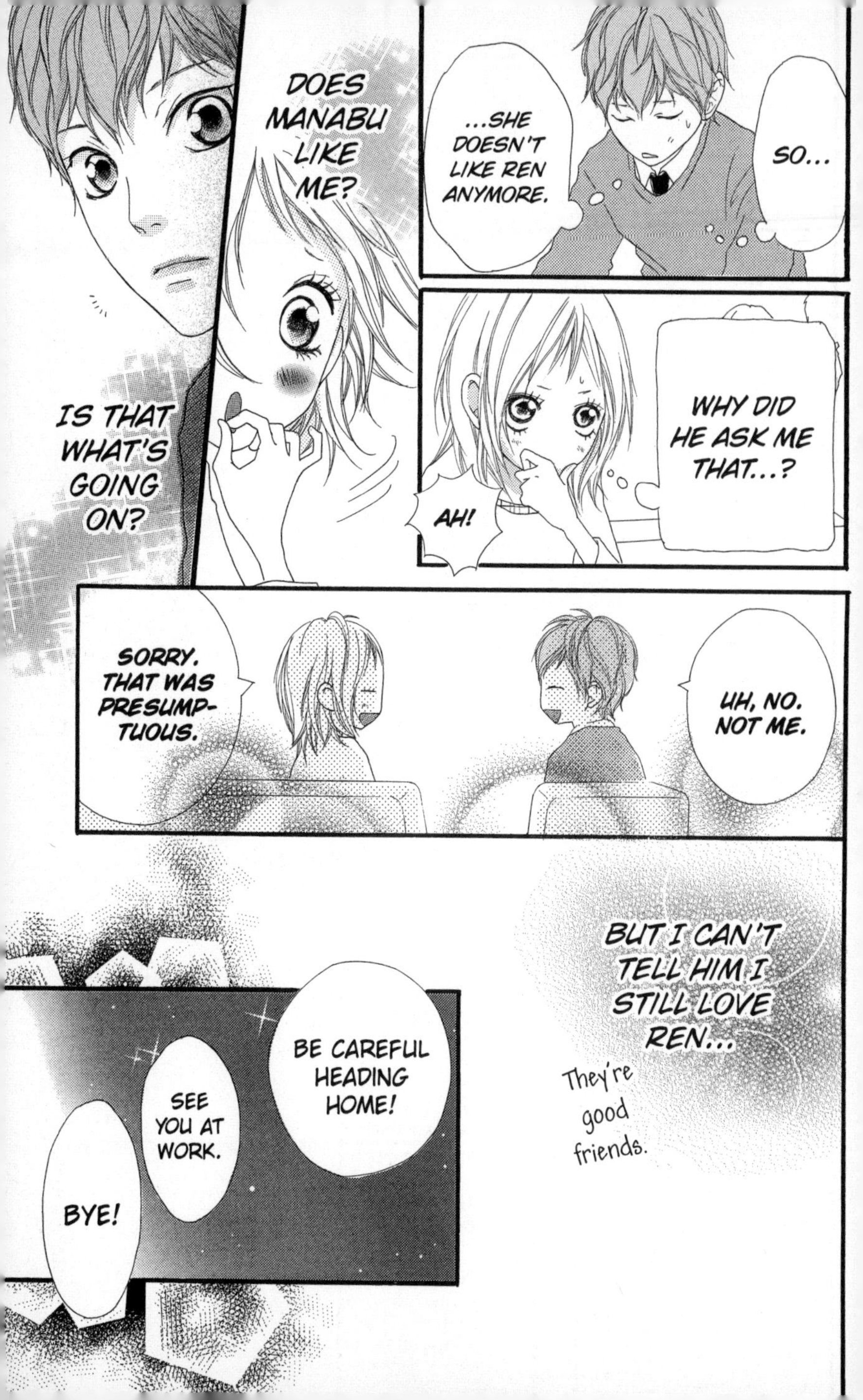
SO...
...SHE DOESN'T LIKE REN ANYMORE.
WHY DID HE ASK ME THAT...?
AH!
DOES MANABU LIKE ME?
IS THAT WHAT'S GOING ON?
UH, NO. NOT ME.
SORRY. THAT WAS PRESUMP-TUOUS.
BUT I CAN'T TELL HIM I STILL LOVE REN...
They're good friends.
BE CAREFUL HEADING HOME!
SEE YOU AT WORK.
BYE!

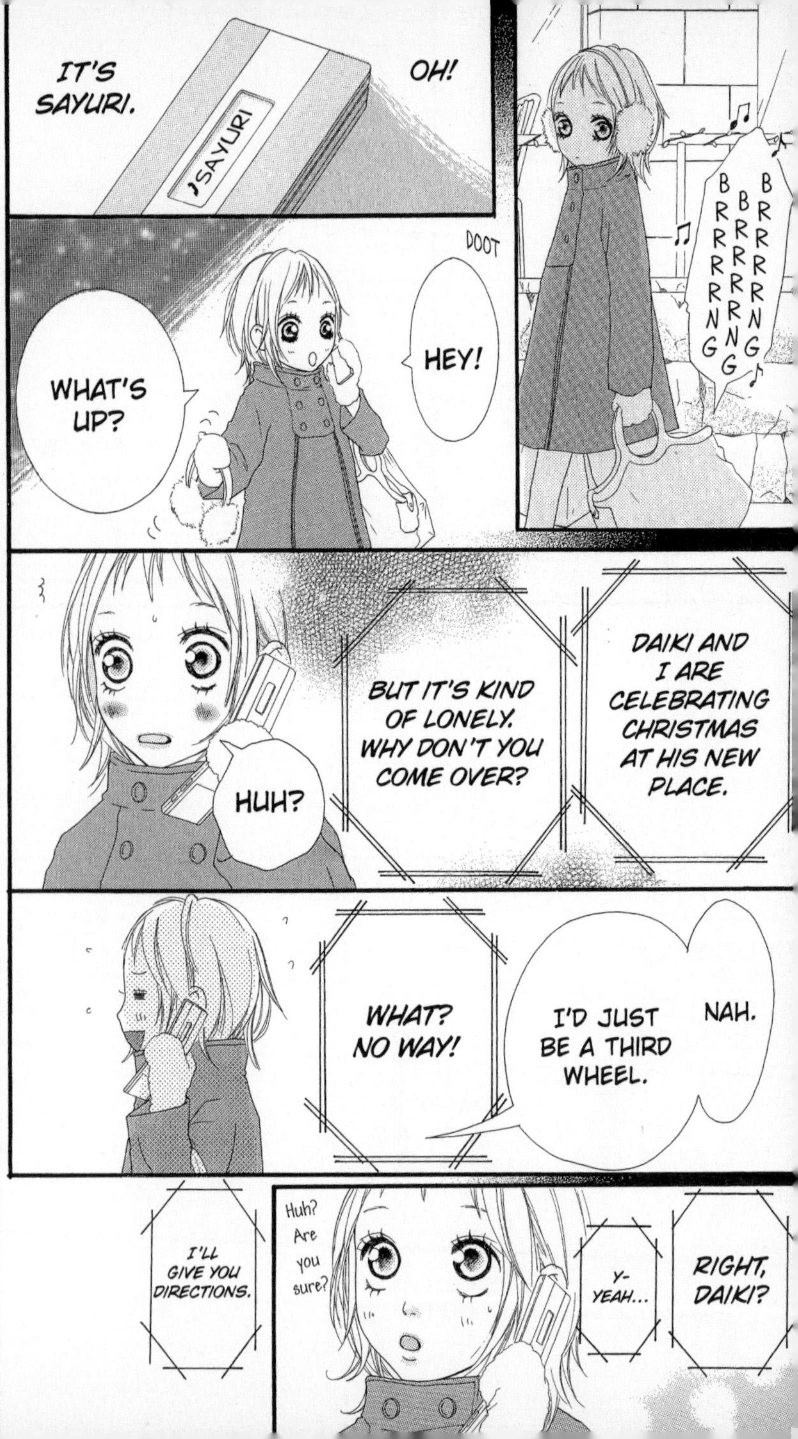
BRRRRRNG
BRRRRNG
BRRRRNG
OH!
♪SAYURI
IT'S SAYURI.
DOOT
HEY!
WHAT'S UP?
DAIKI AND I ARE CELEBRATING CHRISTMAS AT HIS NEW PLACE.
BUT IT'S KIND OF LONELY. WHY DON'T YOU COME OVER?
HUH?
NAH.
I'D JUST BE A THIRD WHEEL.
WHAT? NO WAY!
RIGHT, DAIKI?
Y-YEAH...
Huh? Are you sure?
I'LL GIVE YOU DIRECTIONS.

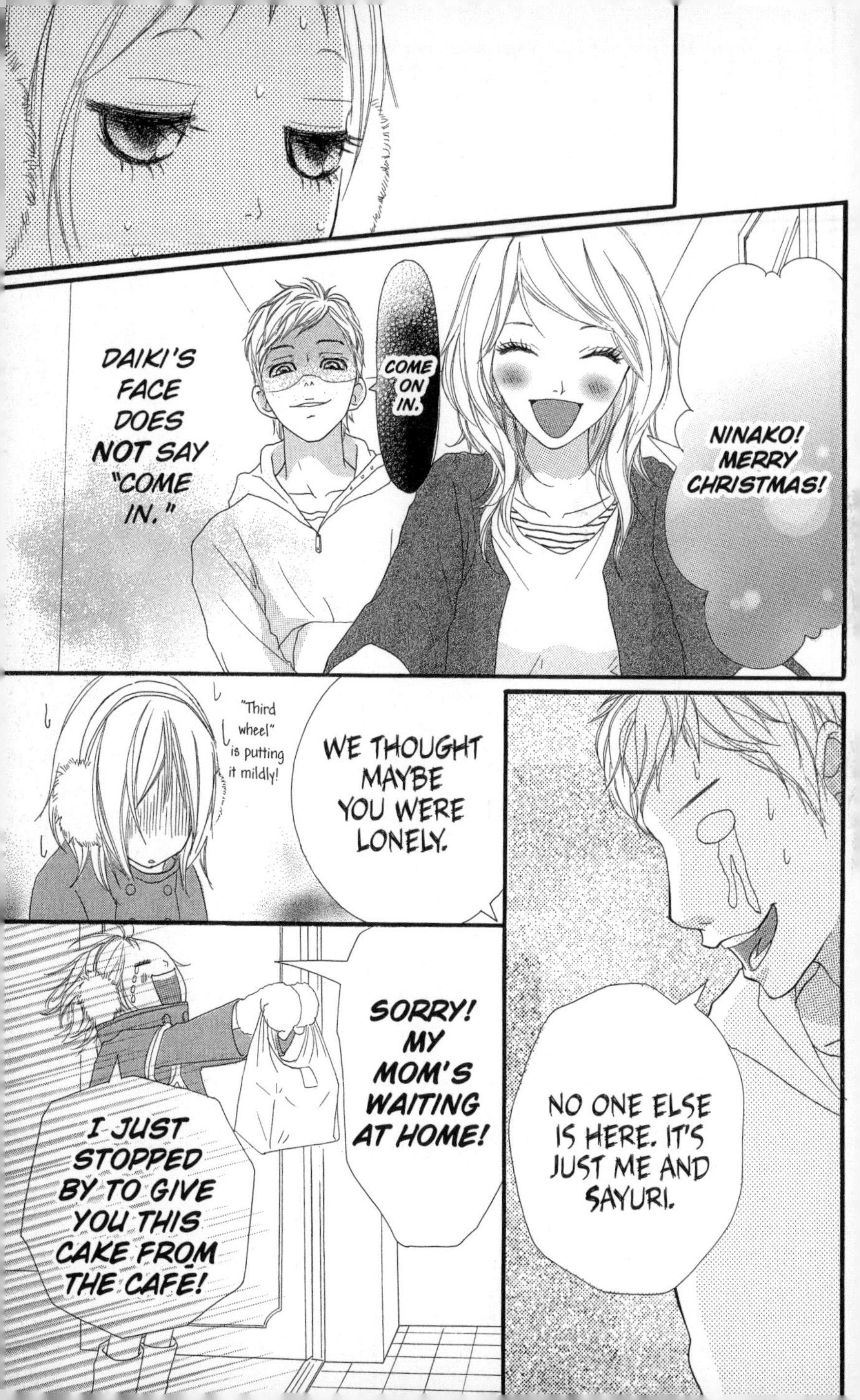
NINAKO! MERRY CHRISTMAS!
COME ON IN.
DAIKI'S FACE DOES NOT SAY "COME IN."
NO ONE ELSE IS HERE. IT'S JUST ME AND SAYURI.
WE THOUGHT MAYBE YOU WERE LONELY.
"Third wheel" is putting it mildly!
SORRY! MY MOM'S WAITING AT HOME!
I JUST STOPPED BY TO GIVE YOU THIS CAKE FROM THE CAFÉ!

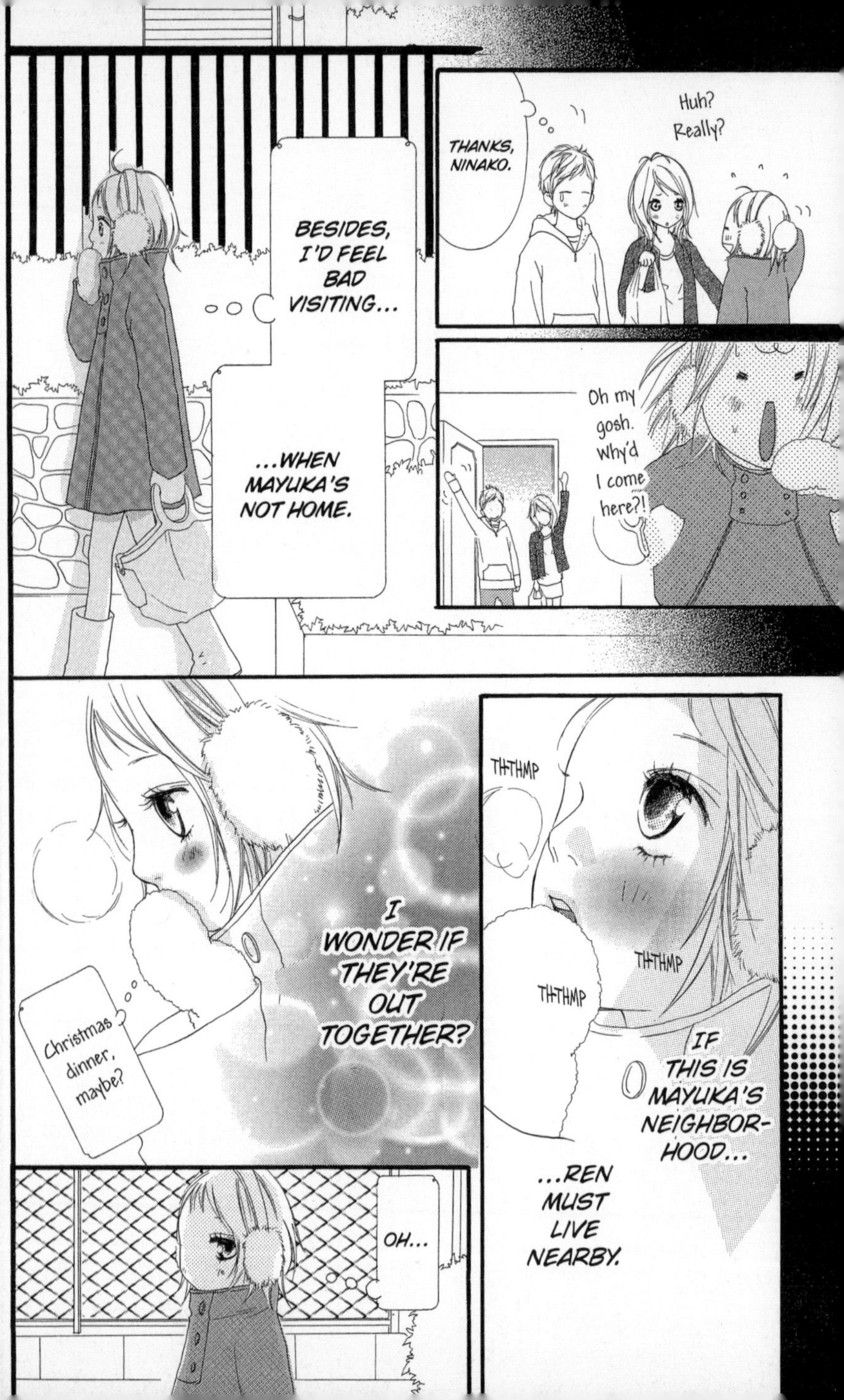
Huh? Really?
THANKS, NINAKO.
Oh my gosh. Why'd I come here?!
BESIDES, I'D FEEL BAD VISITING...
...WHEN MAYUKA'S NOT HOME.
THTHMP
THTHMP
THTHMP
IF THIS IS MAYUKA'S NEIGHBOR-HOOD...
...REN MUST LIVE NEARBY.
I WONDER IF THEY'RE OUT TOGETHER?
Christmas dinner, maybe?
OH...

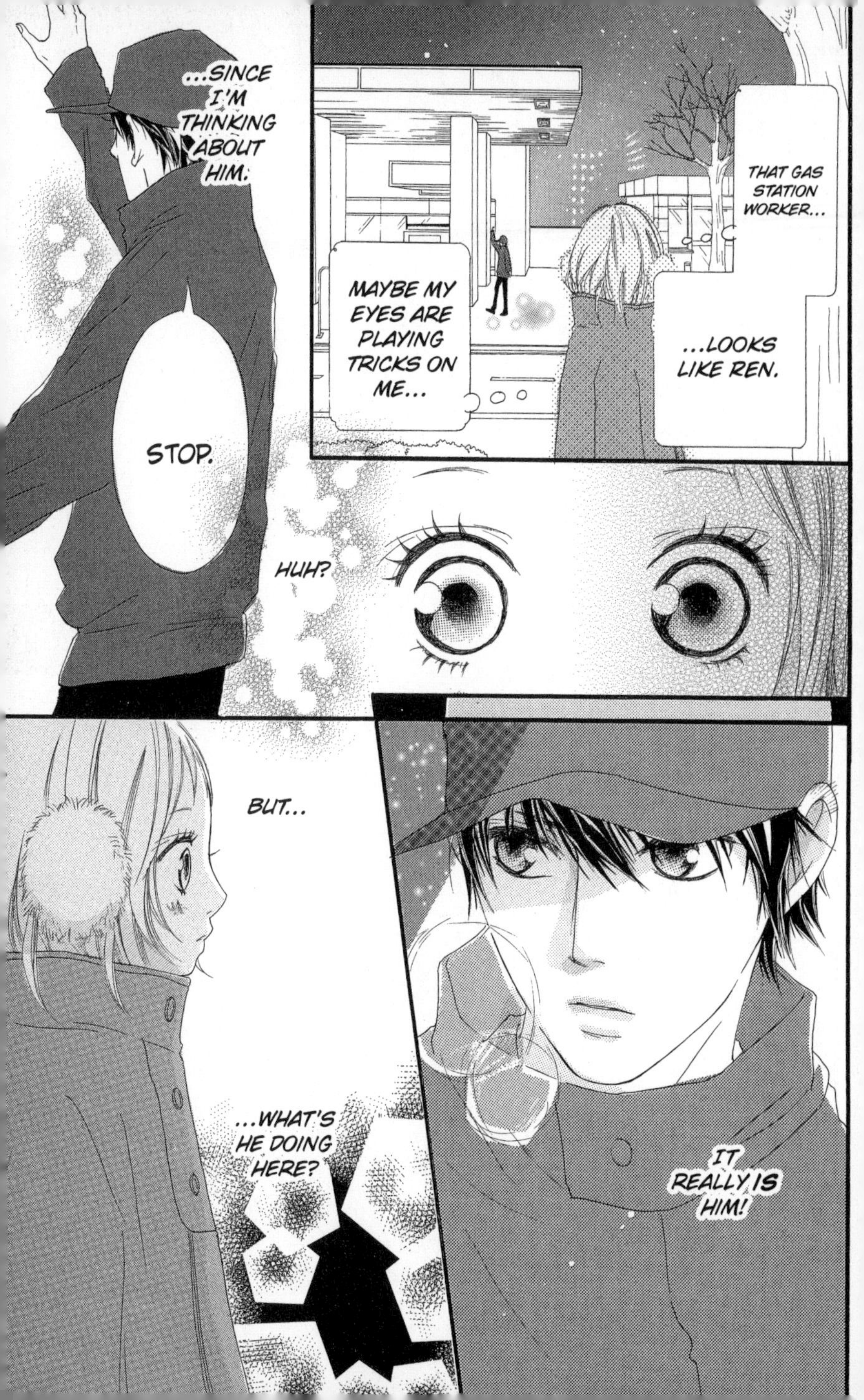
THAT GAS STATION WORKER...
...LOOKS LIKE REN.
MAYBE MY EYES ARE PLAYING TRICKS ON ME...
HUH?
...SINCE I'M THINKING ABOUT HIM.
STOP.
IT REALLY IS HIM!
BUT...
...WHAT'S HE DOING HERE?

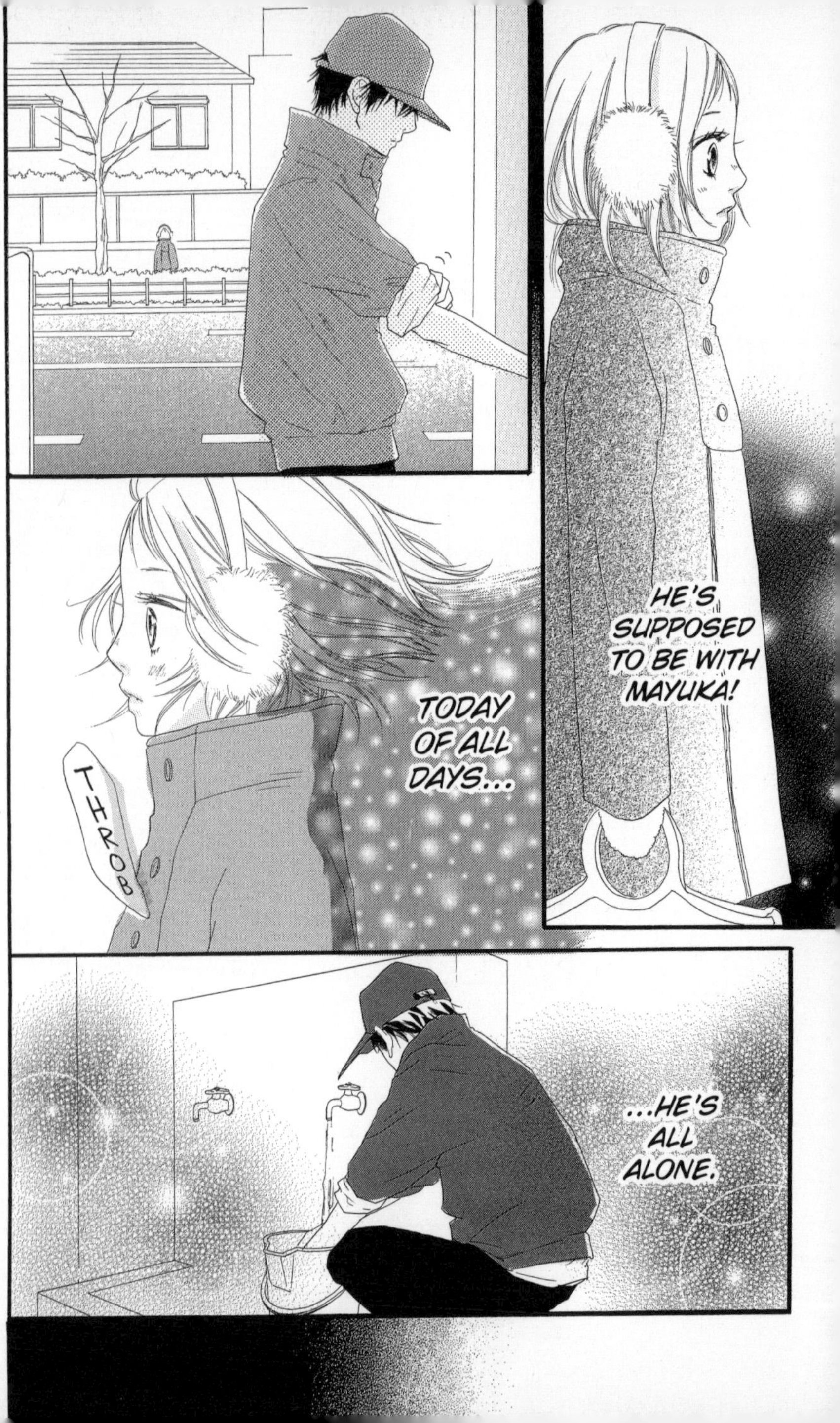
HE'S SUPPOSED TO BE WITH MAYUKA!
TODAY OF ALL DAYS...
THROB
...HE'S ALL ALONE.

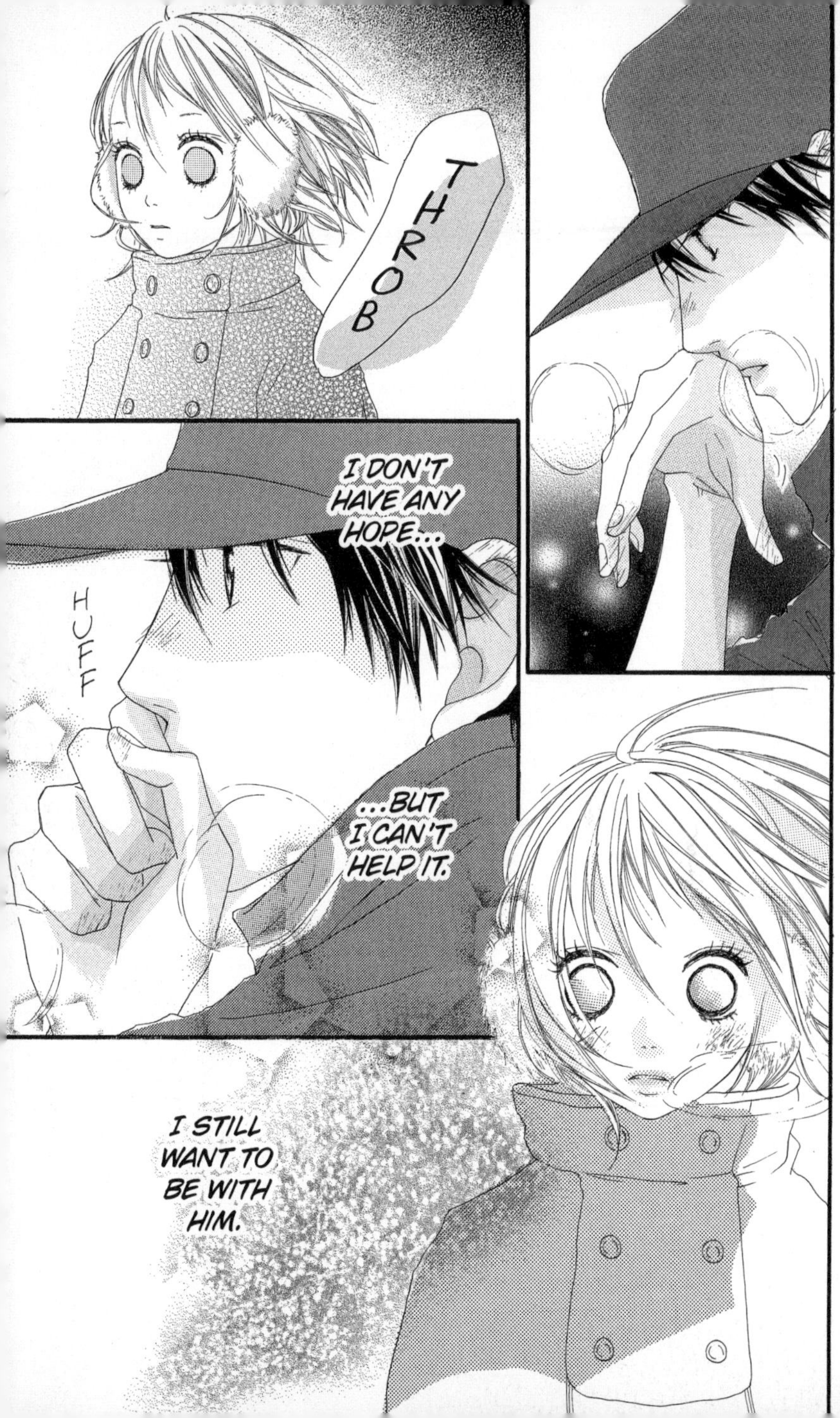
THROB
I DON'T HAVE ANY HOPE...
HUFF
...BUT I CAN'T HELP IT.
I STILL WANT TO BE WITH HIM.

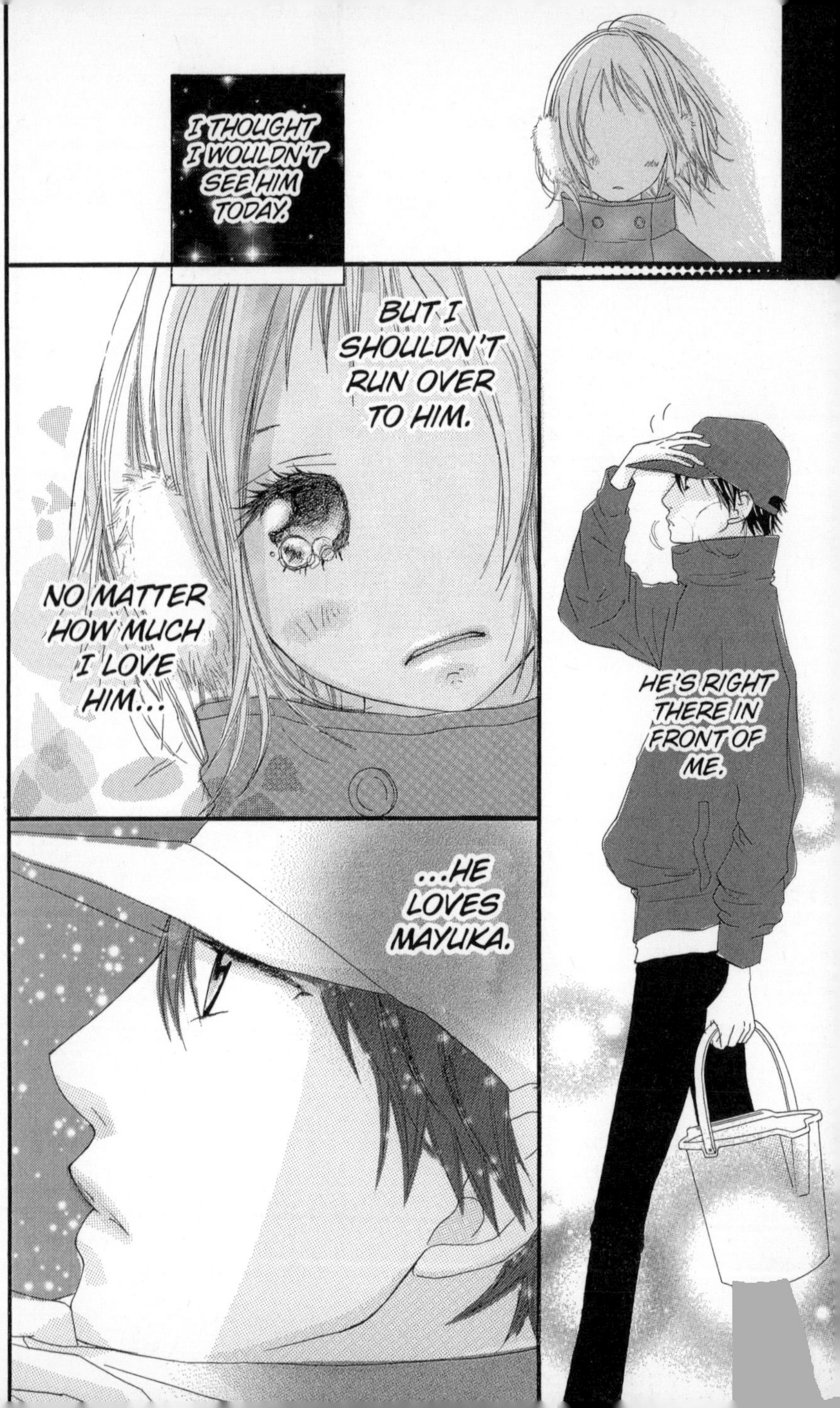
I THOUGHT I WOULDN'T SEE HIM TODAY.
HE'S RIGHT THERE IN FRONT OF ME.
BUT I SHOULDN'T RUN OVER TO HIM.
NO MATTER HOW MUCH I LOVE HIM...
...HE LOVES MAYUKA.

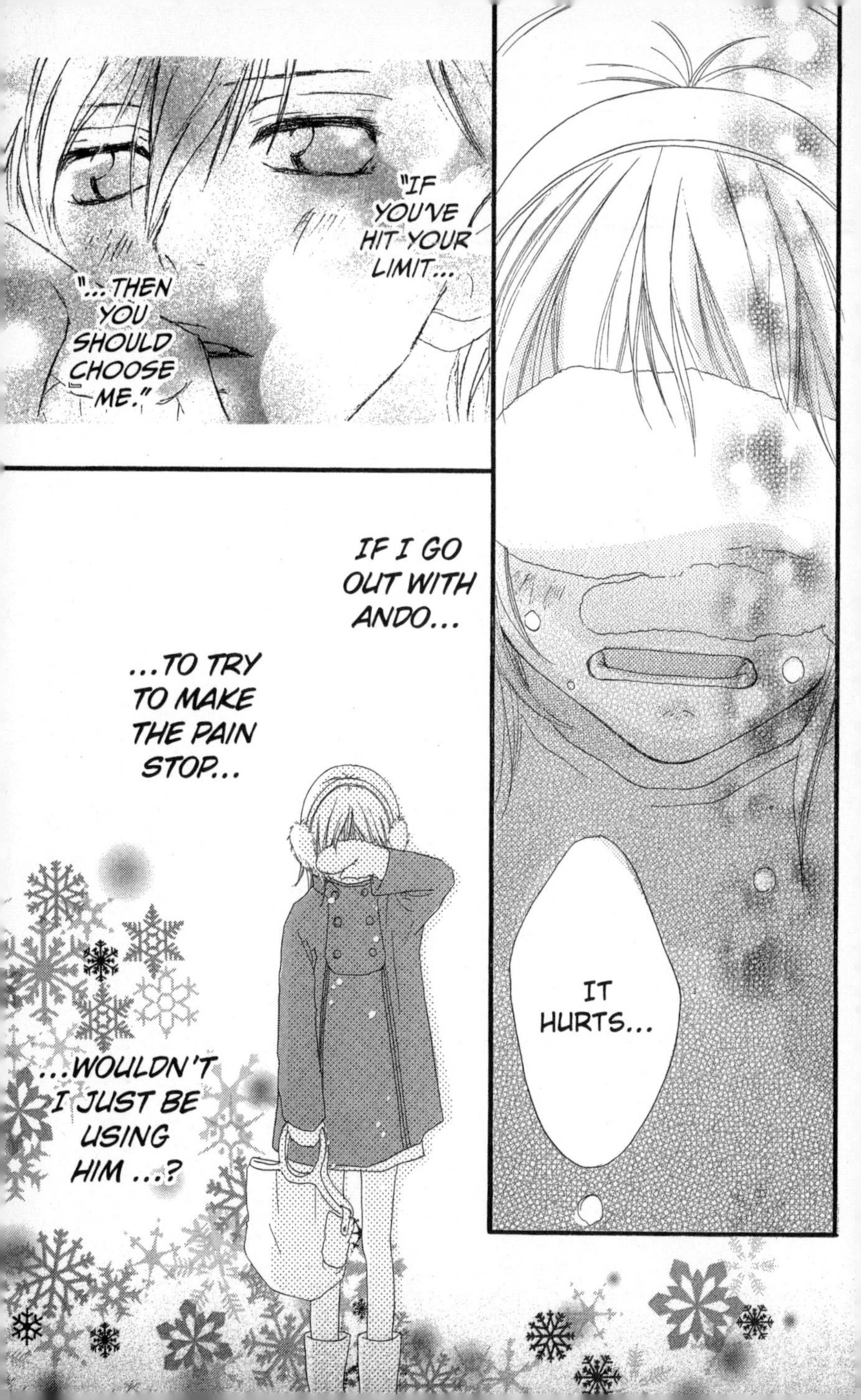
IT HURTS...
"IF YOU'VE HIT YOUR LIMIT...
"...THEN YOU SHOULD CHOOSE ME."
IF I GO OUT WITH ANDO...
...TO TRY TO MAKE THE PAIN STOP...
...WOULDN'T I JUST BE USING HIM ...?

GREETINGS PAGE

Hello! Io Sakisaka here. Thank you for reading *Strobe Edge* volume 5!

We've made it to volume 5! I'm feeling a bit emotional about it. Soon after volume 1 was published, my editor and I had a conversation like this:

Editor: I hope *Strobe Edge* makes it to five volumes or so.

Me: That would be so amazing!

So when I think back on that conversation, I feel like, "Wow, I actually made it to volume 5 *(tears of joy)*," and it seems all the more special. And how did I make it this far? You know the answer! It's all thanks to my readers. I would never have been able to come this far without readers who enjoy *Strobe Edge*. Thank you from the bottom of my heart. That's why, even if I get depressed sometimes, I know I can't be down forever! Even if I'm sad and shedding buckets of tears, I can still turn to my manuscript and move forward with all of you. Further and further into the great beyond!

So let's embark on the *Strobe Edge* volume 5 journey together! Please stick it out to the end!

have a nice trip!
★ Io Sakisaka ★

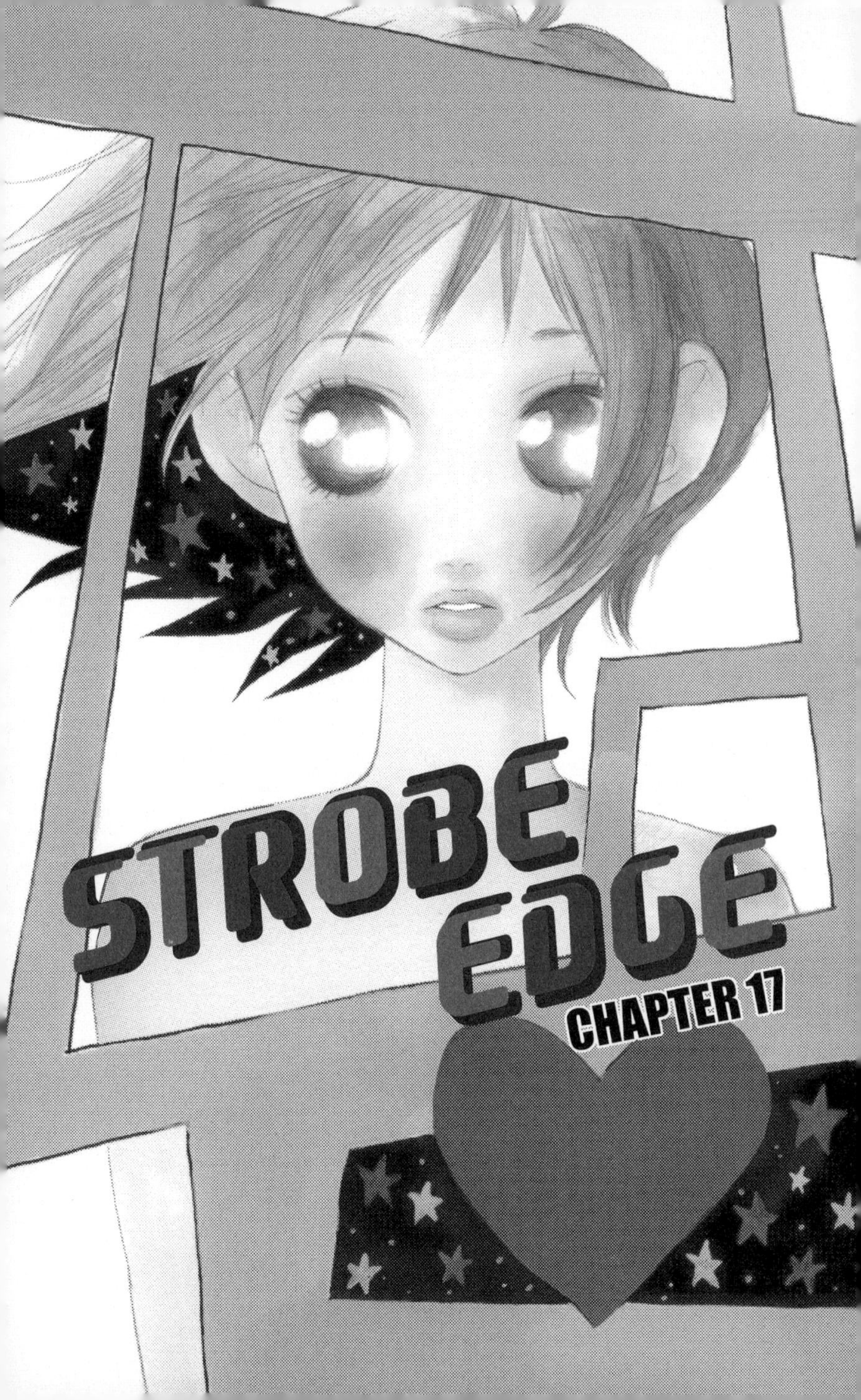
STROBE EDGE
CHAPTER 17

WHAT? NOW? MEET THE SUPPORTING CAST! ♥

Those of you who haven't been officially introduced in the story...
Those of you whose names have never actually been spoken...
I'd like to take the opportunity to introduce you now! Heh heh.

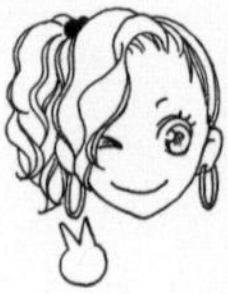

TSUKASA:
No last name. Ninako's classmate. Cheerful and straightforward. Chooses guys entirely based on their looks. Went to the same middle school as Manabu.

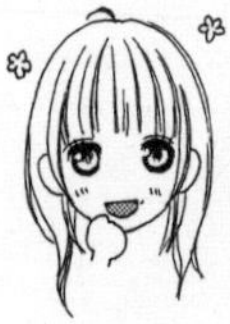

NON-CHAN:
Her real name is Noriko. No last name. Ninako's classmate. Bubbly, but direct when she wants to be.

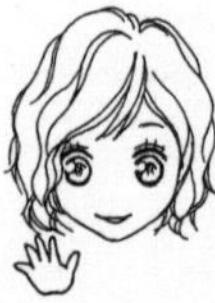

TAMAKI:
Ninako's classmate. Her name hasn't been mentioned even once! But I had a name for her. I love how she seems a bit detached from everything.

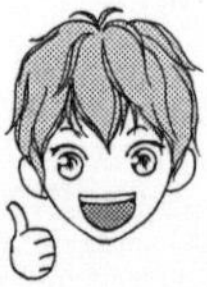

MANABU:
His last name is Miyoshi. There's a scene when he's called by his last name, so I chose this surname for him. Ren's classmate. His personality is kind of "anything goes."

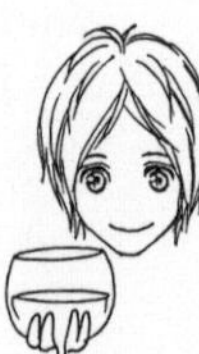

YU:
His real name is Yutaro. While trying to think of a name for him, I happened to see that actor on TV holding a huge brandy glass and mini-blinds. That's where I got his name. Ren's classmate. His job is to keep Manabu in line when he goes too far.

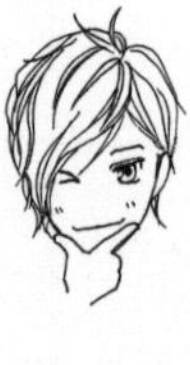

KYO:
His real name is Kyoichi Miyoshi. Owner and manager of the café where Ninako works. Age 27. Manabu's cousin. Currently single. Any takers? But I have to warn you, he has outstanding debts (loans) from when he opened his café.

Why did I do this now? Because I felt like it!

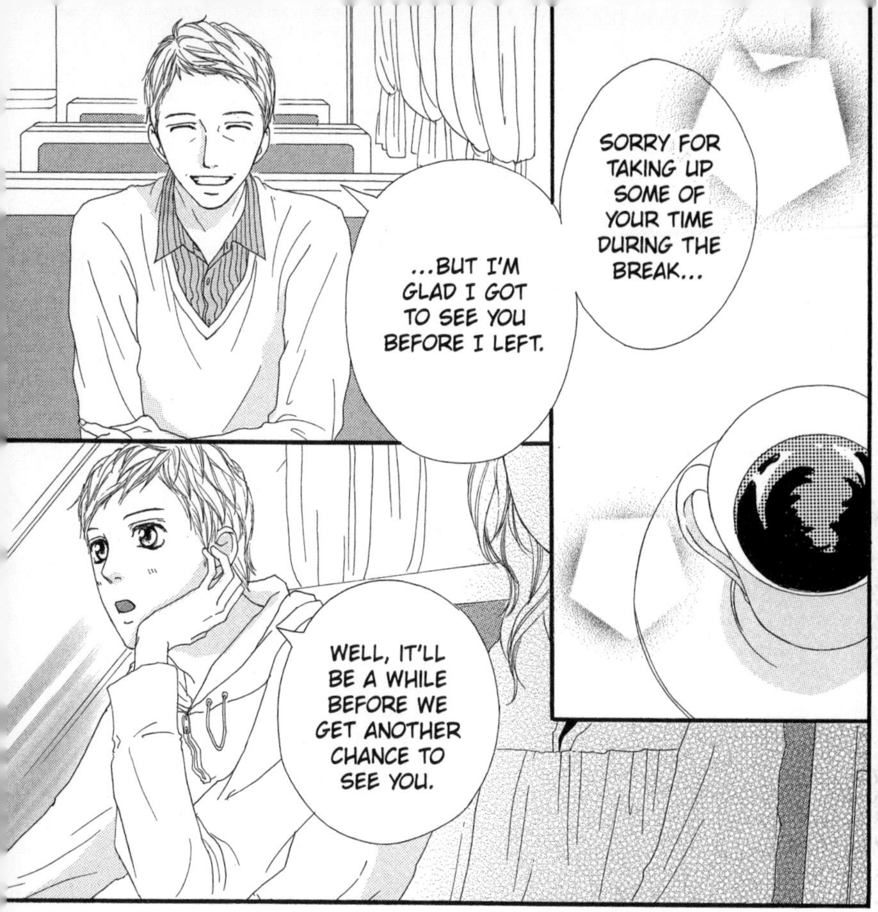
SORRY FOR TAKING UP SOME OF YOUR TIME DURING THE BREAK...
...BUT I'M GLAD I GOT TO SEE YOU BEFORE I LEFT.
WELL, IT'LL BE A WHILE BEFORE WE GET ANOTHER CHANCE TO SEE YOU.

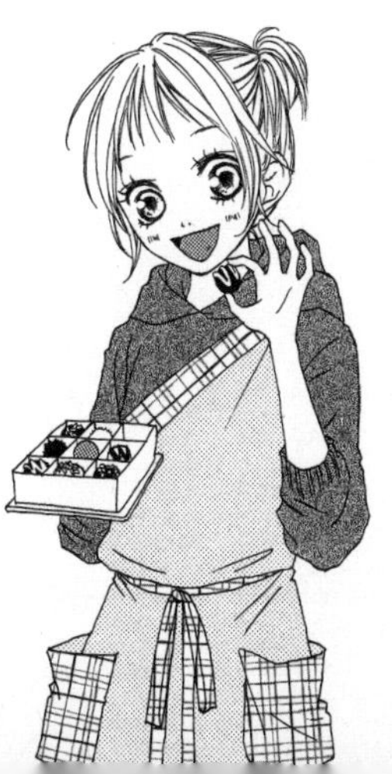

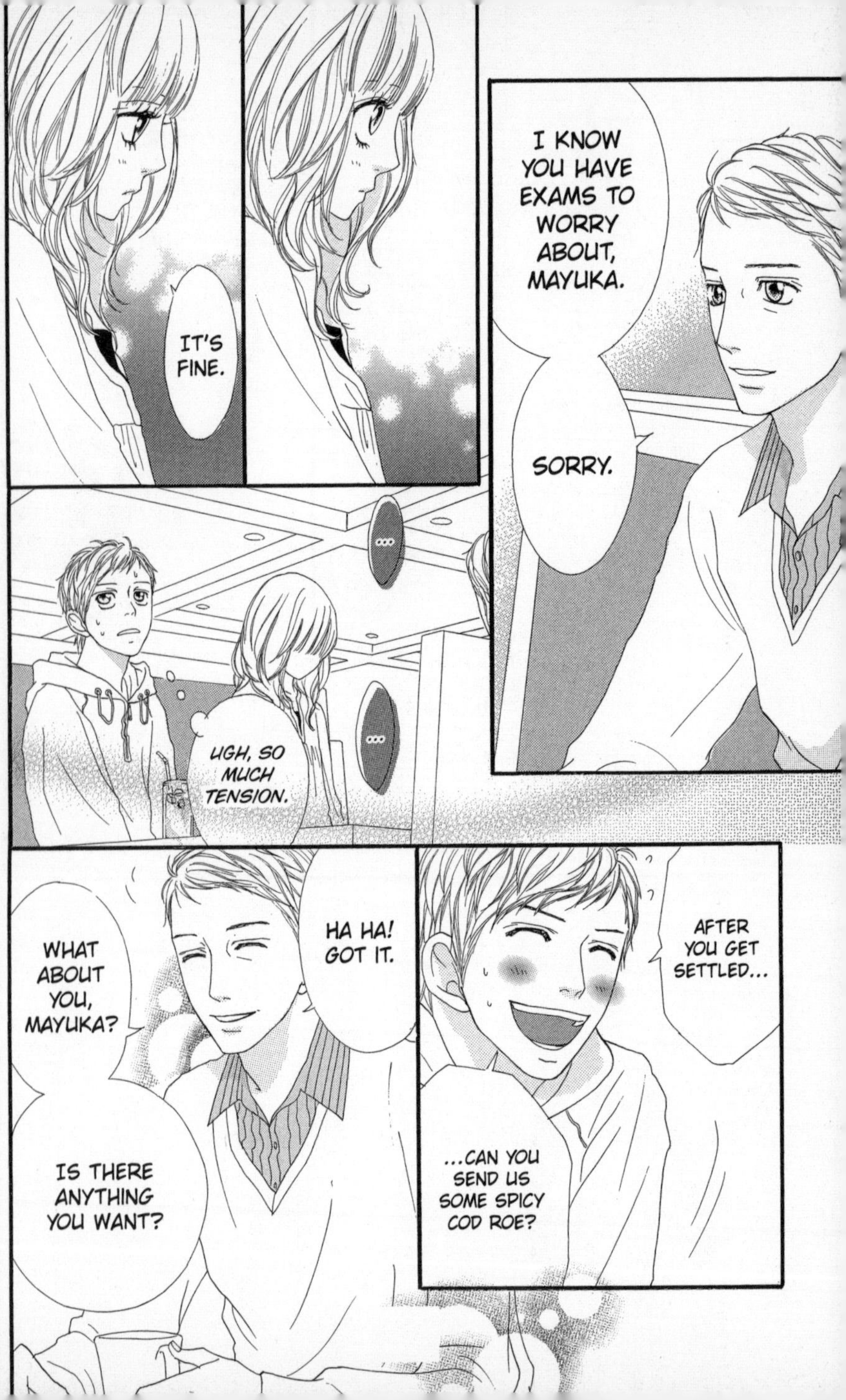
I KNOW YOU HAVE EXAMS TO WORRY ABOUT, MAYUKA.
SORRY.
IT'S FINE.
...
...
UGH, SO MUCH TENSION.
AFTER YOU GET SETTLED...
...CAN YOU SEND US SOME SPICY COD ROE?
HA HA! GOT IT.
WHAT ABOUT YOU, MAYUKA?
IS THERE ANYTHING YOU WANT?

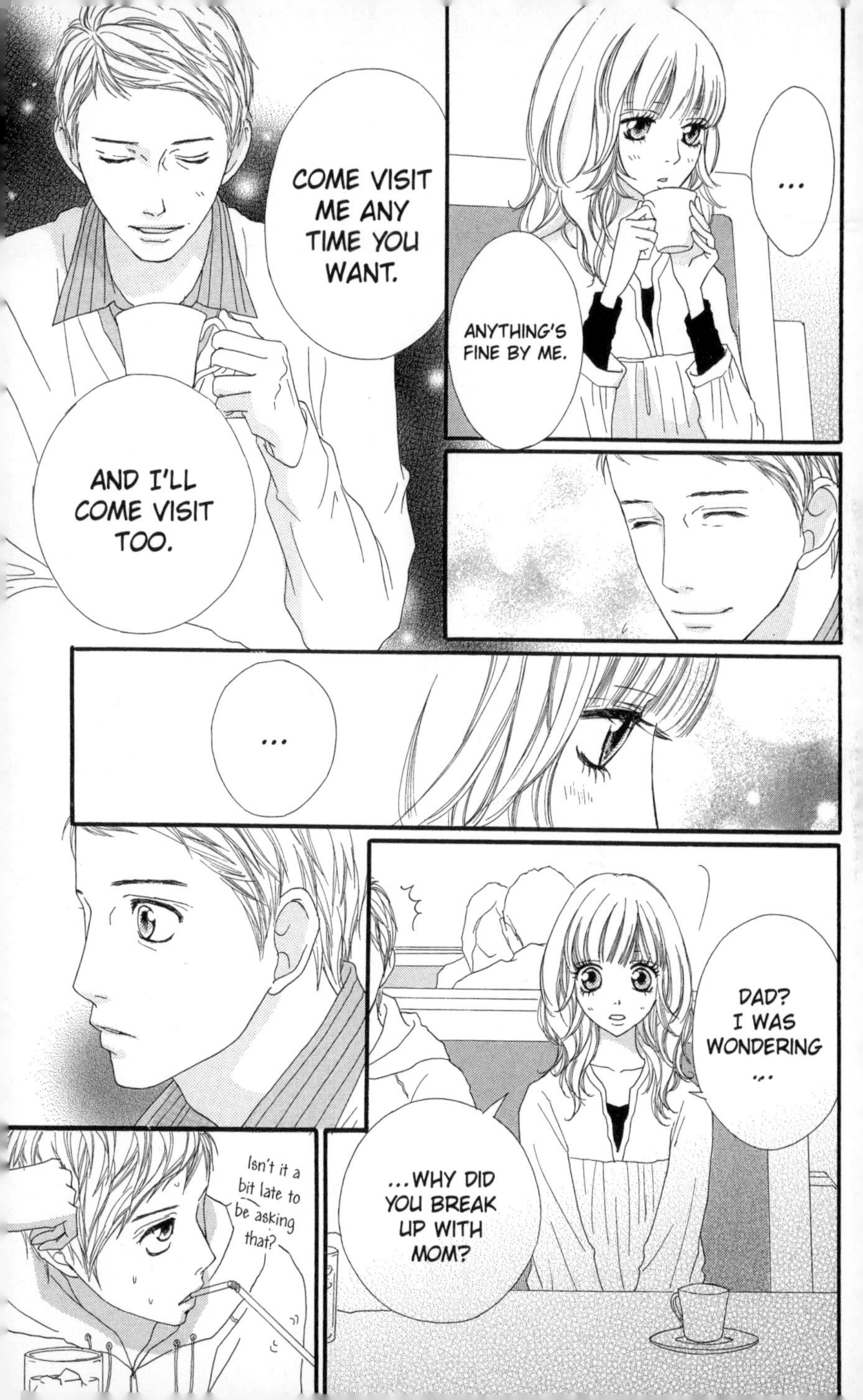
...
ANYTHING'S FINE BY ME.
COME VISIT ME ANY TIME YOU WANT.
AND I'LL COME VISIT TOO.
...
DAD? I WAS WONDERING...
...WHY DID YOU BREAK UP WITH MOM?
Isn't it a bit late to be asking that?

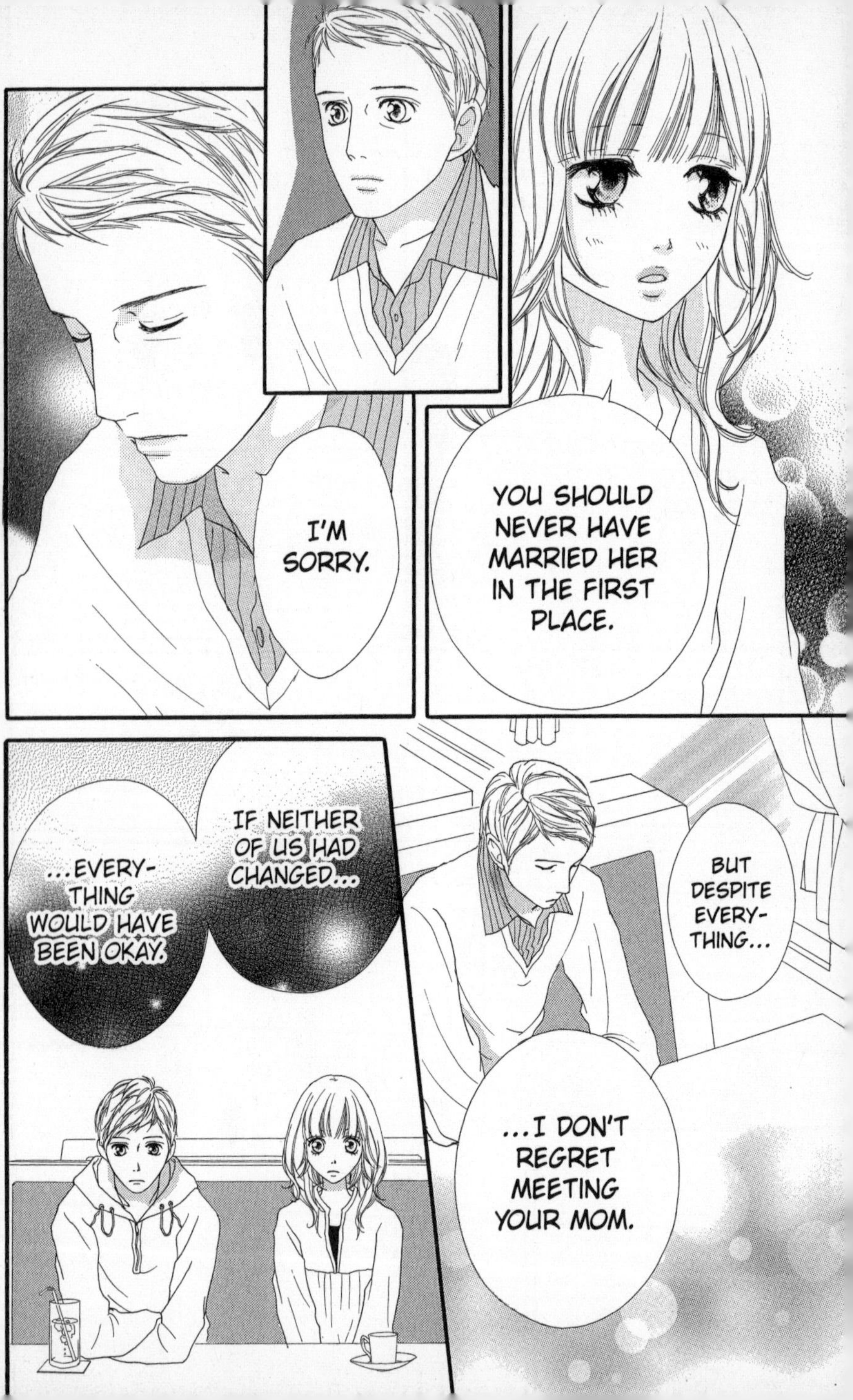
YOU SHOULD NEVER HAVE MARRIED HER IN THE FIRST PLACE.
I'M SORRY.
BUT DESPITE EVERYTHING...
...I DON'T REGRET MEETING YOUR MOM.
IF NEITHER OF US HAD CHANGED...
...EVERYTHING WOULD HAVE BEEN OKAY.

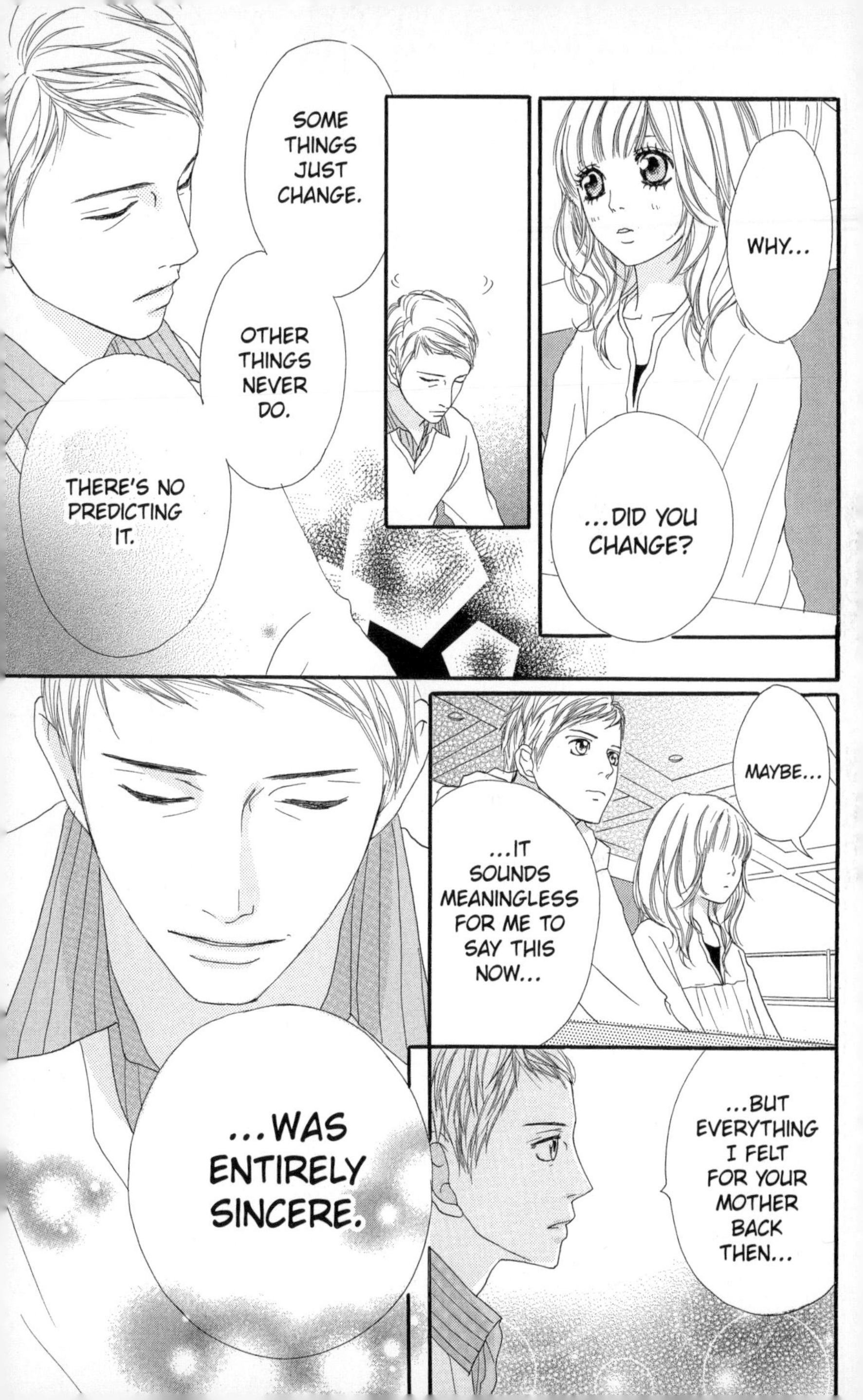
WHY...
...DID YOU CHANGE?
SOME THINGS JUST CHANGE.
OTHER THINGS NEVER DO.
THERE'S NO PREDICTING IT.
MAYBE...
...IT SOUNDS MEANINGLESS FOR ME TO SAY THIS NOW...
...BUT EVERYTHING I FELT FOR YOUR MOTHER BACK THEN...
...WAS ENTIRELY SINCERE.

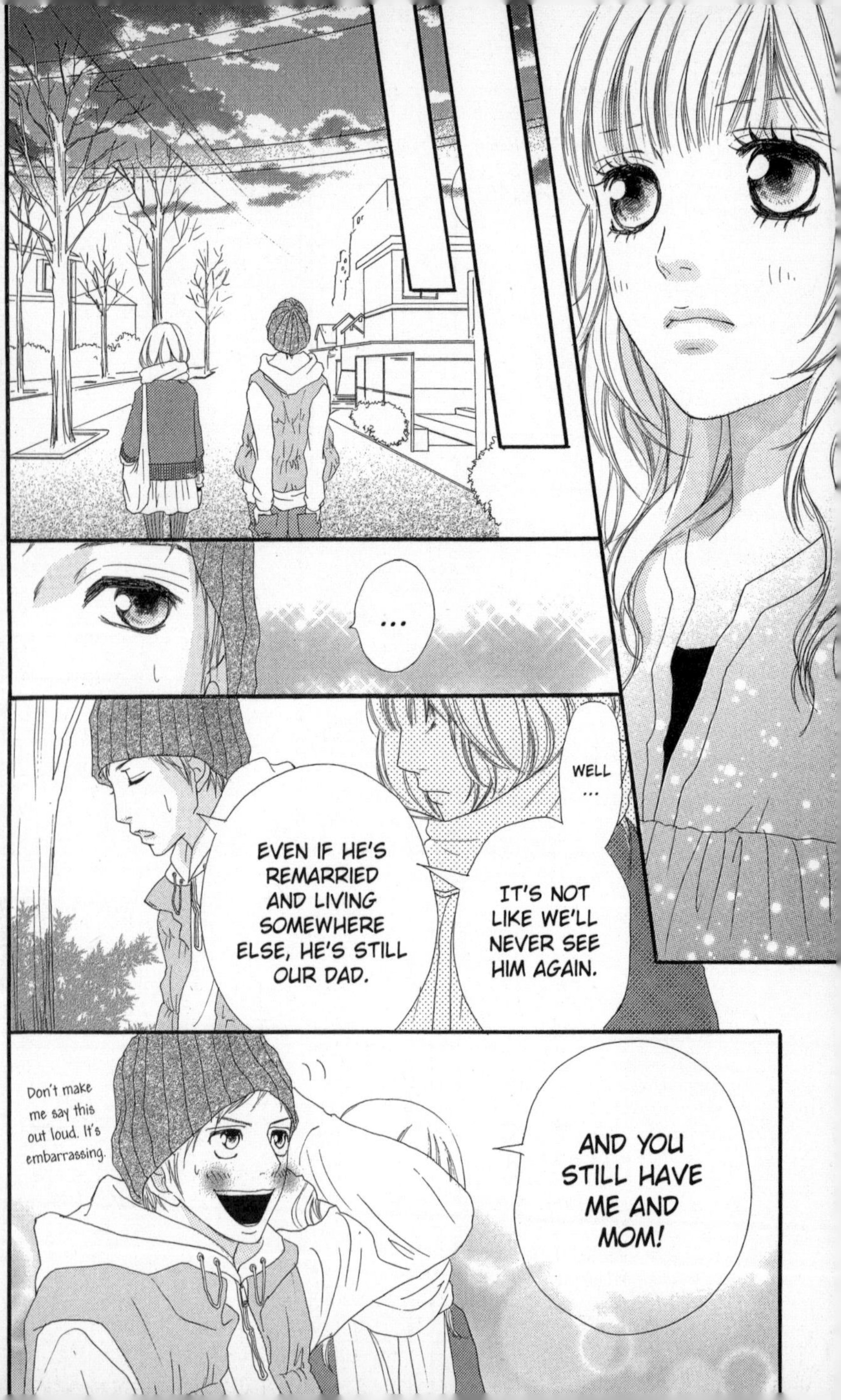
...
WELL ...
IT'S NOT LIKE WE'LL NEVER SEE HIM AGAIN.
EVEN IF HE'S REMARRIED AND LIVING SOMEWHERE ELSE, HE'S STILL OUR DAD.
AND YOU STILL HAVE ME AND MOM!
Don't make me say this out loud. It's embarrassing.

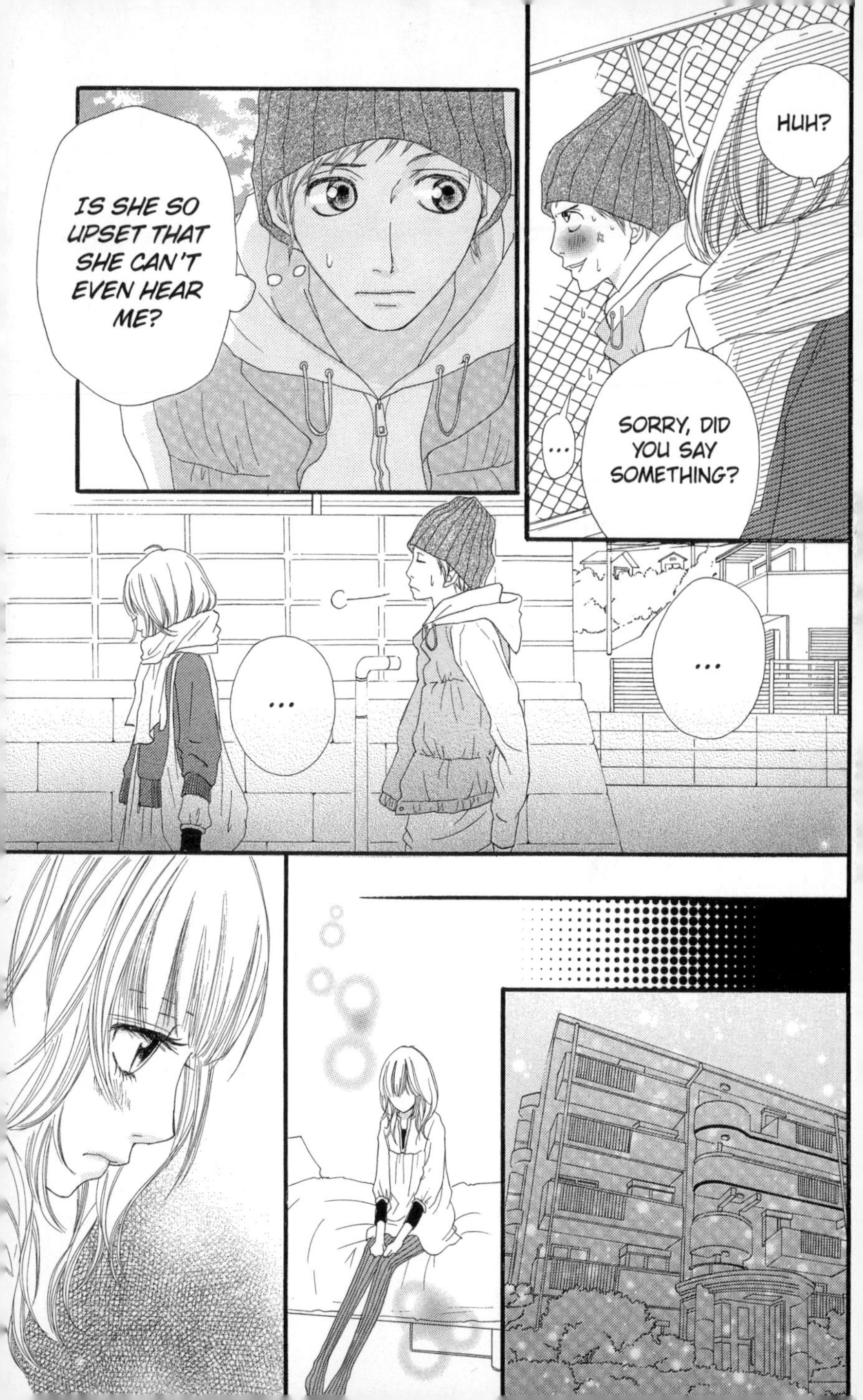
HUH?
SORRY, DID YOU SAY SOMETHING?
...
IS SHE SO UPSET THAT SHE CAN'T EVEN HEAR ME?
...
...

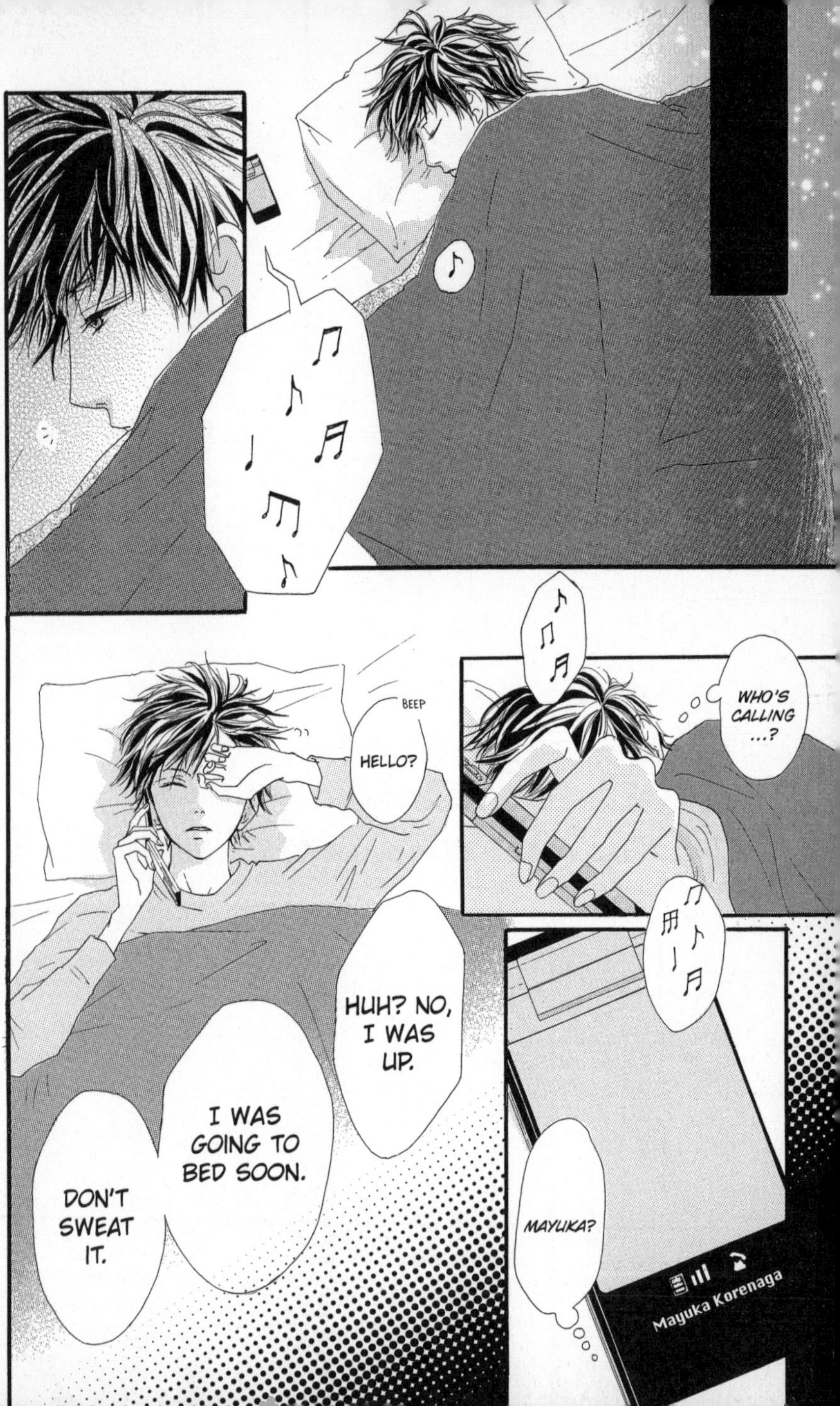
WHO'S CALLING ...?
MAYUKA?
Mayuka Korenaga
BEEP
HELLO?
HUH? NO, I WAS UP.
I WAS GOING TO BED SOON.
DON'T SWEAT IT.

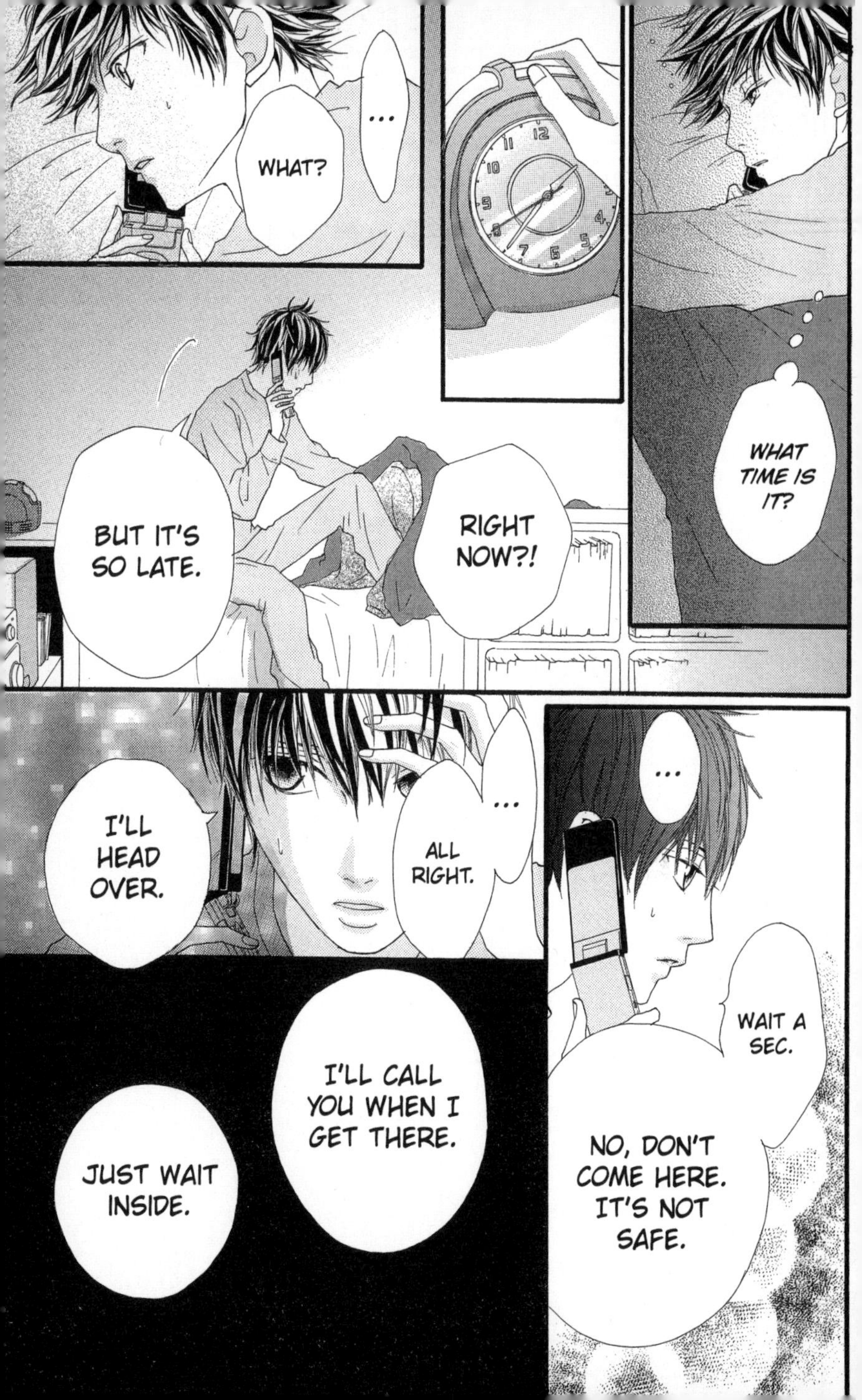
WHAT TIME IS IT?
...
WHAT?
RIGHT NOW?!
BUT IT'S SO LATE.
...
WAIT A SEC.
NO, DON'T COME HERE. IT'S NOT SAFE.
...
ALL RIGHT.
I'LL HEAD OVER.
I'LL CALL YOU WHEN I GET THERE.
JUST WAIT INSIDE.

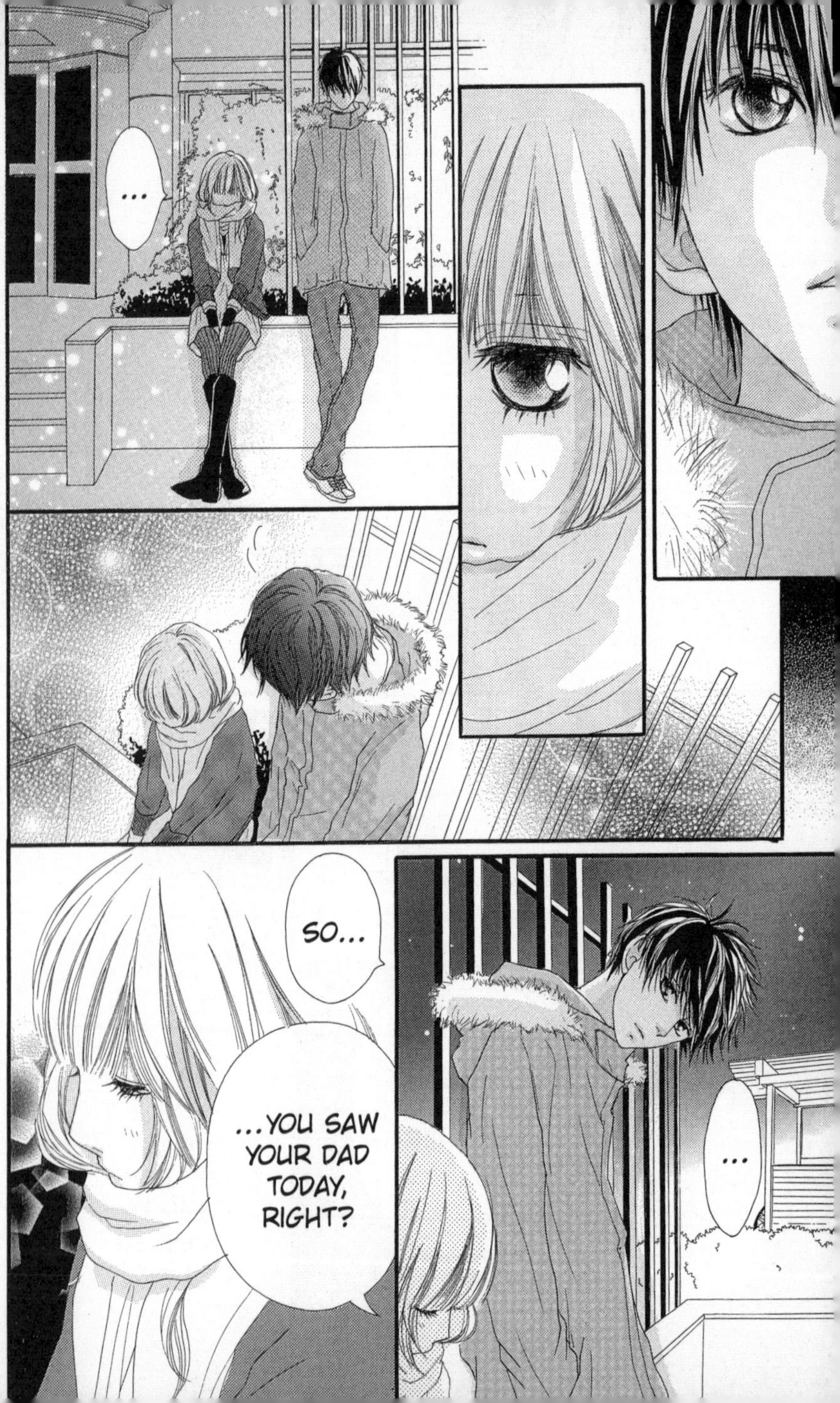
...
SO...
...YOU SAW YOUR DAD TODAY, RIGHT?
...

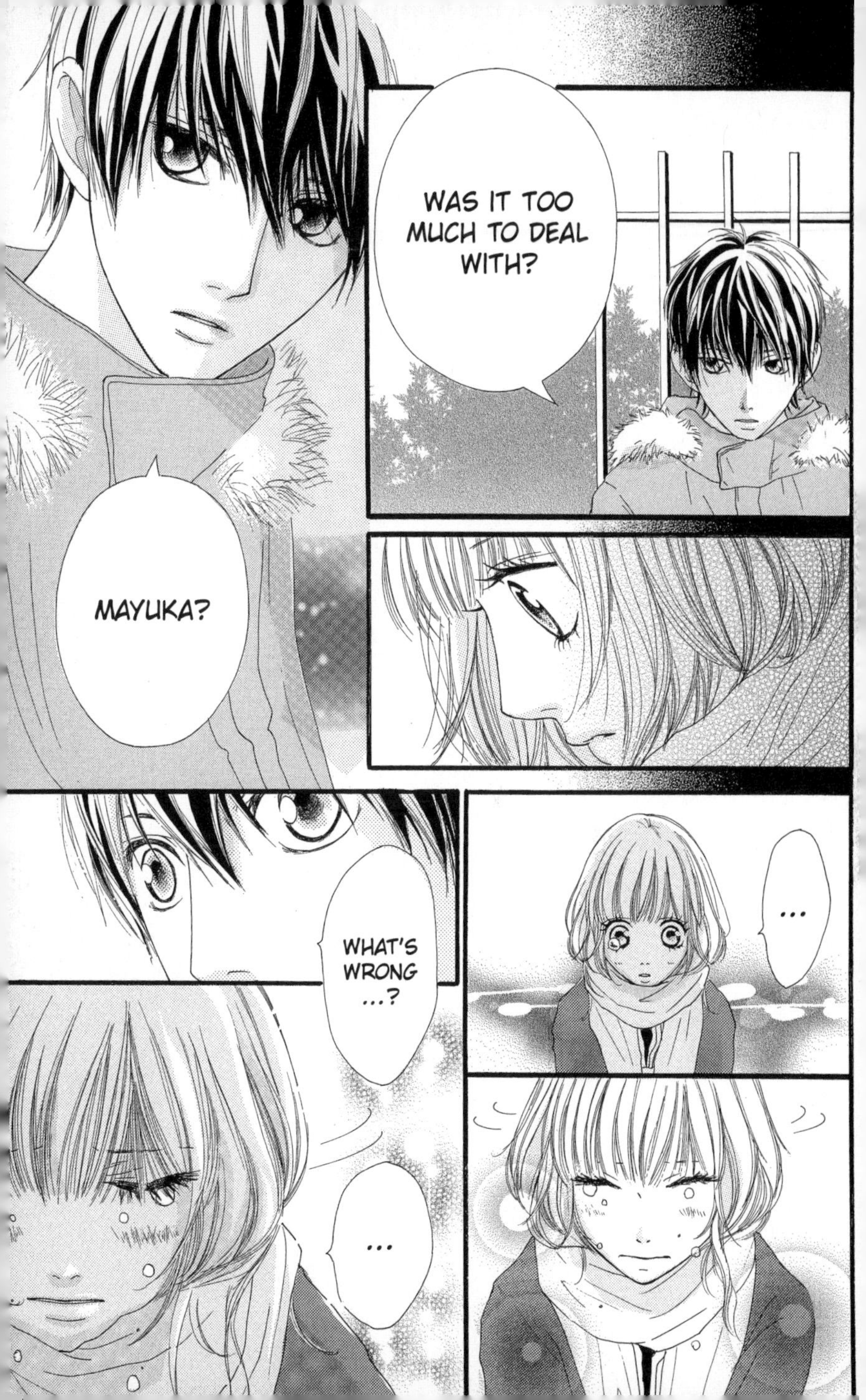
WAS IT TOO MUCH TO DEAL WITH?
MAYUKA?
...
WHAT'S WRONG ...?
...

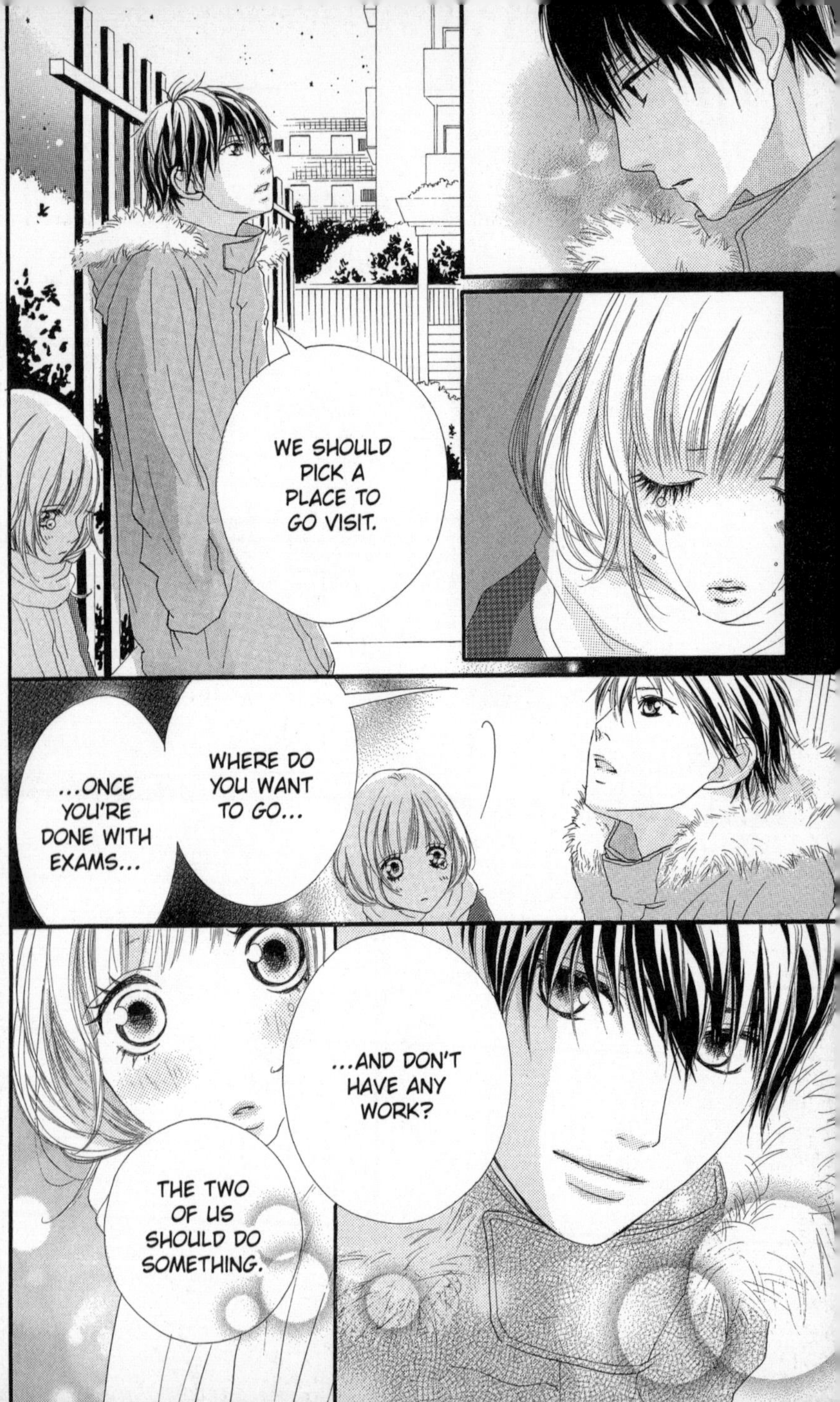
WE SHOULD PICK A PLACE TO GO VISIT.
WHERE DO YOU WANT TO GO...
...ONCE YOU'RE DONE WITH EXAMS...
...AND DON'T HAVE ANY WORK?
THE TWO OF US SHOULD DO SOMETHING.

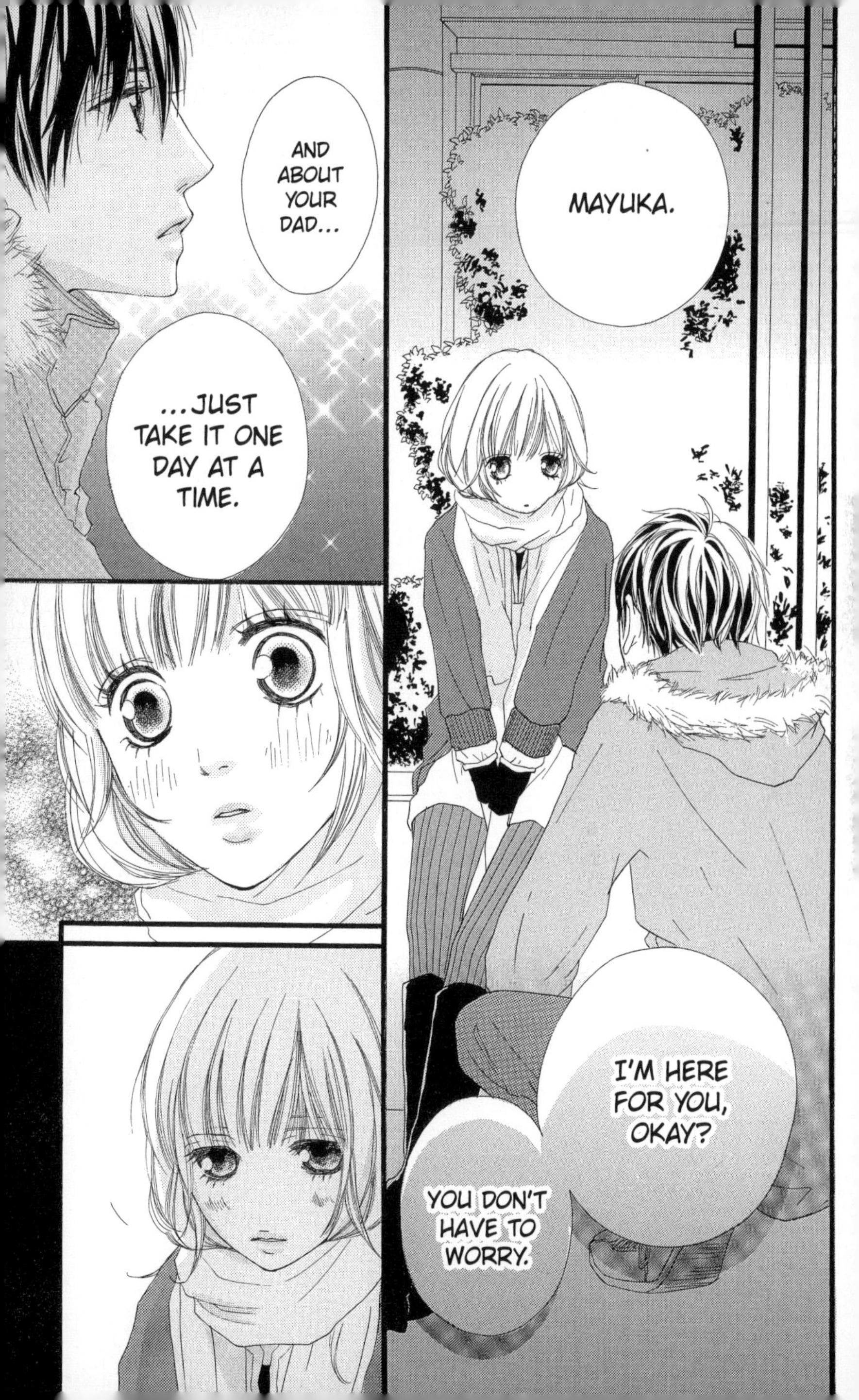
MAYUKA.
I'M HERE FOR YOU, OKAY?
YOU DON'T HAVE TO WORRY.
AND ABOUT YOUR DAD...
...JUST TAKE IT ONE DAY AT A TIME.

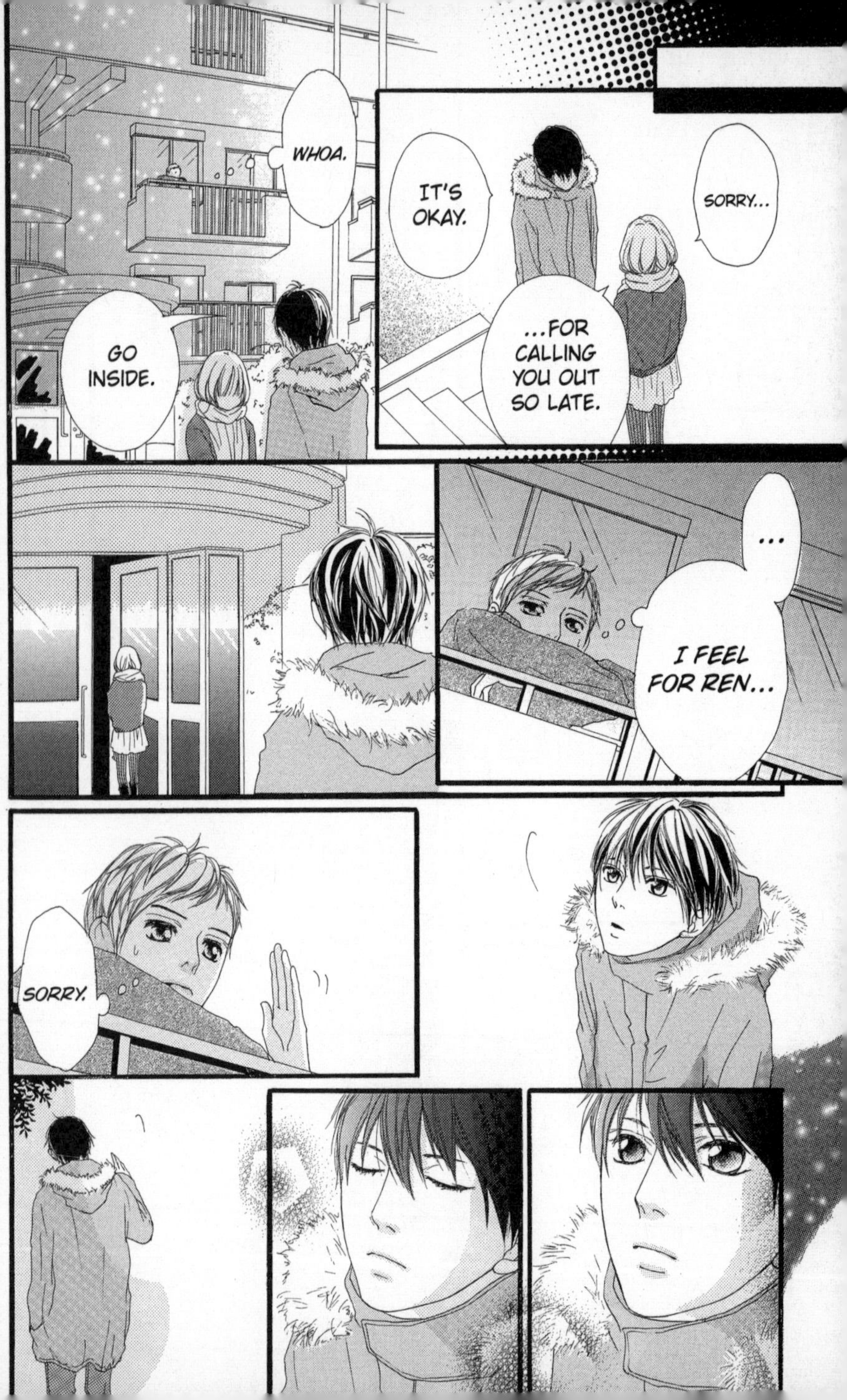
SORRY...
...FOR CALLING YOU OUT SO LATE.
IT'S OKAY.
WHOA.
GO INSIDE.
...
I FEEL FOR REN...
SORRY.

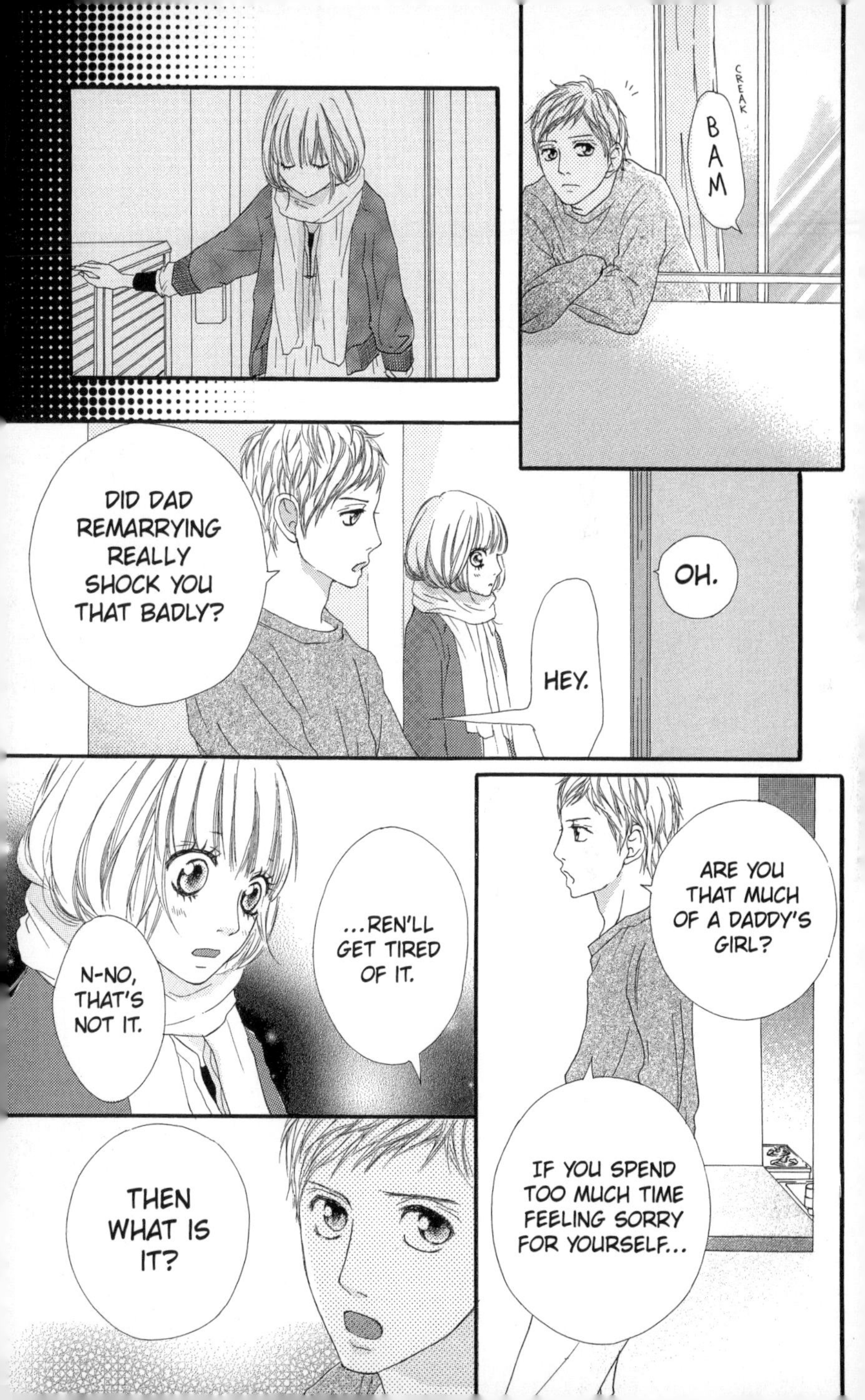
CREAK
BAM
OH.
HEY.
DID DAD REMARRYING REALLY SHOCK YOU THAT BADLY?
ARE YOU THAT MUCH OF A DADDY'S GIRL?
IF YOU SPEND TOO MUCH TIME FEELING SORRY FOR YOURSELF...
...REN'LL GET TIRED OF IT.
N-NO, THAT'S NOT IT.
THEN WHAT IS IT?

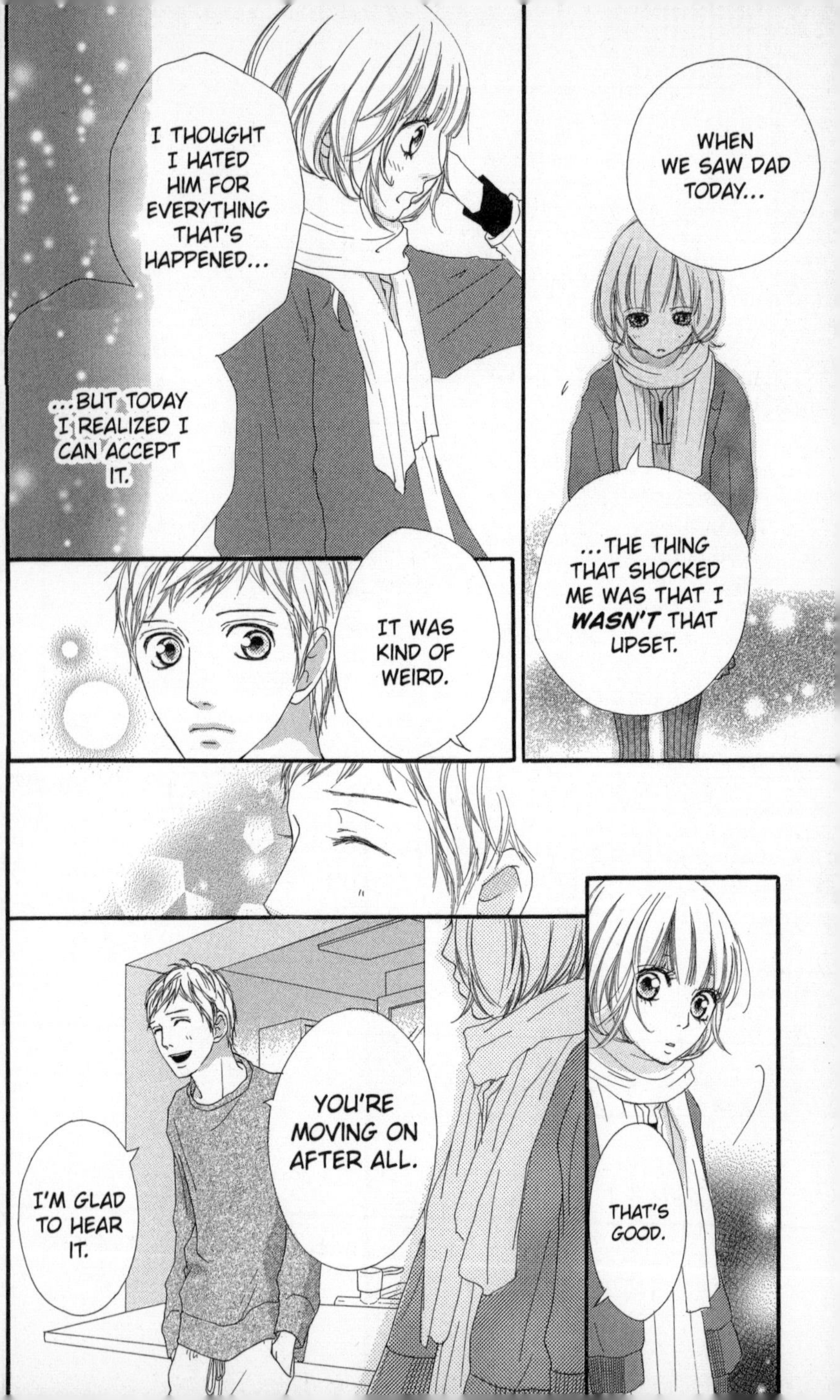
WHEN WE SAW DAD TODAY...
...THE THING THAT SHOCKED ME WAS THAT I **WASN'T** THAT UPSET.
I THOUGHT I HATED HIM FOR EVERYTHING THAT'S HAPPENED...
...BUT TODAY I REALIZED I CAN ACCEPT IT.
IT WAS KIND OF WEIRD.
THAT'S GOOD.
YOU'RE MOVING ON AFTER ALL.
I'M GLAD TO HEAR IT.

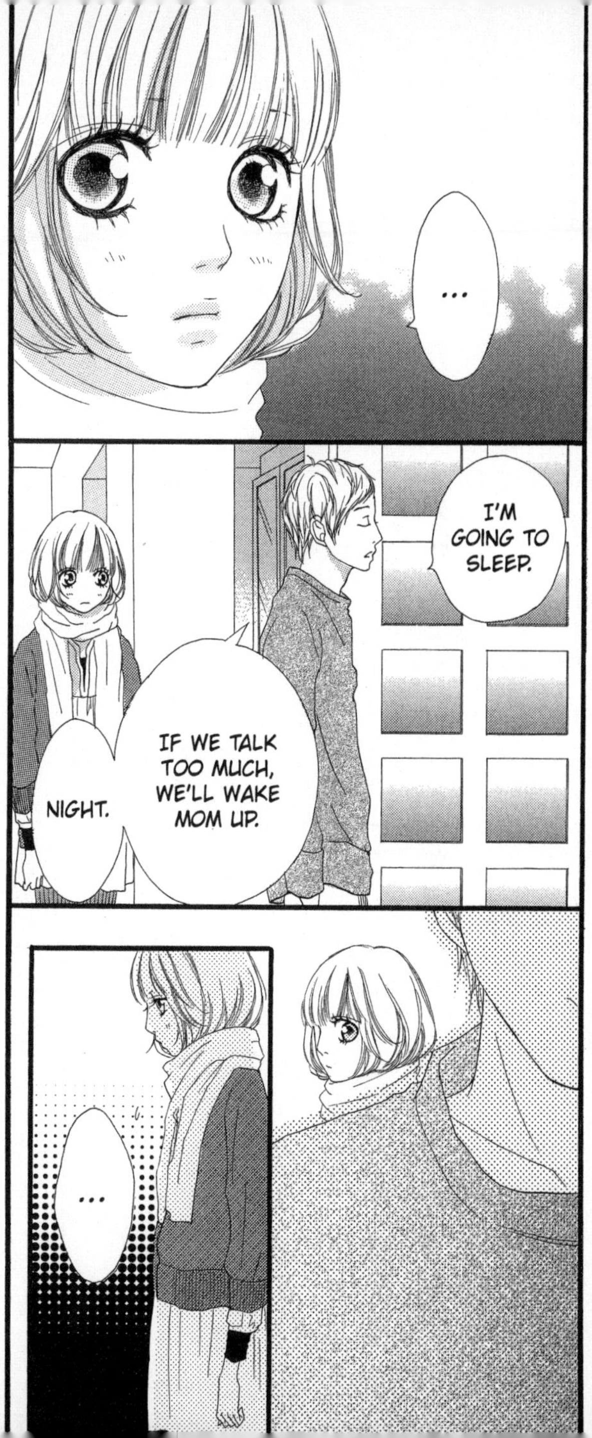
...
I'M GOING TO SLEEP.
IF WE TALK TOO MUCH, WE'LL WAKE MOM UP.
NIGHT.
...

When I have assistants working for me, we often have food delivered. There's this young guy from X Delivery Service who has stunningly beautiful hands. When he's the one who brings our food, I secretly get excited. I can't take my eyes off of his hands. They're slender, refined and nicely shaped. I almost want to scout him as a hand model! But if I creep him out, he may not come anymore. That would be a problem (not really), so I haven't. I just peer at them secretly. Am I harassing him? But what hands—! I can't take my eyes off them. He hardly ever comes, though. I wish it was always him delivering our food. Not that I have a hand fetish or anything...

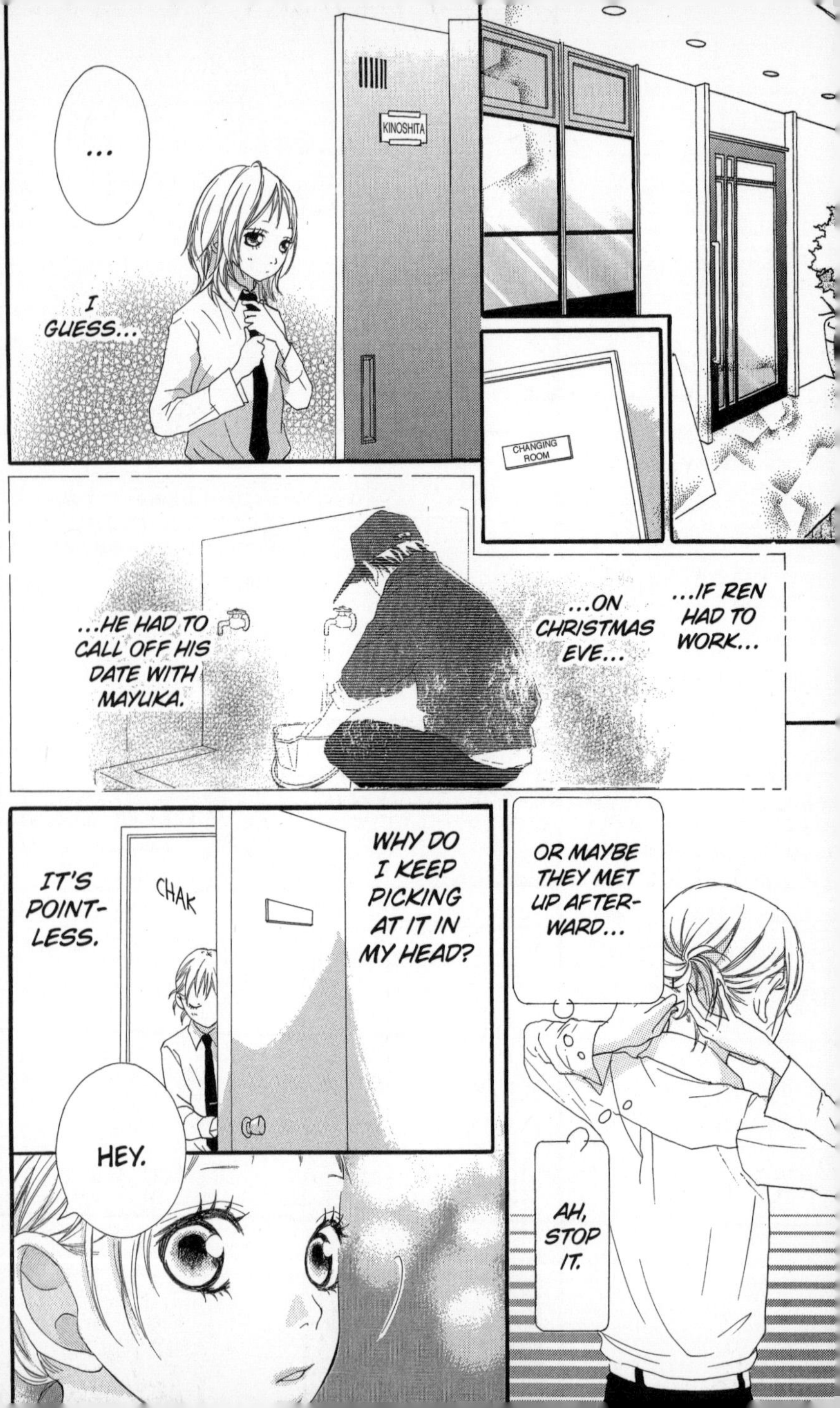
CHANGING ROOM
KINOSHITA
...
I GUESS...
...IF REN HAD TO WORK...
...ON CHRISTMAS EVE...
...HE HAD TO CALL OFF HIS DATE WITH MAYUKA.
OR MAYBE THEY MET UP AFTERWARD...
AH, STOP IT.
WHY DO I KEEP PICKING AT IT IN MY HEAD?
IT'S POINTLESS.
CHAK
HEY.

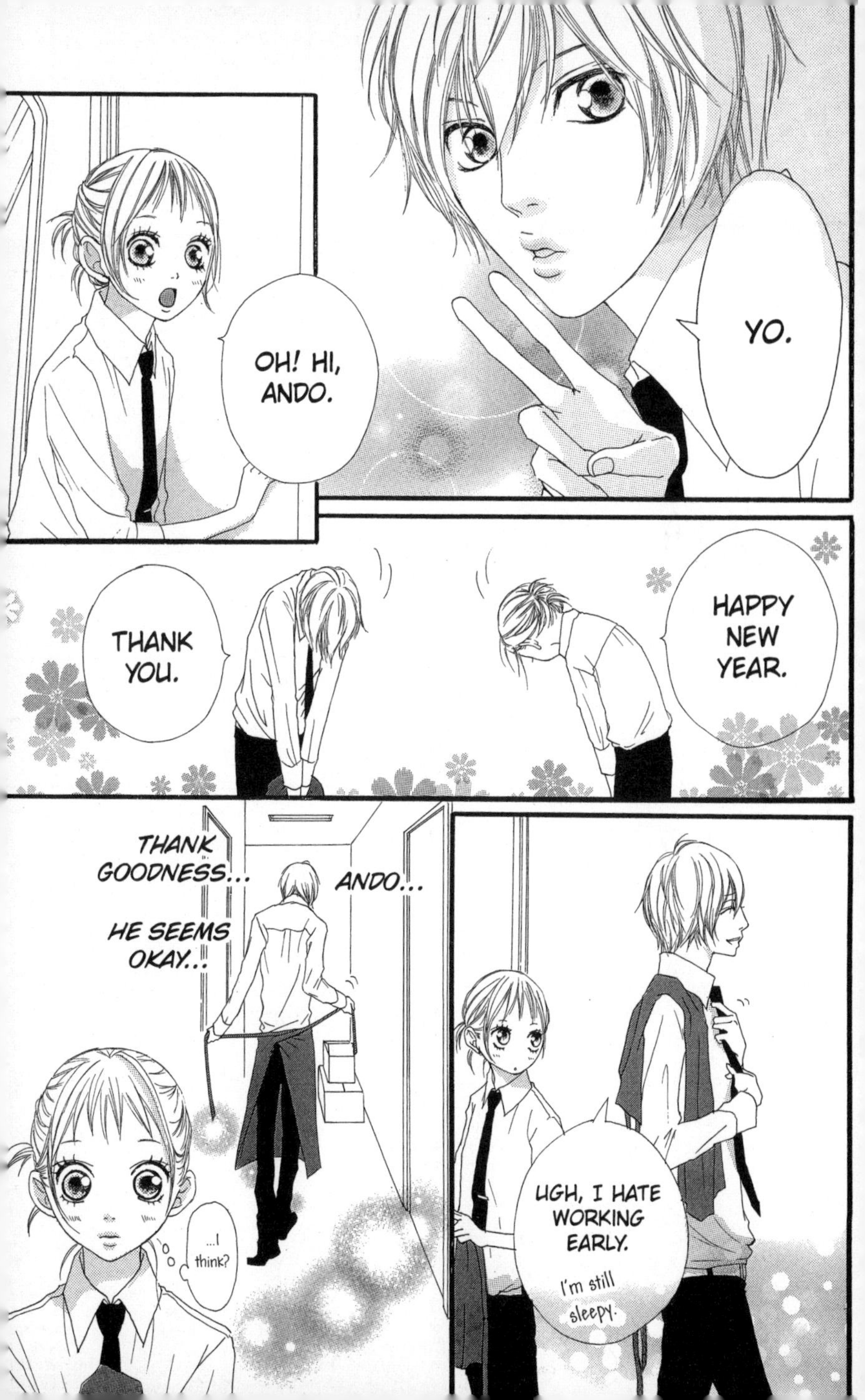
YO.
OH! HI, ANDO.
HAPPY NEW YEAR.
THANK YOU.
UGH, I HATE WORKING EARLY.
I'm still sleepy.
ANDO...
THANK GOODNESS...
HE SEEMS OKAY...
...I think?

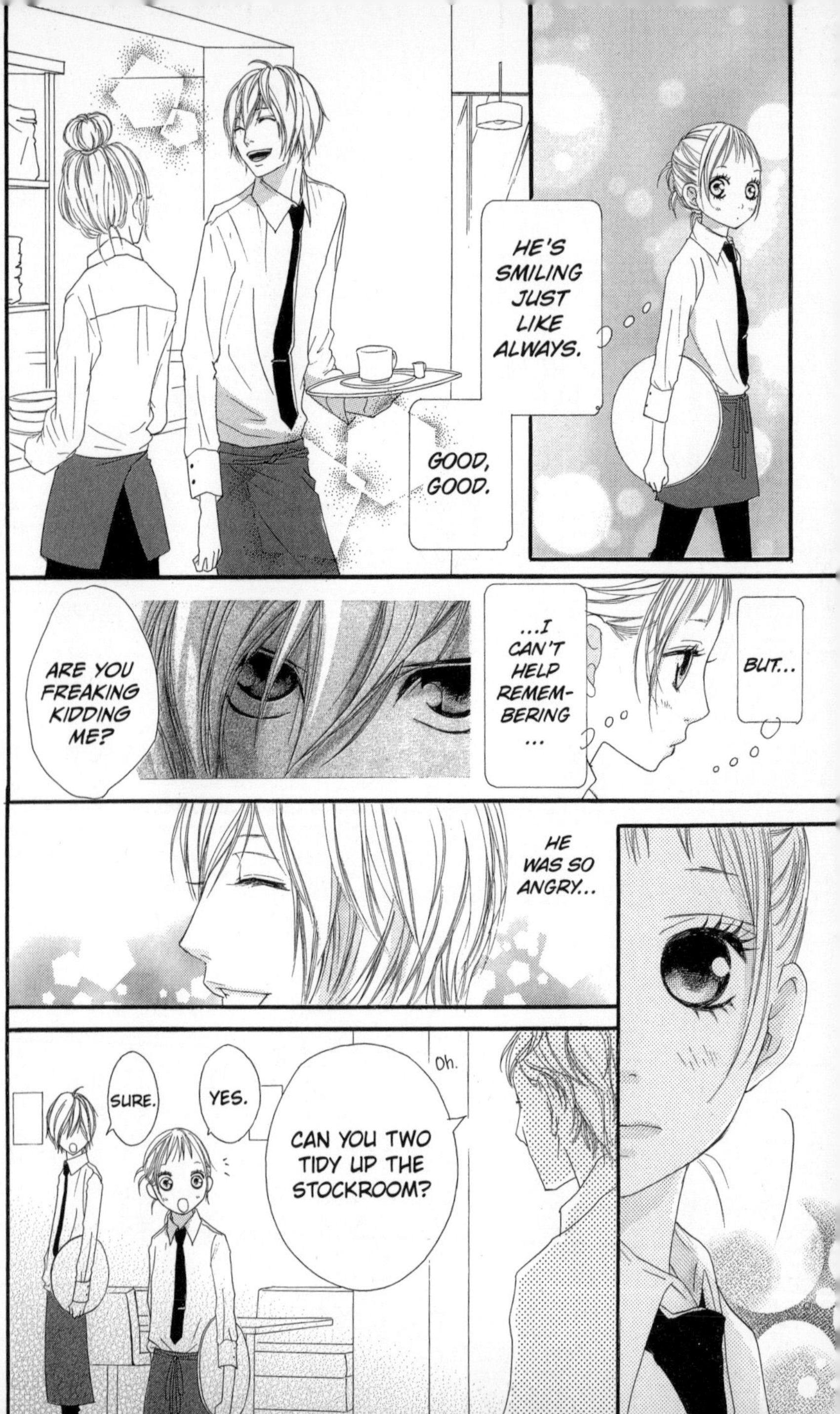
HE'S SMILING JUST LIKE ALWAYS.
GOOD, GOOD.
BUT...
...I CAN'T HELP REMEMBERING...
ARE YOU FREAKING KIDDING ME?
HE WAS SO ANGRY...
Oh.
CAN YOU TWO TIDY UP THE STOCKROOM?
YES.
SURE.

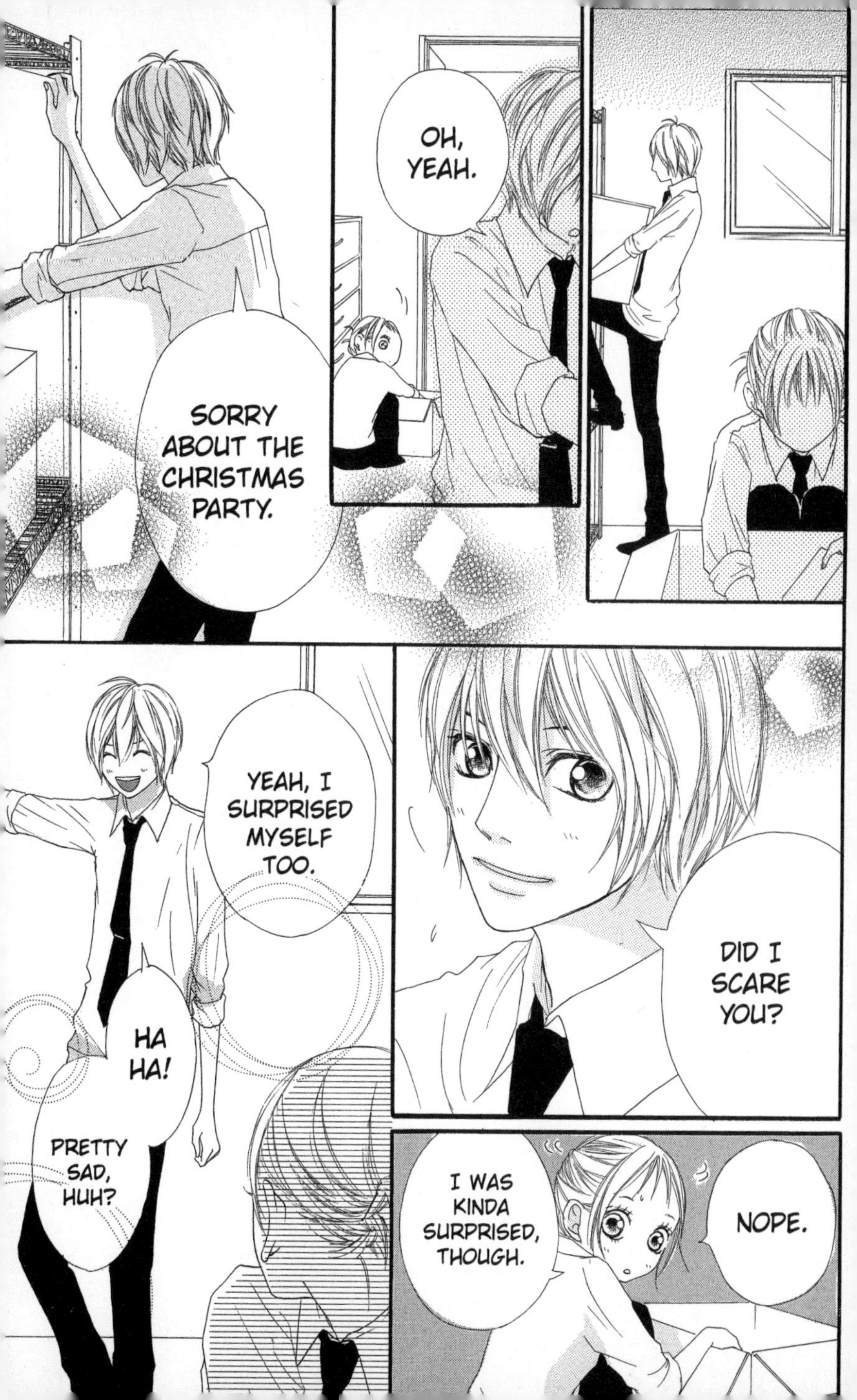
OH, YEAH.
SORRY ABOUT THE CHRISTMAS PARTY.
DID I SCARE YOU?
NOPE.
I WAS KINDA SURPRISED, THOUGH.
YEAH, I SURPRISED MYSELF TOO.
HA HA!
PRETTY SAD, HUH?

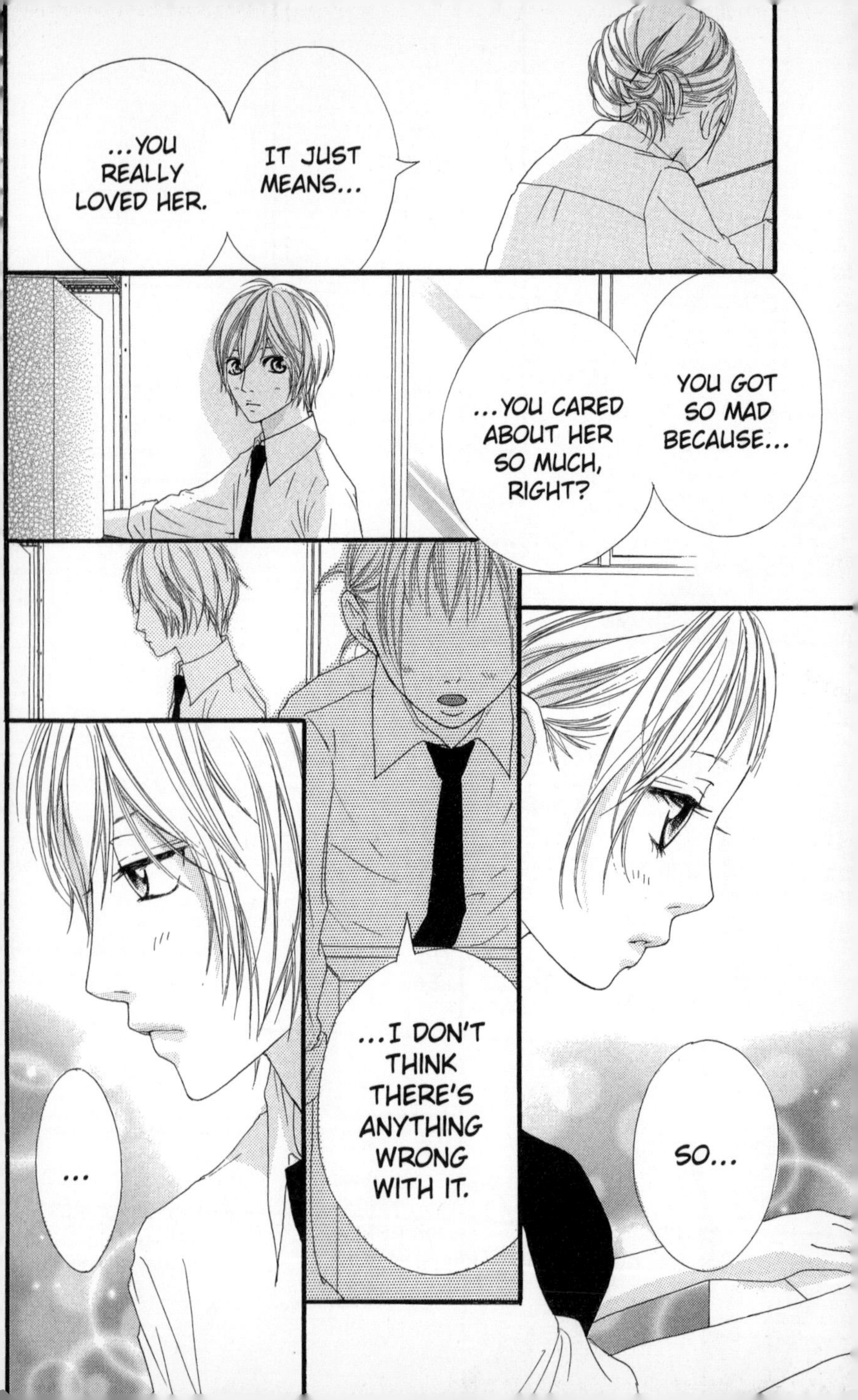
IT JUST MEANS...
...YOU REALLY LOVED HER.
YOU GOT SO MAD BECAUSE...
...YOU CARED ABOUT HER SO MUCH, RIGHT?
SO...
...I DON'T THINK THERE'S ANYTHING WRONG WITH IT.
...

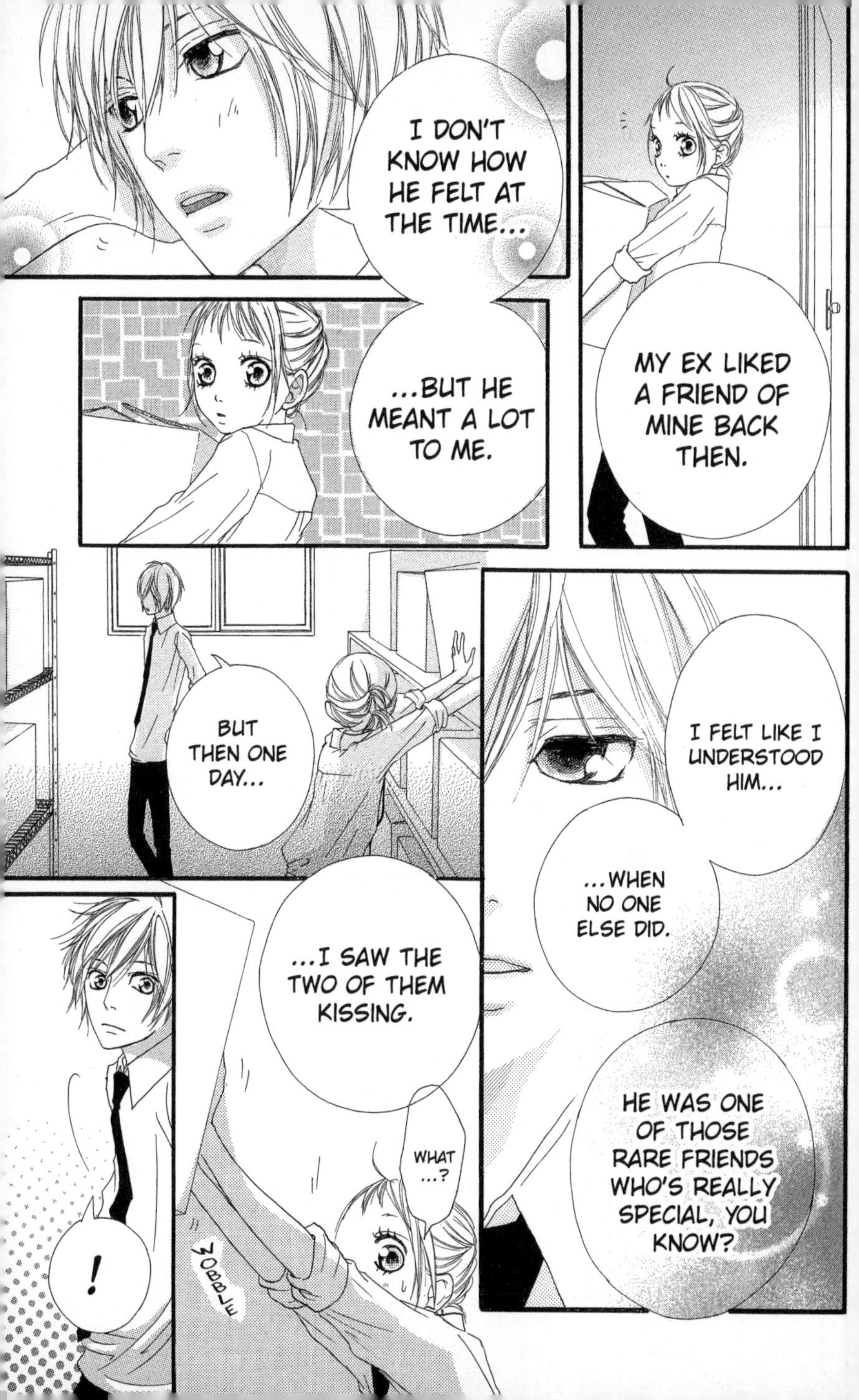
MY EX LIKED A FRIEND OF MINE BACK THEN.
I DON'T KNOW HOW HE FELT AT THE TIME...
...BUT HE MEANT A LOT TO ME.
I FELT LIKE I UNDERSTOOD HIM...
...WHEN NO ONE ELSE DID.
HE WAS ONE OF THOSE RARE FRIENDS WHO'S REALLY SPECIAL, YOU KNOW?
BUT THEN ONE DAY...
...I SAW THE TWO OF THEM KISSING.
WHAT ...?
WOBBLE
!

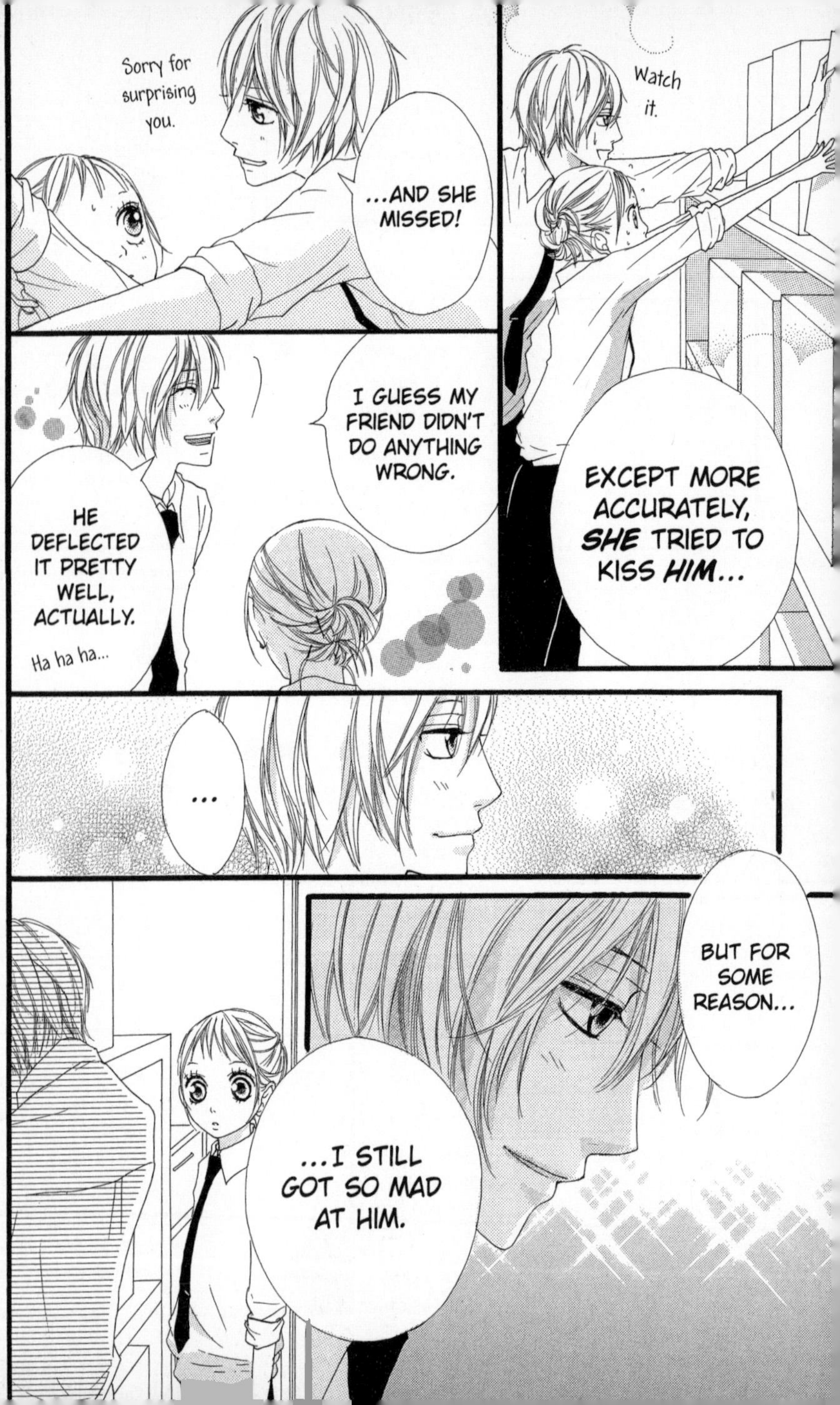
Watch it.
EXCEPT MORE ACCURATELY, *SHE* TRIED TO KISS *HIM*...
...AND SHE MISSED!
Sorry for surprising you.
I GUESS MY FRIEND DIDN'T DO ANYTHING WRONG.
HE DEFLECTED IT PRETTY WELL, ACTUALLY.
Ha ha ha...
...
BUT FOR SOME REASON...
...I STILL GOT SO MAD AT HIM.

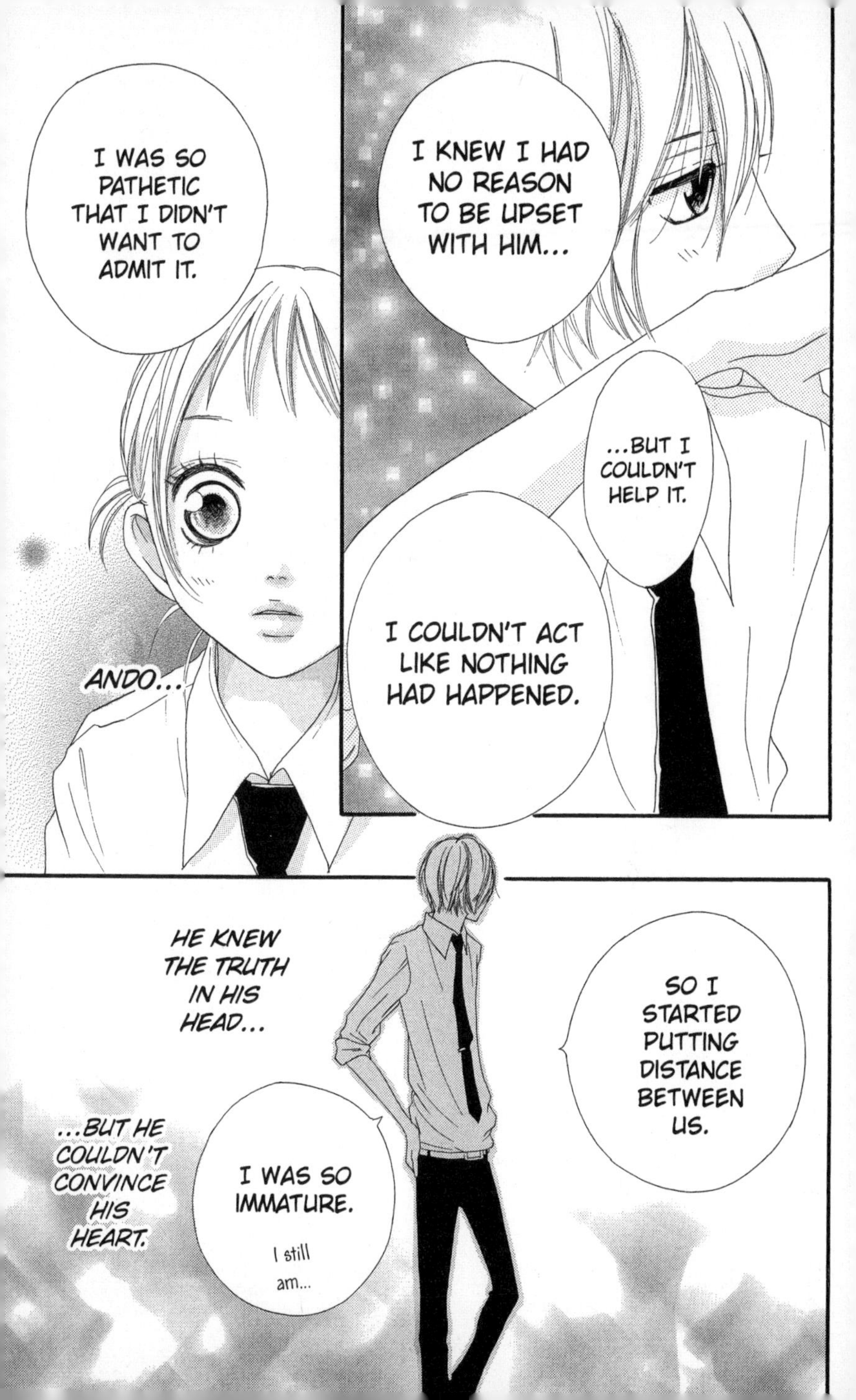
I KNEW I HAD NO REASON TO BE UPSET WITH HIM...
...BUT I COULDN'T HELP IT.
I COULDN'T ACT LIKE NOTHING HAD HAPPENED.
I WAS SO PATHETIC THAT I DIDN'T WANT TO ADMIT IT.
ANDO...
SO I STARTED PUTTING DISTANCE BETWEEN US.
HE KNEW THE TRUTH IN HIS HEAD...
I WAS SO IMMATURE.
I still am...
...BUT HE COULDN'T CONVINCE HIS HEART.

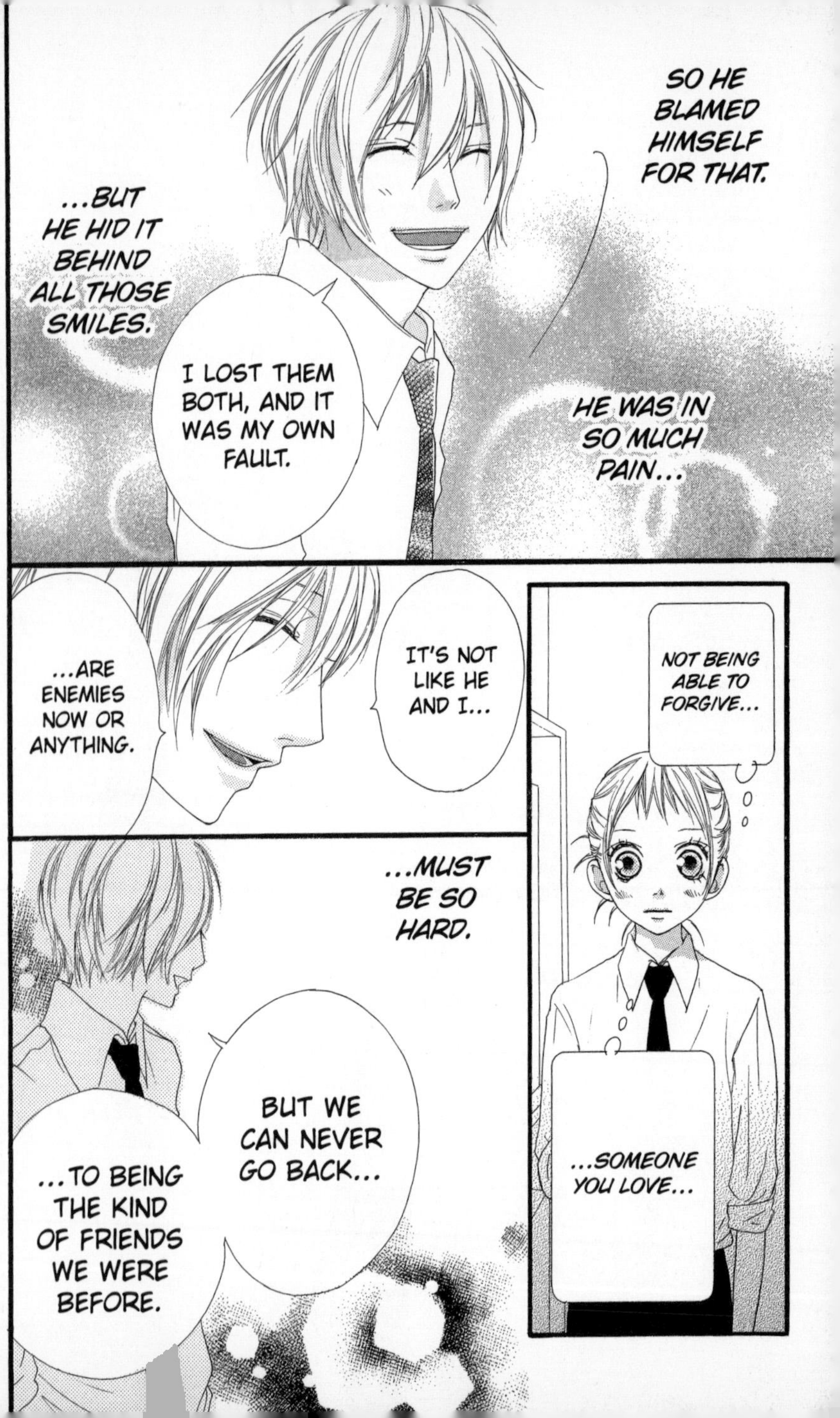
SO HE BLAMED HIMSELF FOR THAT.
I LOST THEM BOTH, AND IT WAS MY OWN FAULT.
HE WAS IN SO MUCH PAIN...
...BUT HE HID IT BEHIND ALL THOSE SMILES.
NOT BEING ABLE TO FORGIVE...
...SOMEONE YOU LOVE...
IT'S NOT LIKE HE AND I...
...ARE ENEMIES NOW OR ANYTHING.
...MUST BE SO HARD.
BUT WE CAN NEVER GO BACK...
...TO BEING THE KIND OF FRIENDS WE WERE BEFORE.

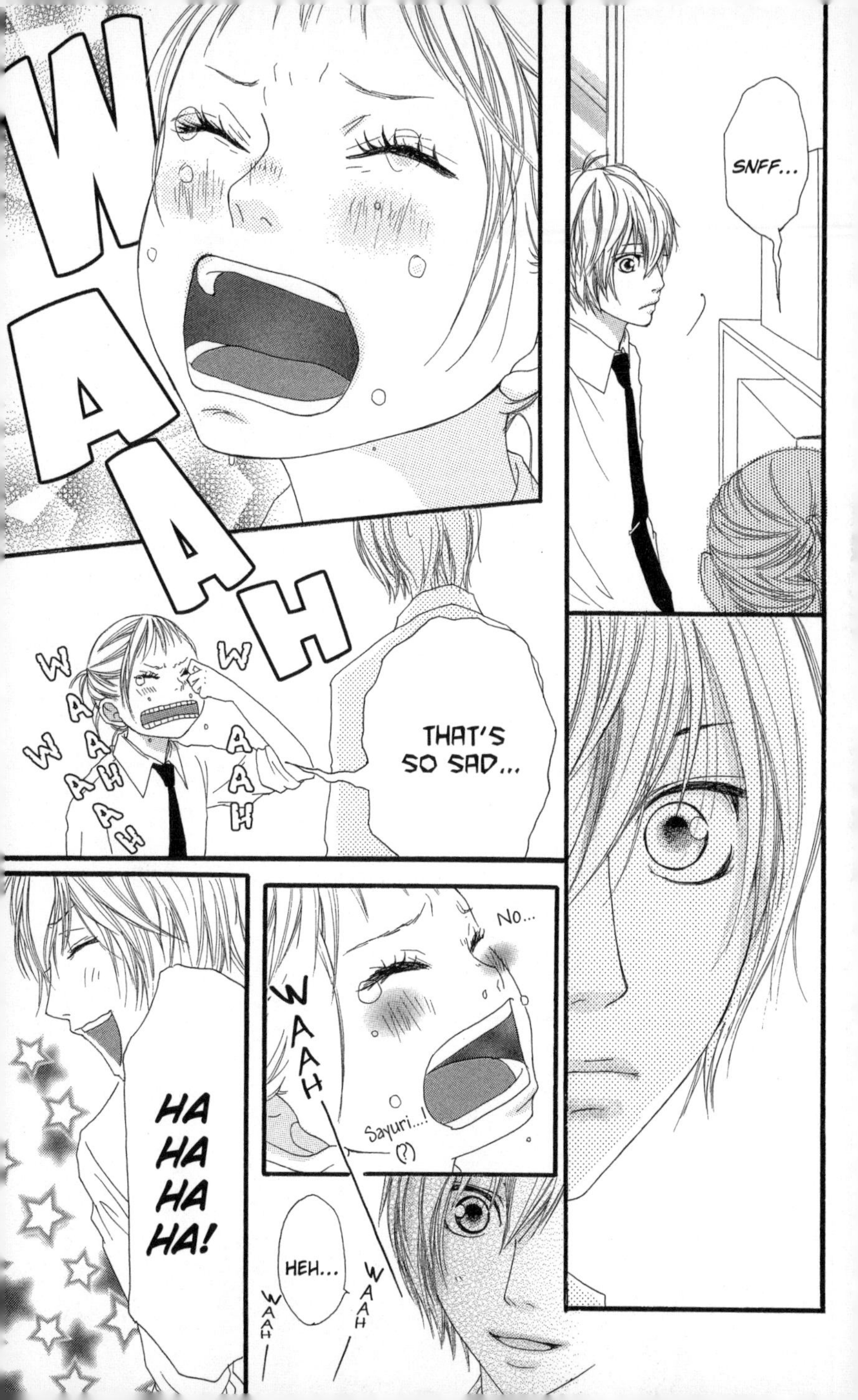

SNFF...
WAAAH
WAAAH
WAAAH
THAT'S SO SAD...
No...
WAAH
Sayuri...! (?)
HEH...
WAAH
WAAH
HA HA HA HA HA HA HA!

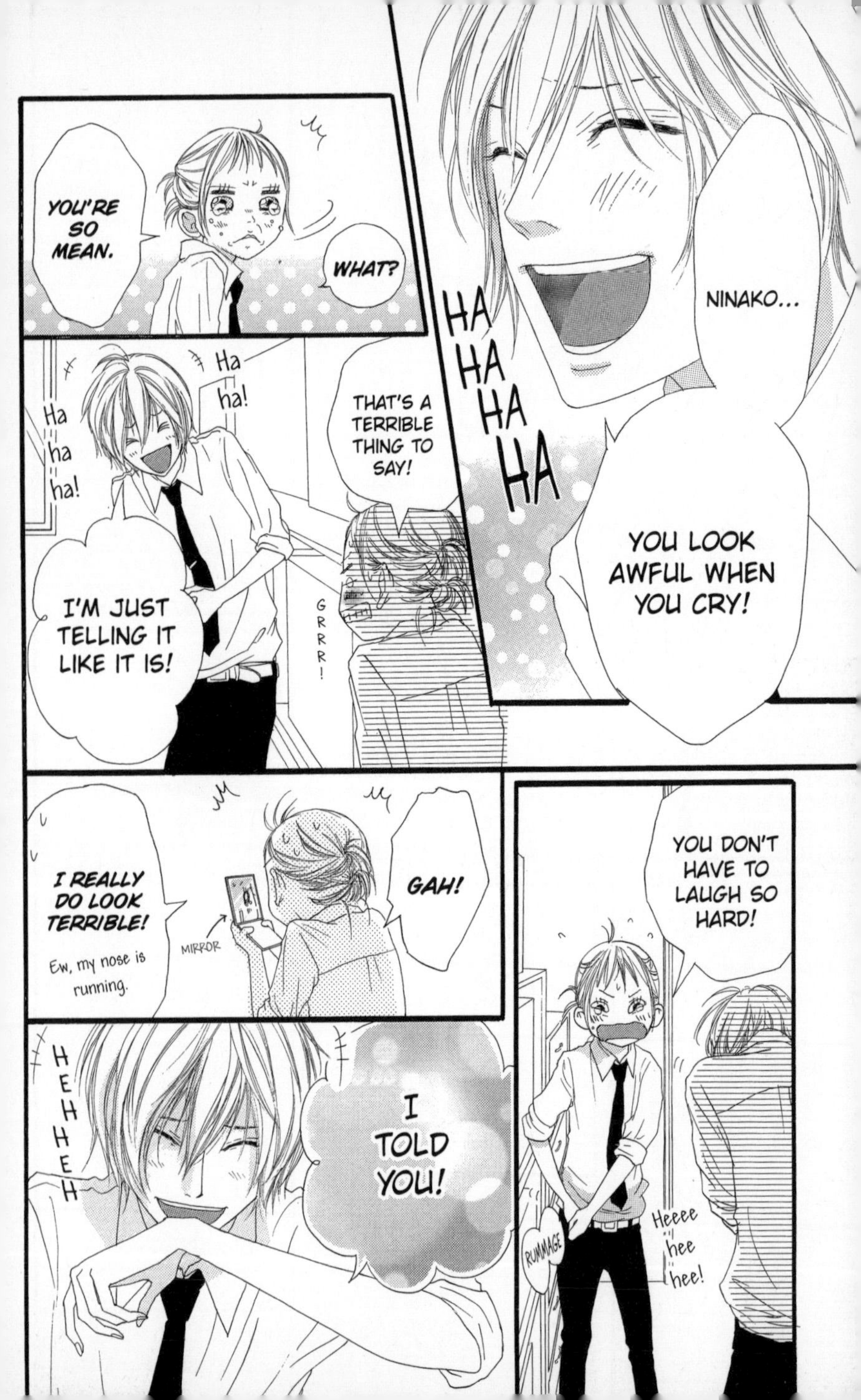
NINAKO...
HA HA HA HA
YOU LOOK AWFUL WHEN YOU CRY!
WHAT?
YOU'RE SO MEAN.
THAT'S A TERRIBLE THING TO SAY!
Ha ha!
GRRR!
Ha ha ha!
I'M JUST TELLING IT LIKE IT IS!
YOU DON'T HAVE TO LAUGH SO HARD!
Heeee hee hee!
RUMMAGE
GAH!
MIRROR
I REALLY DO LOOK TERRIBLE!
Ew, my nose is running.
I TOLD YOU!
HEHHEHEH

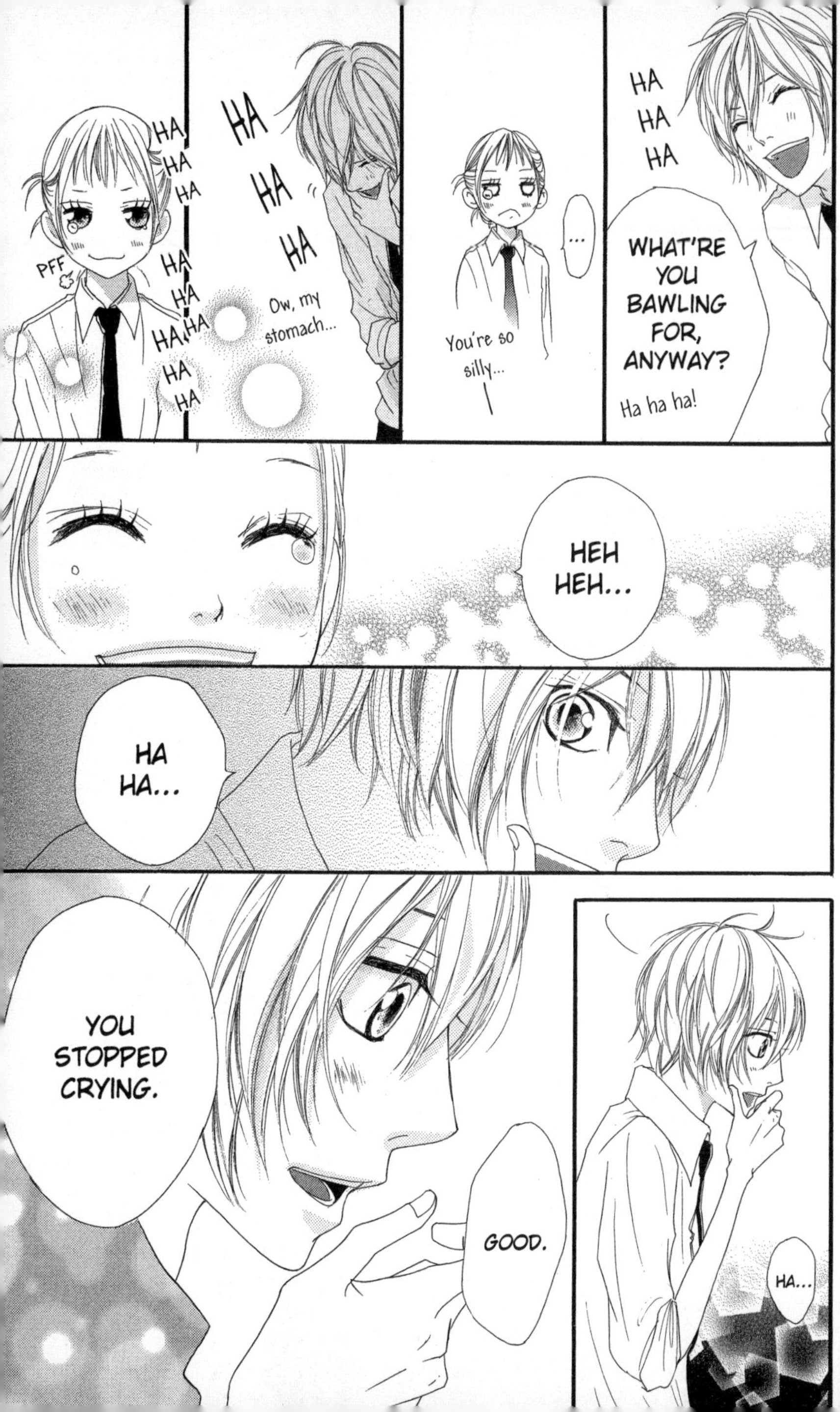
HA HA HA
WHAT'RE YOU BAWLING FOR, ANYWAY?
Ha ha ha!
...
You're so silly...
HA HA HA
Ow, my stomach...
HA HA HA
PFF
HA HA HA HA HA HA HA
HEH HEH...
HA HA...
HA...
YOU STOPPED CRYING.
GOOD.

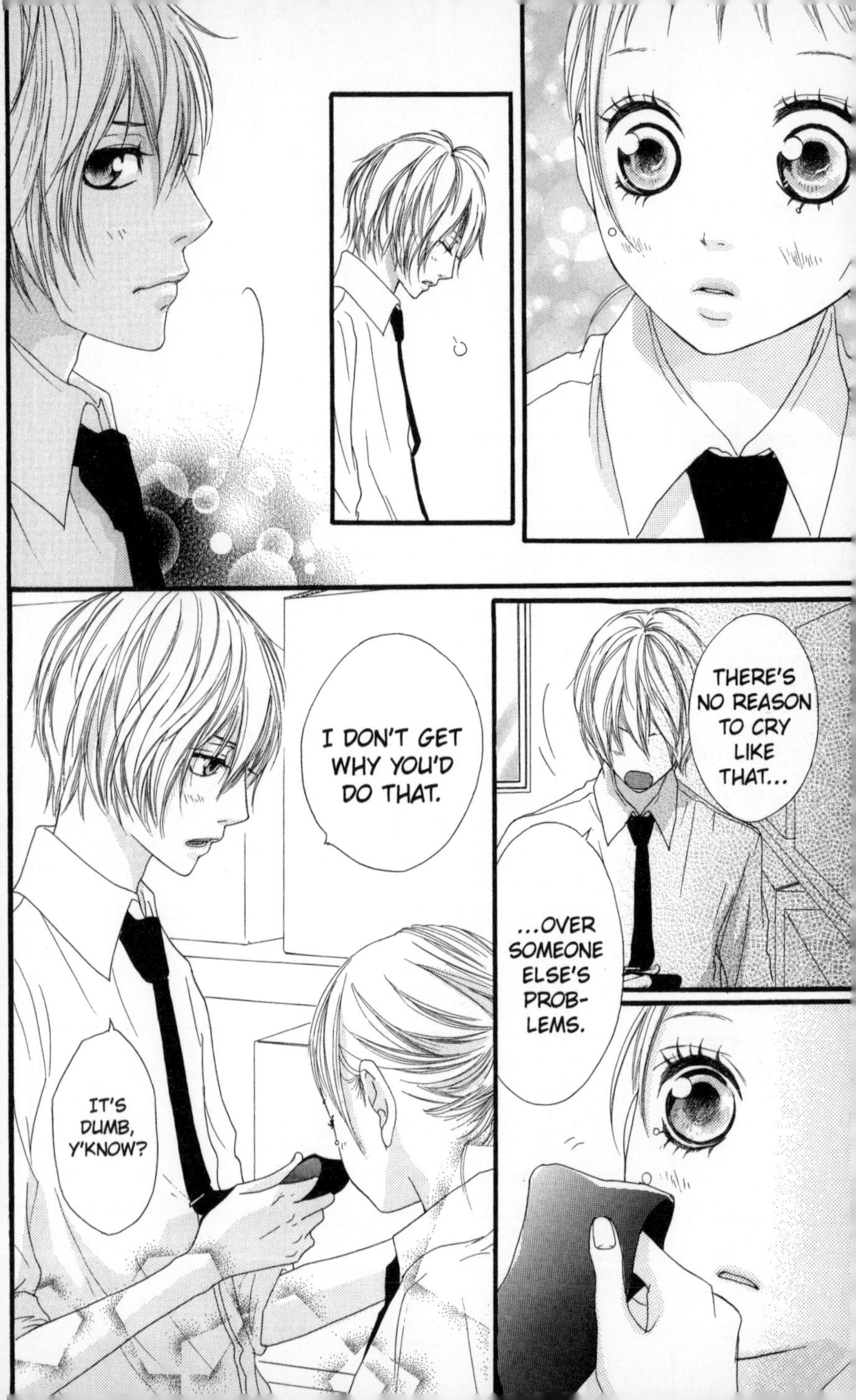
THERE'S NO REASON TO CRY LIKE THAT...
...OVER SOMEONE ELSE'S PROB-LEMS.
I DON'T GET WHY YOU'D DO THAT.
IT'S DUMB, Y'KNOW?

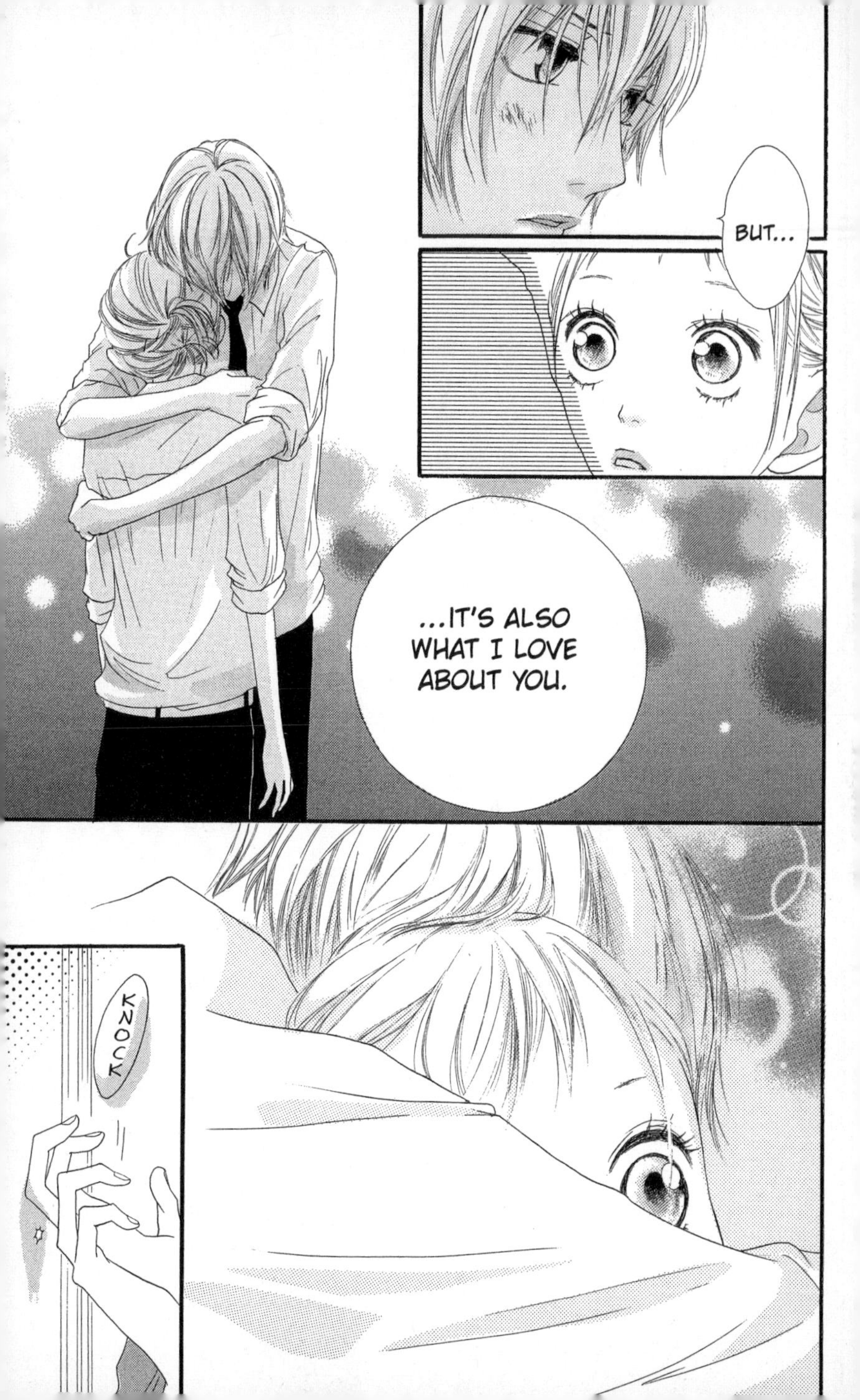
BUT...
...IT'S ALSO WHAT I LOVE ABOUT YOU.
KNOCK

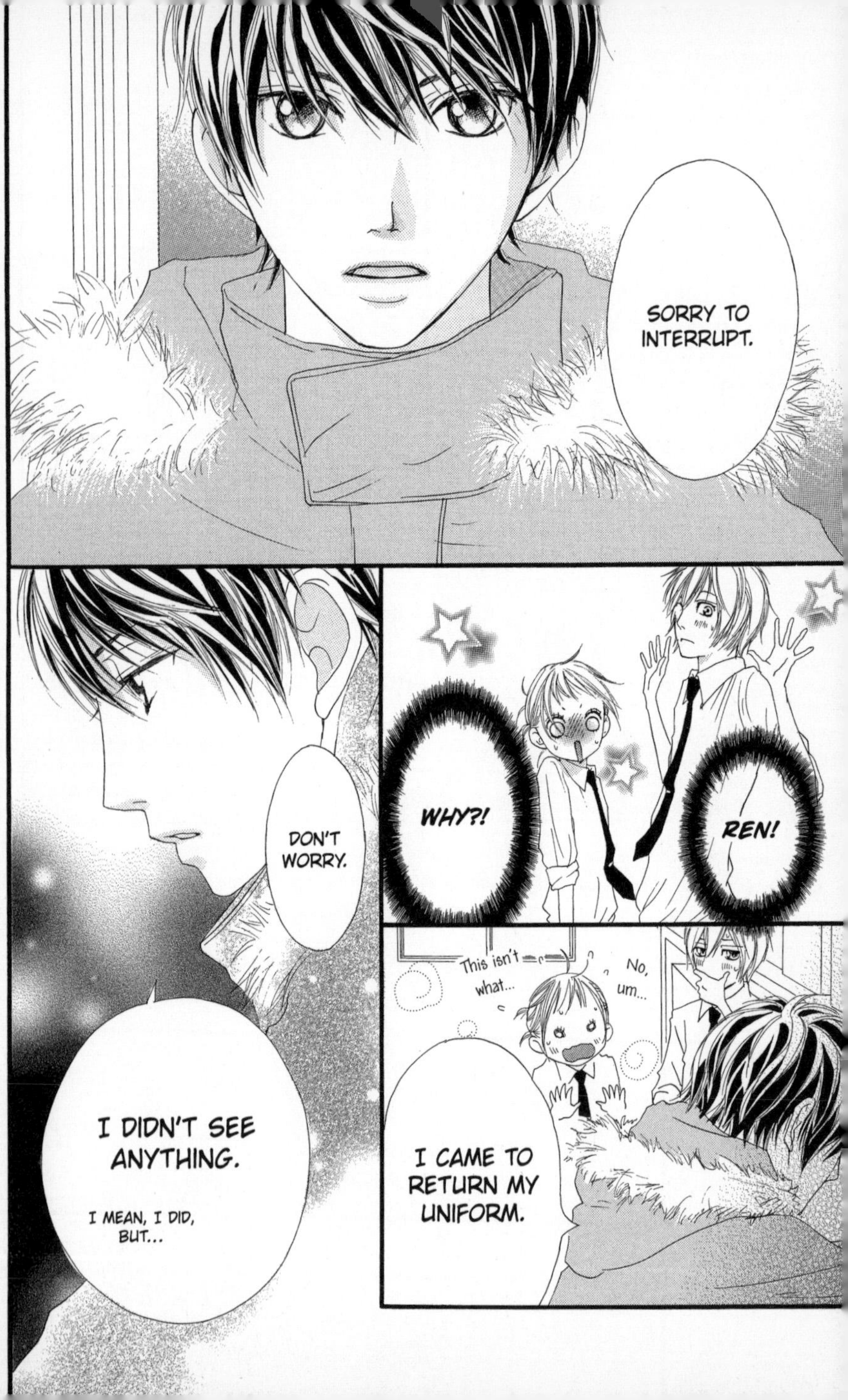
SORRY TO INTERRUPT.
REN!
WHY?!
No, um...
This isn't what...
I CAME TO RETURN MY UNIFORM.
DON'T WORRY.
I DIDN'T SEE ANYTHING.
I MEAN, I DID, BUT...

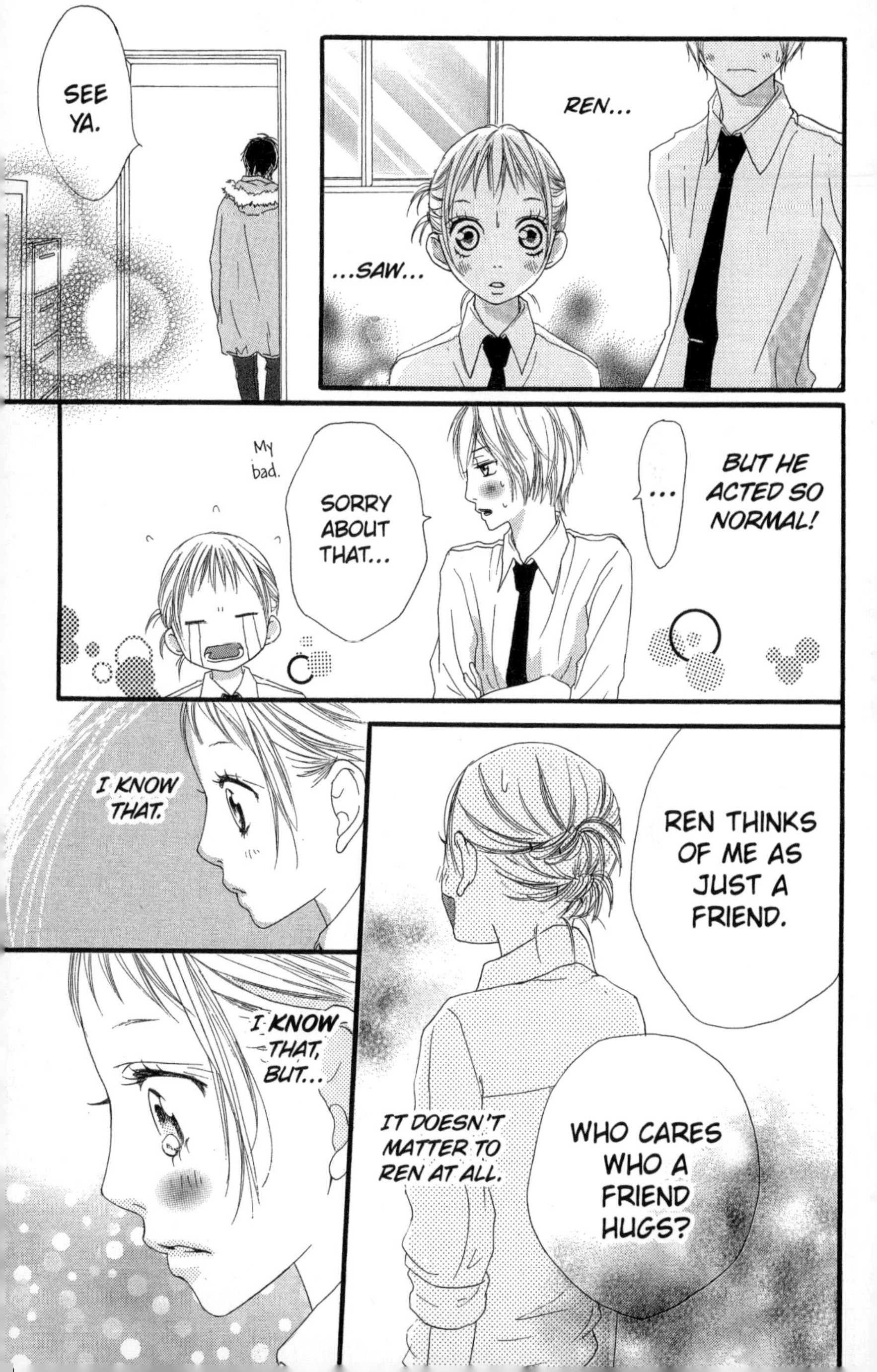
REN...
...SAW...
SEE YA.
BUT HE ACTED SO NORMAL!
...
SORRY ABOUT THAT...
My bad.
REN THINKS OF ME AS JUST A FRIEND.
WHO CARES WHO A FRIEND HUGS?
IT DOESN'T MATTER TO REN AT ALL.
I KNOW THAT.
I KNOW THAT, BUT...

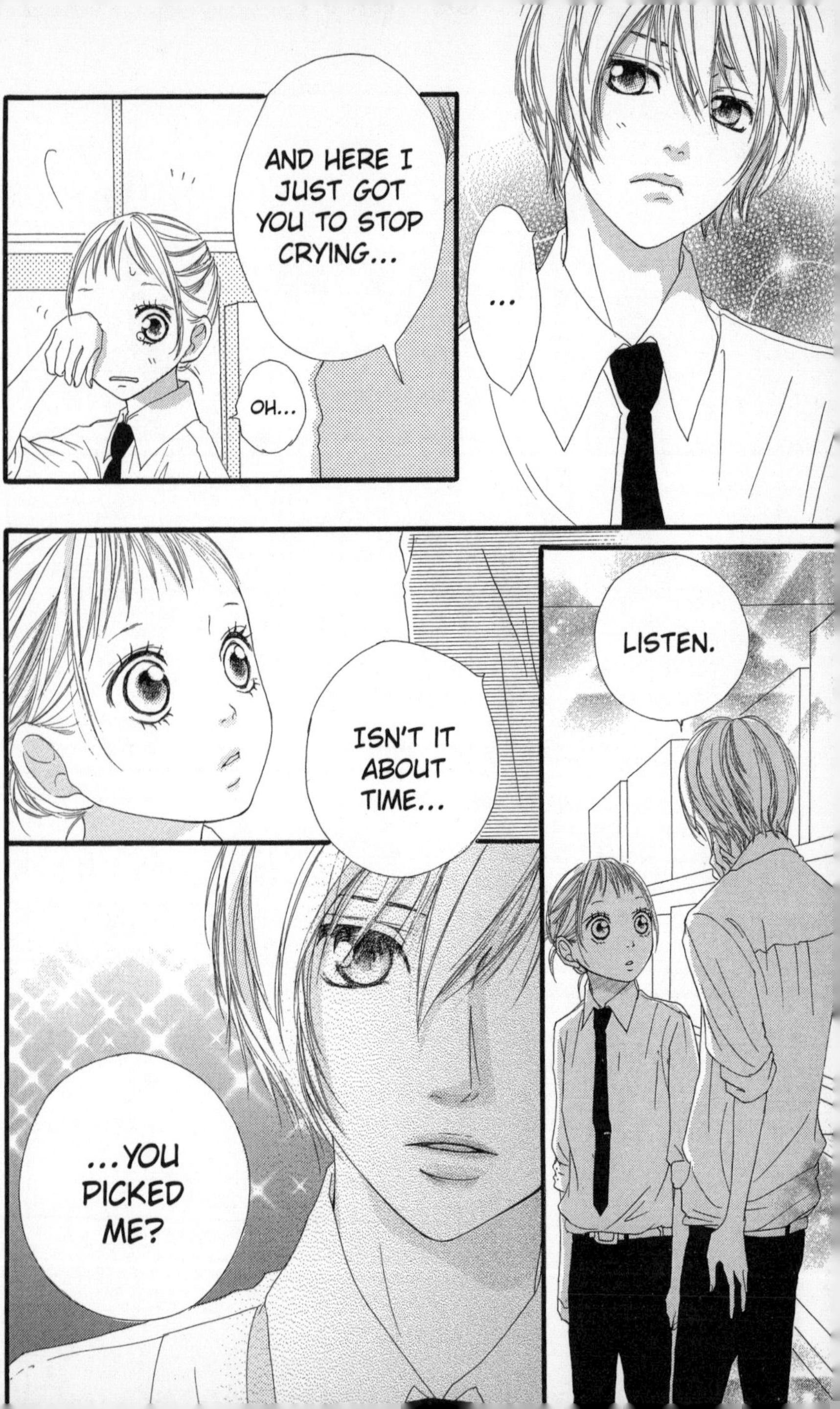
...
AND HERE I JUST GOT YOU TO STOP CRYING...
OH...
LISTEN.
ISN'T IT ABOUT TIME...
...YOU PICKED ME?

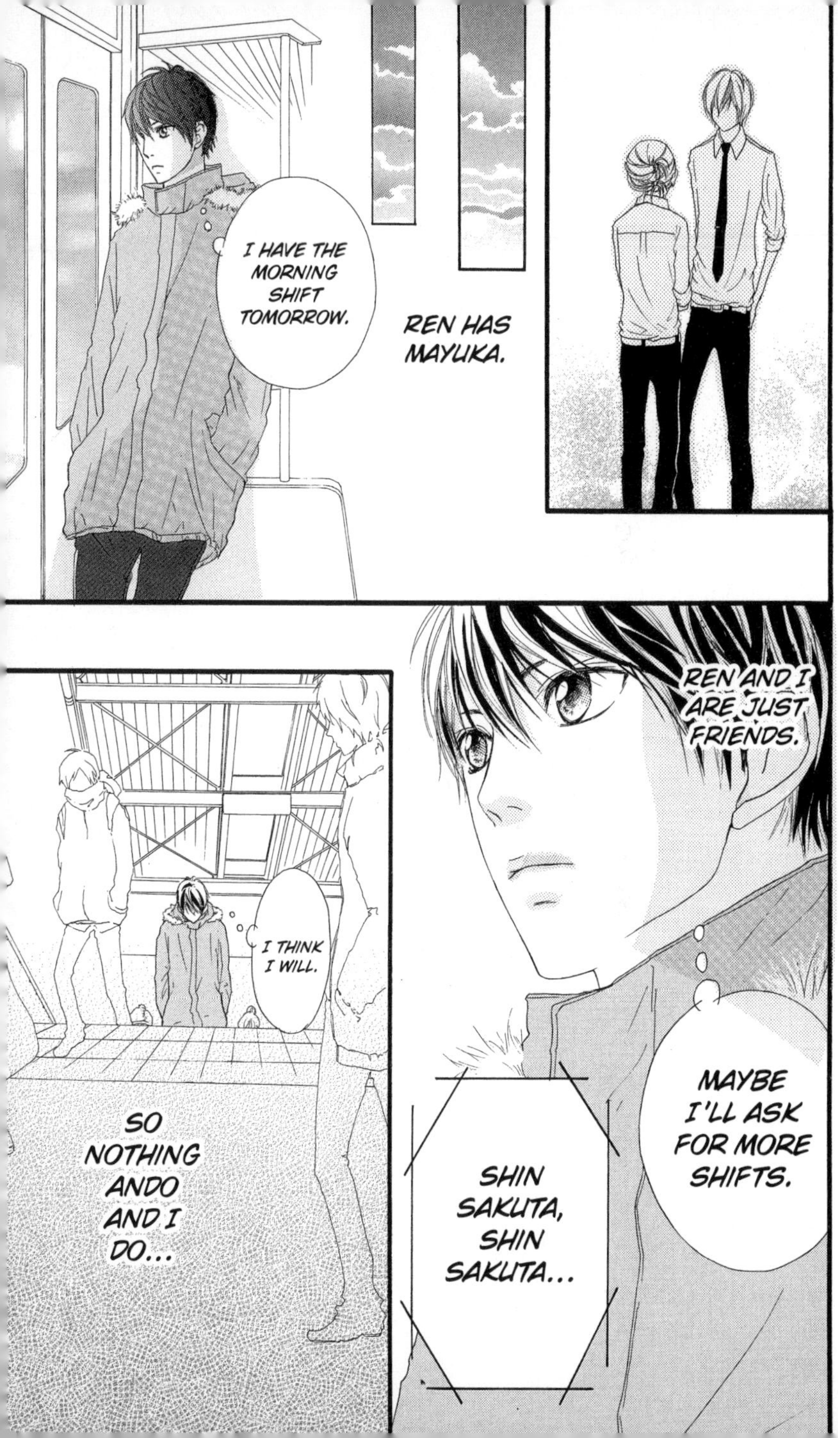
REN HAS MAYUKA.
I HAVE THE MORNING SHIFT TOMORROW.
REN AND I ARE JUST FRIENDS.
MAYBE I'LL ASK FOR MORE SHIFTS.
SHIN SAKUTA, SHIN SAKUTA...
I THINK I WILL.
SO NOTHING ANDO AND I DO...

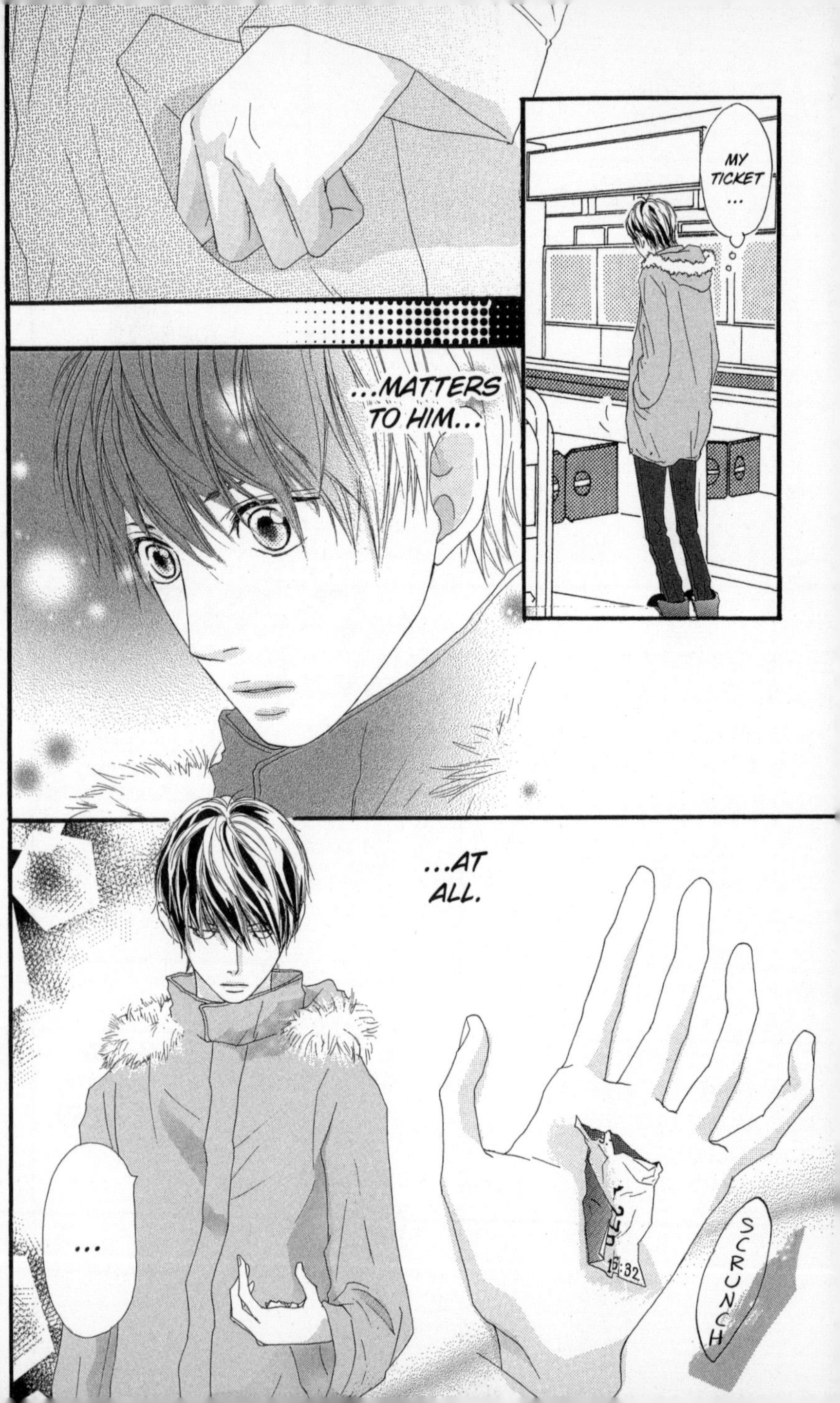
MY TICKET ...
...MATTERS TO HIM...
...AT ALL.
SCRUNCH
...

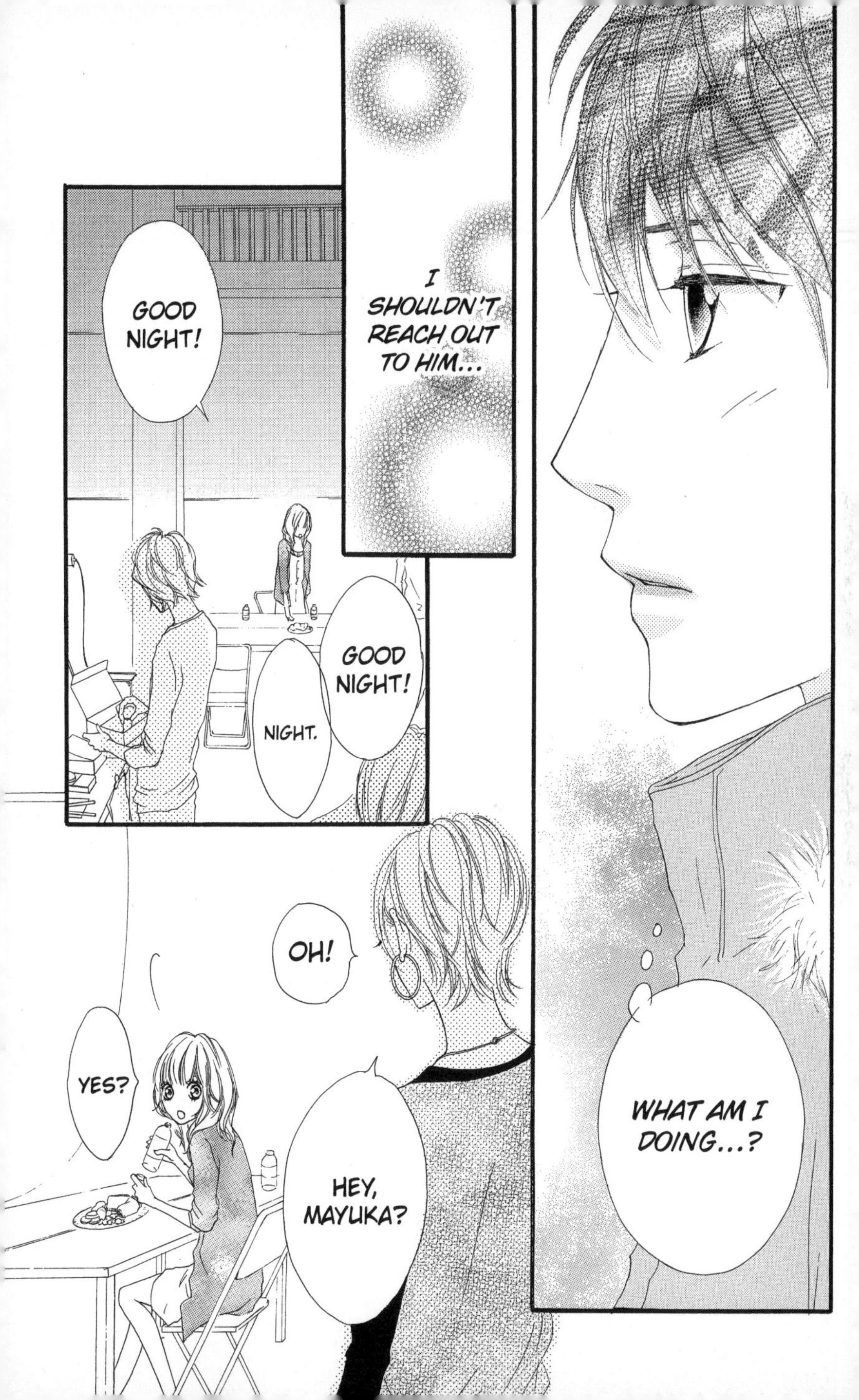
I SHOULDN'T REACH OUT TO HIM...
GOOD NIGHT!
GOOD NIGHT!
NIGHT.
WHAT AM I DOING...?
OH!
HEY, MAYUKA?
YES?

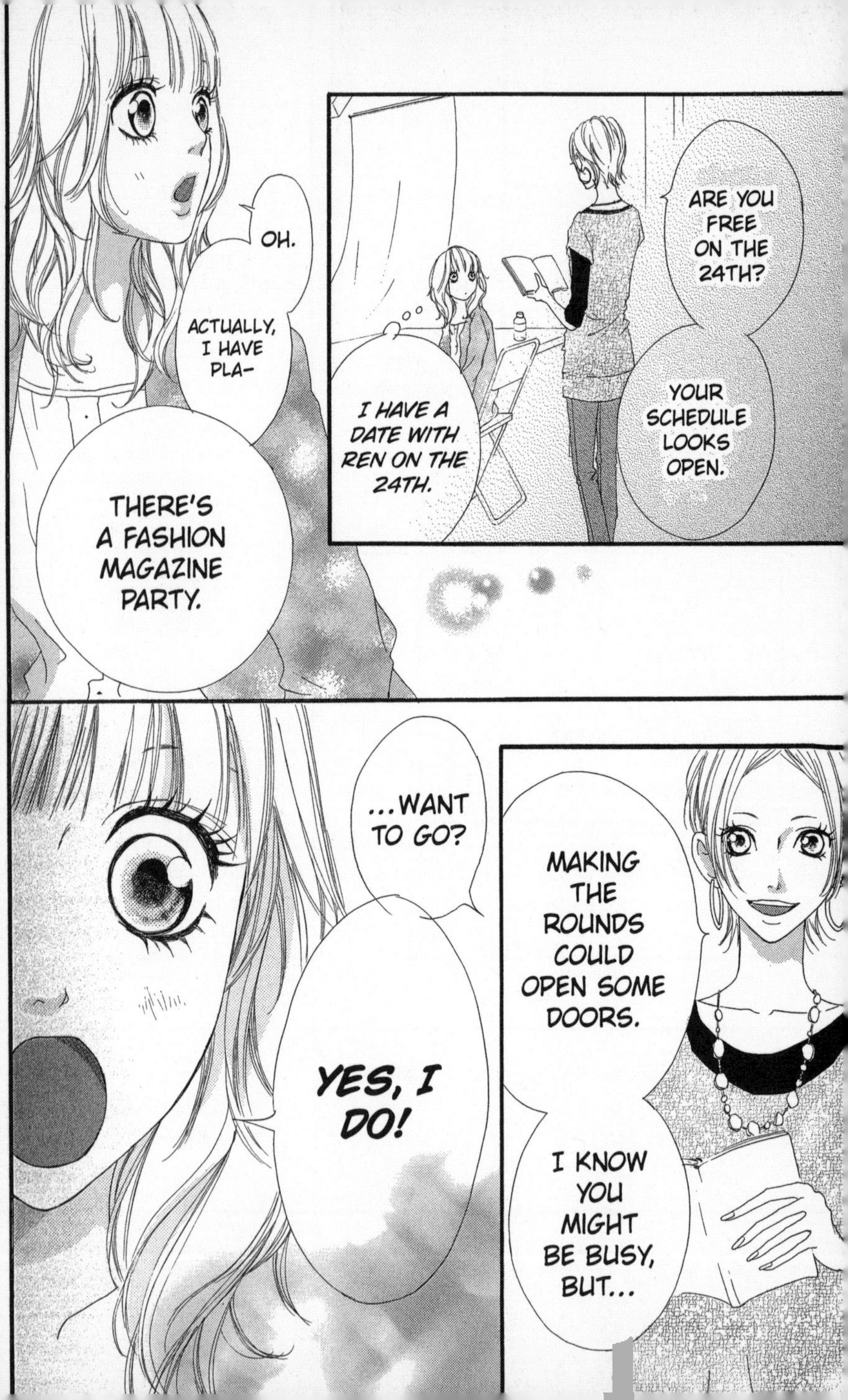
ARE YOU FREE ON THE 24TH?
YOUR SCHEDULE LOOKS OPEN.
I HAVE A DATE WITH REN ON THE 24TH.
OH.
ACTUALLY, I HAVE PLA-
THERE'S A FASHION MAGAZINE PARTY.
MAKING THE ROUNDS COULD OPEN SOME DOORS.
I KNOW YOU MIGHT BE BUSY, BUT...
...WANT TO GO?
YES, I DO!

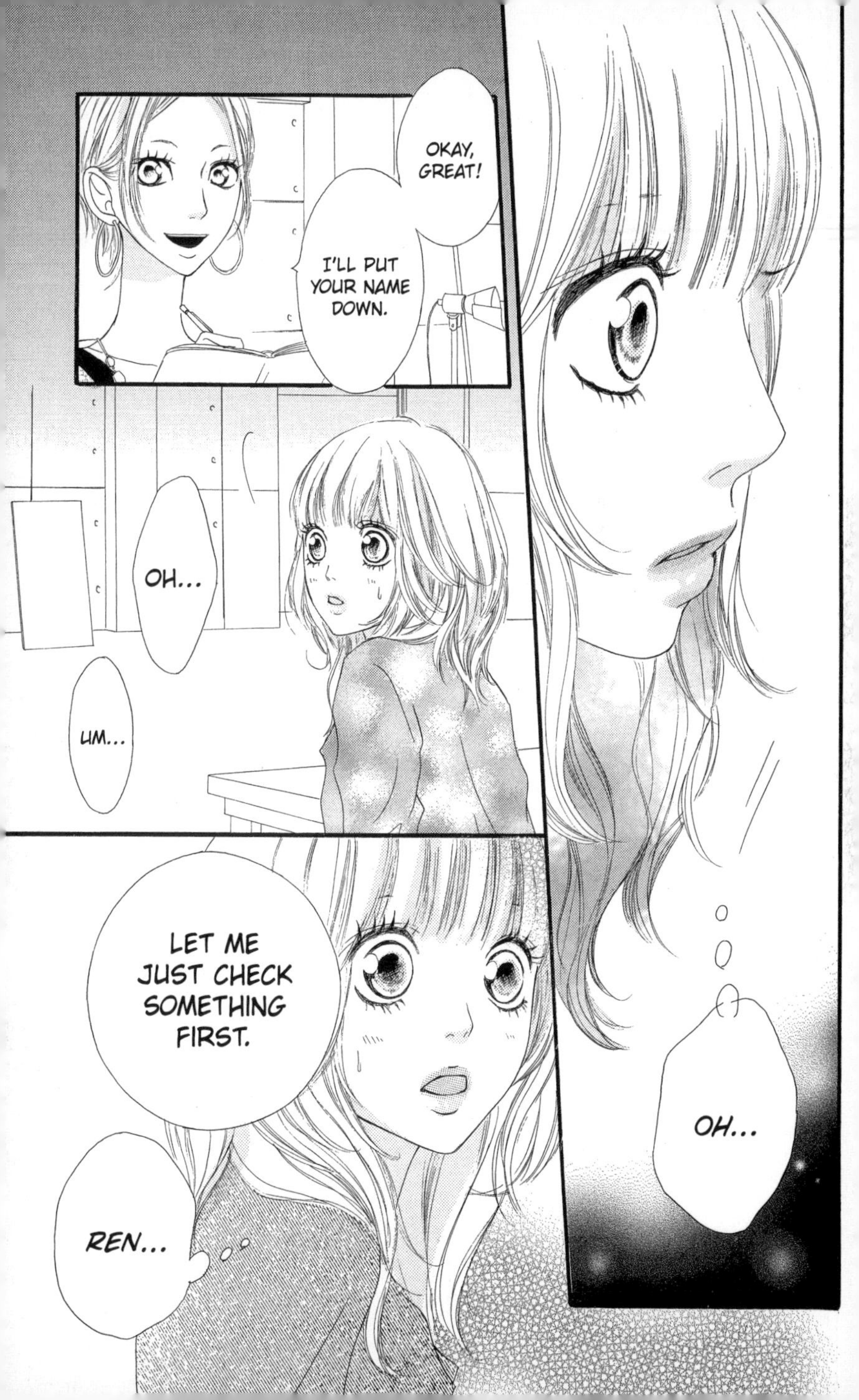
OH...
OKAY, GREAT!
I'LL PUT YOUR NAME DOWN.
OH...
UM...
LET ME JUST CHECK SOMETHING FIRST.
REN...

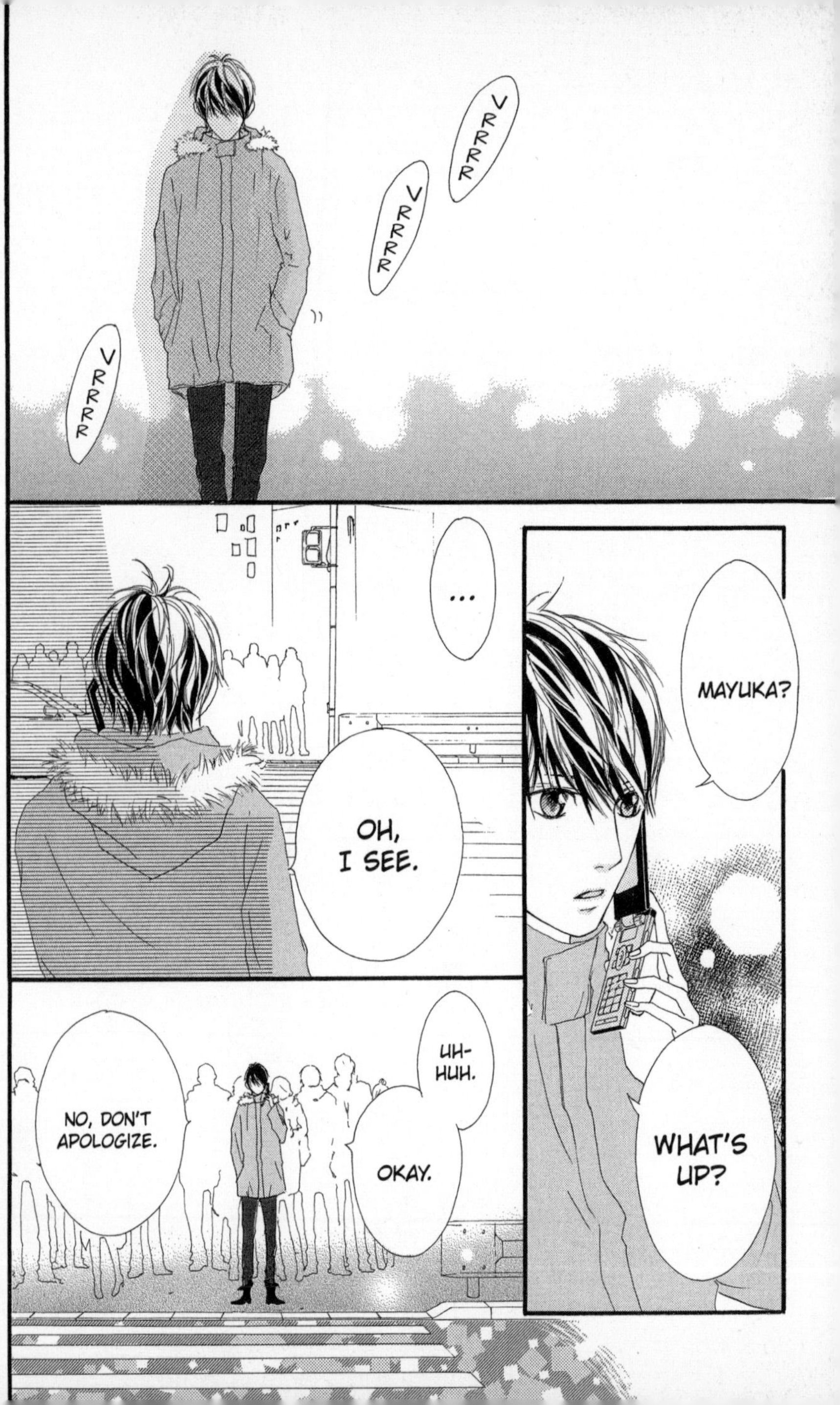
VRRRR
VRRRR
VRRRR
MAYUKA?
WHAT'S UP?
...
OH, I SEE.
UH-HUH.
OKAY.
NO, DON'T APOLOGIZE.

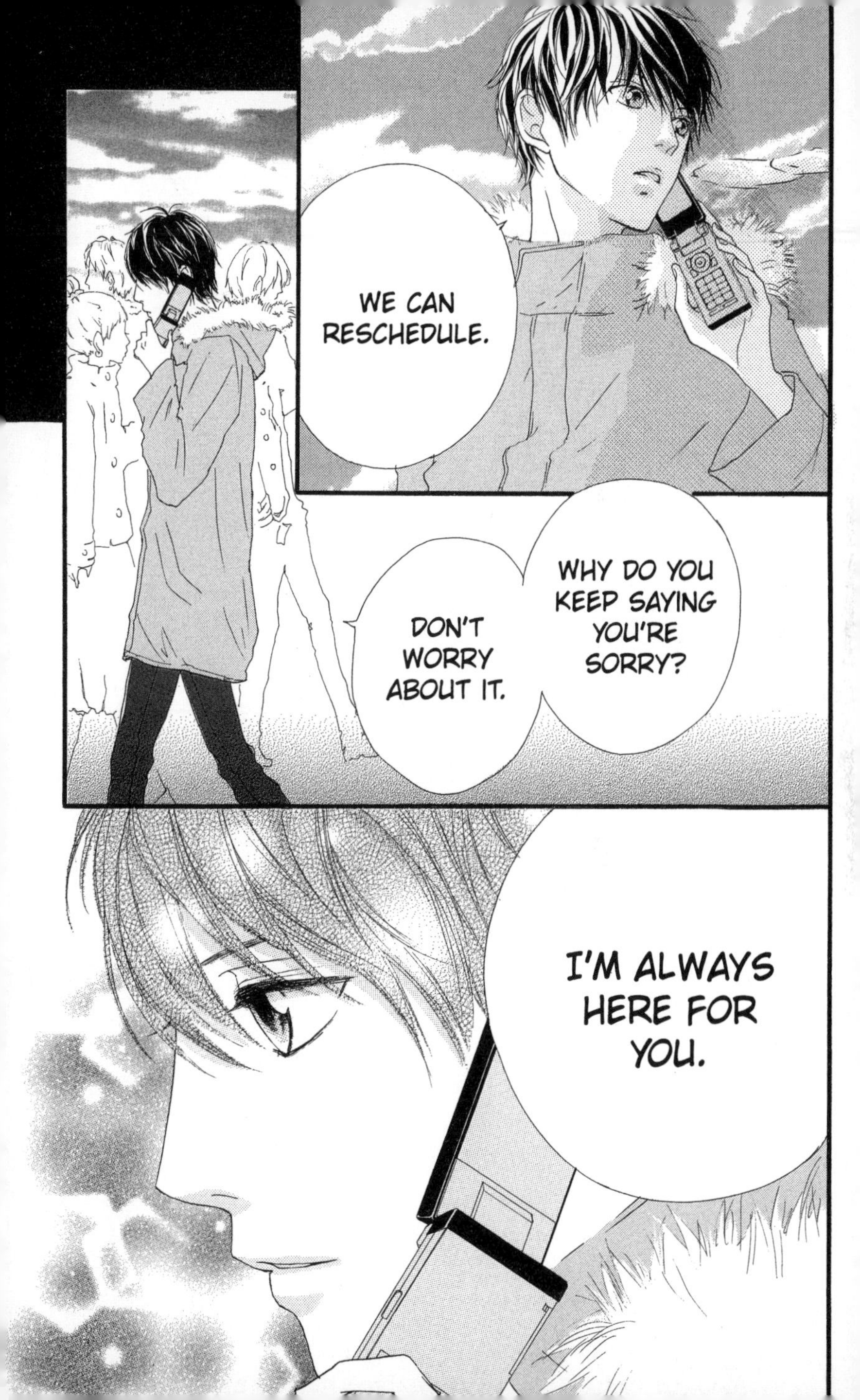
WE CAN RESCHEDULE.
WHY DO YOU KEEP SAYING YOU'RE SORRY?
DON'T WORRY ABOUT IT.
I'M ALWAYS HERE FOR YOU.

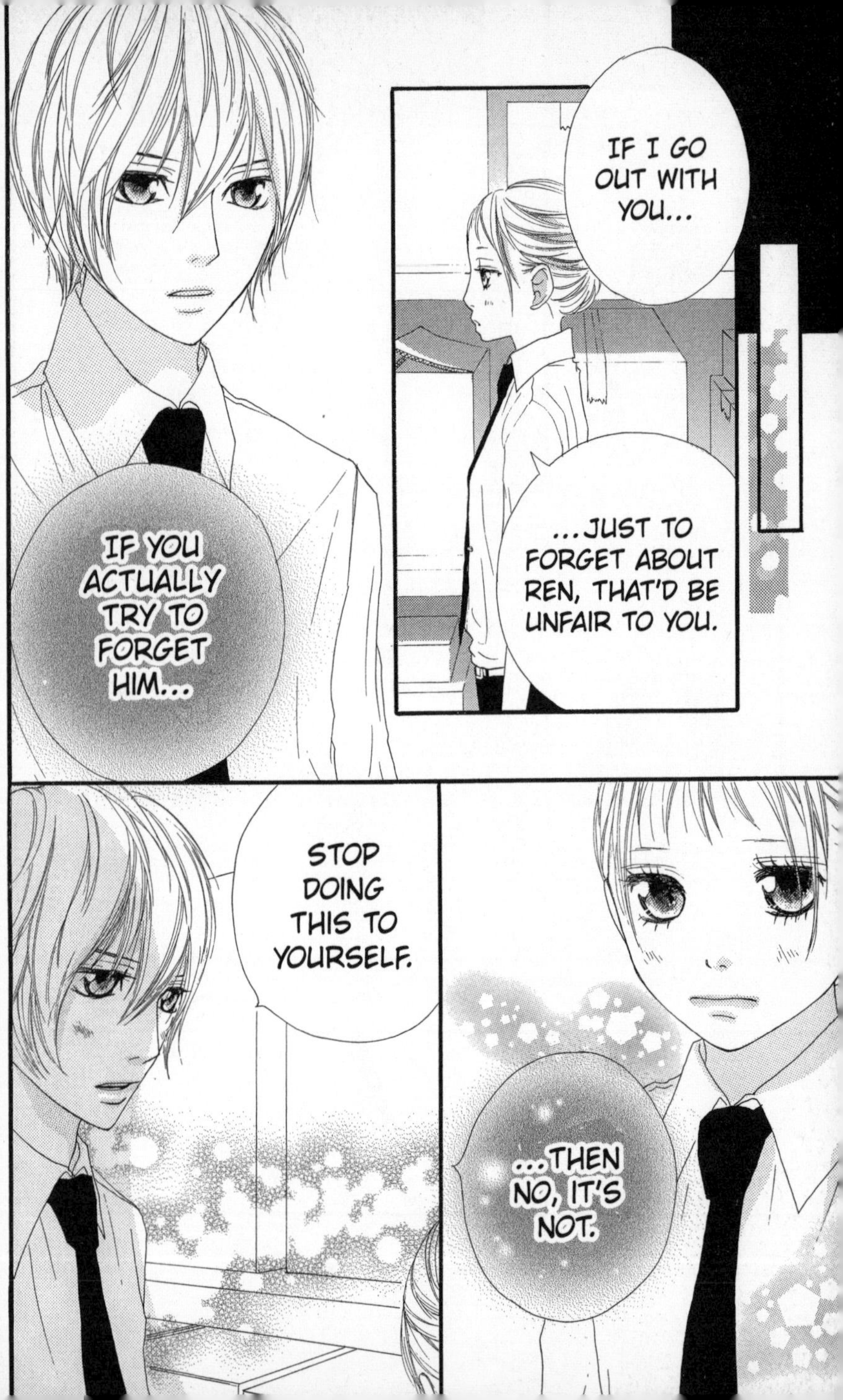
IF I GO OUT WITH YOU...
...JUST TO FORGET ABOUT REN, THAT'D BE UNFAIR TO YOU.
IF YOU ACTUALLY TRY TO FORGET HIM...
...THEN NO, IT'S NOT.
STOP DOING THIS TO YOURSELF.

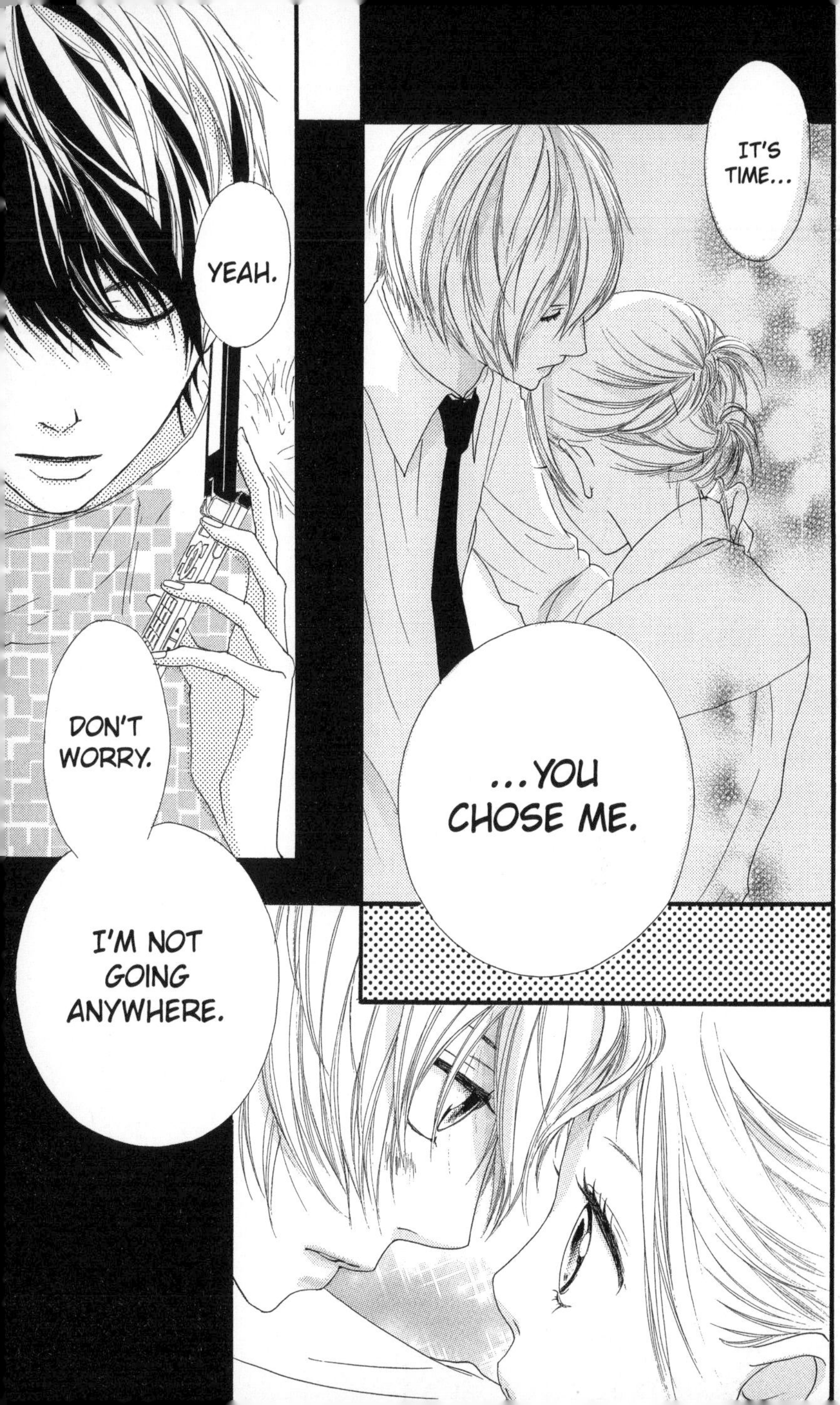
IT'S TIME...
...YOU CHOSE ME.
YEAH.
DON'T WORRY.
I'M NOT GOING ANYWHERE.

WHIMSICAL DIARY by. S. S. S. S.

Super Special Speedy Sakisaka

Month X Day Y
I was supposed to turn in my work, but I got the time when I was supposed to meet my editor wrong. "Crap! I messed up!" I cried, as I rushed to our meeting place. Then...

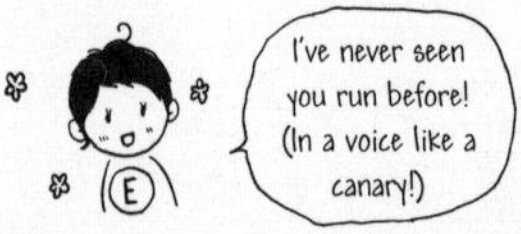
E
I've never seen you run before! (In a voice like a canary!)

It was a refreshing reaction. And funny. Sorry for being so late!

Month X Day Y
I left a document in the photocopier at the convenience store and lost it. Both embarrassing and sad. Incidentally, it was a rough draft for "Unfinished Map." Goodbye...!

The title page

Month X Day Y
I read the kanji character "Raijin" (God of Thunder) as "Kaminari-sama" (Mr. Thunder) and embarrassed myself.

Month X Day Y
My X-Acto knife rolled off my desk! It would've cut my foot, but my extraordinary reflexes deftly averted the near disaster.

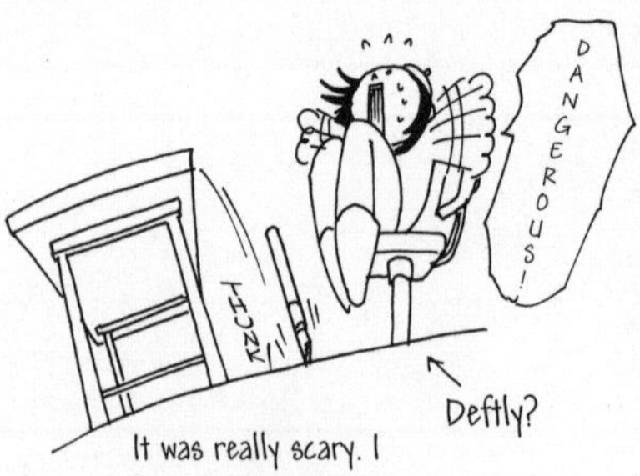
DANGEROUS!
THUNK
Deftly?

It was really scary. I mean, I often slash the palm of my hand...

Day X Month Y
My work chair is deteriorating more every day. I suspect it's almost time to say goodbye.

Month X Day Y
But I'm still using it.

Month X Day Y
Because I'm too lazy to buy a new one.

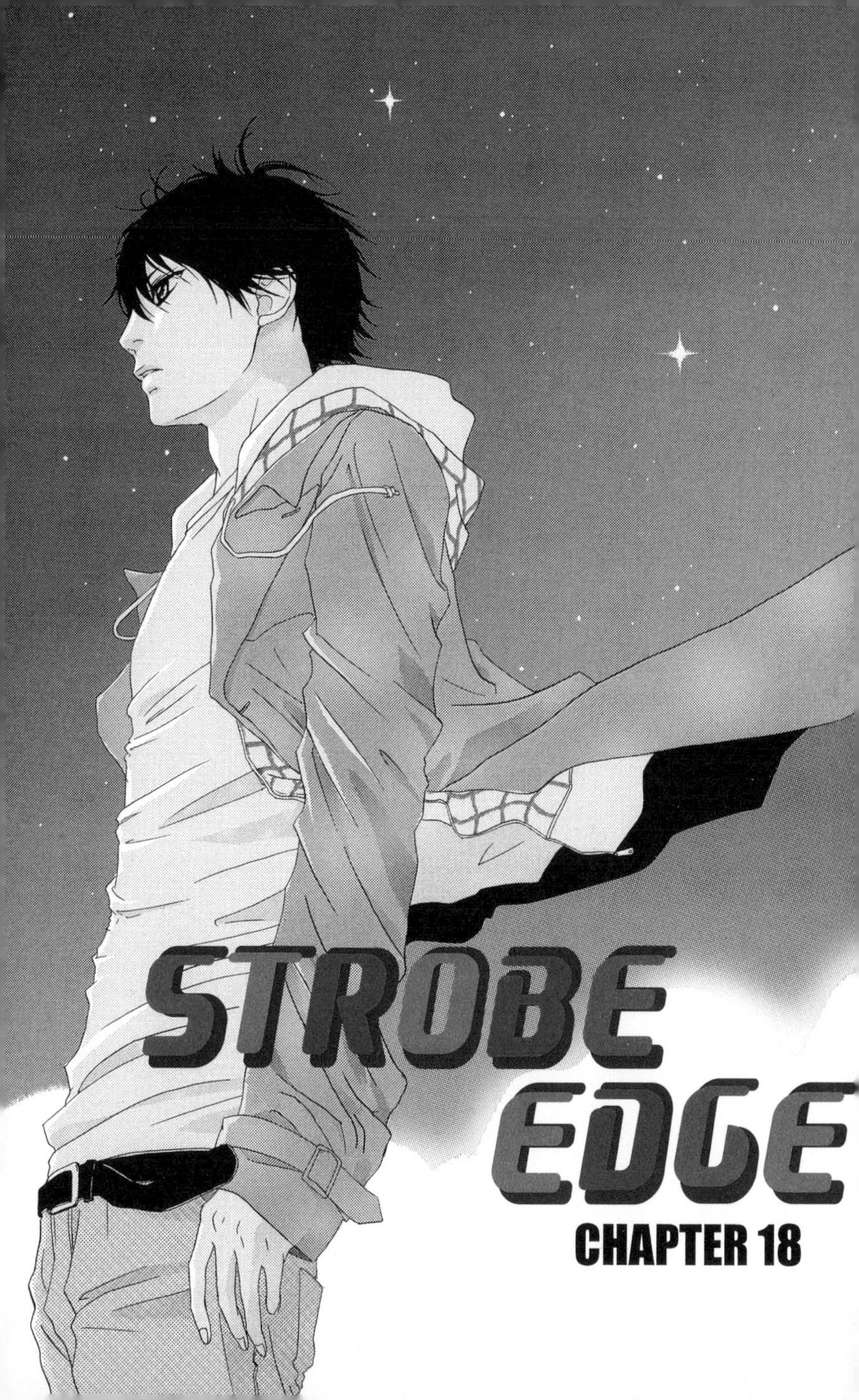
STROBE EDGE
CHAPTER 18

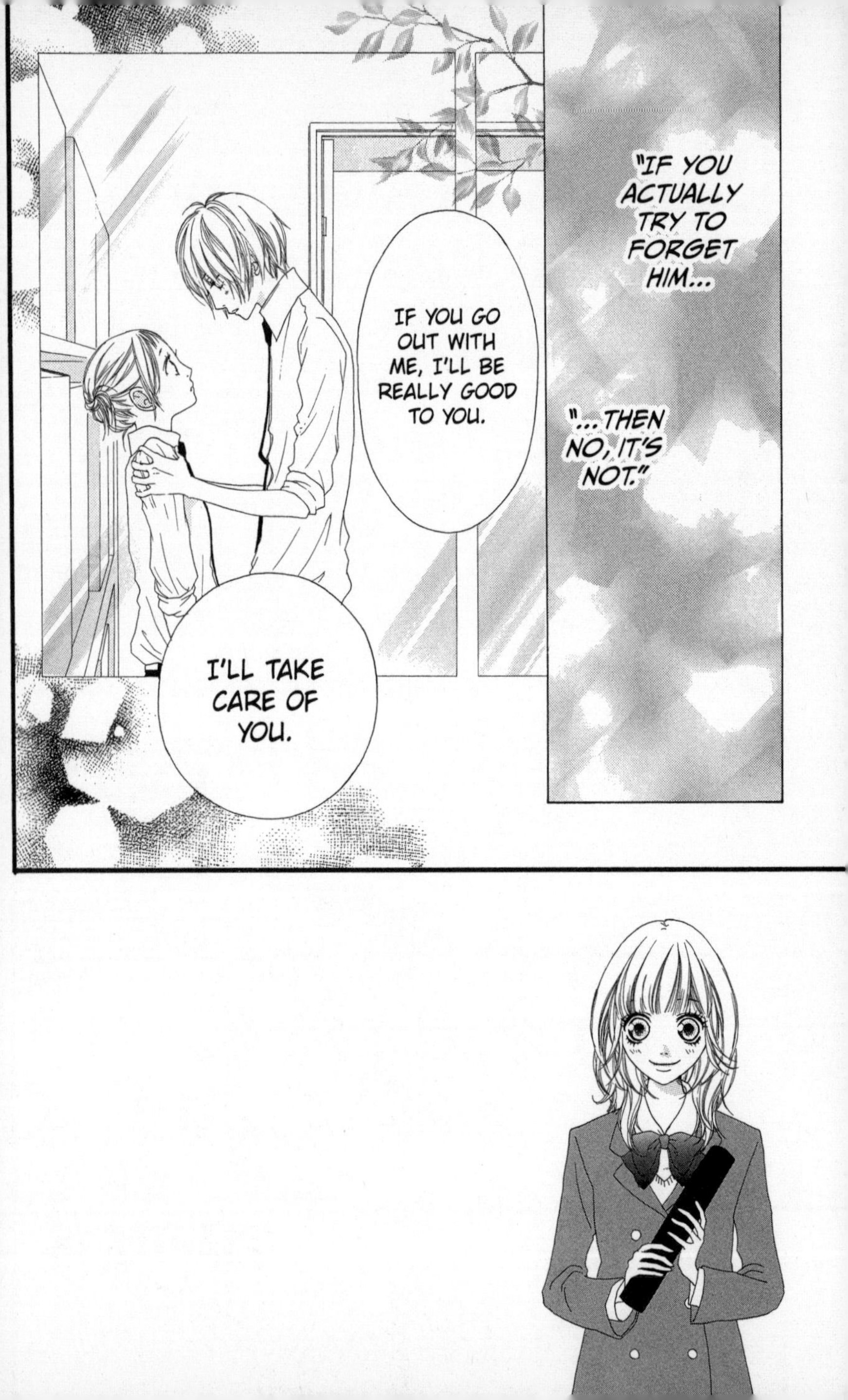
"IF YOU ACTUALLY TRY TO FORGET HIM...
"...THEN NO, IT'S NOT."
IF YOU GO OUT WITH ME, I'LL BE REALLY GOOD TO YOU.
I'LL TAKE CARE OF YOU.

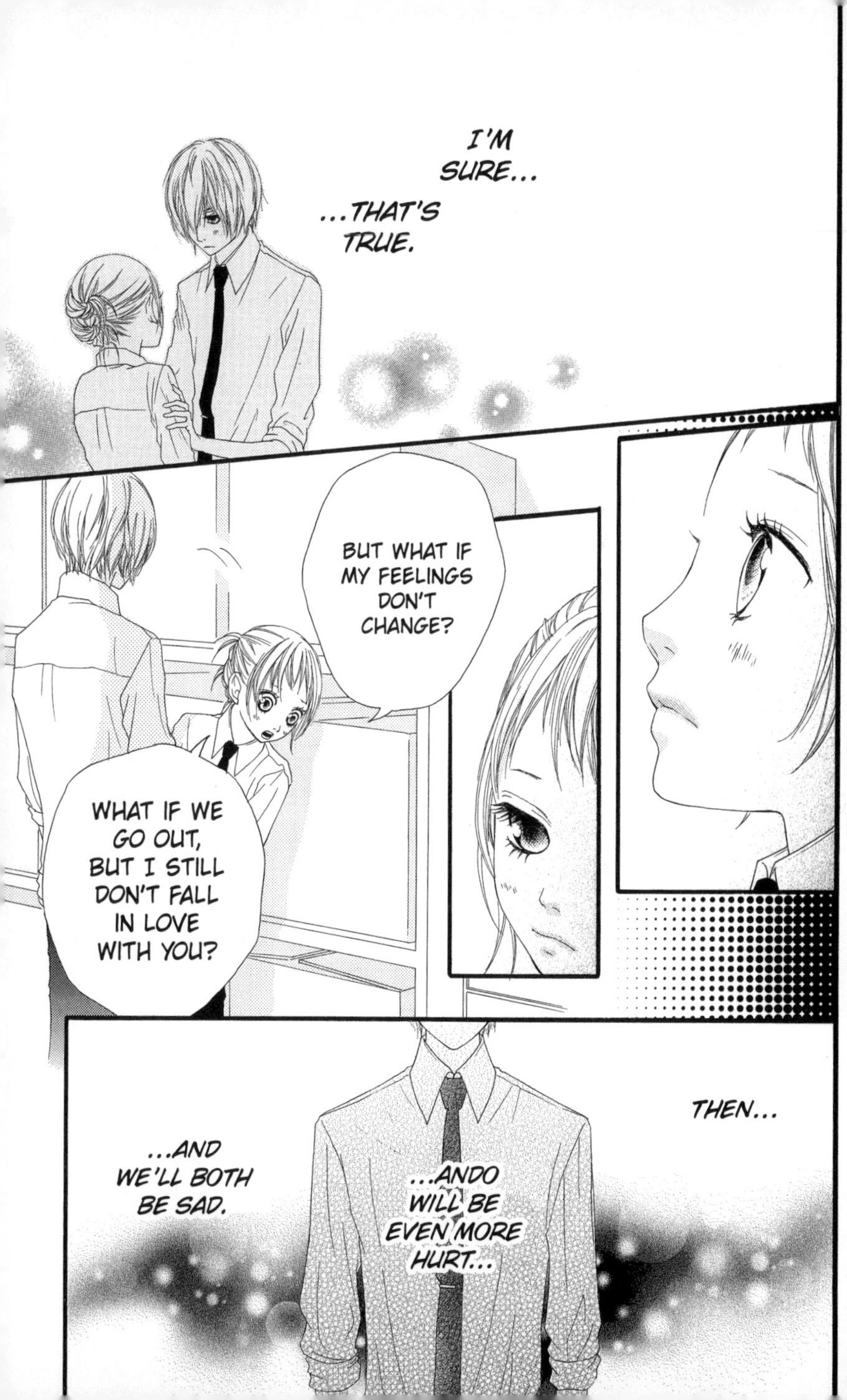
I'M SURE...
...THAT'S TRUE.
BUT WHAT IF MY FEELINGS DON'T CHANGE?
WHAT IF WE GO OUT, BUT I STILL DON'T FALL IN LOVE WITH YOU?
THEN...
...ANDO WILL BE EVEN MORE HURT...
...AND WE'LL BOTH BE SAD.

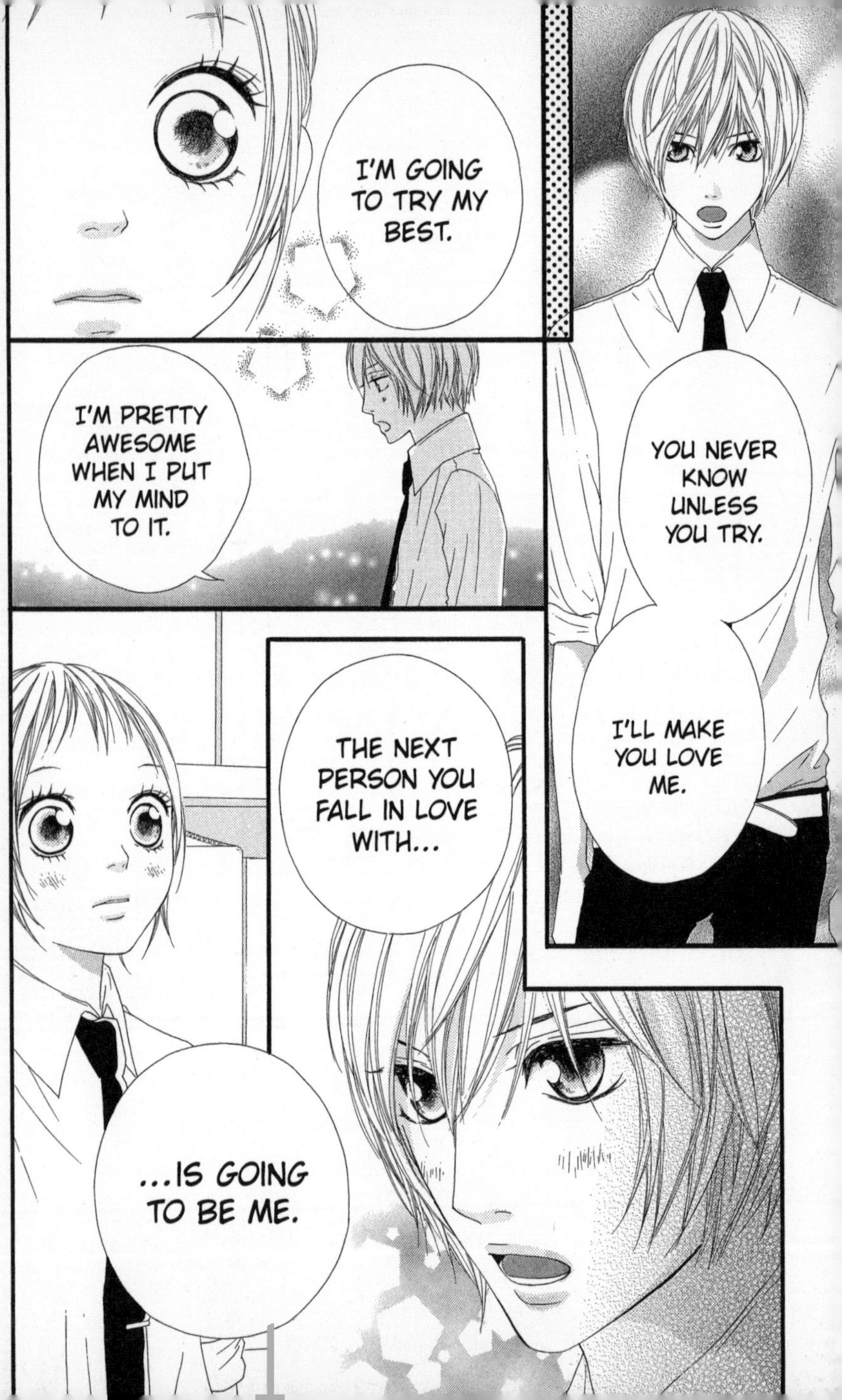
YOU NEVER KNOW UNLESS YOU TRY.
I'LL MAKE YOU LOVE ME.
I'M GOING TO TRY MY BEST.
I'M PRETTY AWESOME WHEN I PUT MY MIND TO IT.
THE NEXT PERSON YOU FALL IN LOVE WITH...
...IS GOING TO BE ME.

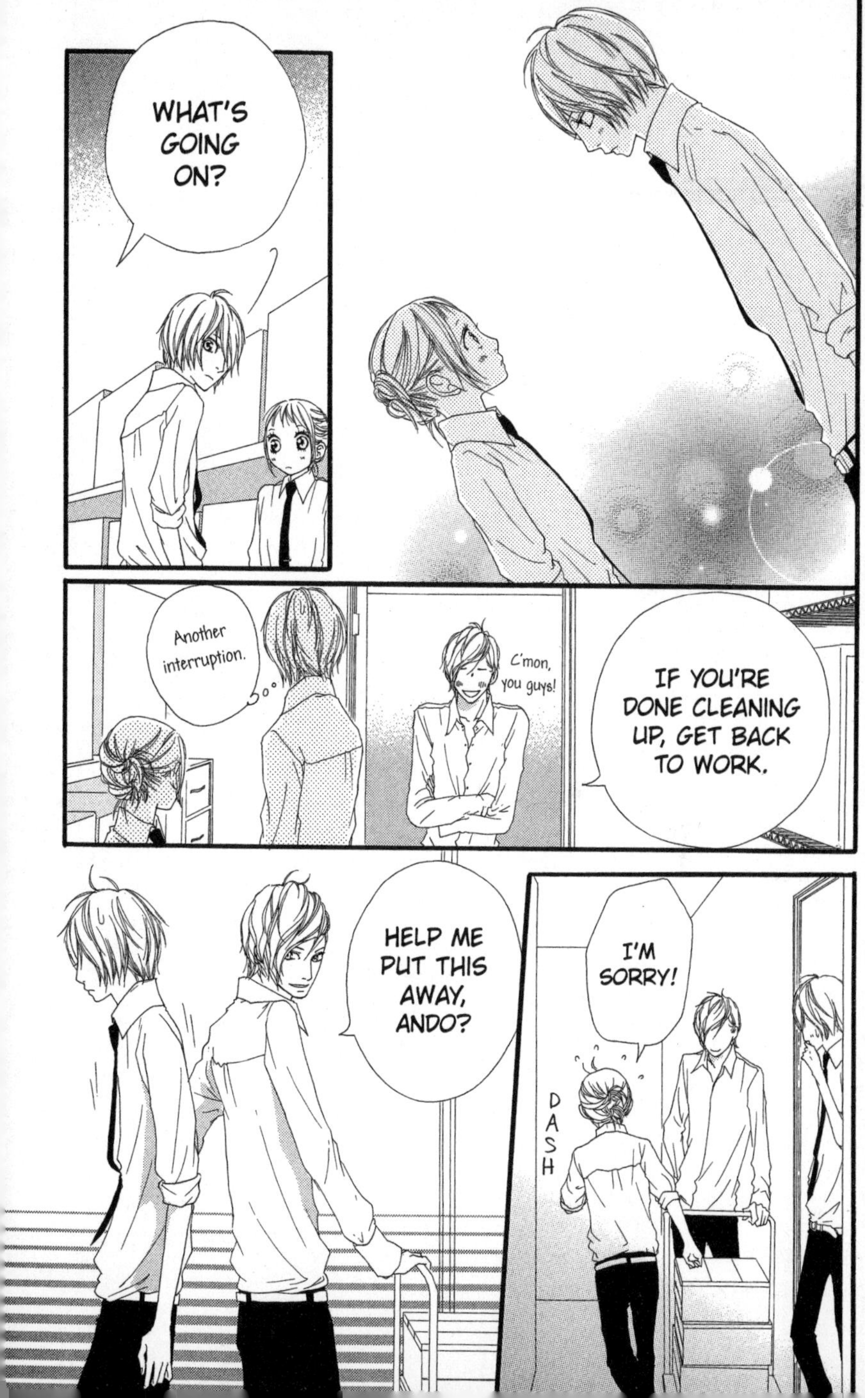
WHAT'S GOING ON?
IF YOU'RE DONE CLEANING UP, GET BACK TO WORK.
C'mon, you guys!
Another interruption.
I'M SORRY!
DASH
HELP ME PUT THIS AWAY, ANDO?

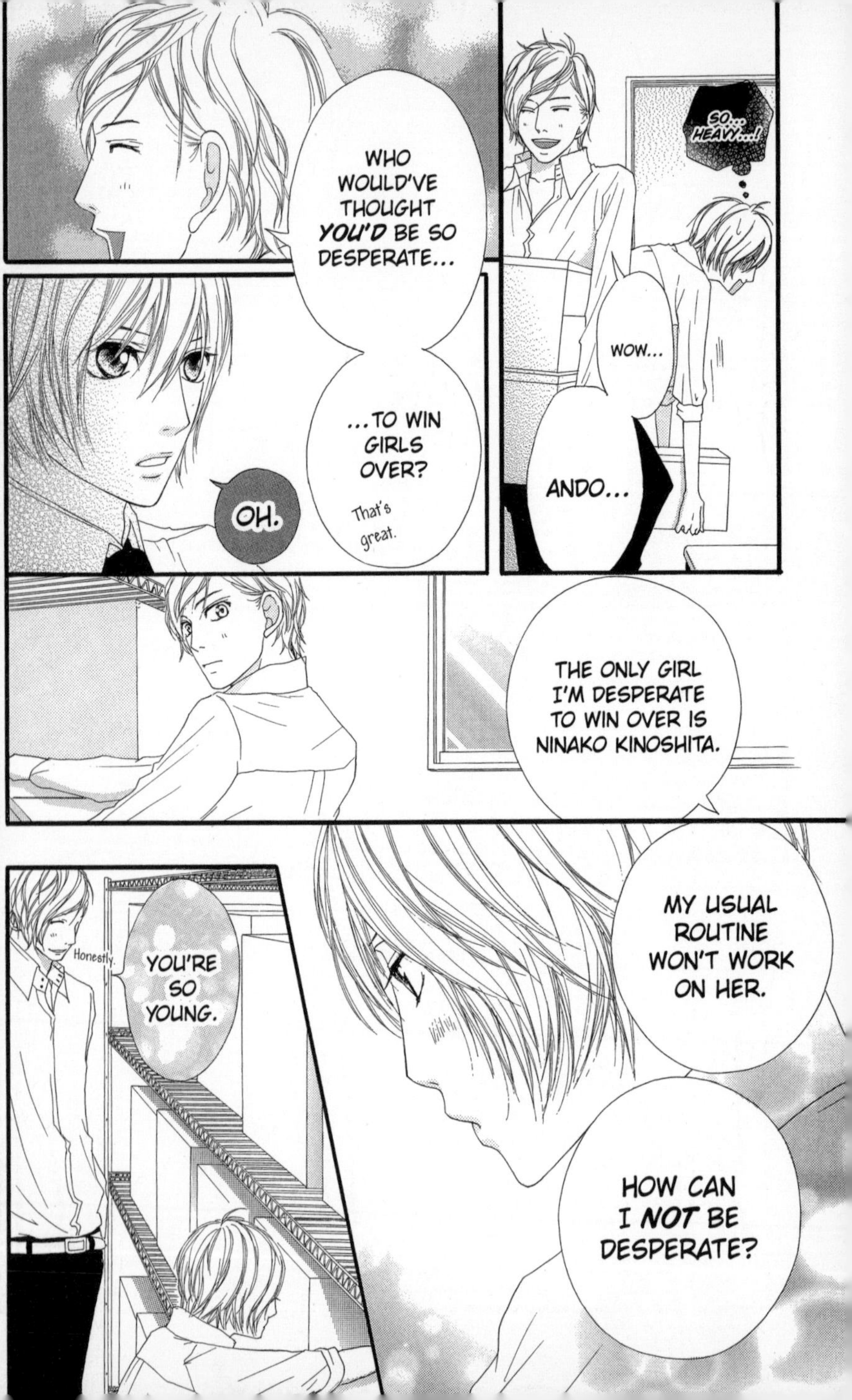
SO... HEAVY...!
WOW...
ANDO...
WHO WOULD'VE THOUGHT *YOU'D* BE SO DESPERATE...
...TO WIN GIRLS OVER?
That's great.
OH.
THE ONLY GIRL I'M DESPERATE TO WIN OVER IS NINAKO KINOSHITA.
MY USUAL ROUTINE WON'T WORK ON HER.
HOW CAN I *NOT* BE DESPERATE?
YOU'RE SO YOUNG.
Honestly.

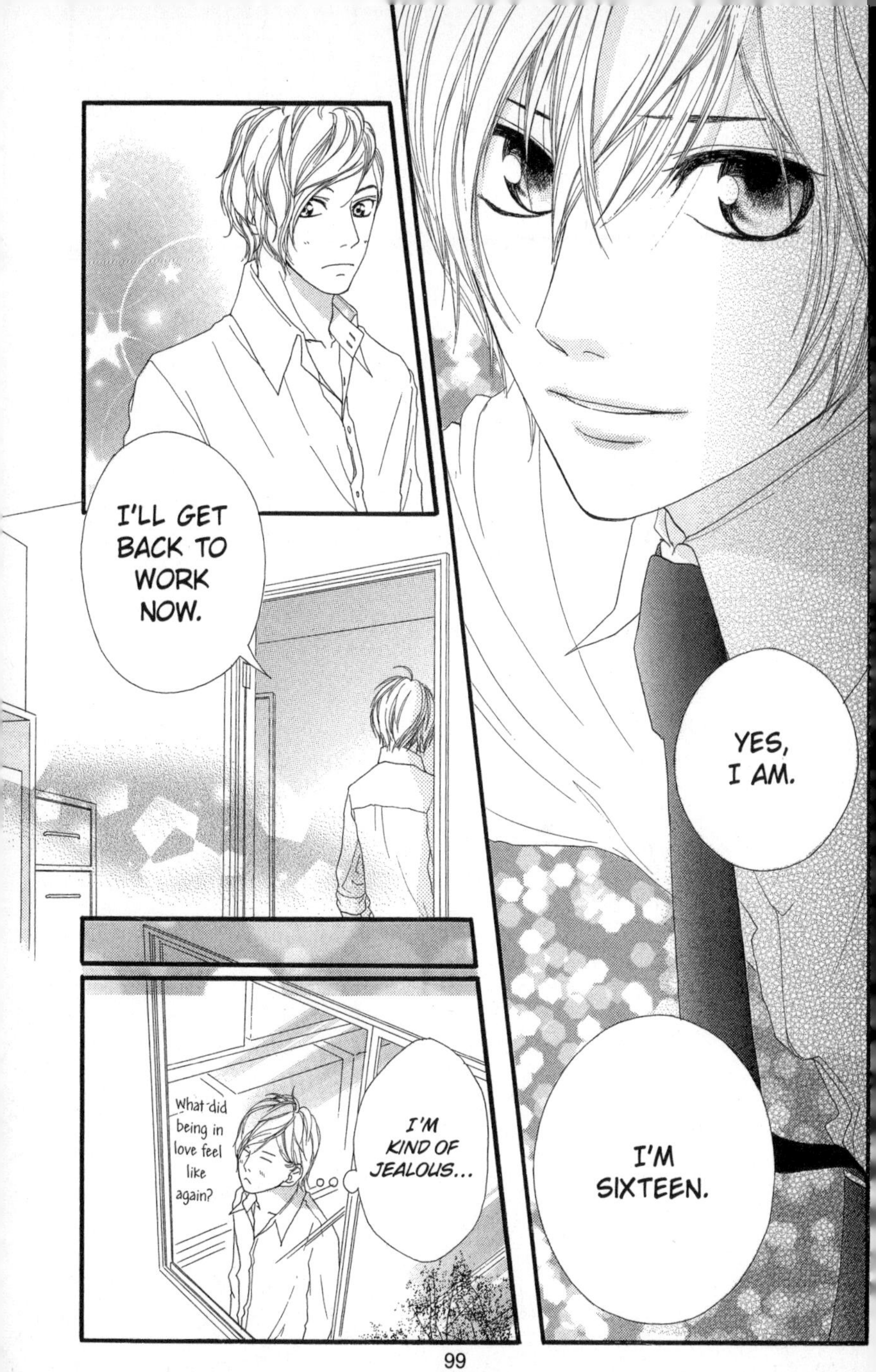
YES, I AM.
I'M SIXTEEN.
I'LL GET BACK TO WORK NOW.
I'M KIND OF JEALOUS...
What did being in love feel like again?

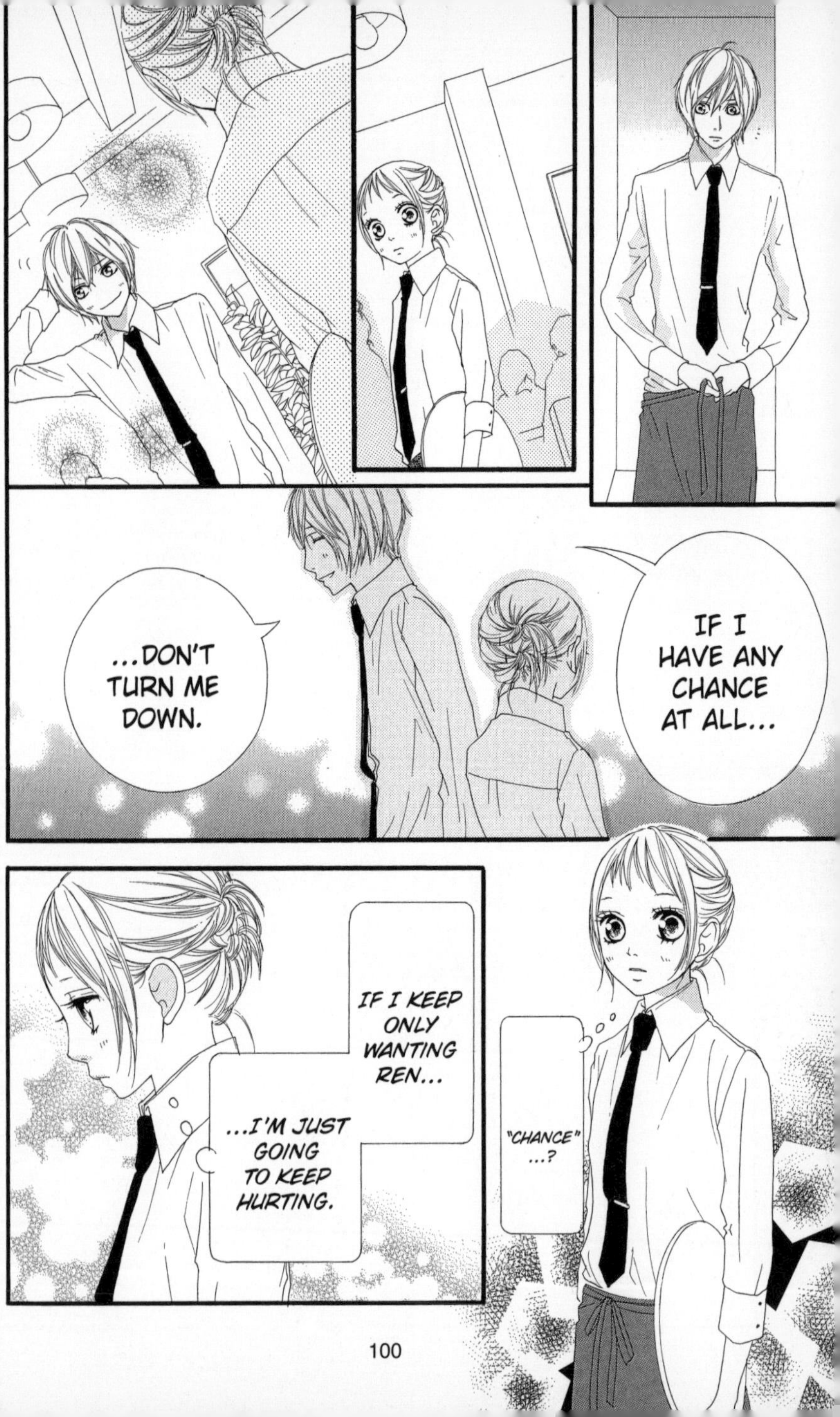

IF I HAVE ANY CHANCE AT ALL...
...DON'T TURN ME DOWN.
"CHANCE" ...?
IF I KEEP ONLY WANTING REN...
...I'M JUST GOING TO KEEP HURTING.

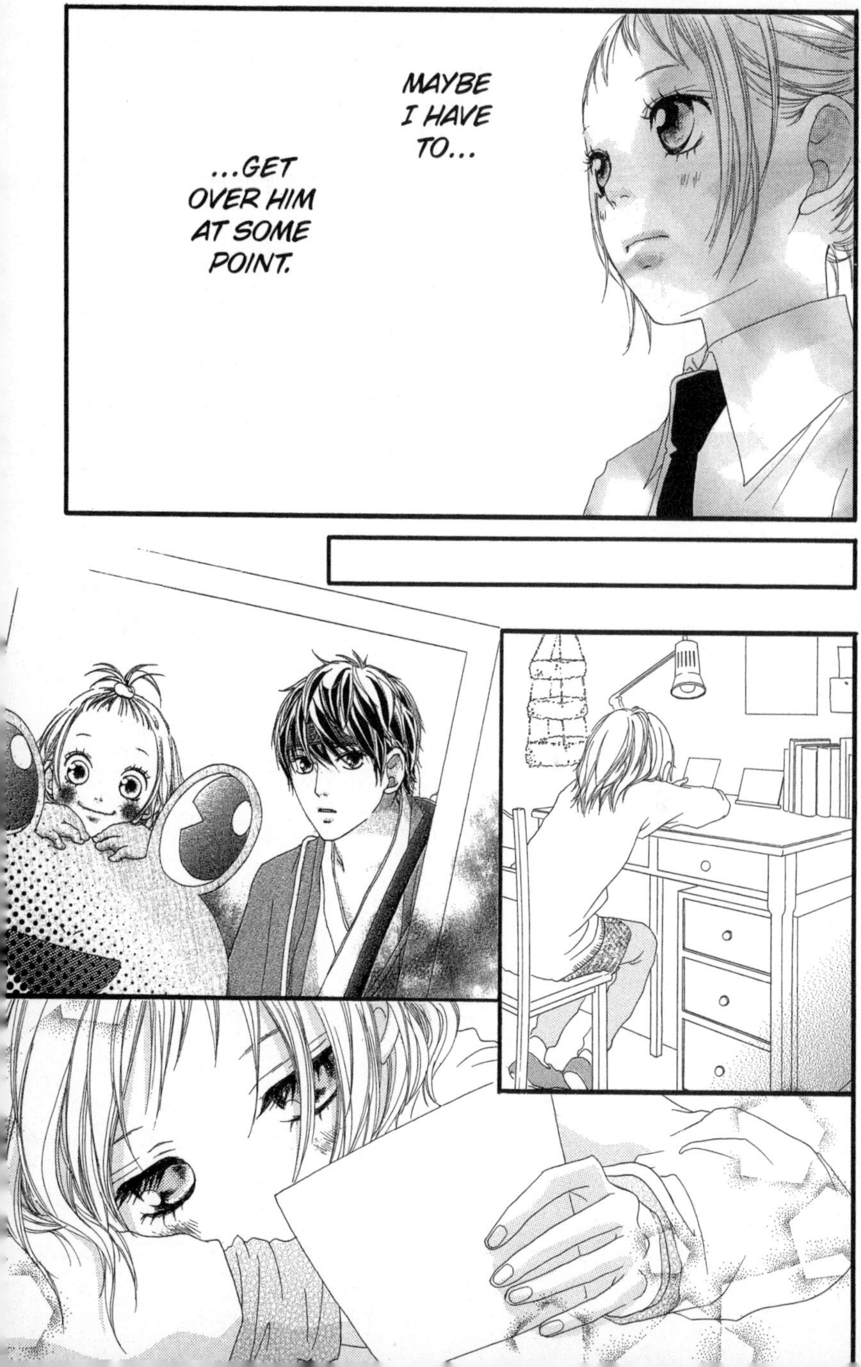
MAYBE I HAVE TO...
...GET OVER HIM AT SOME POINT.

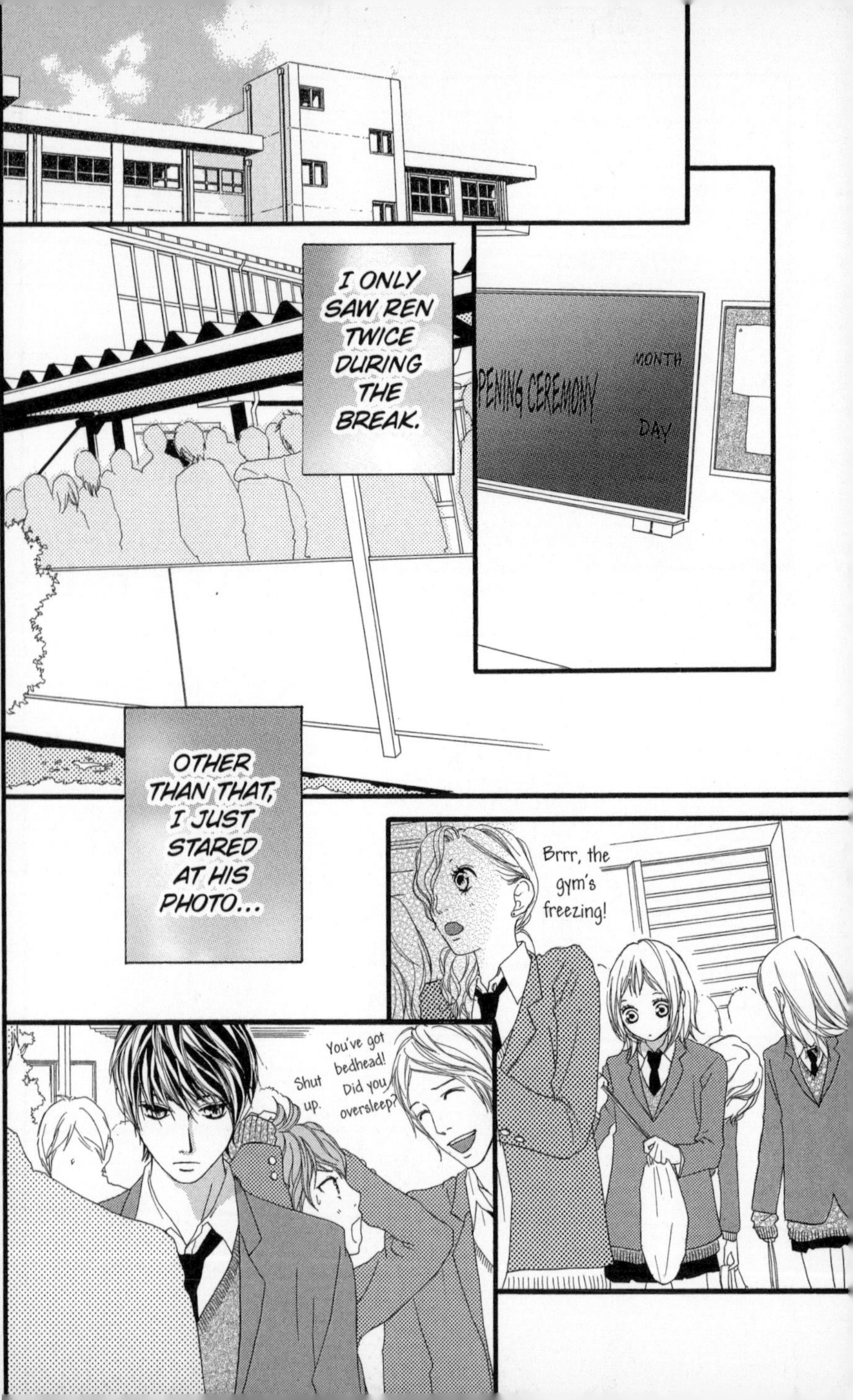
PENING CEREMONY
MONTH
DAY
I ONLY SAW REN TWICE DURING THE BREAK.
OTHER THAN THAT, I JUST STARED AT HIS PHOTO...
Brrr, the gym's freezing!
You've got bedhead! Did you oversleep?
Shut up.

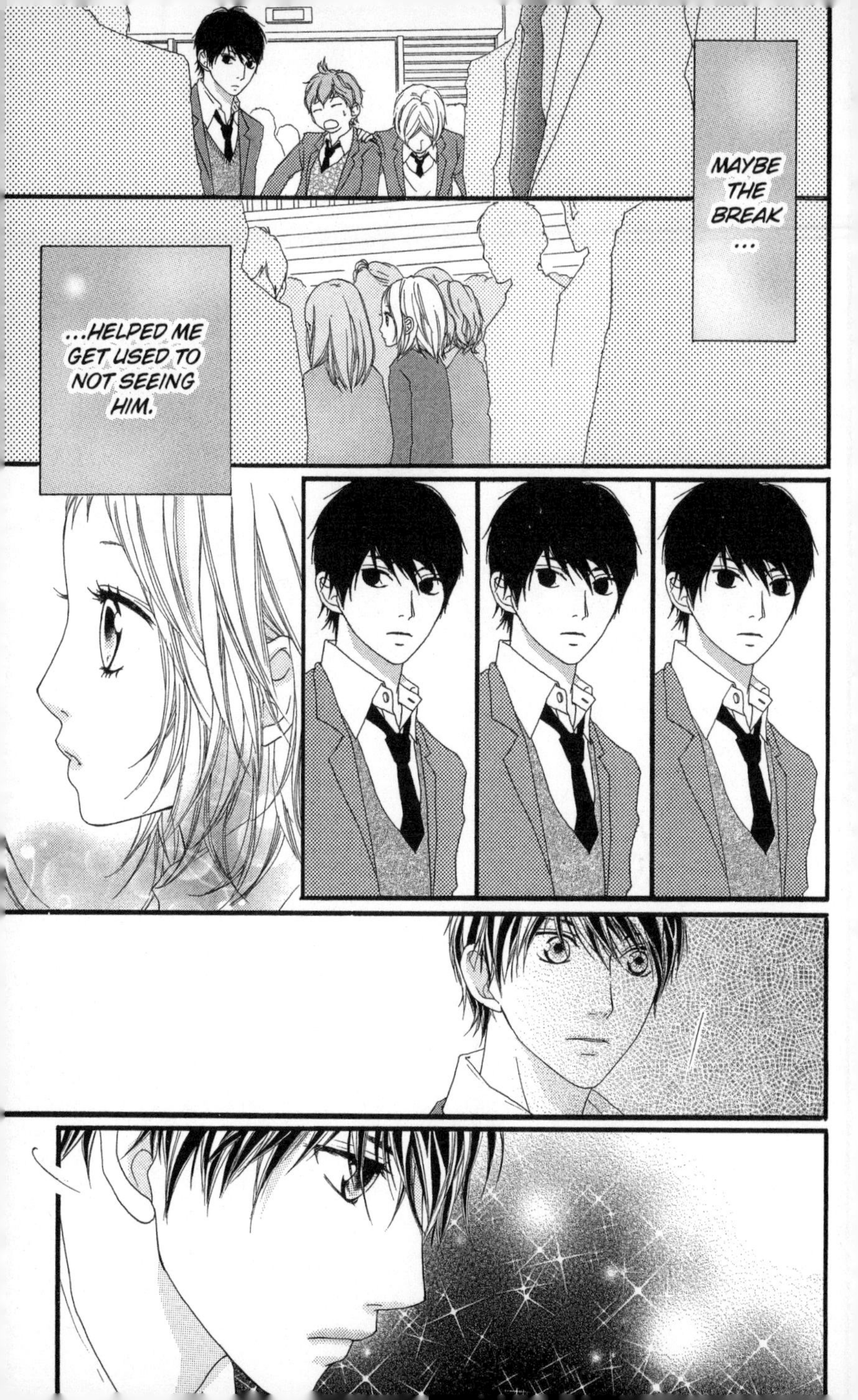
MAYBE THE BREAK ...
...HELPED ME GET USED TO NOT SEEING HIM.

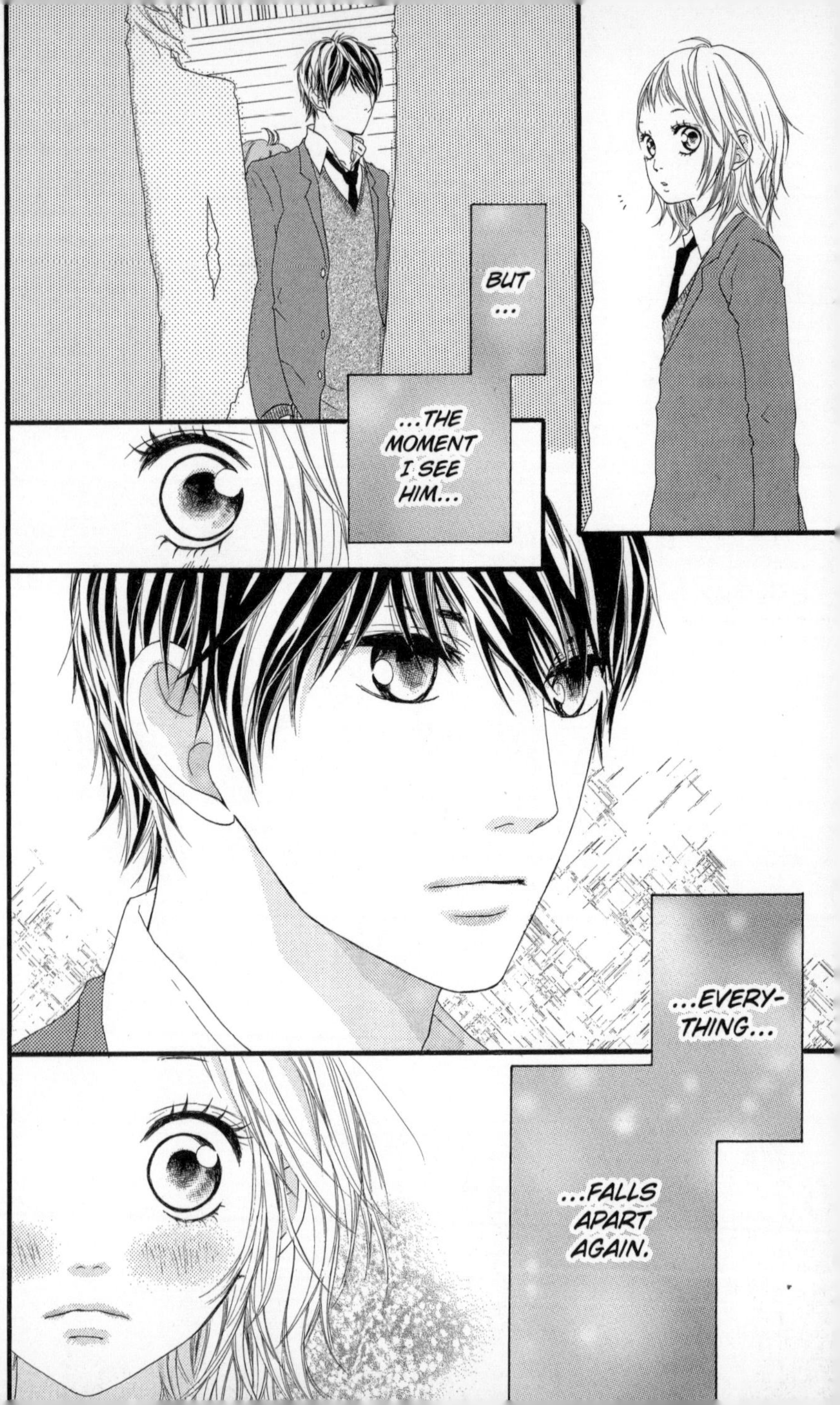
BUT ...
...THE MOMENT I SEE HIM...
...EVERY-THING...
...FALLS APART AGAIN.

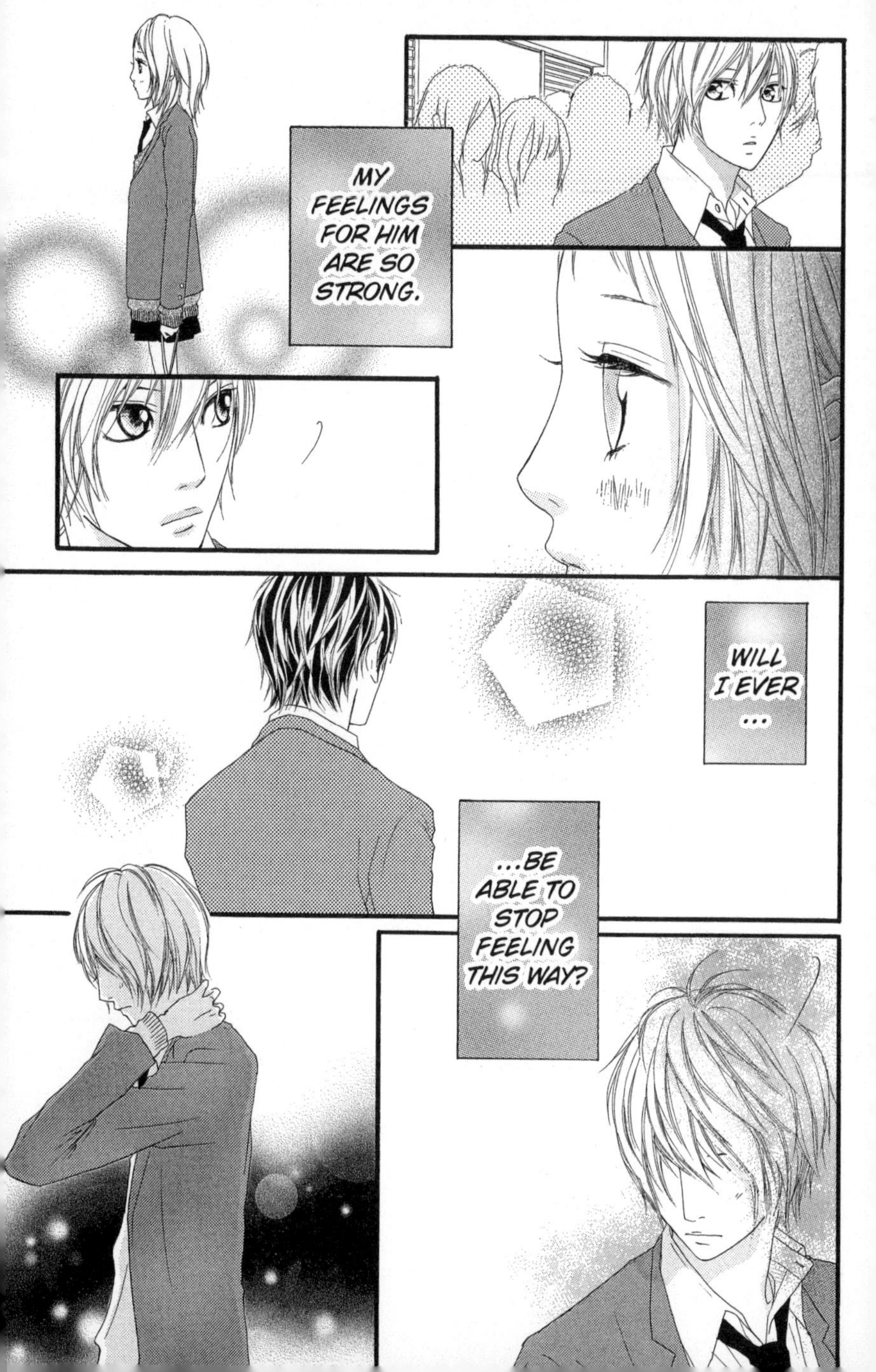
MY FEELINGS FOR HIM ARE SO STRONG.
WILL I EVER ...
...BE ABLE TO STOP FEELING THIS WAY?

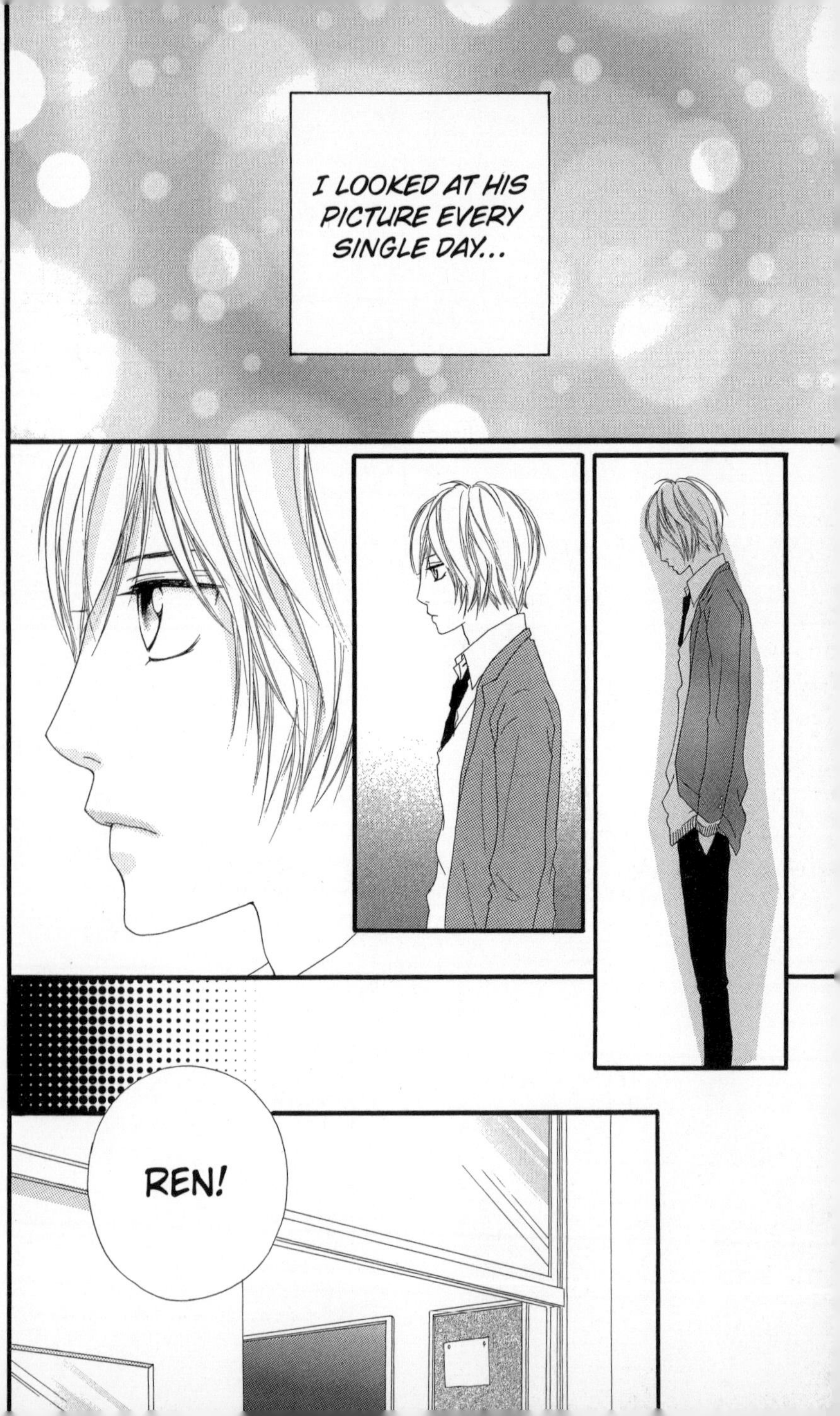
I LOOKED AT HIS PICTURE EVERY SINGLE DAY...
REN!

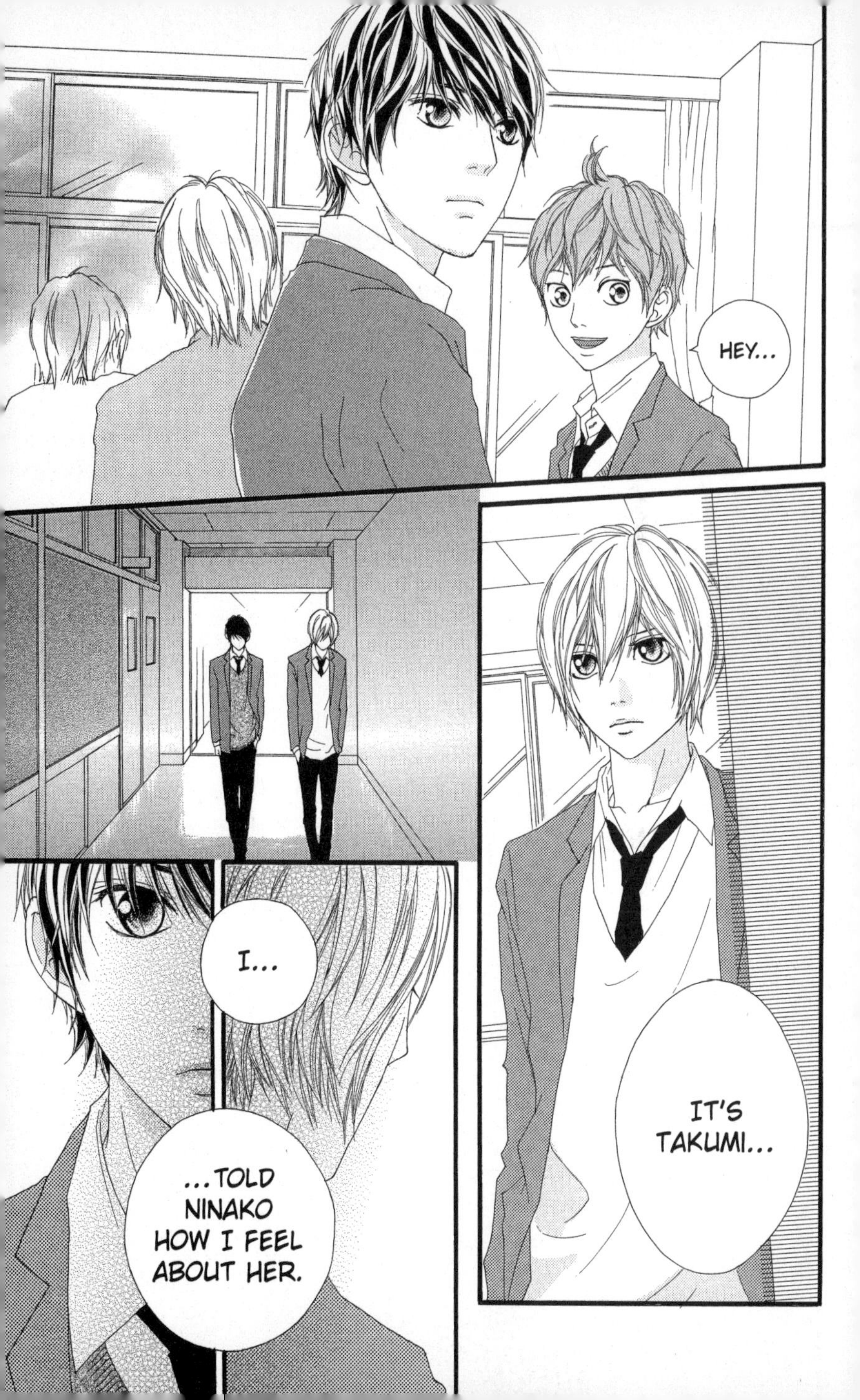
HEY...
IT'S TAKUMI...
I...
...TOLD NINAKO HOW I FEEL ABOUT HER.

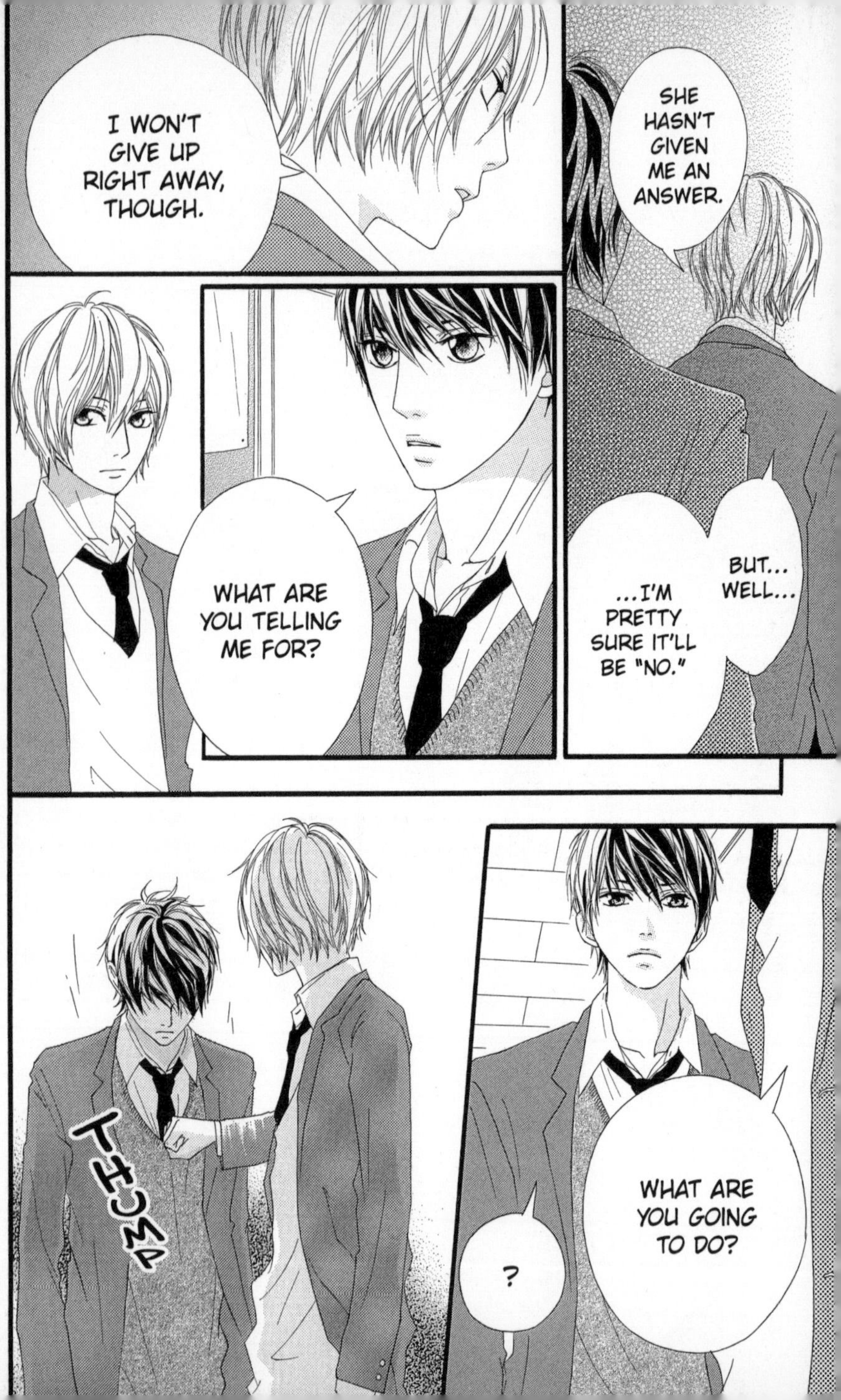
SHE HASN'T GIVEN ME AN ANSWER.
BUT... WELL...
...I'M PRETTY SURE IT'LL BE "NO."
I WON'T GIVE UP RIGHT AWAY, THOUGH.
WHAT ARE YOU TELLING ME FOR?
WHAT ARE YOU GOING TO DO?
?
THUMP

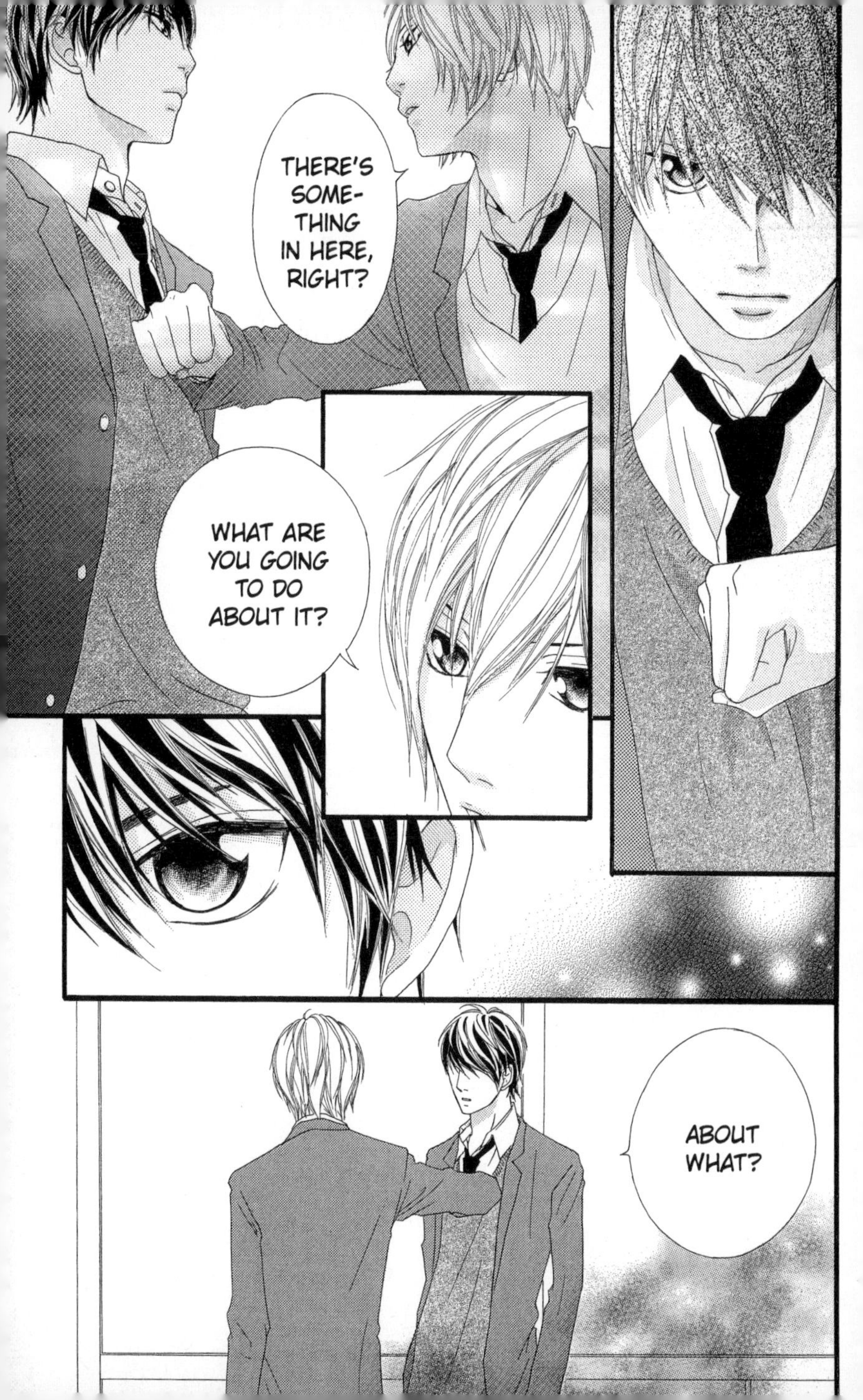
THERE'S SOMETHING IN HERE, RIGHT?
WHAT ARE YOU GOING TO DO ABOUT IT?
ABOUT WHAT?

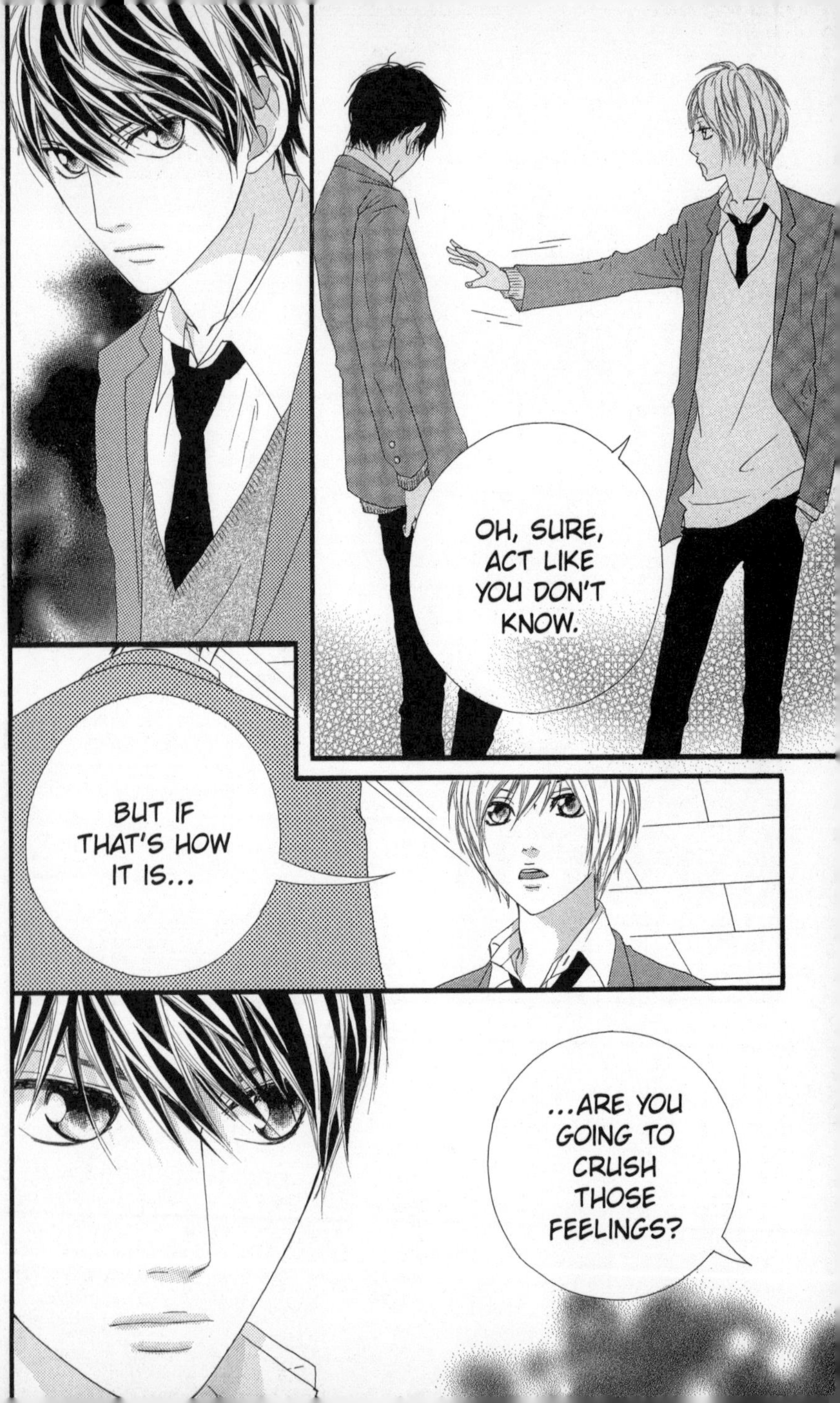
OH, SURE, ACT LIKE YOU DON'T KNOW.
BUT IF THAT'S HOW IT IS...
...ARE YOU GOING TO CRUSH THOSE FEELINGS?

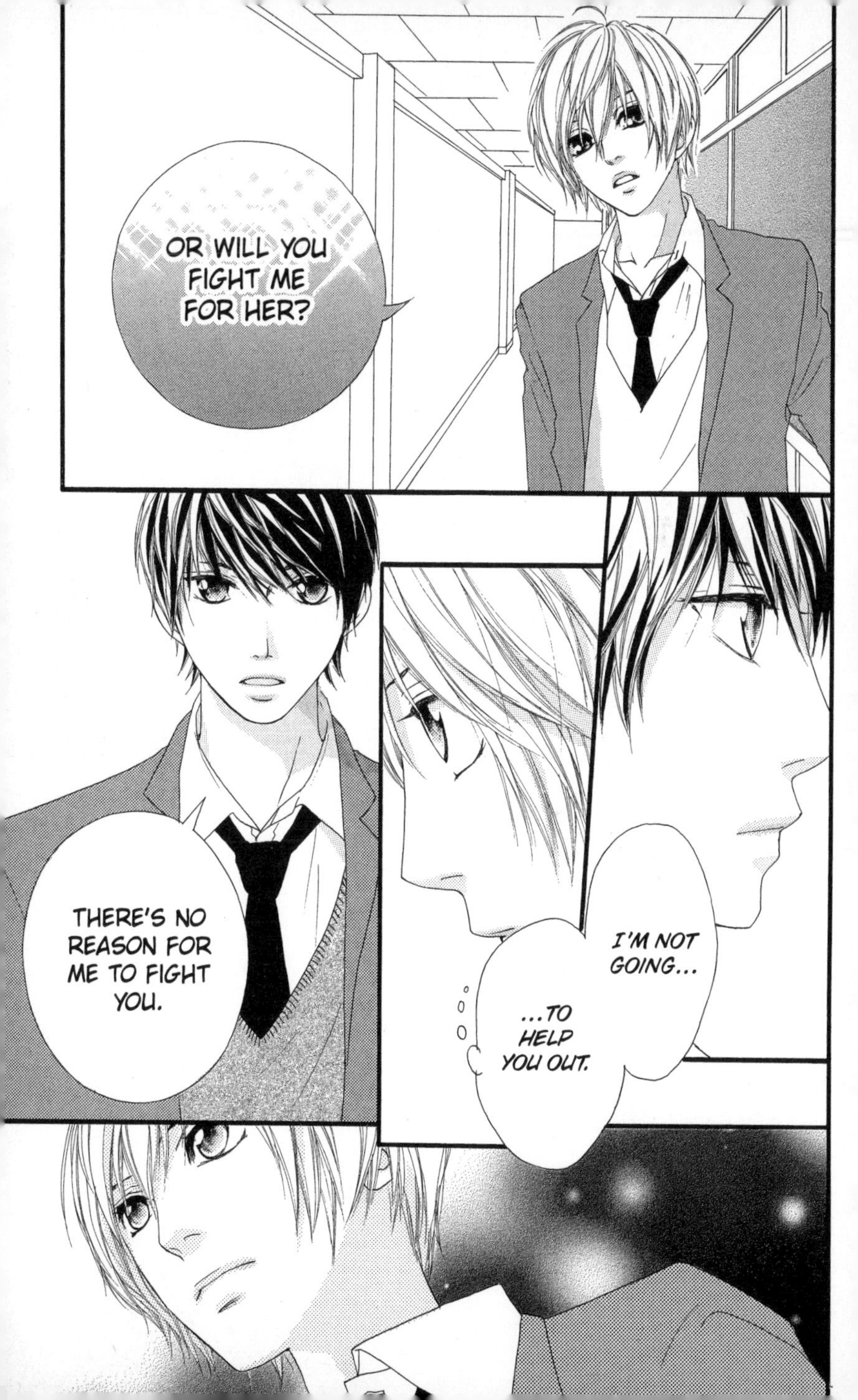
OR WILL YOU FIGHT ME FOR HER?
I'M NOT GOING... ...TO HELP YOU OUT.
THERE'S NO REASON FOR ME TO FIGHT YOU.

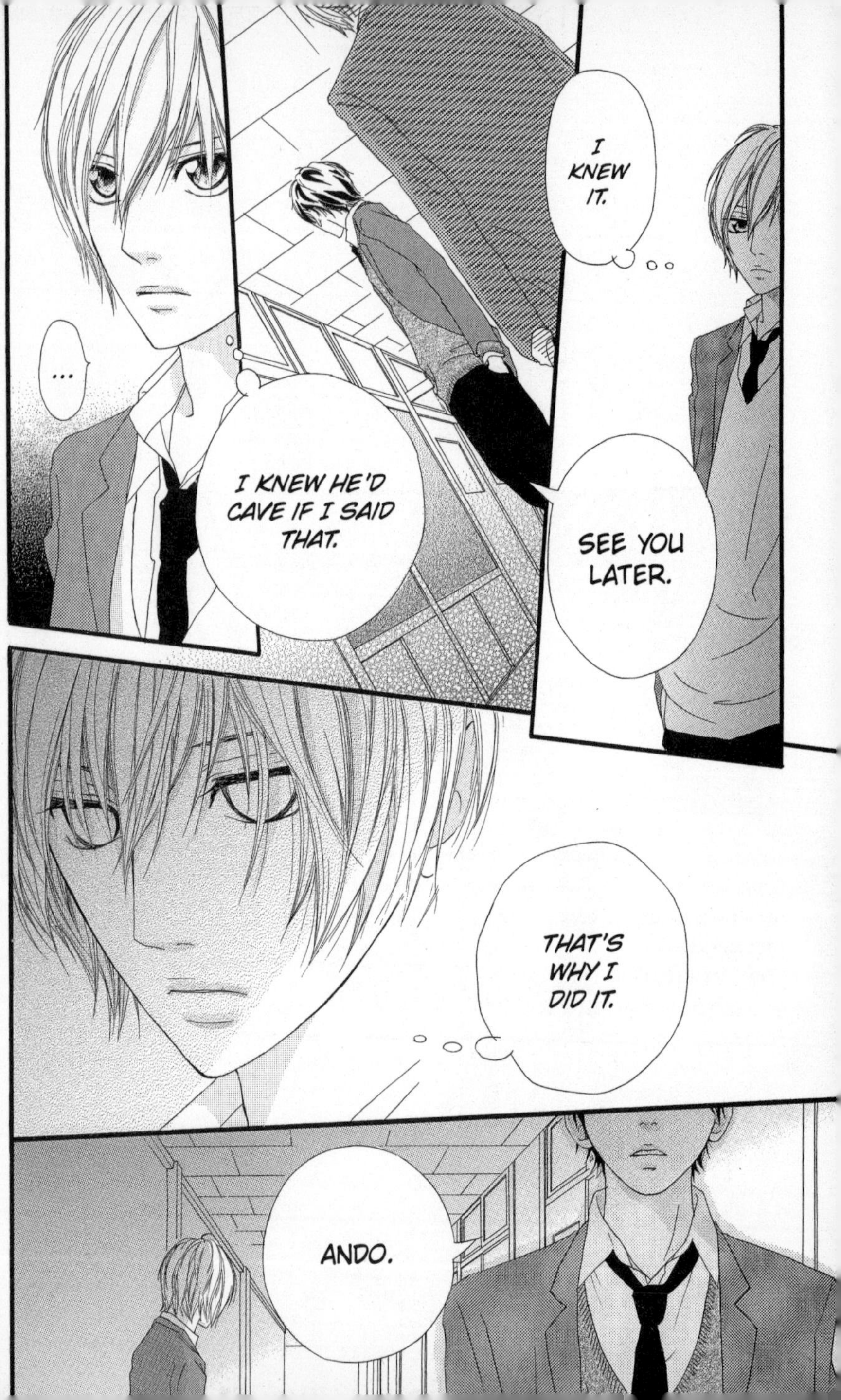
I KNEW IT.
SEE YOU LATER.
...
I KNEW HE'D CAVE IF I SAID THAT.
THAT'S WHY I DID IT.
ANDO.

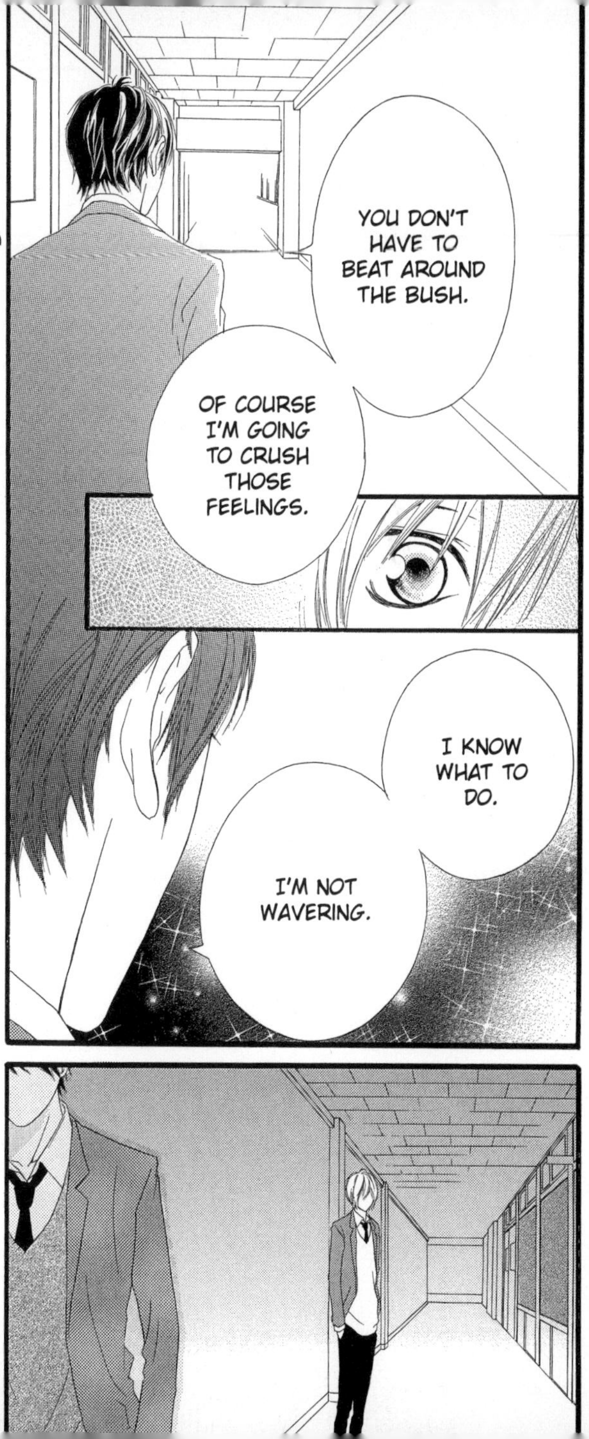
YOU DON'T HAVE TO BEAT AROUND THE BUSH.
OF COURSE I'M GOING TO CRUSH THOSE FEELINGS.
I KNOW WHAT TO DO.
I'M NOT WAVERING.

I got to watch a VOMIC recording session!

In VOMICs, voice actors deliver the lines of manga characters. *Strobe Edge* was made into a VOMIC. (Chapters 5 and 6 from volume 2.)

It was my first time going to a studio and meeting voice actors. I was so excited! But as it turned out, during both the rehearsal and actual recording, I had to check the script, so I could only catch glimpses of the voice actors. Phooey! I really wanted to see them in action.

But their voices were amazing. They are voice actors, after all! We got to take a commemorative photo afterward, and I was surrounded by beautiful voices! What is this? Wow!

You may still be able to catch back-issues on the Internet. Please try searching "VOMIC."

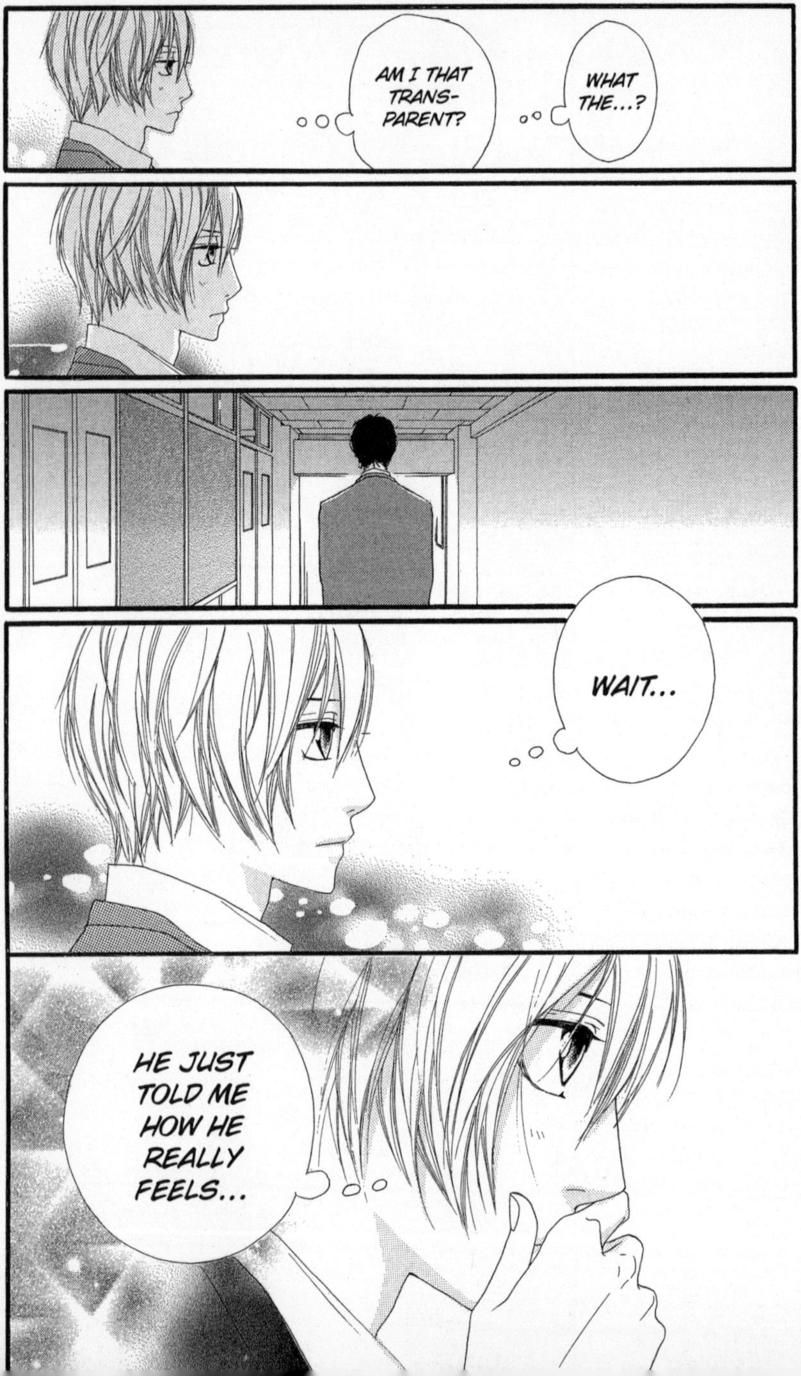
WHAT THE...?
AM I THAT TRANS-PARENT?
WAIT...
HE JUST TOLD ME HOW HE REALLY FEELS...

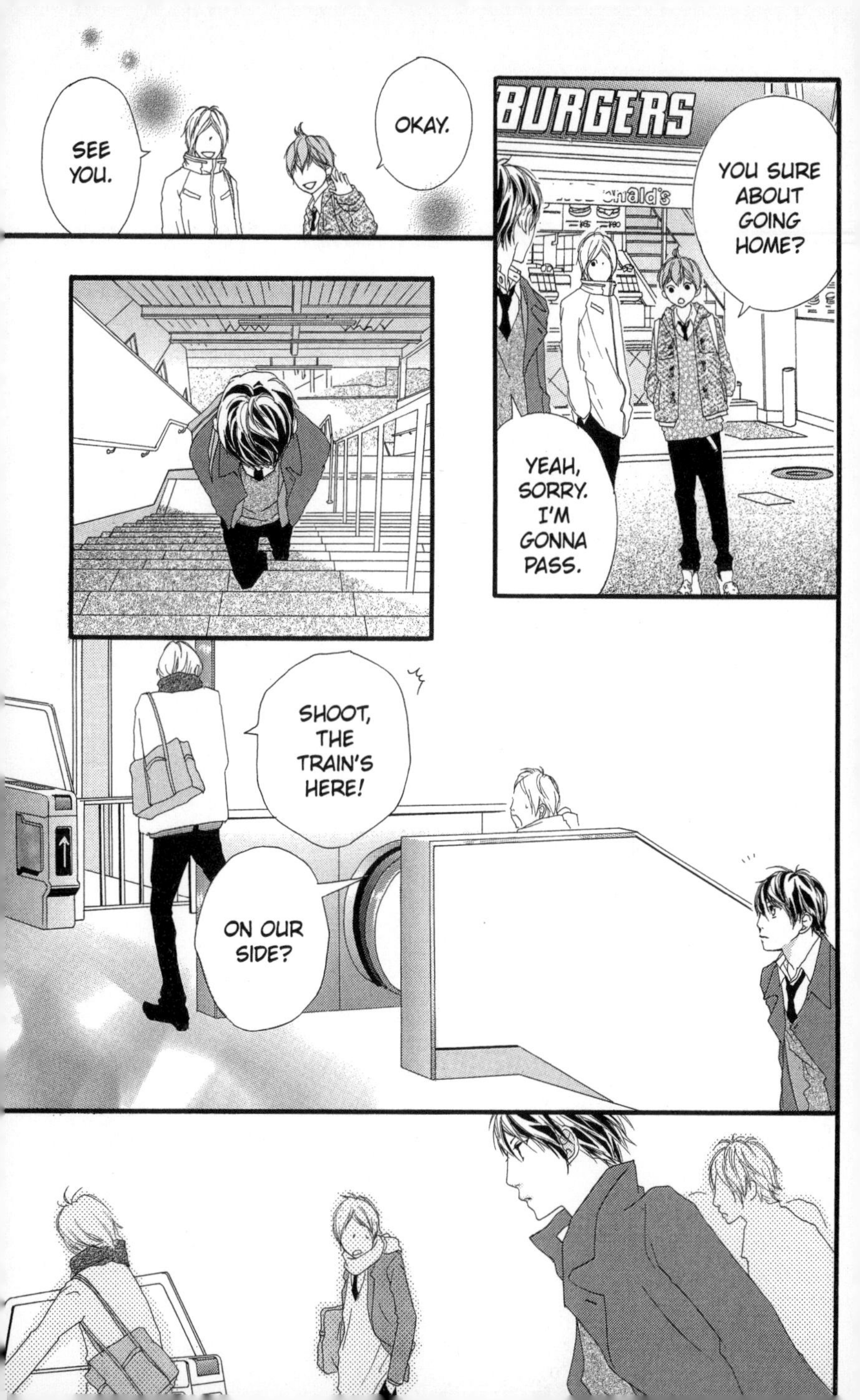
BURGERS
YOU SURE ABOUT GOING HOME?
YEAH, SORRY. I'M GONNA PASS.
SEE YOU.
OKAY.
SHOOT, THE TRAIN'S HERE!
ON OUR SIDE?

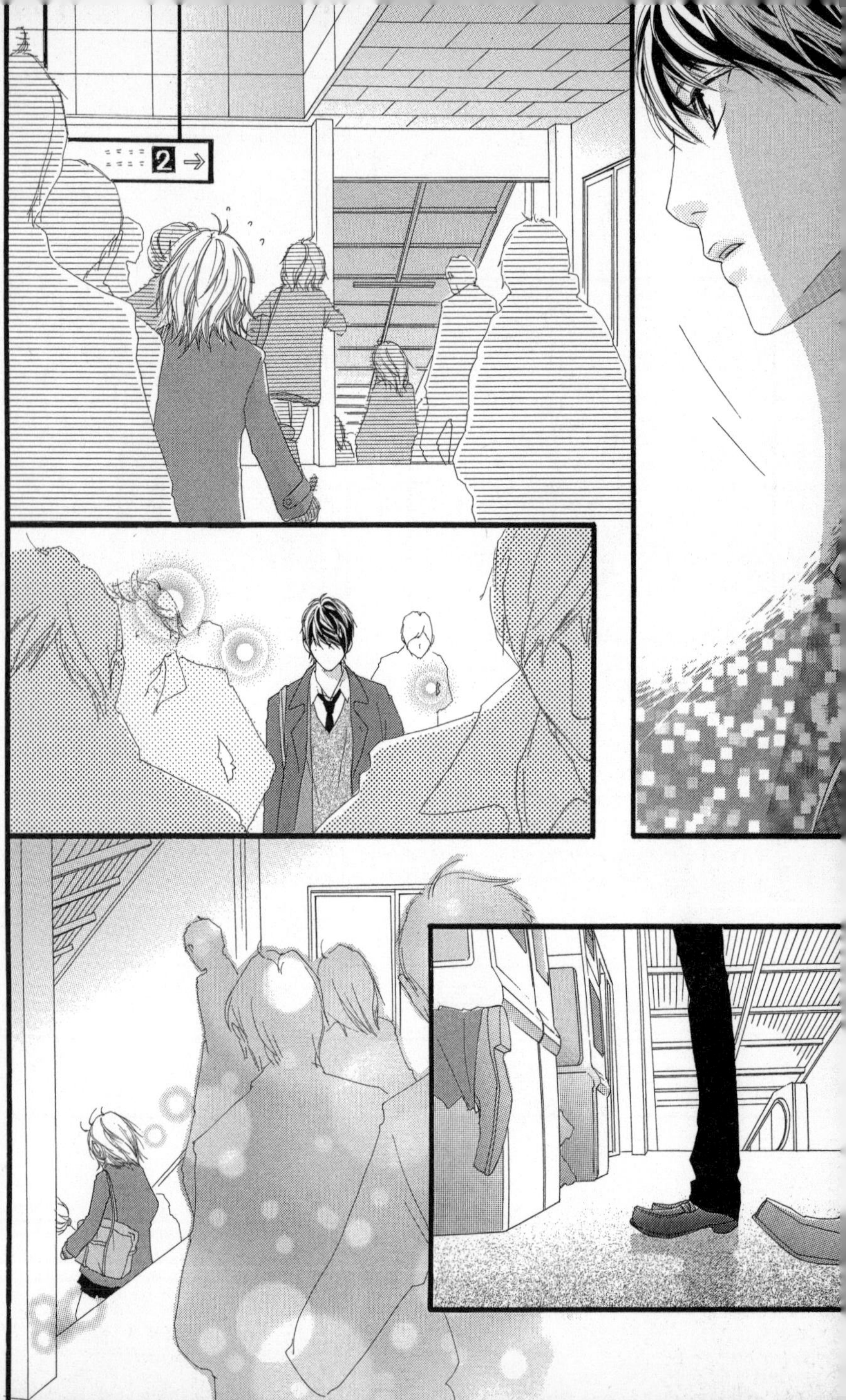
2

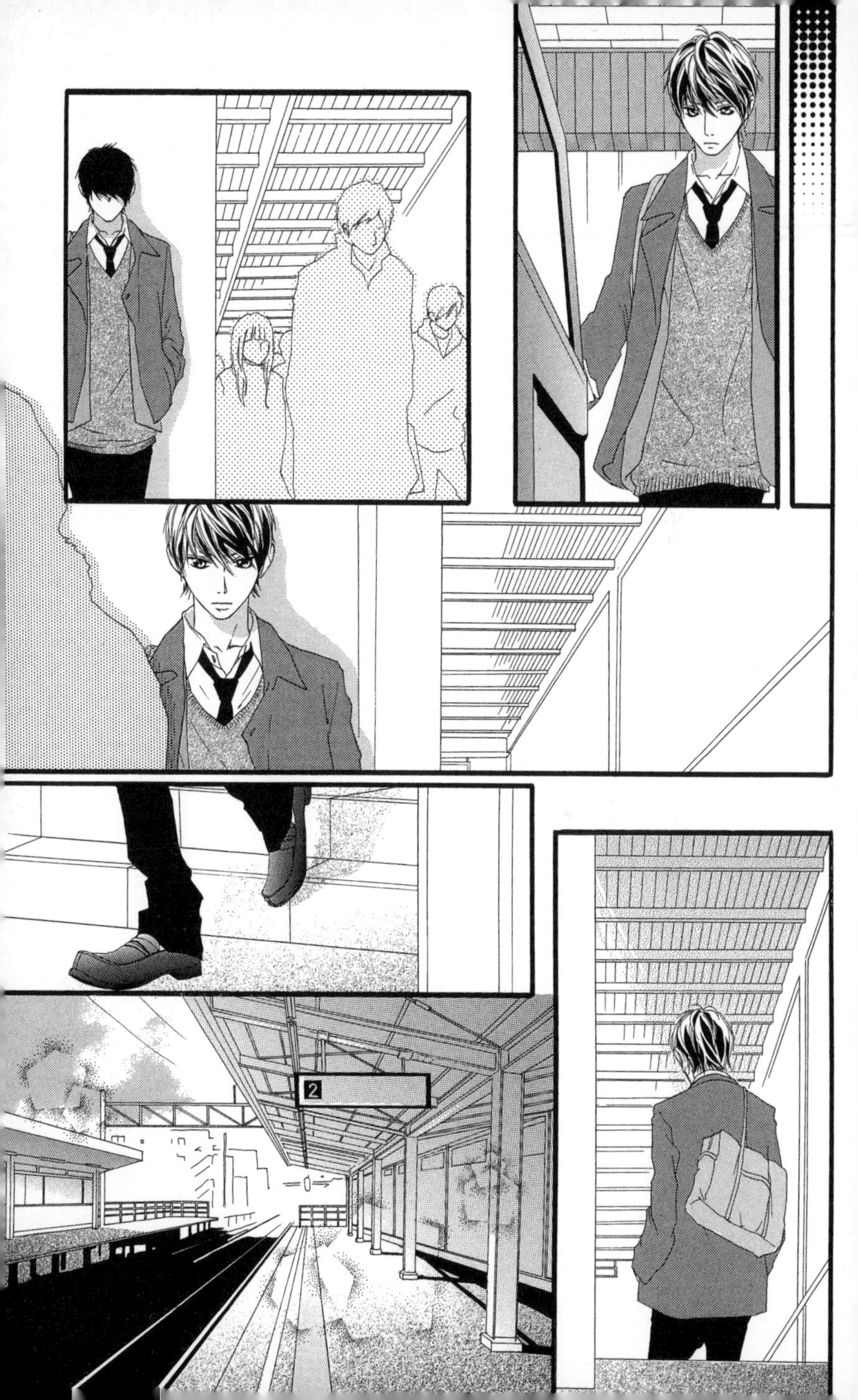
2

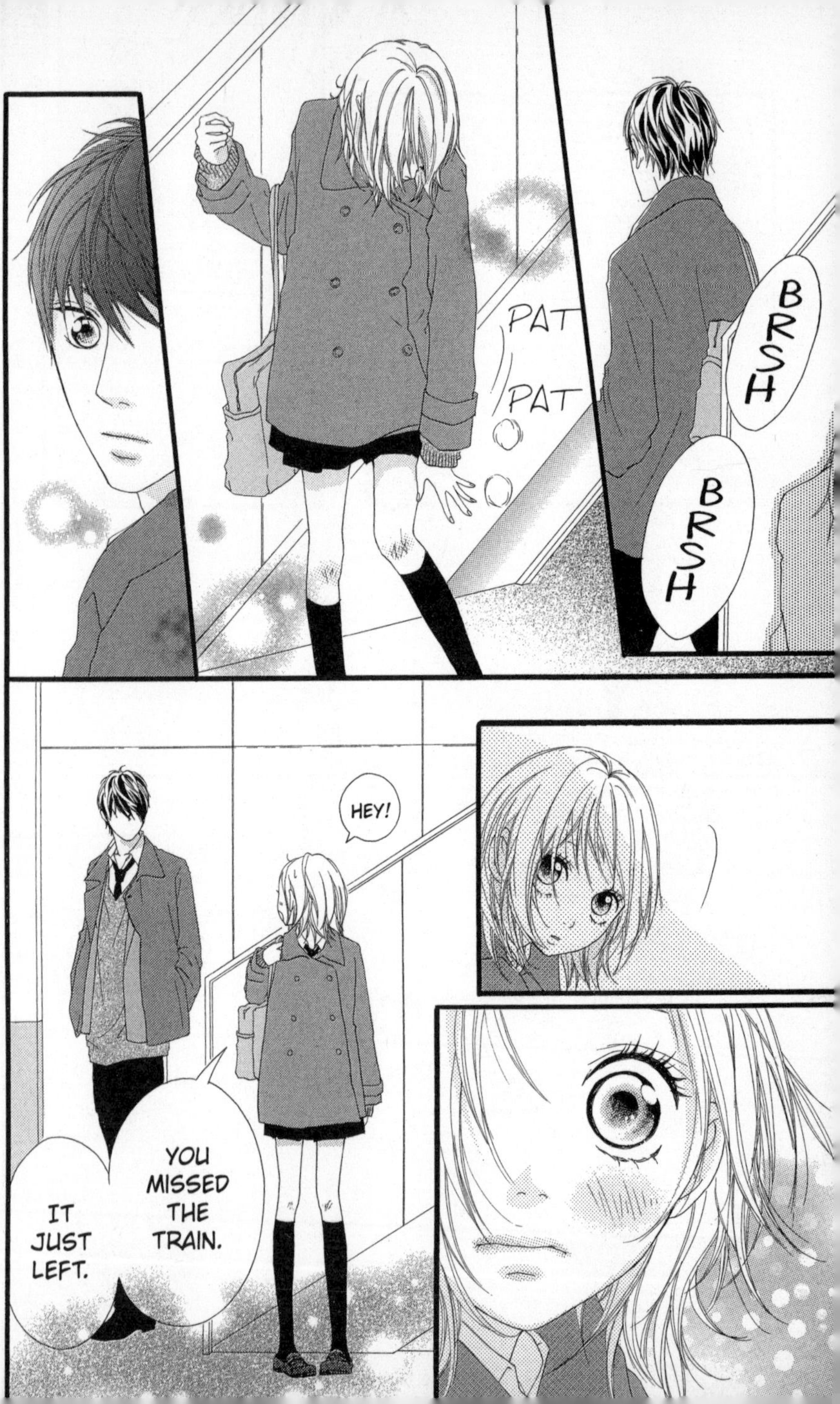
BRSH
BRSH
PAT
PAT
HEY!
YOU MISSED THE TRAIN.
IT JUST LEFT.

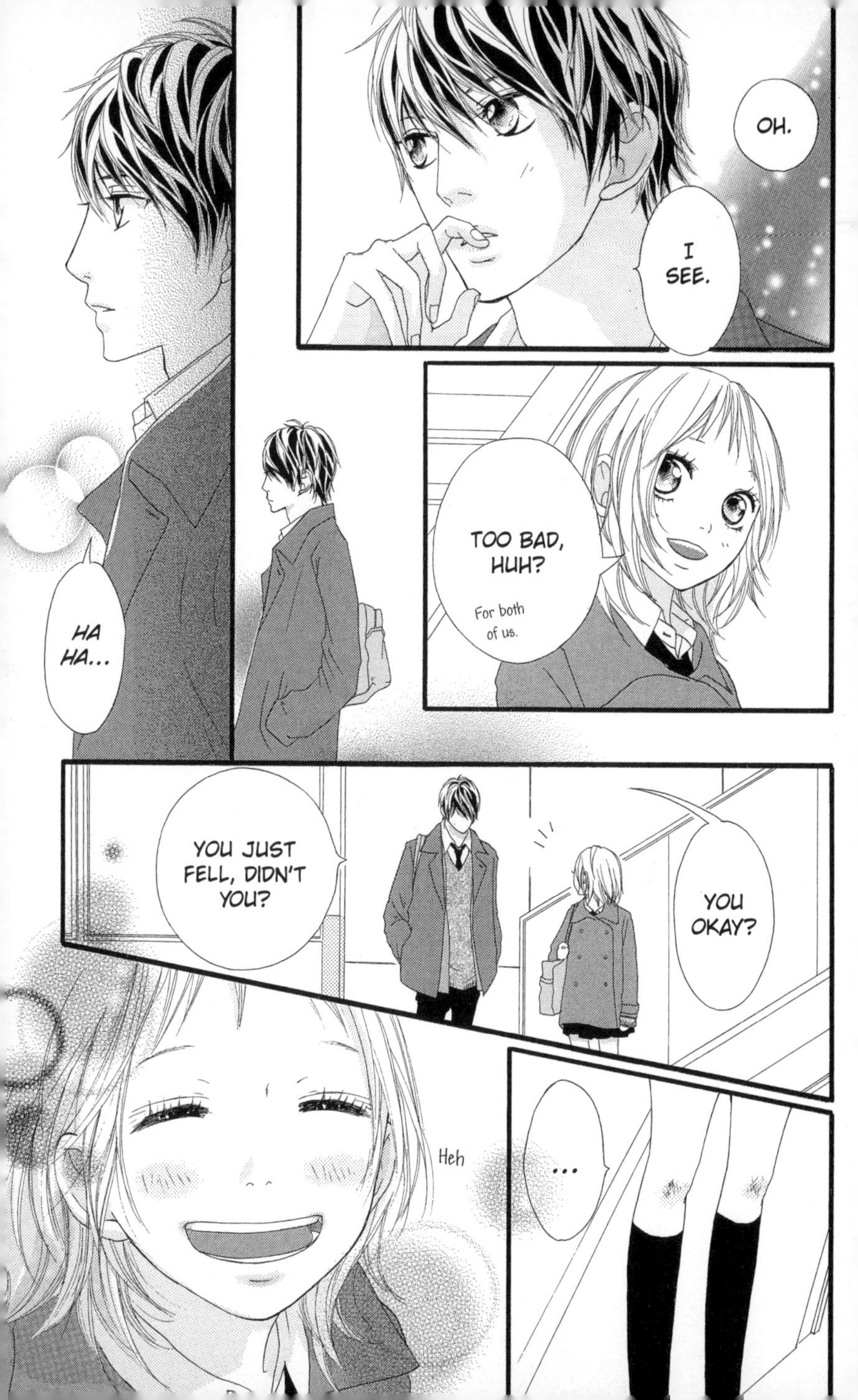
OH.
I SEE.
TOO BAD, HUH?
For both of us.
HA HA...
YOU OKAY?
YOU JUST FELL, DIDN'T YOU?
...
Heh

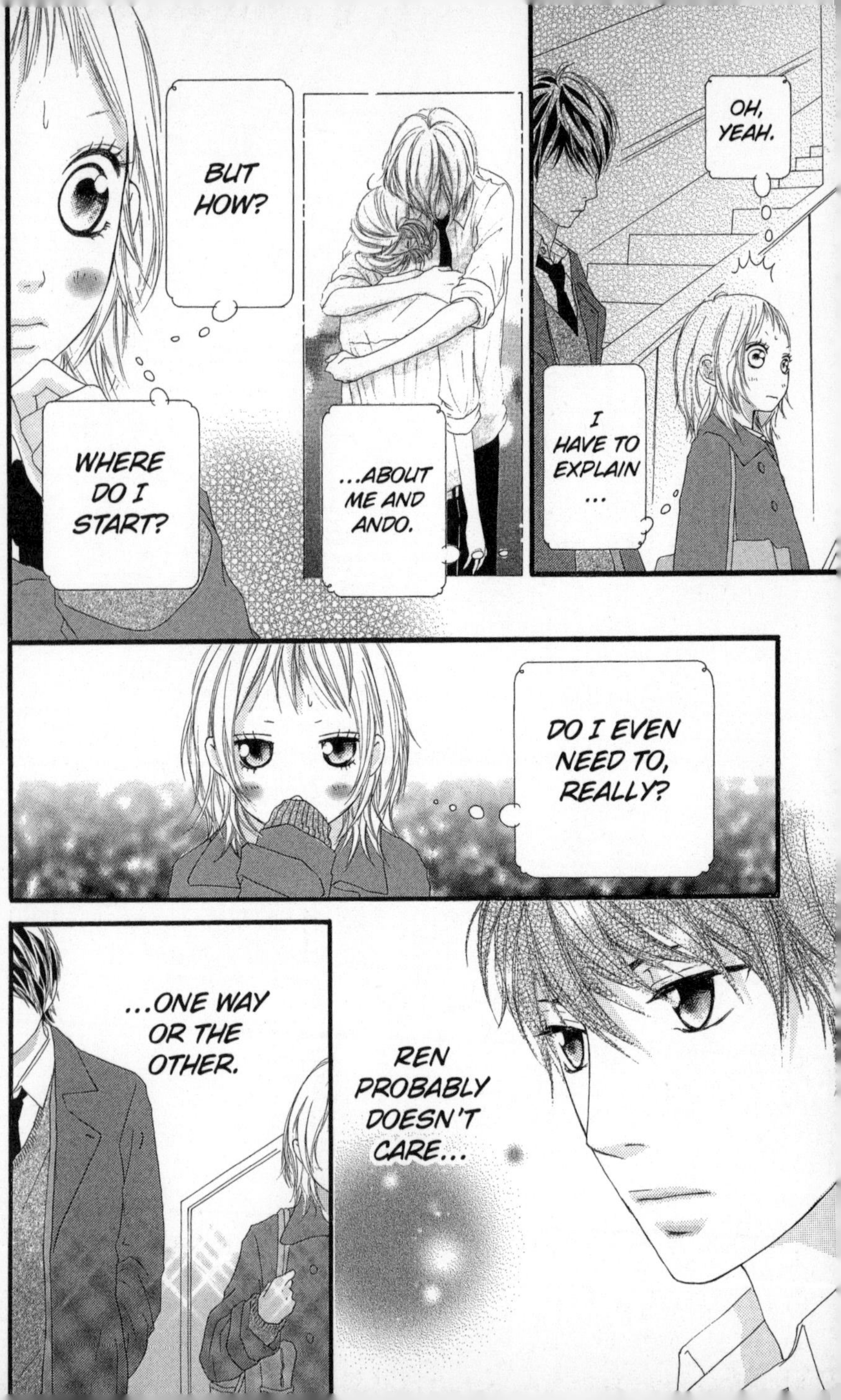
OH, YEAH.
I HAVE TO EXPLAIN ...
...ABOUT ME AND ANDO.
BUT HOW?
WHERE DO I START?
DO I EVEN NEED TO, REALLY?
REN PROBABLY DOESN'T CARE...
...ONE WAY OR THE OTHER.

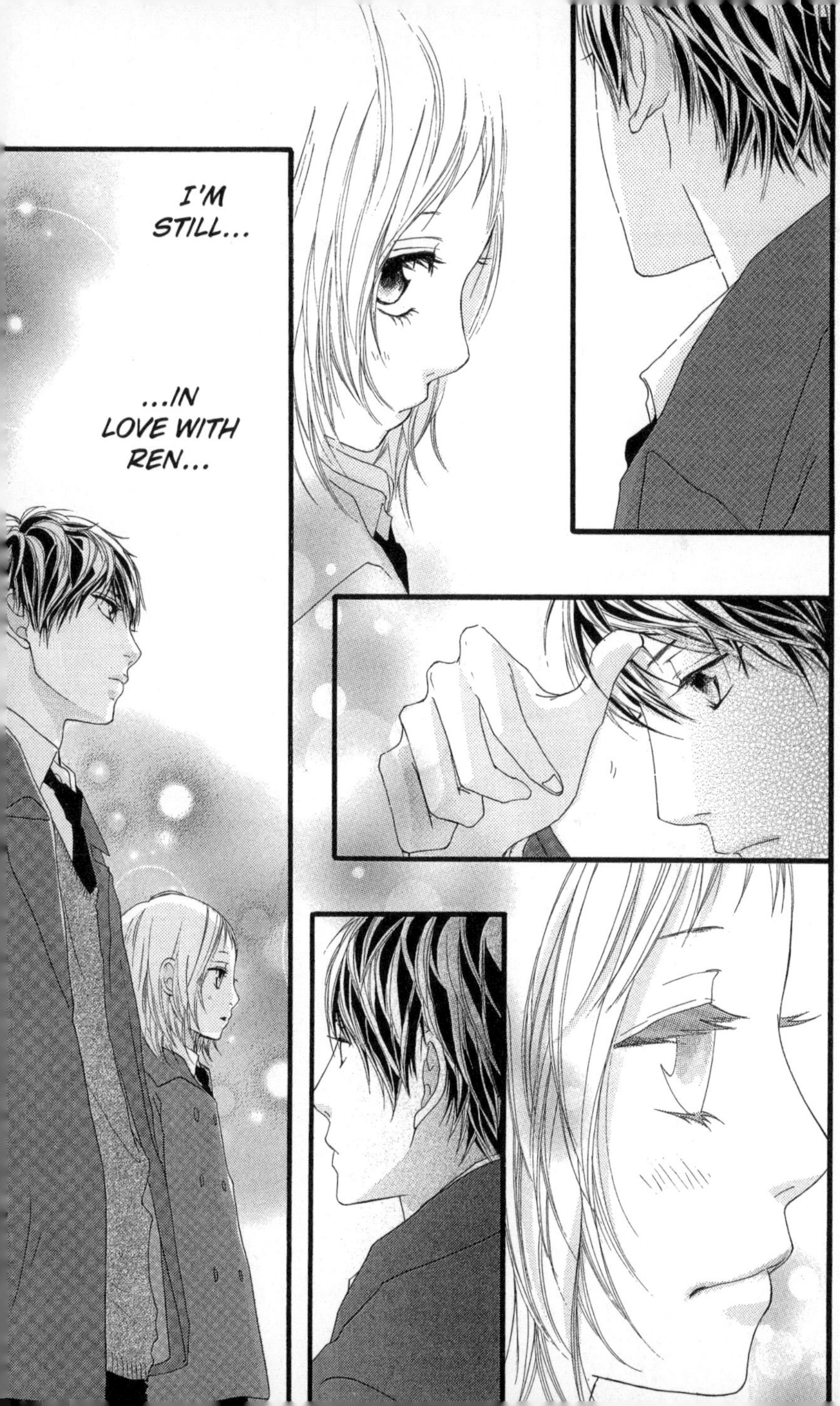
I'M STILL...
...IN LOVE WITH REN...

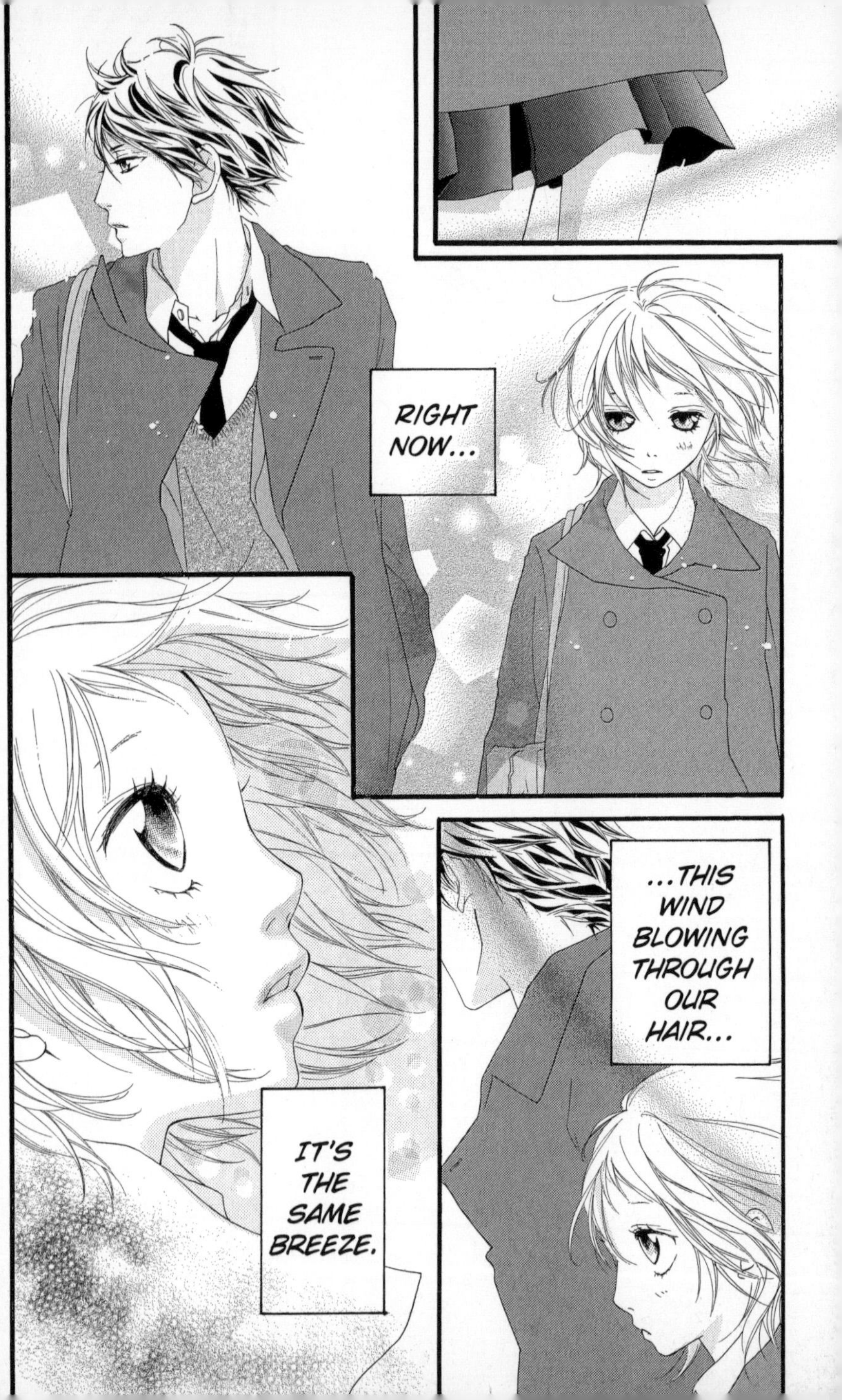
RIGHT NOW...
...THIS WIND BLOWING THROUGH OUR HAIR...
IT'S THE SAME BREEZE.

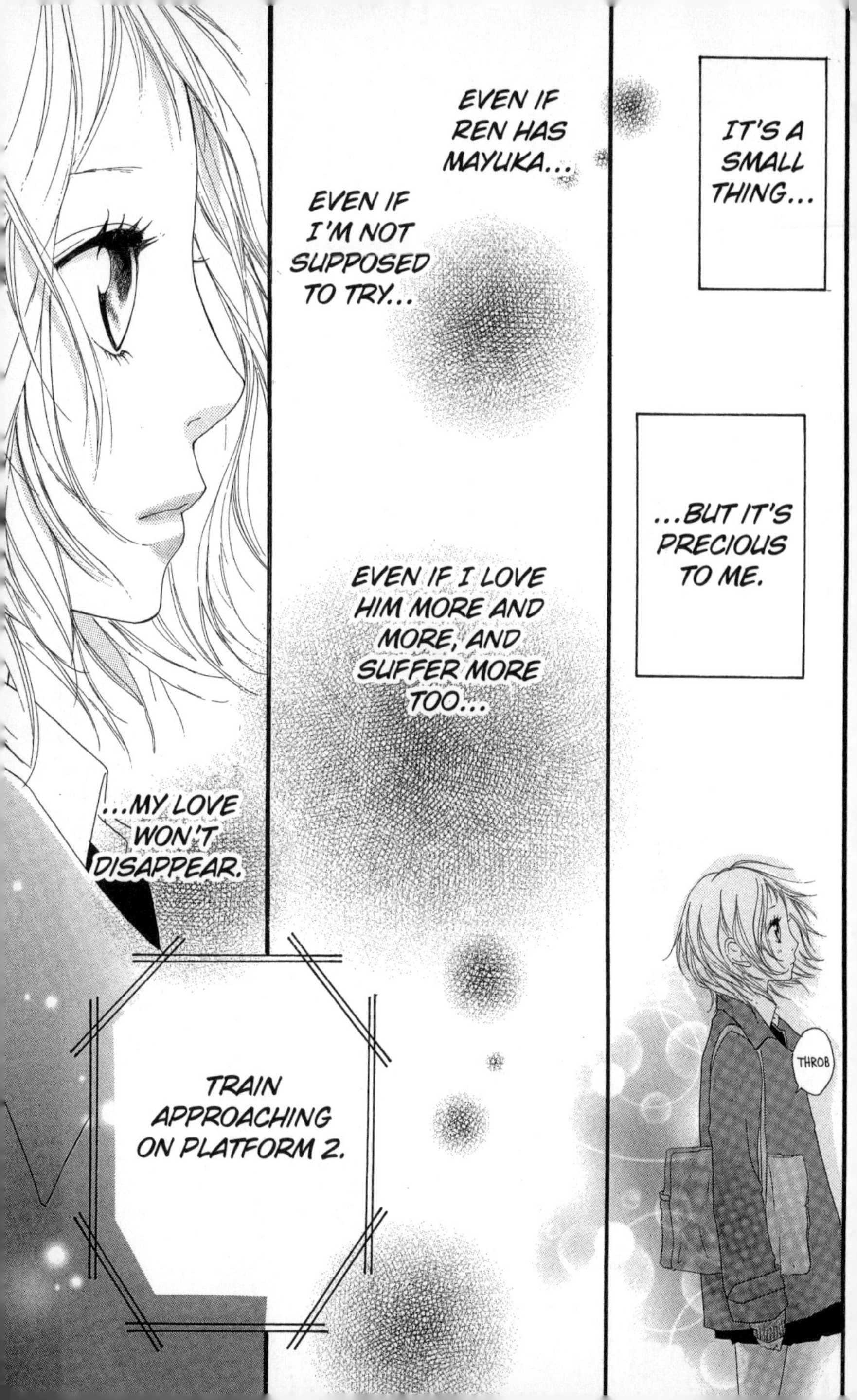
IT'S A SMALL THING...
...BUT IT'S PRECIOUS TO ME.
THROB
EVEN IF REN HAS MAYUKA...
EVEN IF I'M NOT SUPPOSED TO TRY...
EVEN IF I LOVE HIM MORE AND MORE, AND SUFFER MORE TOO...
...MY LOVE WON'T DISAPPEAR.
TRAIN APPROACHING ON PLATFORM 2.

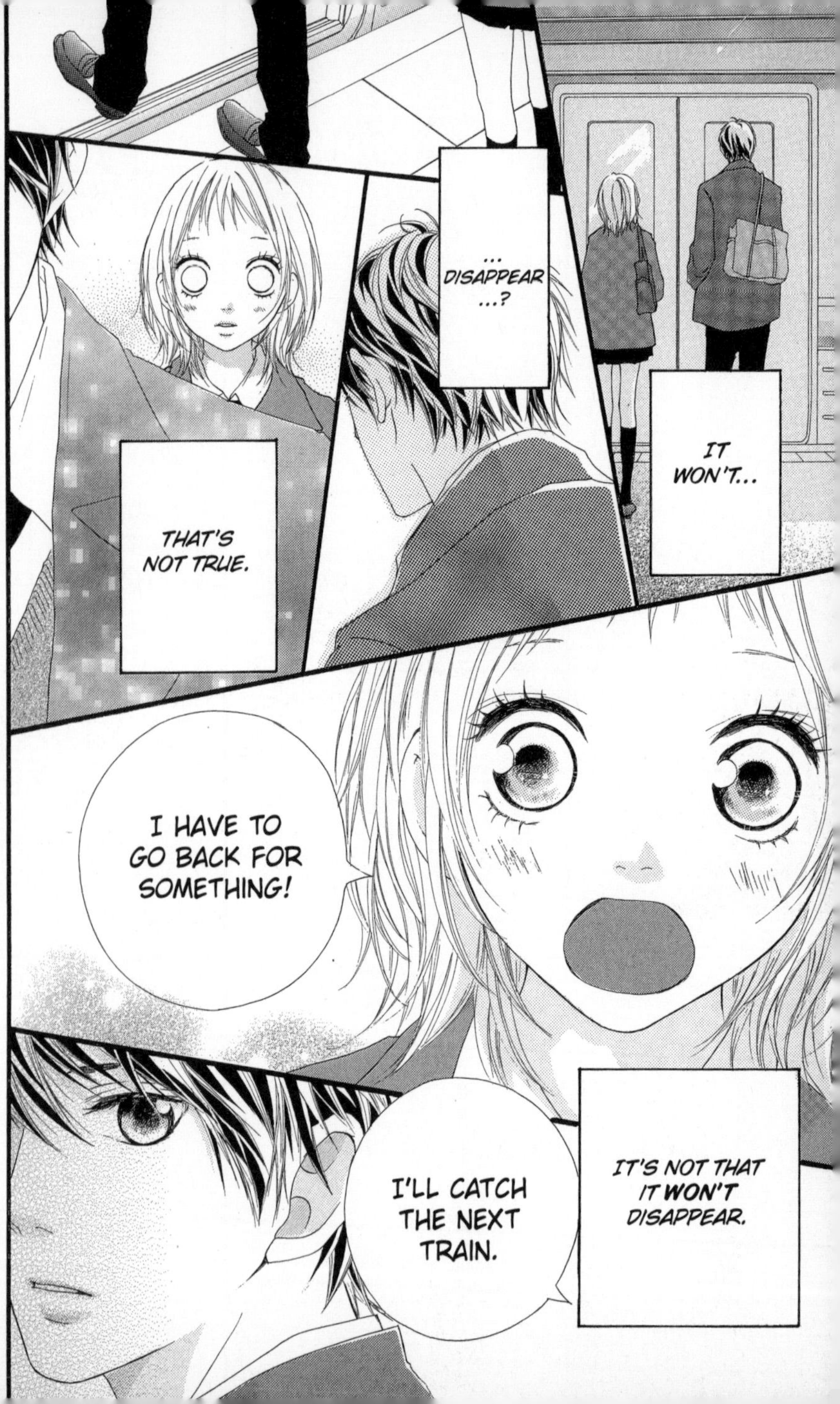
IT WON'T...
...DISAPPEAR...?
THAT'S NOT TRUE.
I HAVE TO GO BACK FOR SOMETHING!
IT'S NOT THAT IT WON'T DISAPPEAR.
I'LL CATCH THE NEXT TRAIN.

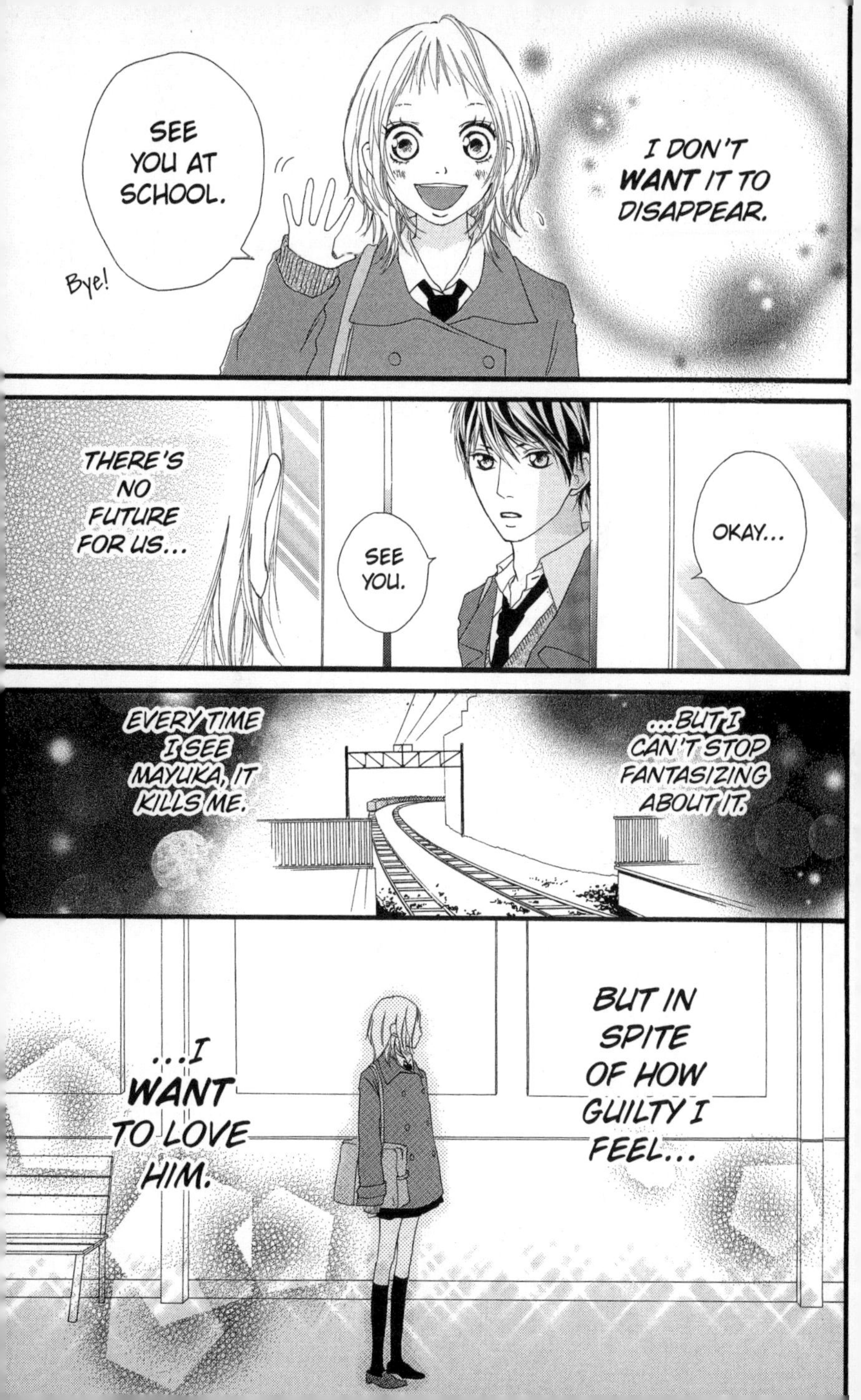
I DON'T WANT IT TO DISAPPEAR.
SEE YOU AT SCHOOL.
Bye!
OKAY...
SEE YOU.
THERE'S NO FUTURE FOR US...
...BUT I CAN'T STOP FANTASIZING ABOUT IT.
EVERY TIME I SEE MAYUKA, IT KILLS ME.
BUT IN SPITE OF HOW GUILTY I FEEL...
...I WANT TO LOVE HIM.

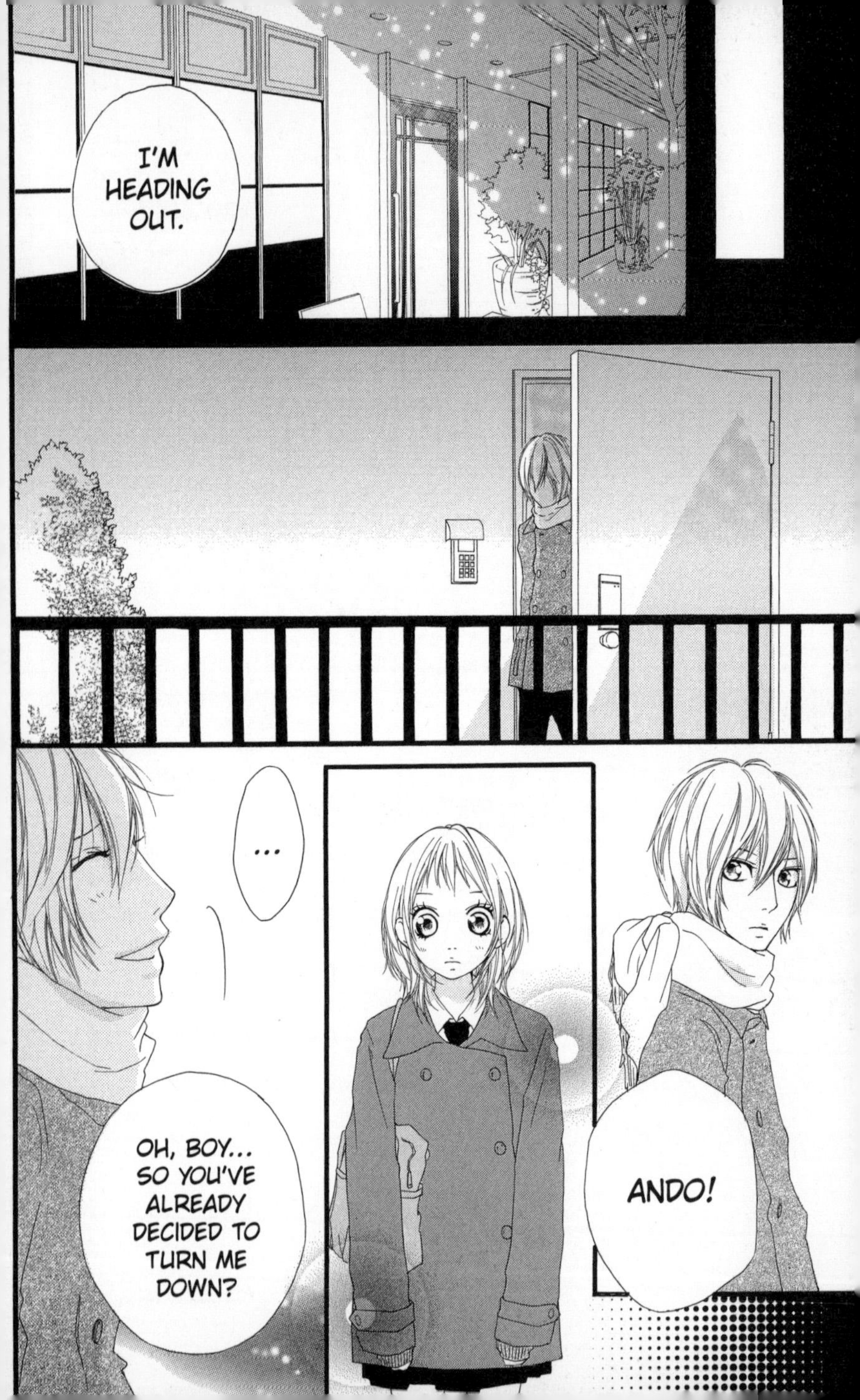
I'M HEADING OUT.
ANDO!
...
OH, BOY... SO YOU'VE ALREADY DECIDED TO TURN ME DOWN?

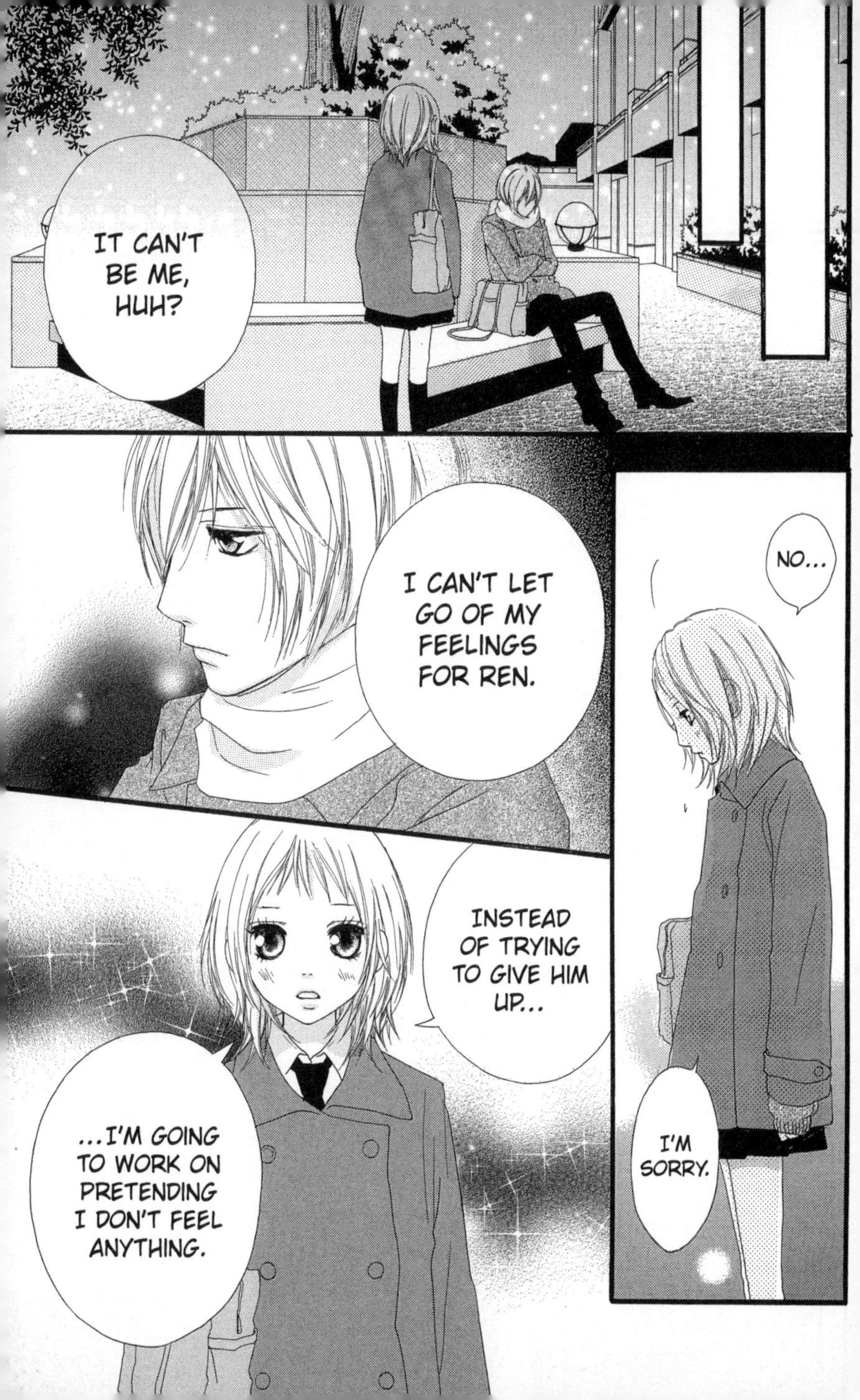
IT CAN'T BE ME, HUH?
NO...
I'M SORRY.
I CAN'T LET GO OF MY FEELINGS FOR REN.
INSTEAD OF TRYING TO GIVE HIM UP...
...I'M GOING TO WORK ON PRETENDING I DON'T FEEL ANYTHING.

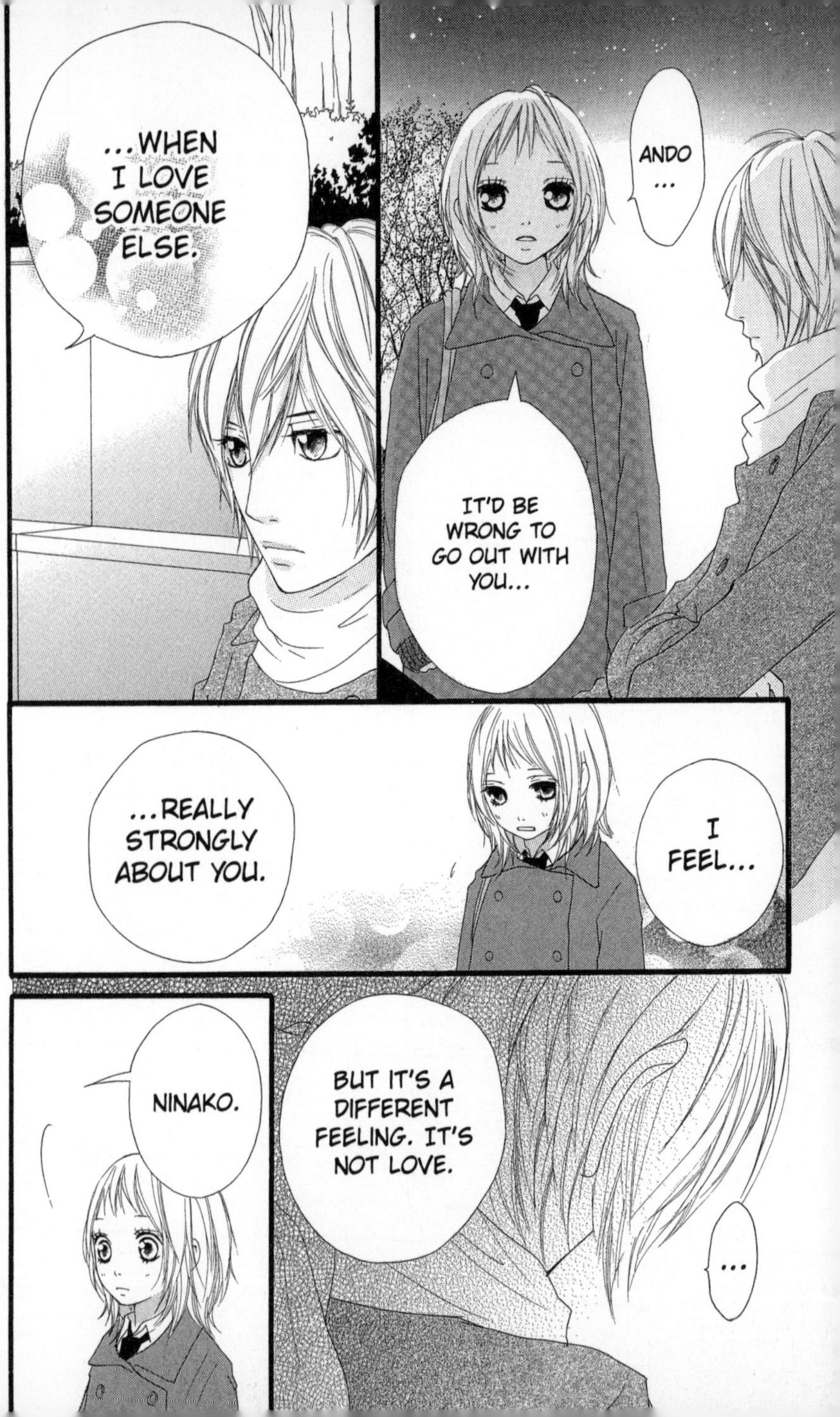
ANDO ...
IT'D BE WRONG TO GO OUT WITH YOU...
...WHEN I LOVE SOMEONE ELSE.
I FEEL...
...REALLY STRONGLY ABOUT YOU.
BUT IT'S A DIFFERENT FEELING. IT'S NOT LOVE.
...
NINAKO.

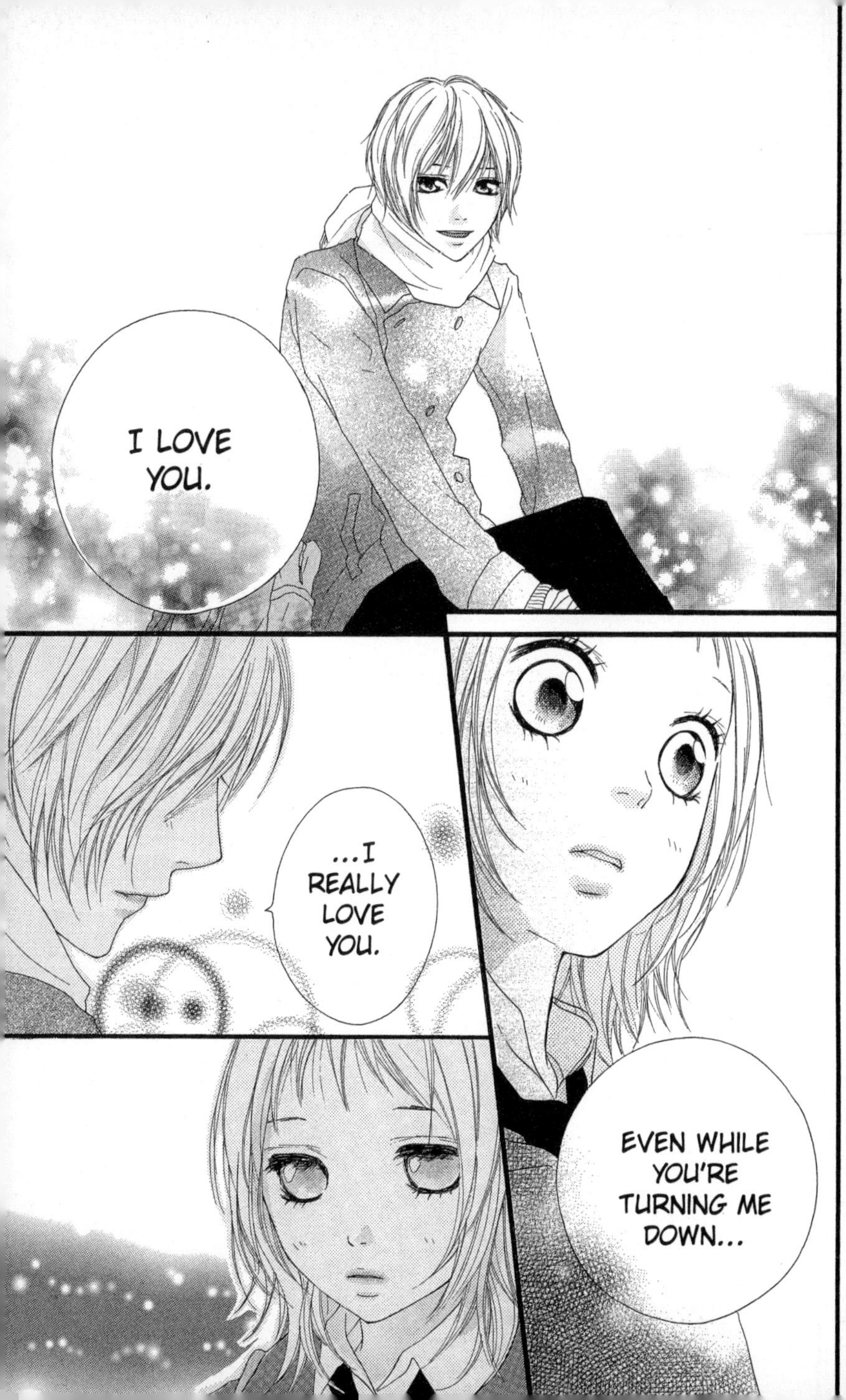
I LOVE YOU.
...I REALLY LOVE YOU.
EVEN WHILE YOU'RE TURNING ME DOWN...

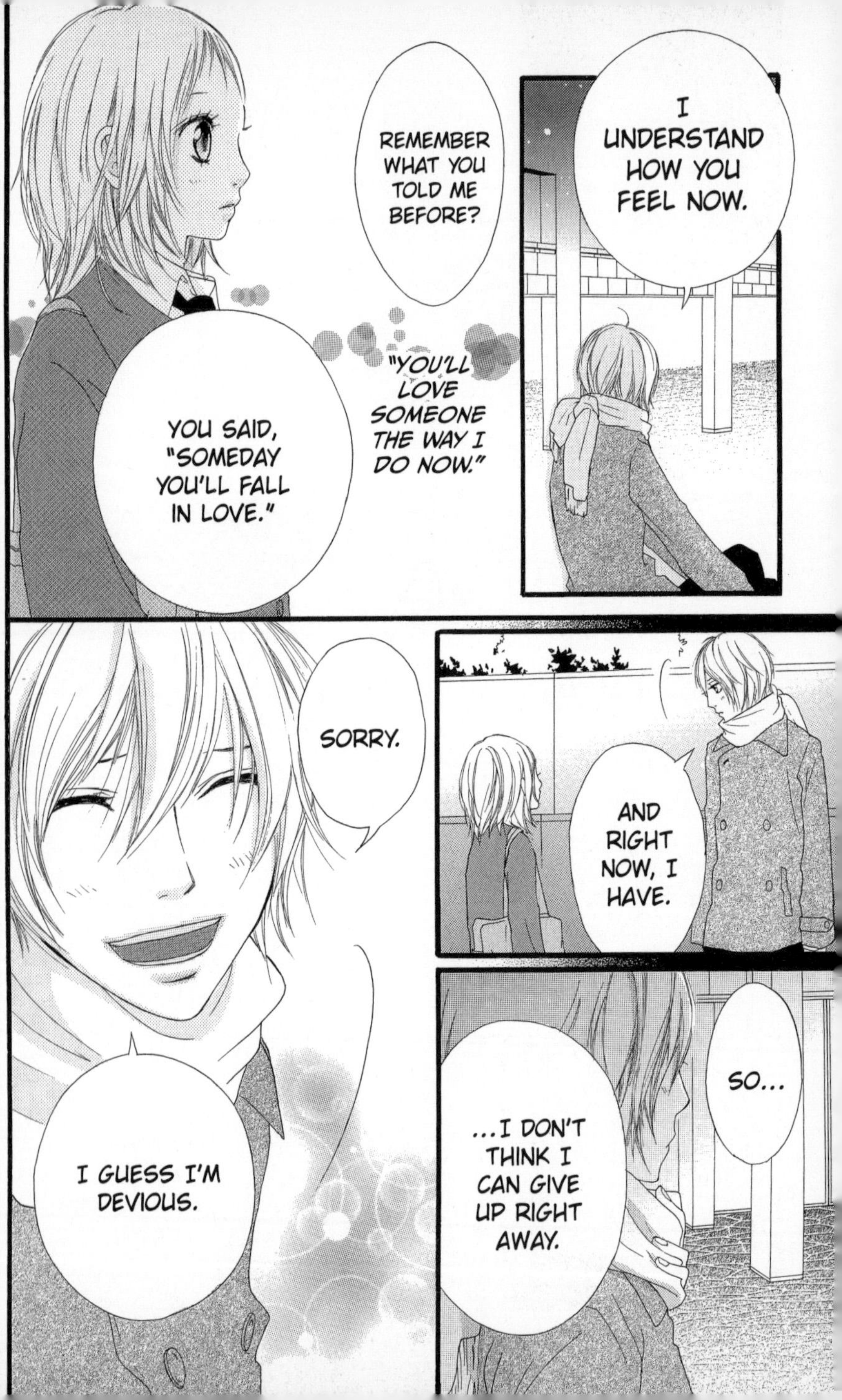
I UNDERSTAND HOW YOU FEEL NOW.
REMEMBER WHAT YOU TOLD ME BEFORE?
YOU SAID, "SOMEDAY YOU'LL FALL IN LOVE."
"YOU'LL LOVE SOMEONE THE WAY I DO NOW."
AND RIGHT NOW, I HAVE.
SO...
...I DON'T THINK I CAN GIVE UP RIGHT AWAY.
SORRY.
I GUESS I'M DEVIOUS.

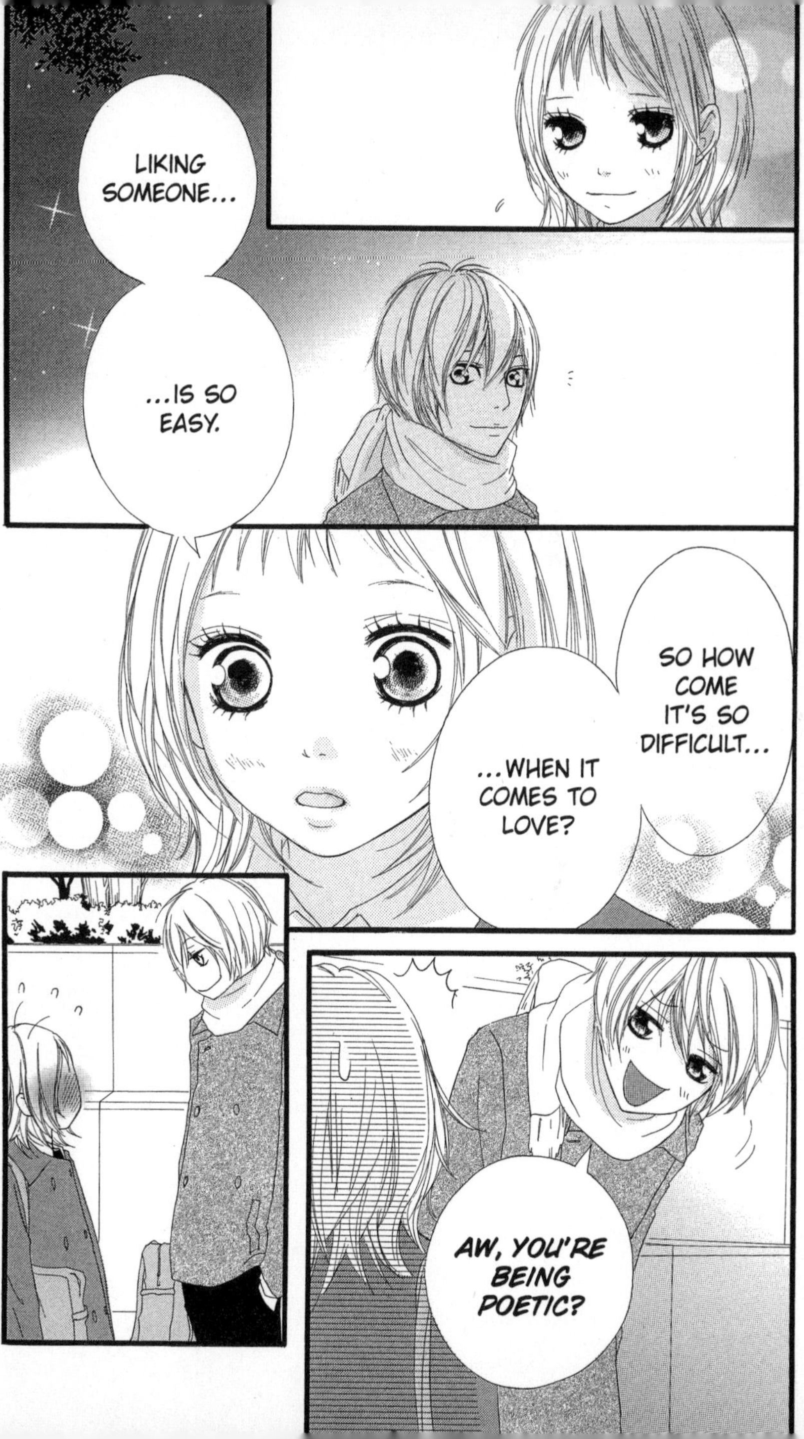
LIKING SOMEONE...
...IS SO EASY.
SO HOW COME IT'S SO DIFFICULT...
...WHEN IT COMES TO LOVE?
AW, YOU'RE BEING POETIC?

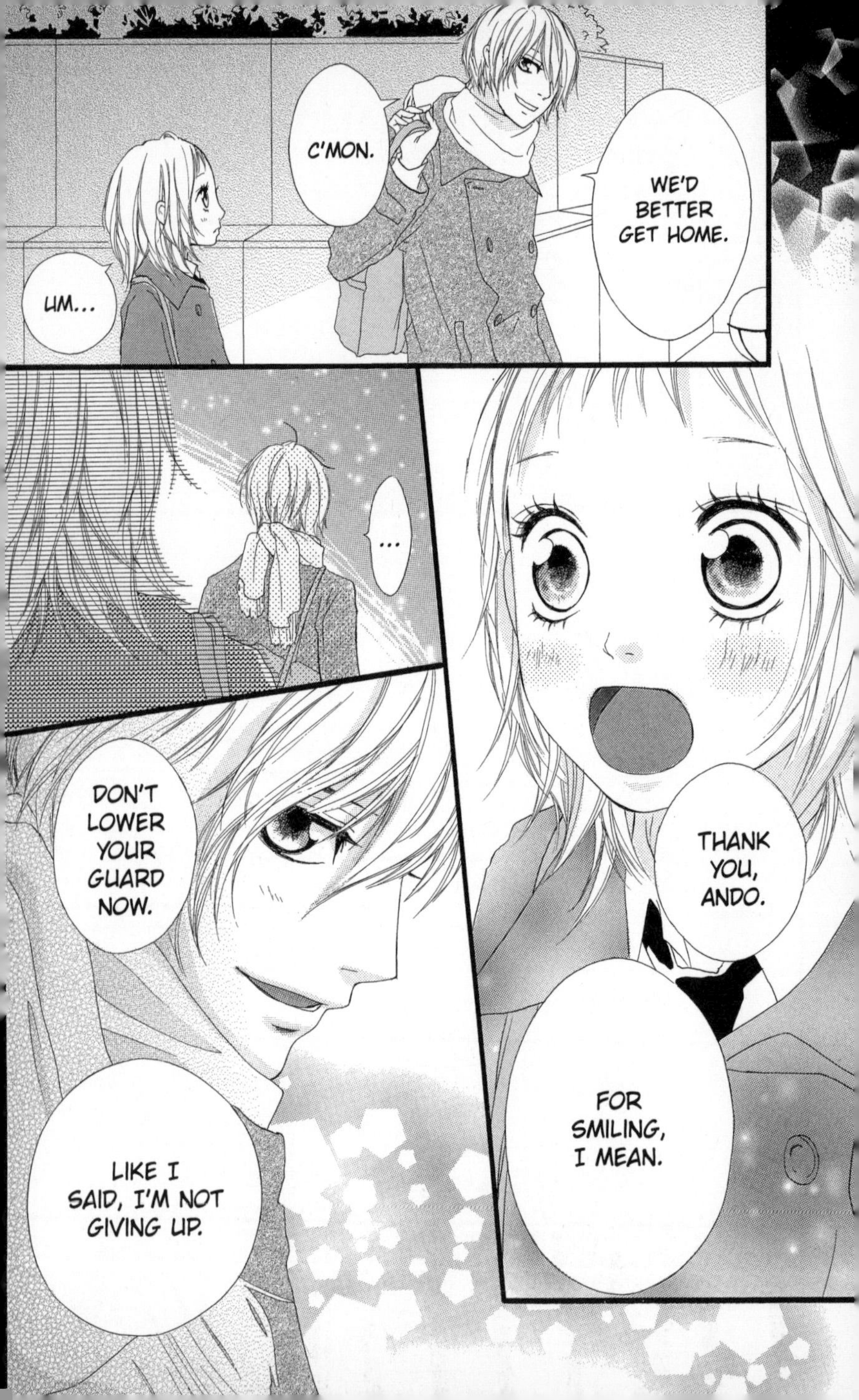

WE'D BETTER GET HOME.
C'MON.
UM...
THANK YOU, ANDO.
FOR SMILING, I MEAN.
...
DON'T LOWER YOUR GUARD NOW.
LIKE I SAID, I'M NOT GIVING UP.

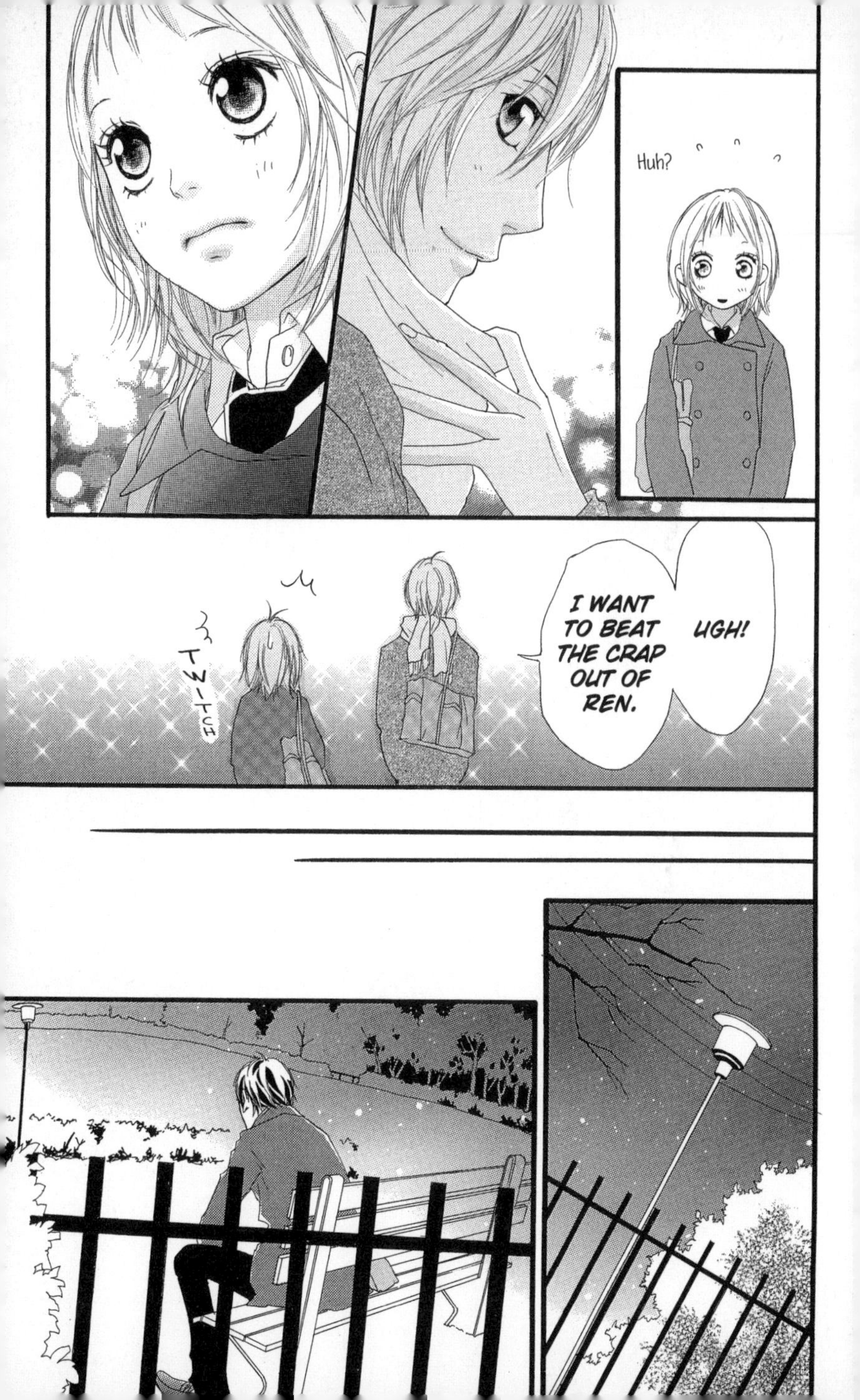
Huh?
UGH!
I WANT TO BEAT THE CRAP OUT OF REN.
TWITCH

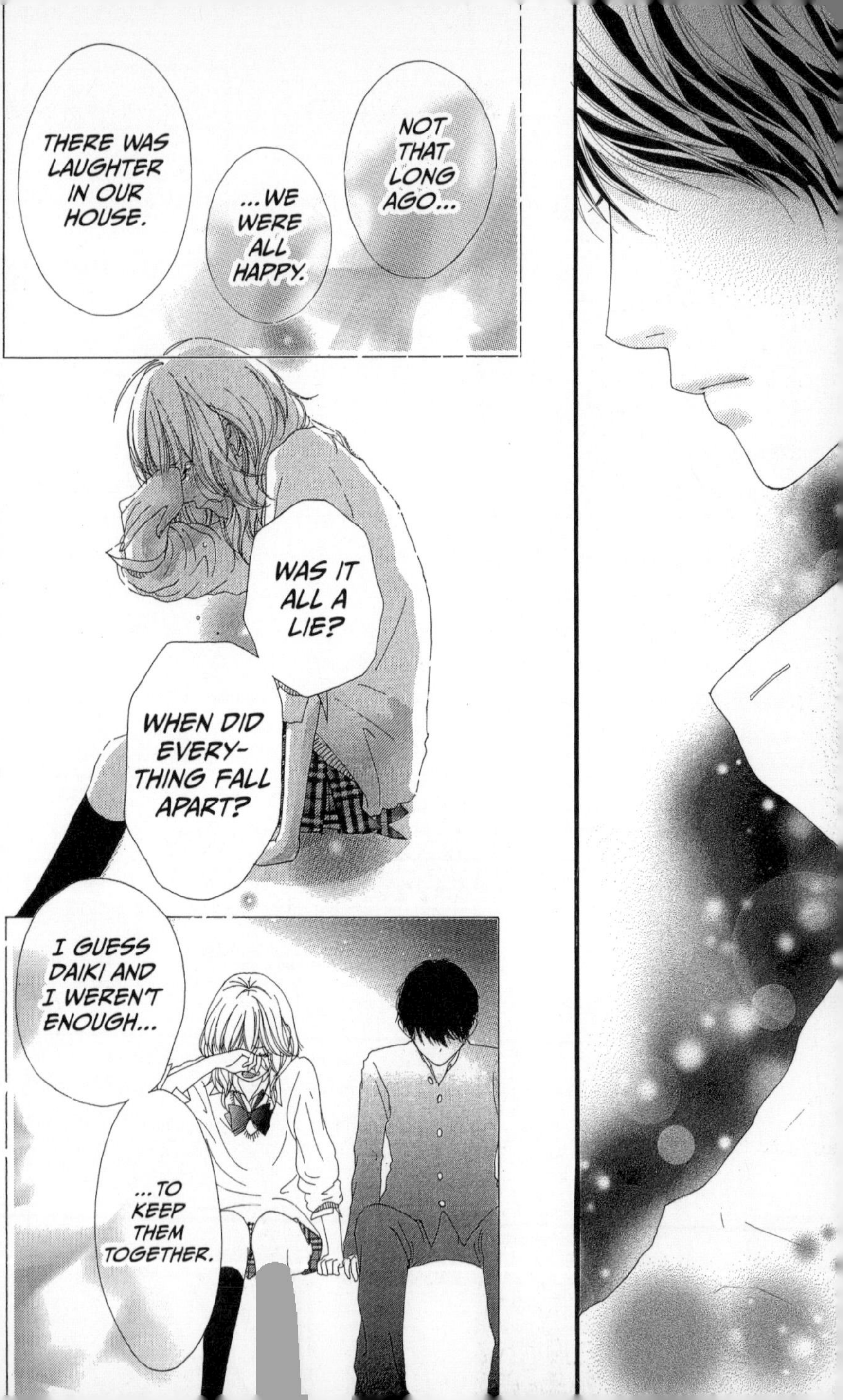
NOT THAT LONG AGO...
...WE WERE ALL HAPPY.
THERE WAS LAUGHTER IN OUR HOUSE.
WAS IT ALL A LIE?
WHEN DID EVERY-THING FALL APART?
I GUESS DAIKI AND I WEREN'T ENOUGH...
...TO KEEP THEM TOGETHER.

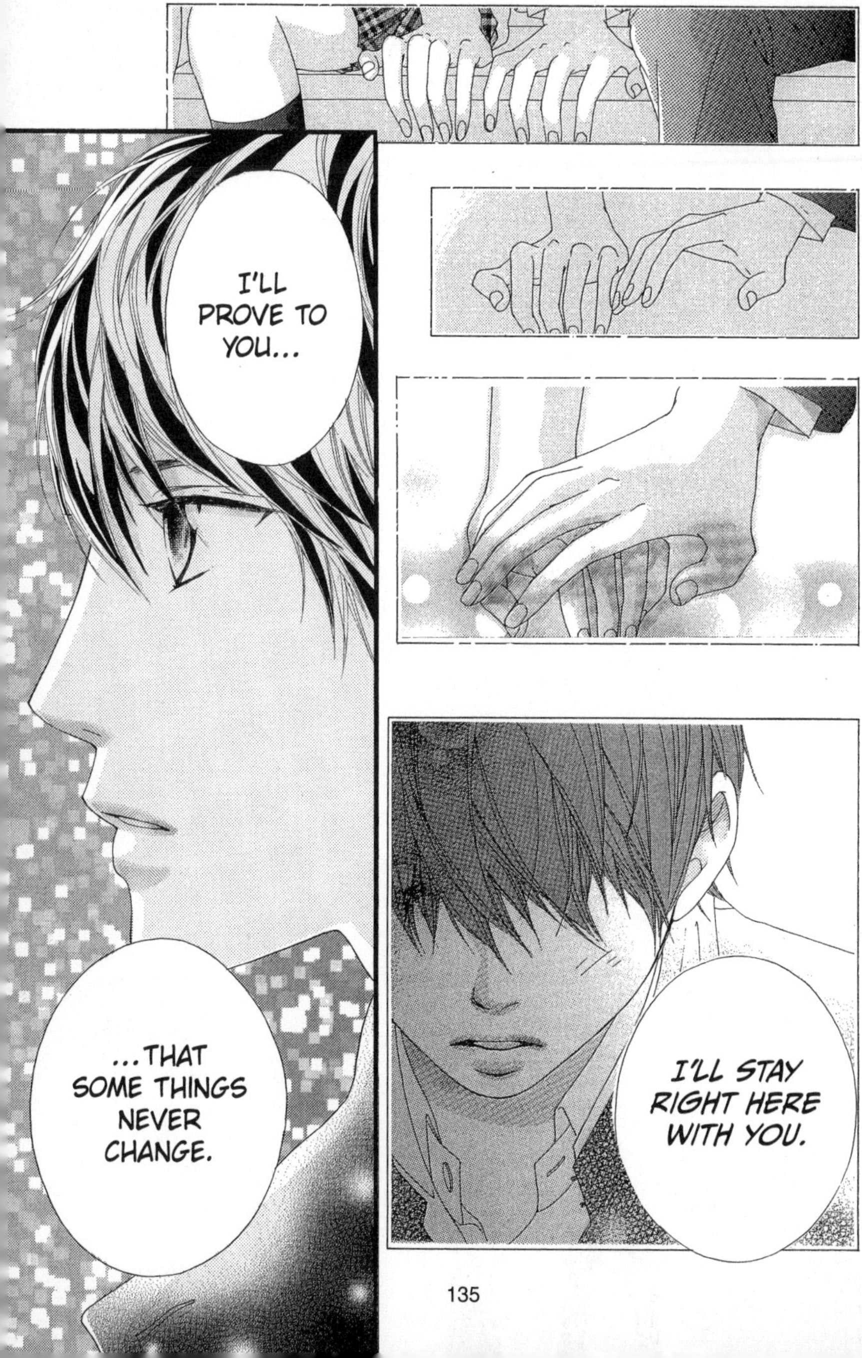
I'LL STAY RIGHT HERE WITH YOU.
I'LL PROVE TO YOU...
...THAT SOME THINGS NEVER CHANGE.

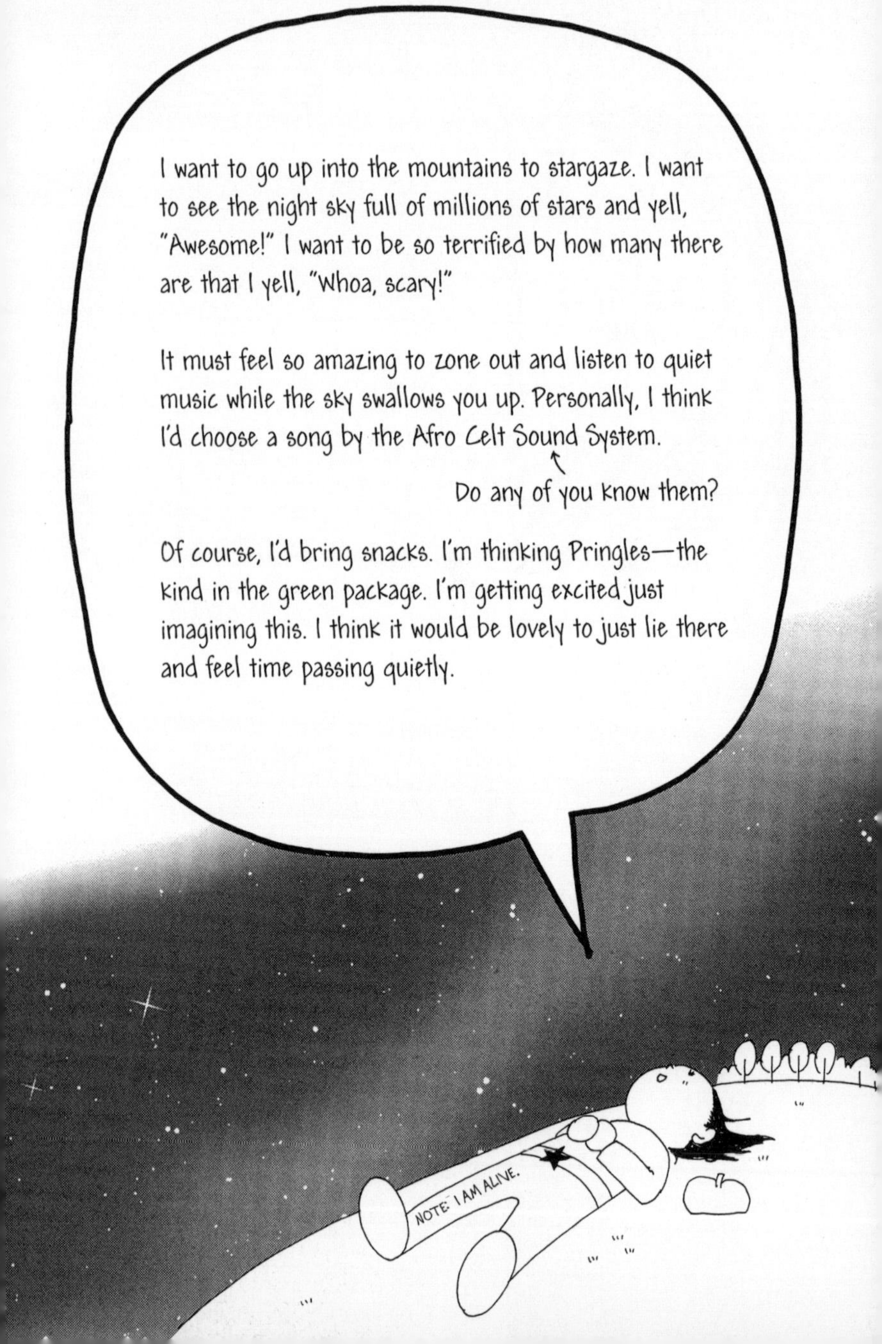
I want to go up into the mountains to stargaze. I want to see the night sky full of millions of stars and yell, "Awesome!" I want to be so terrified by how many there are that I yell, "Whoa, scary!"
It must feel so amazing to zone out and listen to quiet music while the sky swallows you up. Personally, I think I'd choose a song by the Afro Celt Sound System.
Do any of you know them?
Of course, I'd bring snacks. I'm thinking Pringles—the kind in the green package. I'm getting excited just imagining this. I think it would be lovely to just lie there and feel time passing quietly.
NOTE: I AM ALIVE.

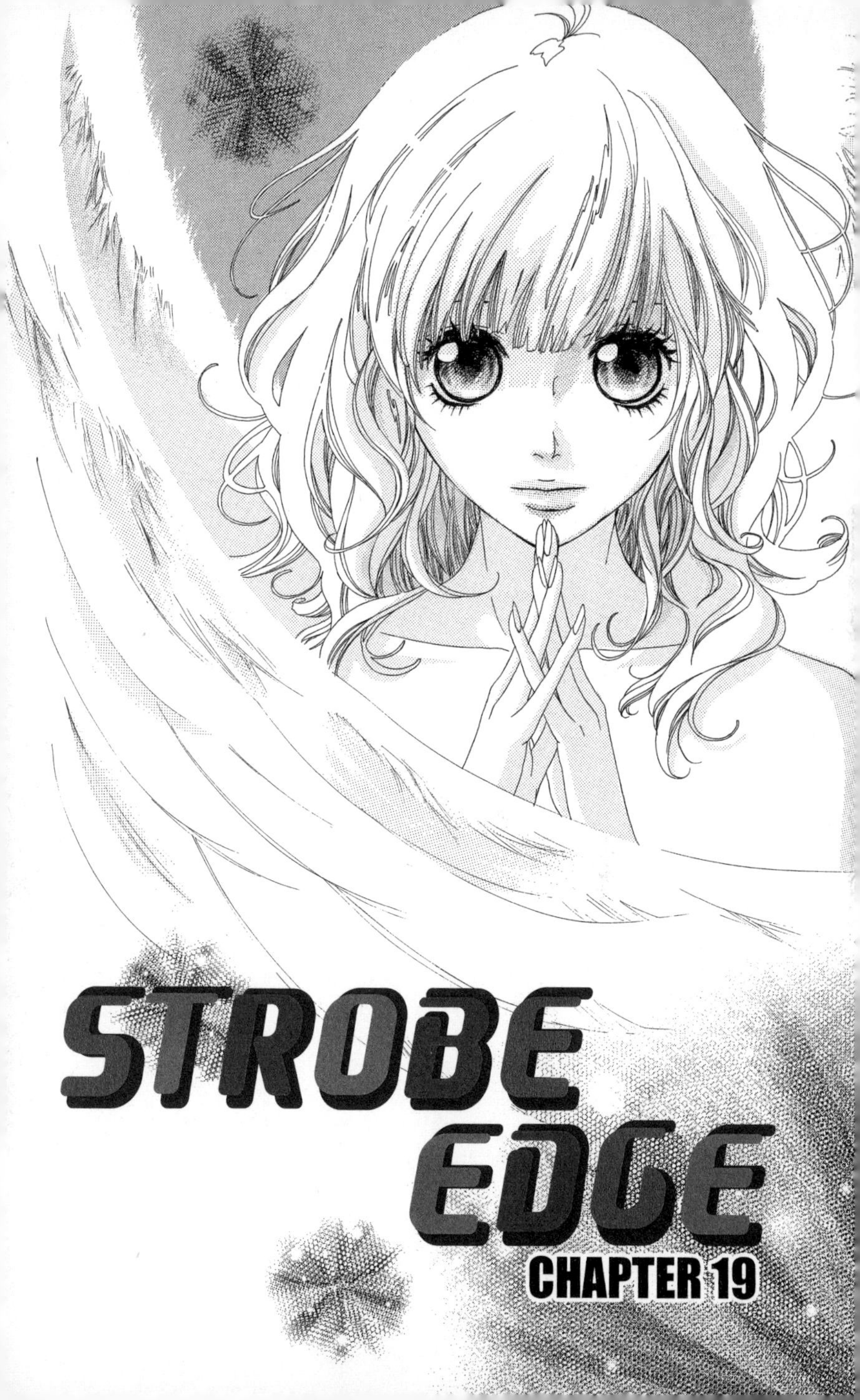
STROBE EDGE
CHAPTER 19

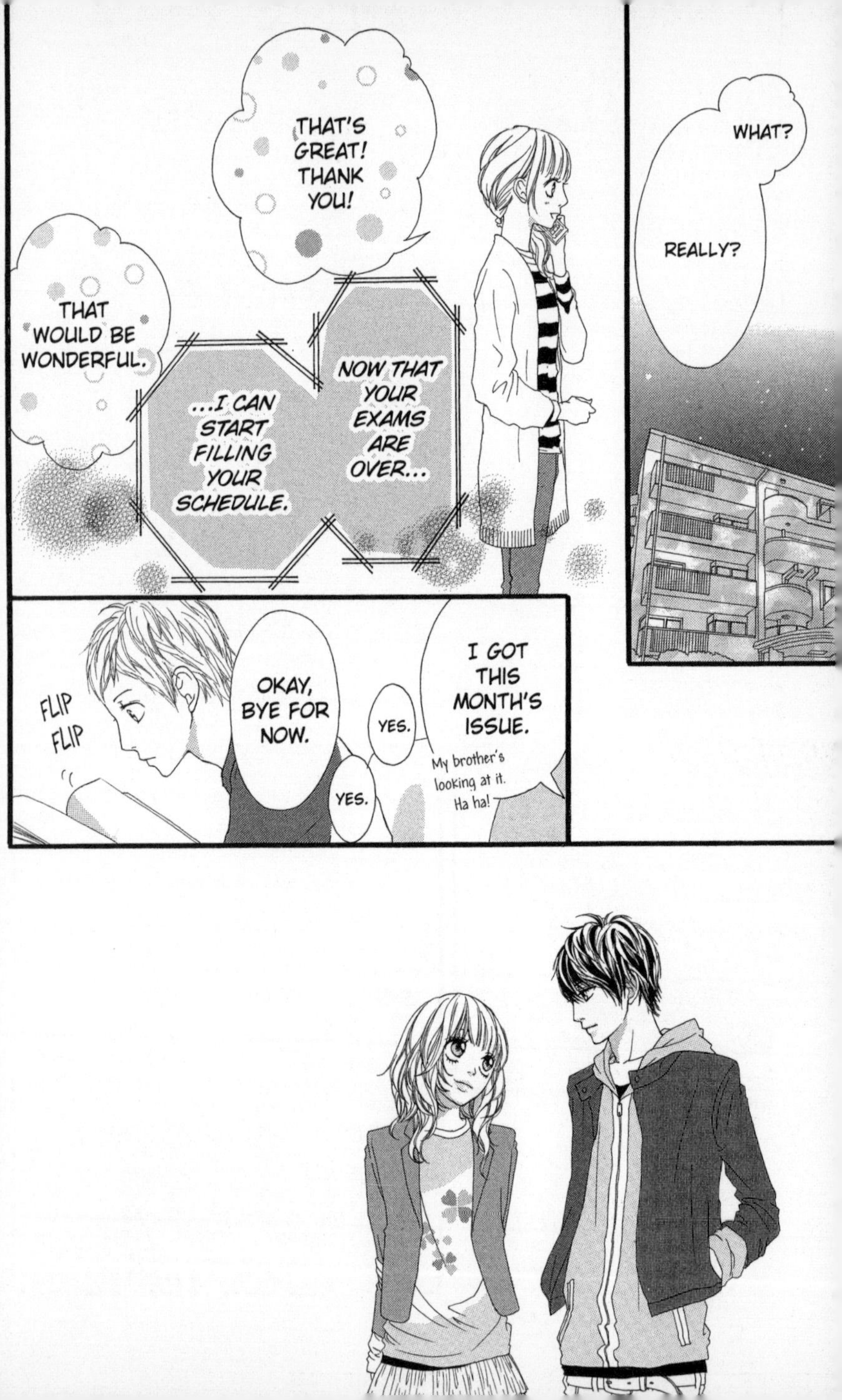
WHAT?
REALLY?
THAT'S GREAT! THANK YOU!
NOW THAT YOUR EXAMS ARE OVER...
...I CAN START FILLING YOUR SCHEDULE.
THAT WOULD BE WONDERFUL.
I GOT THIS MONTH'S ISSUE.
My brother's looking at it. Ha ha!
YES.
YES.
OKAY, BYE FOR NOW.
FLIP FLIP

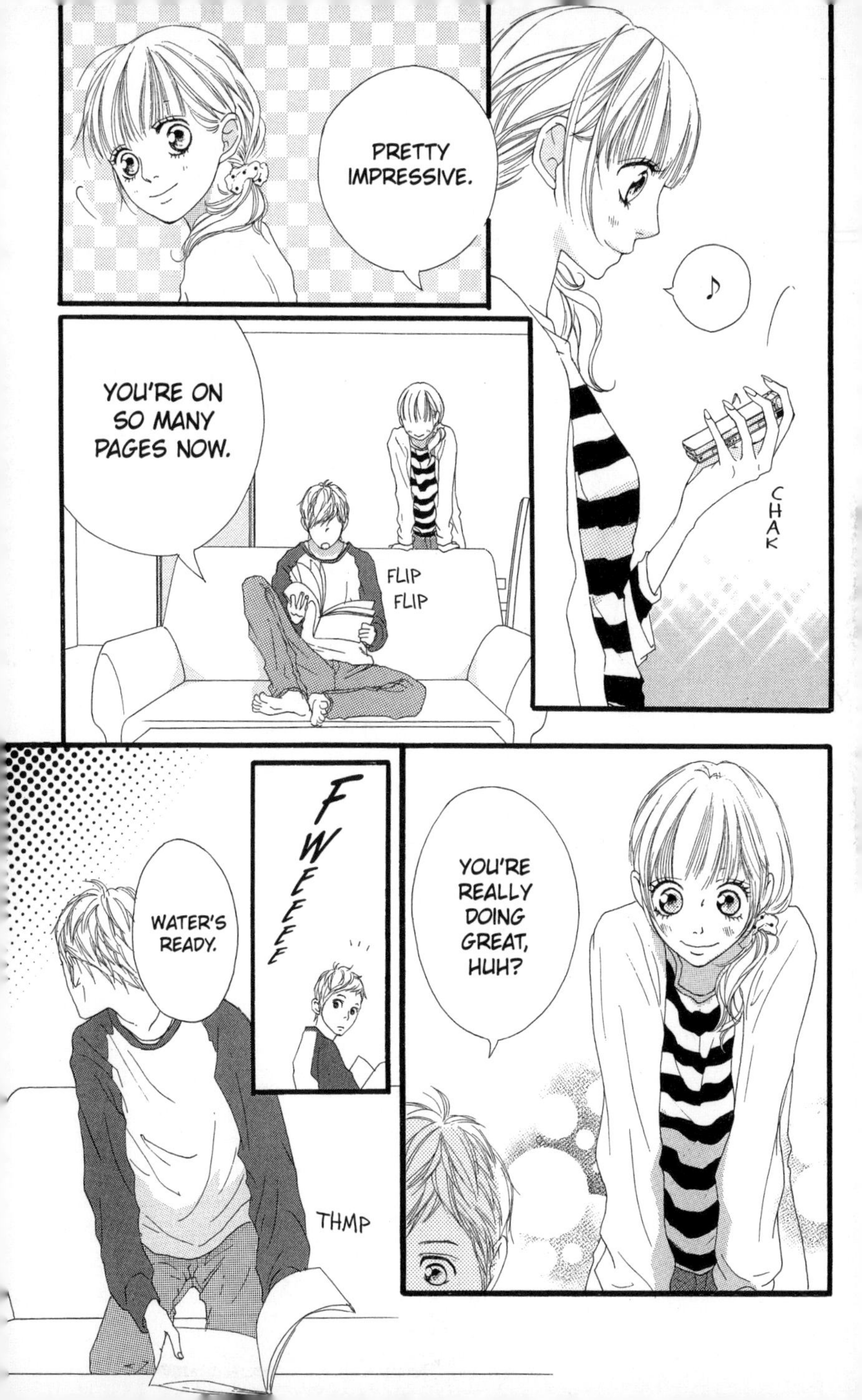
♪
CHAK
PRETTY IMPRESSIVE.
YOU'RE ON SO MANY PAGES NOW.
FLIP FLIP
YOU'RE REALLY DOING GREAT, HUH?
FWEEEEE
WATER'S READY.
THMP

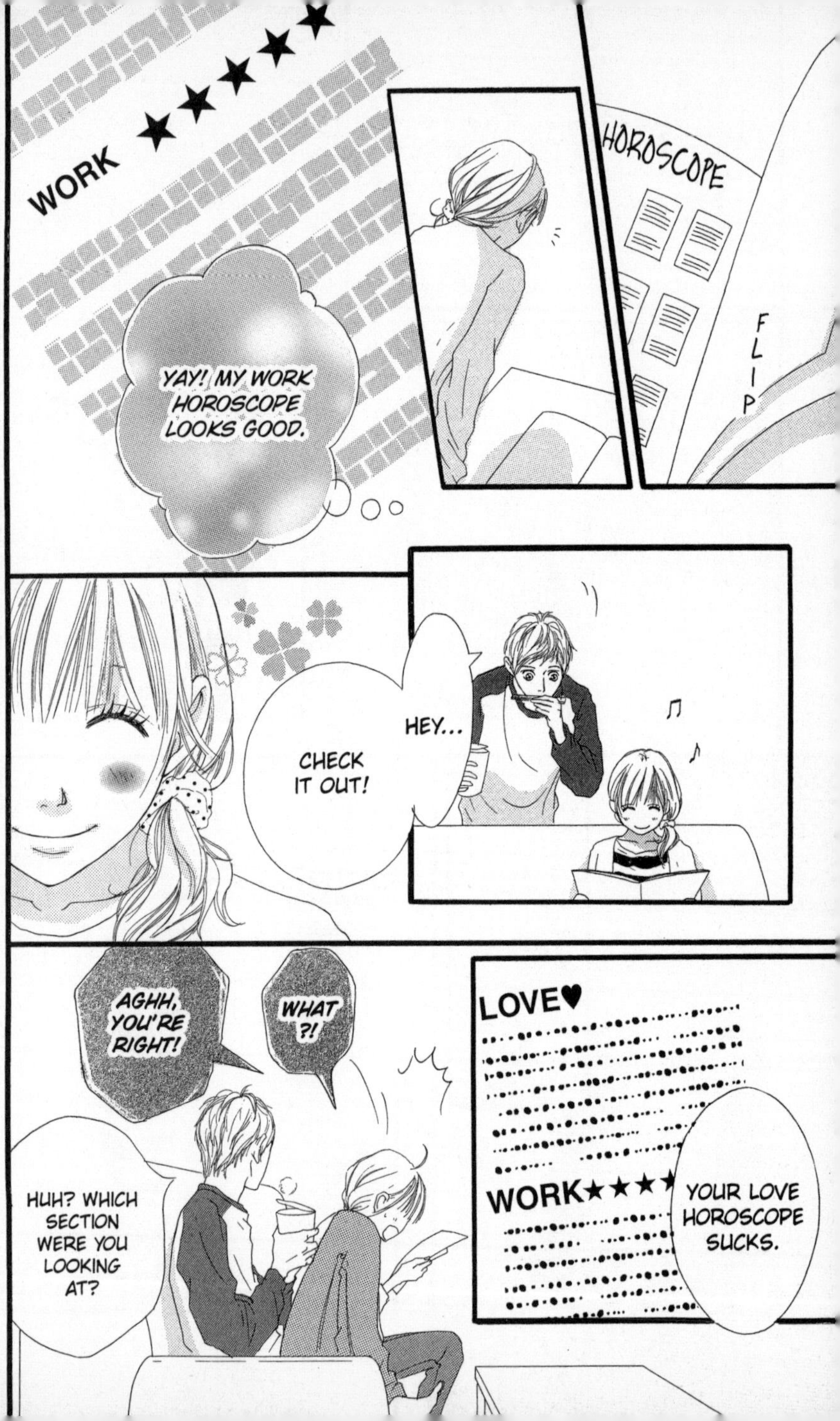
HOROSCOPE
FLIP
WORK ★★★★★
YAY! MY WORK HOROSCOPE LOOKS GOOD.
HEY...
CHECK IT OUT!
LOVE♥
WORK★★★★
YOUR LOVE HOROSCOPE SUCKS.
WHAT?!
AGHH, YOU'RE RIGHT!
HUH? WHICH SECTION WERE YOU LOOKING AT?

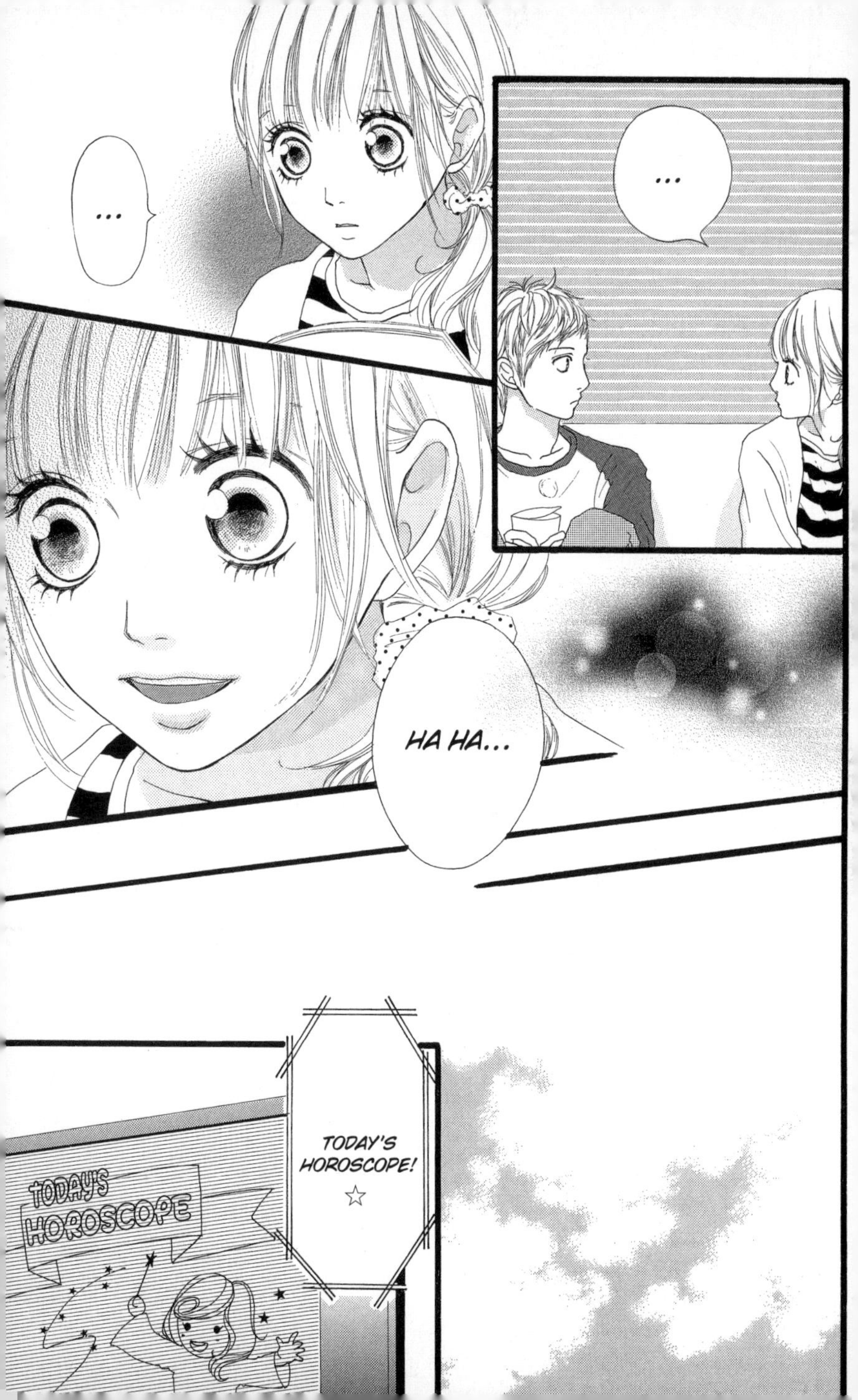
...
...
HA HA...
TODAY'S HOROSCOPE! ☆
TODAY'S HOROSCOPE

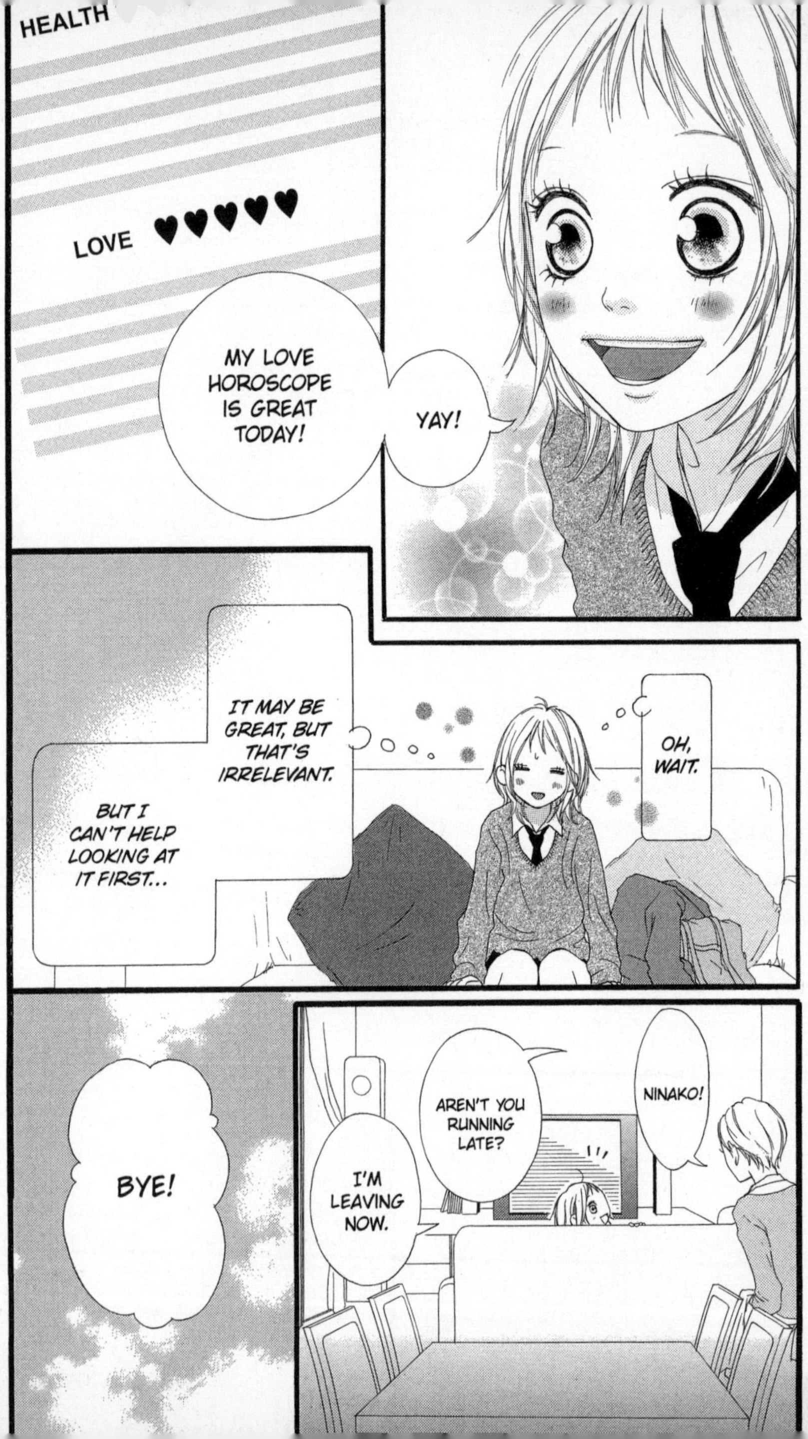
YAY!
MY LOVE HOROSCOPE IS GREAT TODAY!
HEALTH
LOVE ♥♥♥♥♥
OH, WAIT.
IT MAY BE GREAT, BUT THAT'S IRRELEVANT.
BUT I CAN'T HELP LOOKING AT IT FIRST...
NINAKO!
AREN'T YOU RUNNING LATE?
I'M LEAVING NOW.
BYE!

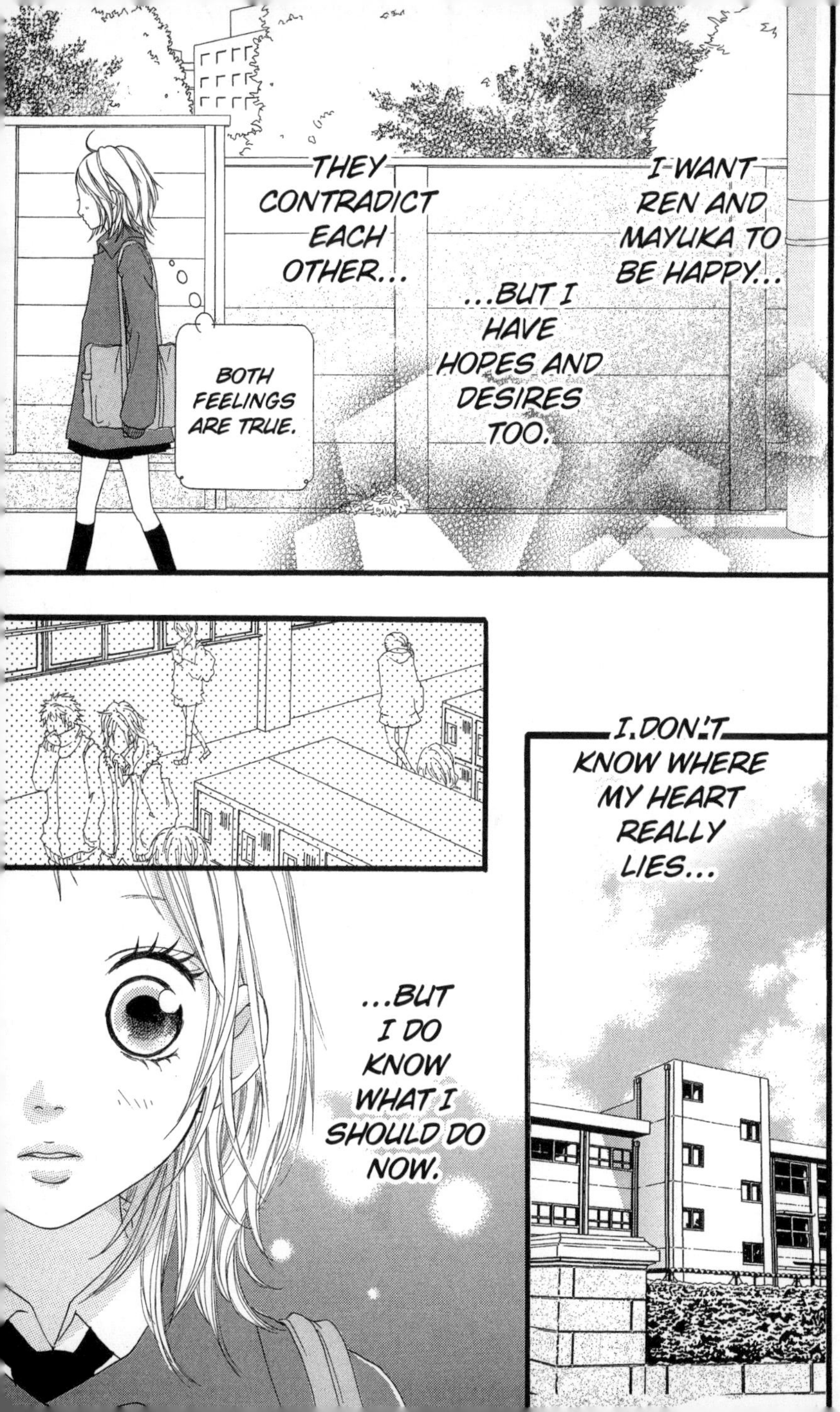
I WANT REN AND MAYUKA TO BE HAPPY...
...BUT I HAVE HOPES AND DESIRES TOO.
THEY CONTRADICT EACH OTHER...
BOTH FEELINGS ARE TRUE.
I DON'T KNOW WHERE MY HEART REALLY LIES...
...BUT I DO KNOW WHAT I SHOULD DO NOW.

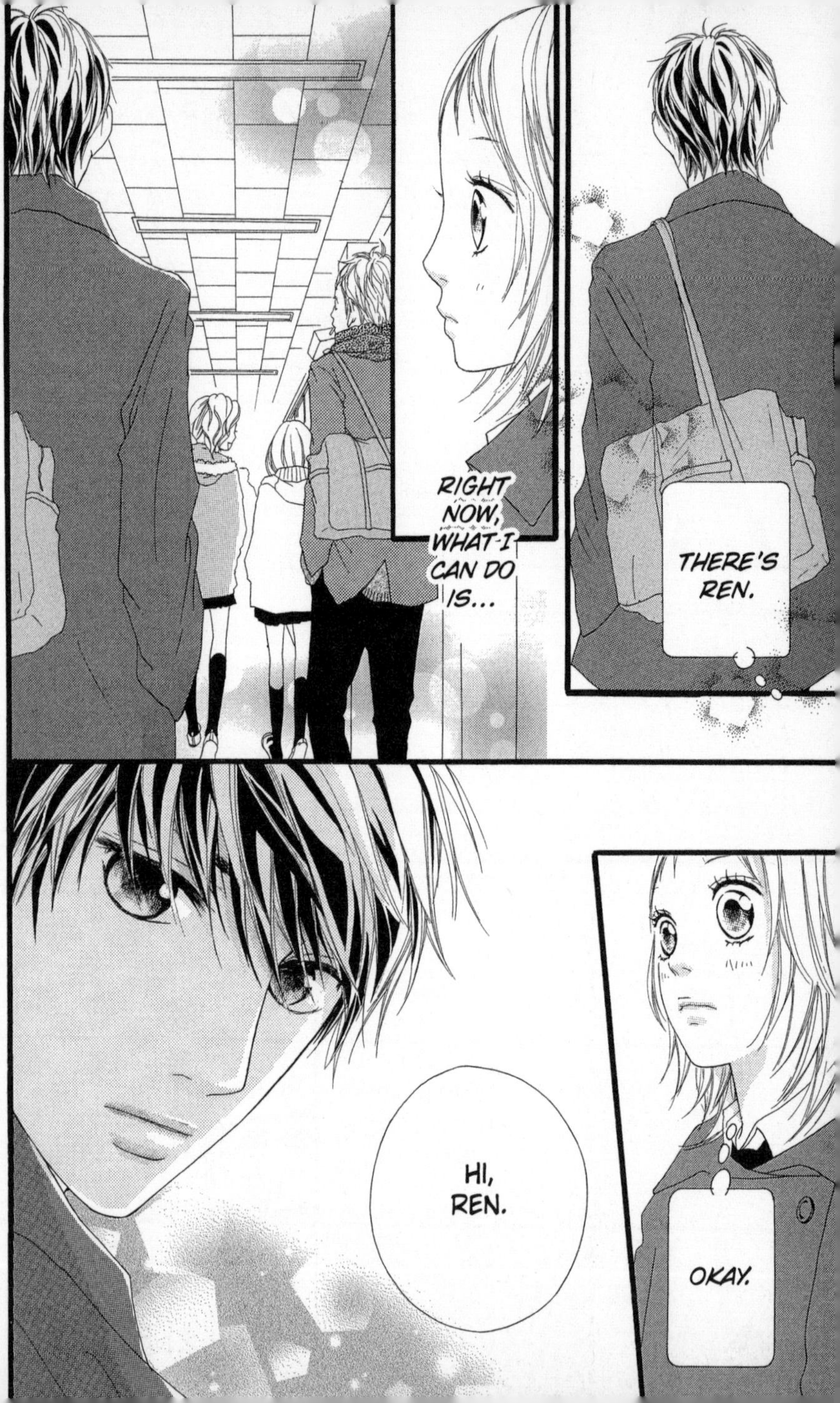
THERE'S REN.
RIGHT NOW, WHAT I CAN DO IS...
OKAY.
HI, REN.

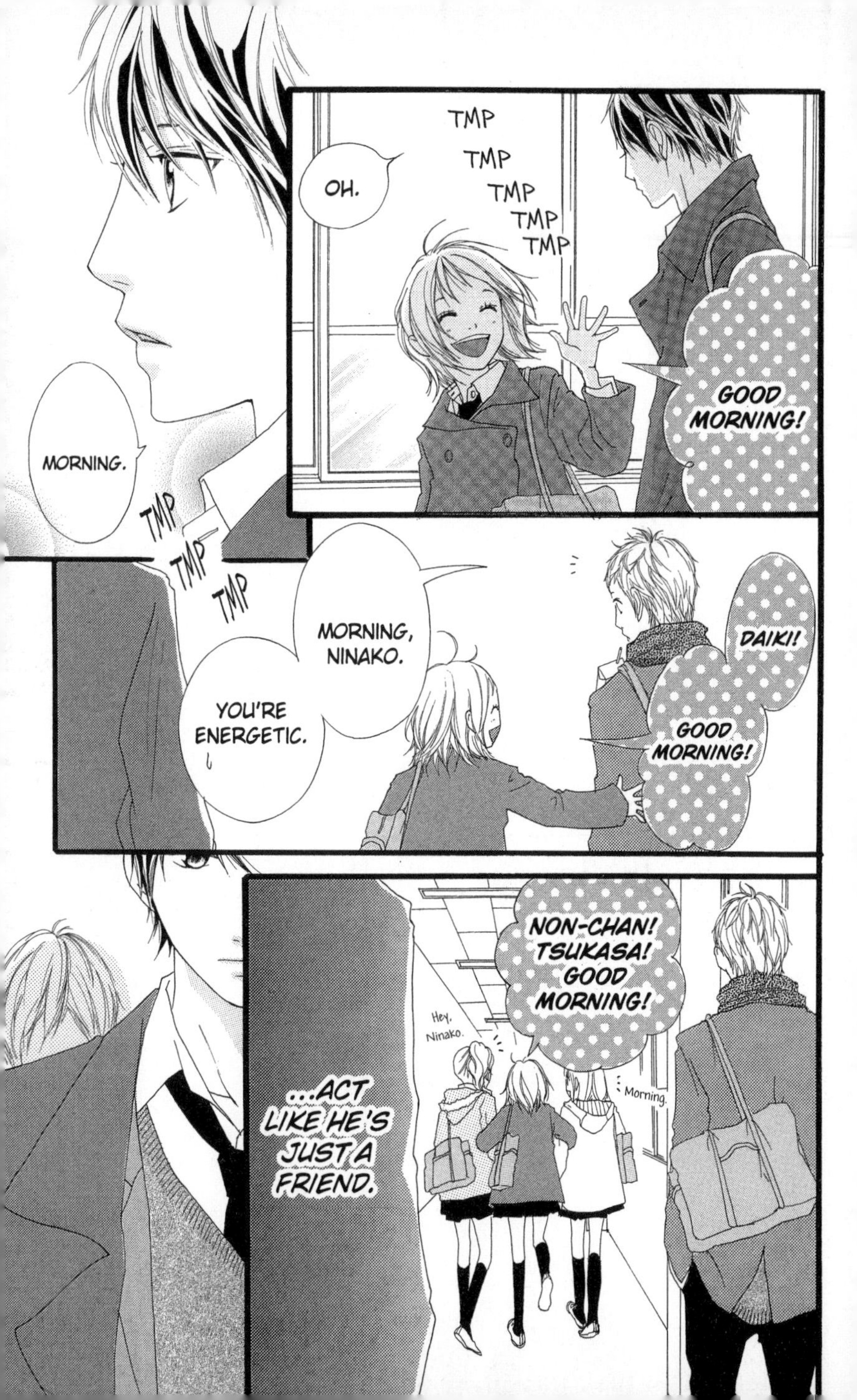
TMP
TMP
TMP
TMP
TMP
GOOD MORNING!
OH.
MORNING.
TMP
TMP
TMP
DAIKI!
GOOD MORNING!
MORNING, NINAKO.
YOU'RE ENERGETIC.
NON-CHAN! TSUKASA! GOOD MORNING!
Morning.
Hey, Ninako.
...ACT LIKE HE'S JUST A FRIEND.

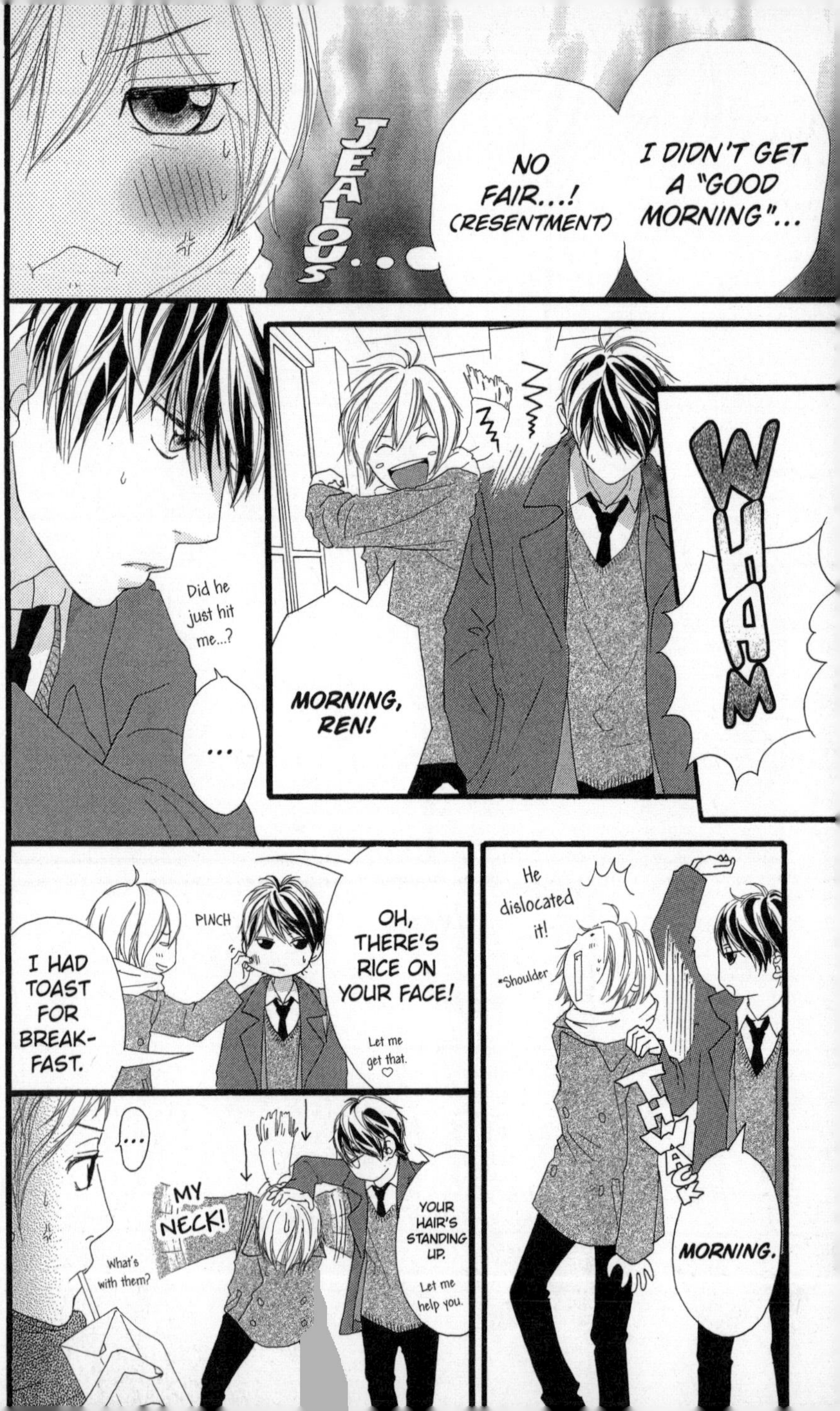
I DIDN'T GET A "GOOD MORNING"...
NO FAIR...! (RESENTMENT)
JEALOUS...
WHAM
MORNING, REN!
Did he just hit me...?
...
MORNING.
THWACK
He dislocated it!
*Shoulder
OH, THERE'S RICE ON YOUR FACE!
Let me get that. ♡
PINCH
I HAD TOAST FOR BREAK-FAST.
YOUR HAIR'S STANDING UP.
Let me help you.
MY NECK!
...
What's with them?

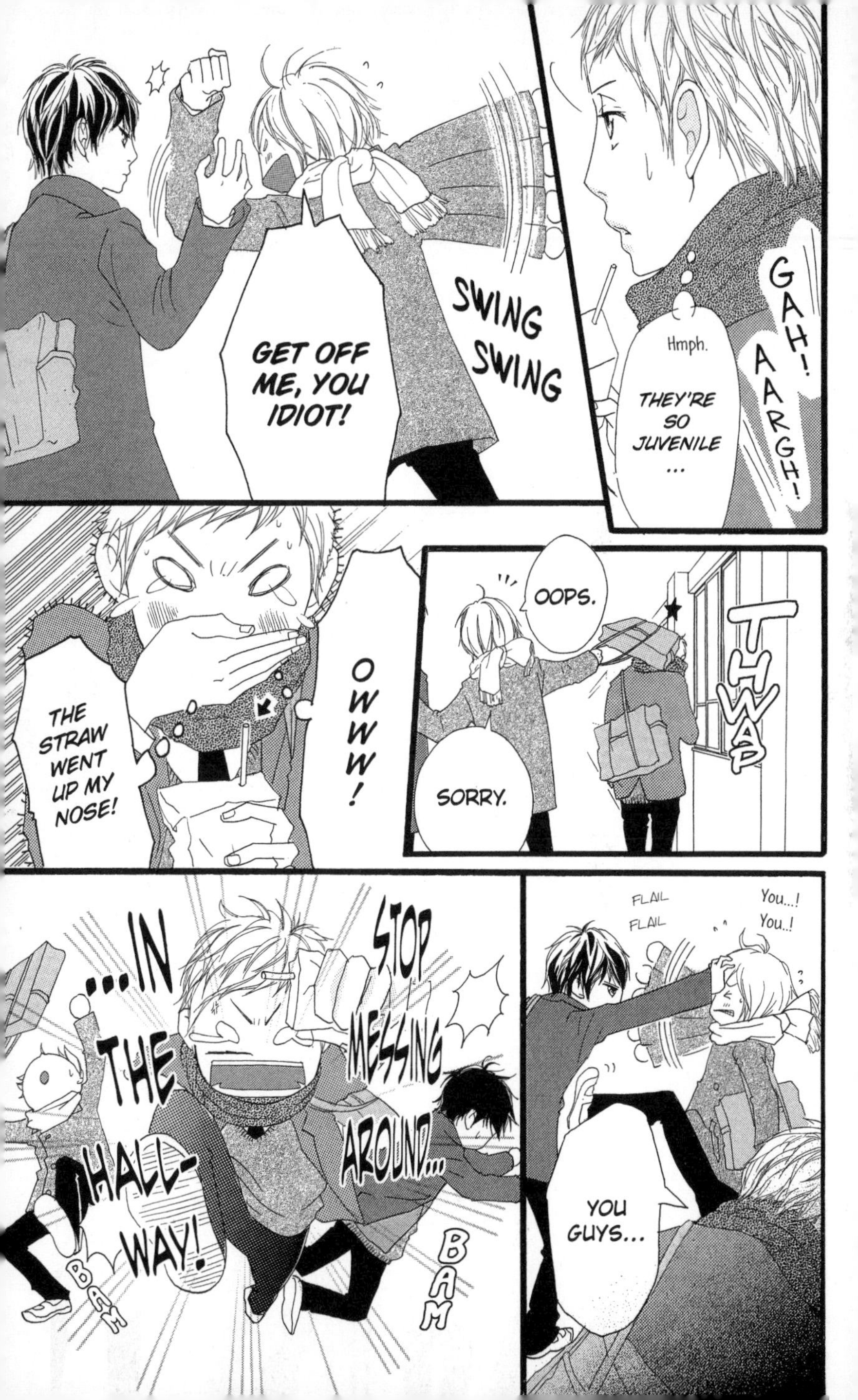
GAH! AARGH!
Hmph.
THEY'RE SO JUVENILE...
SWING SWING
GET OFF ME, YOU IDIOT!
THWAP
OOPS.
SORRY.
OWWWW!
THE STRAW WENT UP MY NOSE!
You...! You..!
FLAIL FLAIL
YOU GUYS...
STOP MESSING AROUND...
...IN THE HALL-WAY!
BAM
BAM

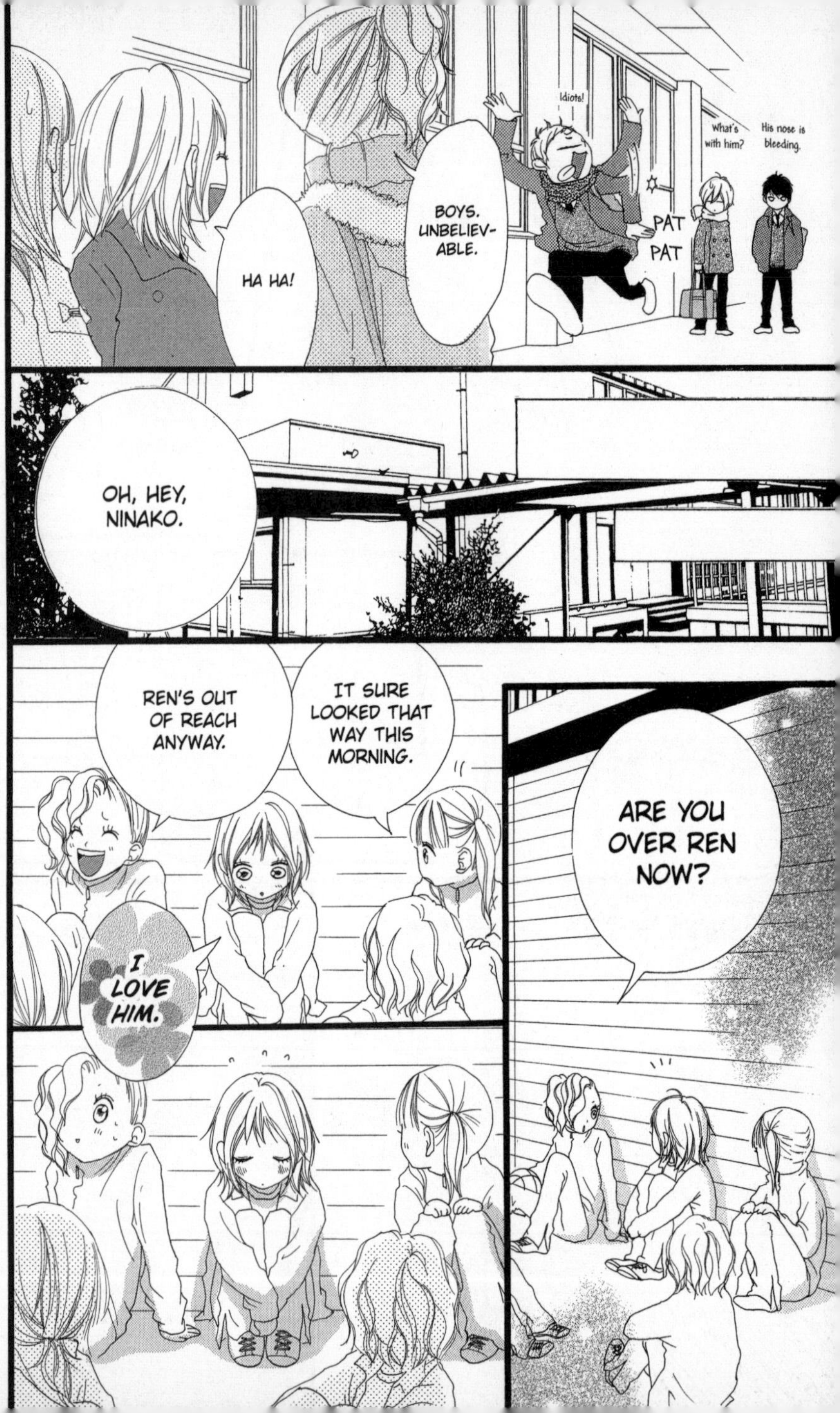
Idiots!
His nose is bleeding.
What's with him?
PAT PAT
BOYS. UNBELIEV-ABLE.
HA HA!
OH, HEY, NINAKO.
ARE YOU OVER REN NOW?
IT SURE LOOKED THAT WAY THIS MORNING.
REN'S OUT OF REACH ANYWAY.
I LOVE HIM.

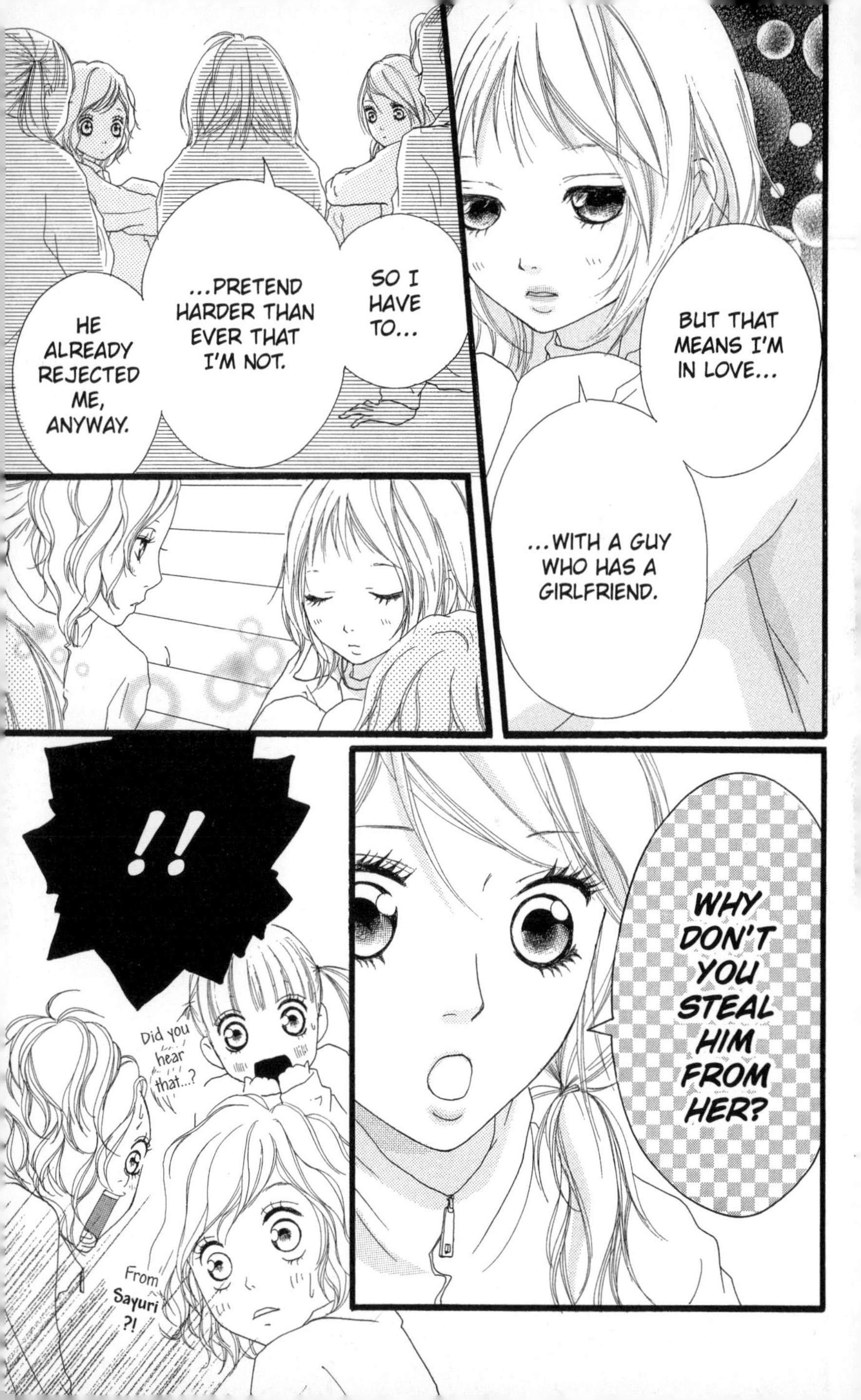
BUT THAT MEANS I'M IN LOVE...
...WITH A GUY WHO HAS A GIRLFRIEND.
SO I HAVE TO...
...PRETEND HARDER THAN EVER THAT I'M NOT.
HE ALREADY REJECTED ME, ANYWAY.
WHY DON'T YOU STEAL HIM FROM HER?
!!
Did you hear that...?
From Sayuri?!

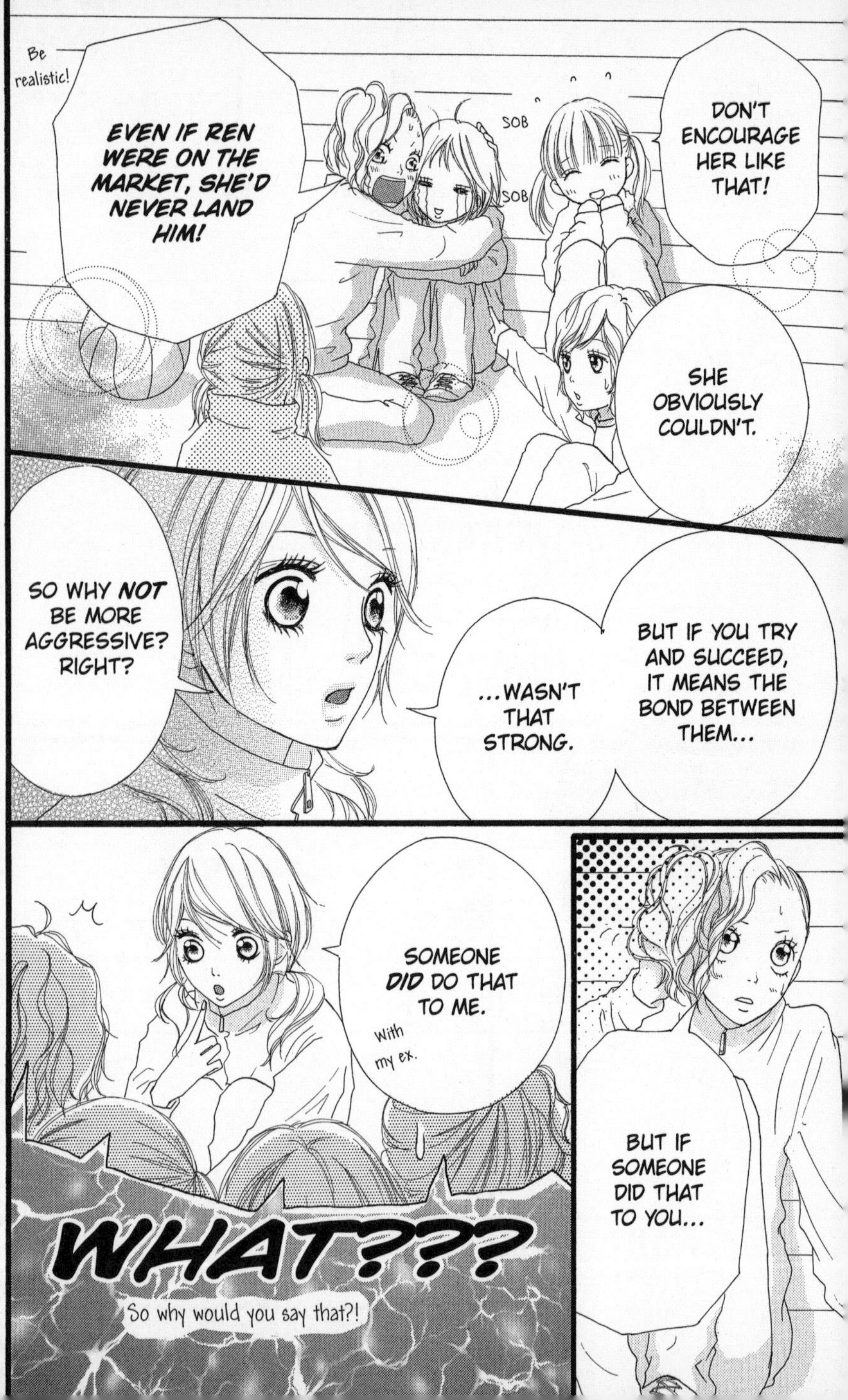
DON'T ENCOURAGE HER LIKE THAT!
SOB SOB
Be realistic!
EVEN IF REN WERE ON THE MARKET, SHE'D NEVER LAND HIM!
SHE OBVIOUSLY COULDN'T.
BUT IF YOU TRY AND SUCCEED, IT MEANS THE BOND BETWEEN THEM...
...WASN'T THAT STRONG.
SO WHY NOT BE MORE AGGRESSIVE? RIGHT?
BUT IF SOMEONE DID THAT TO YOU...
SOMEONE DID DO THAT TO ME.
With my ex.
WHAT???
So why would you say that?!

These people helped me with my work:

Moto Harui

Hami Ayase

Satomi Sera

Sayu Kanno

Yuniko Honda

Naomi Minamoto

Yurie Ono

Thank you so much! Without you guys, I wouldn't get any sleep. You're all lifesavers! I enjoy work because of you.

Sorry our workspace is so tight. Sorry we always have to order takeout. Sorry there aren't many buses on my route. Sorry about everything...!

*The marks are for my "Tabasco buddies" who love Tabasco sauce.

Yay, Tabasco!

Thank you!!

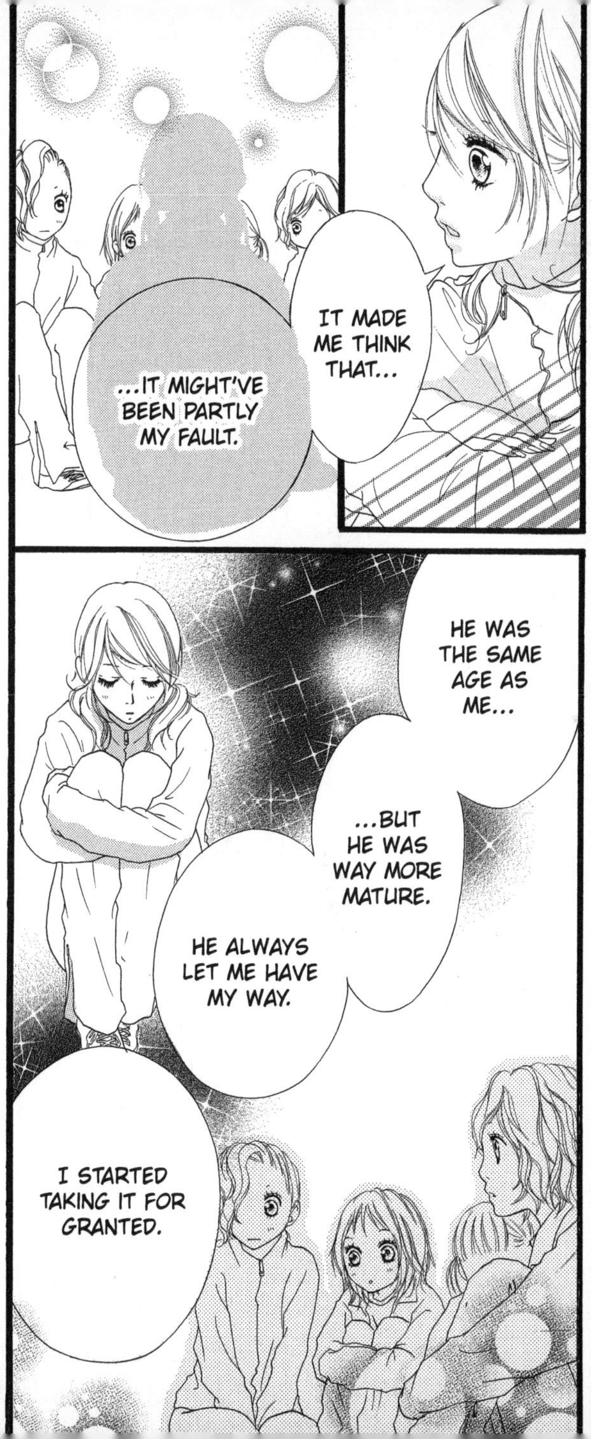
IT MADE ME THINK THAT...
...IT MIGHT'VE BEEN PARTLY MY FAULT.
HE WAS THE SAME AGE AS ME...
...BUT HE WAS WAY MORE MATURE.
HE ALWAYS LET ME HAVE MY WAY.
I STARTED TAKING IT FOR GRANTED.

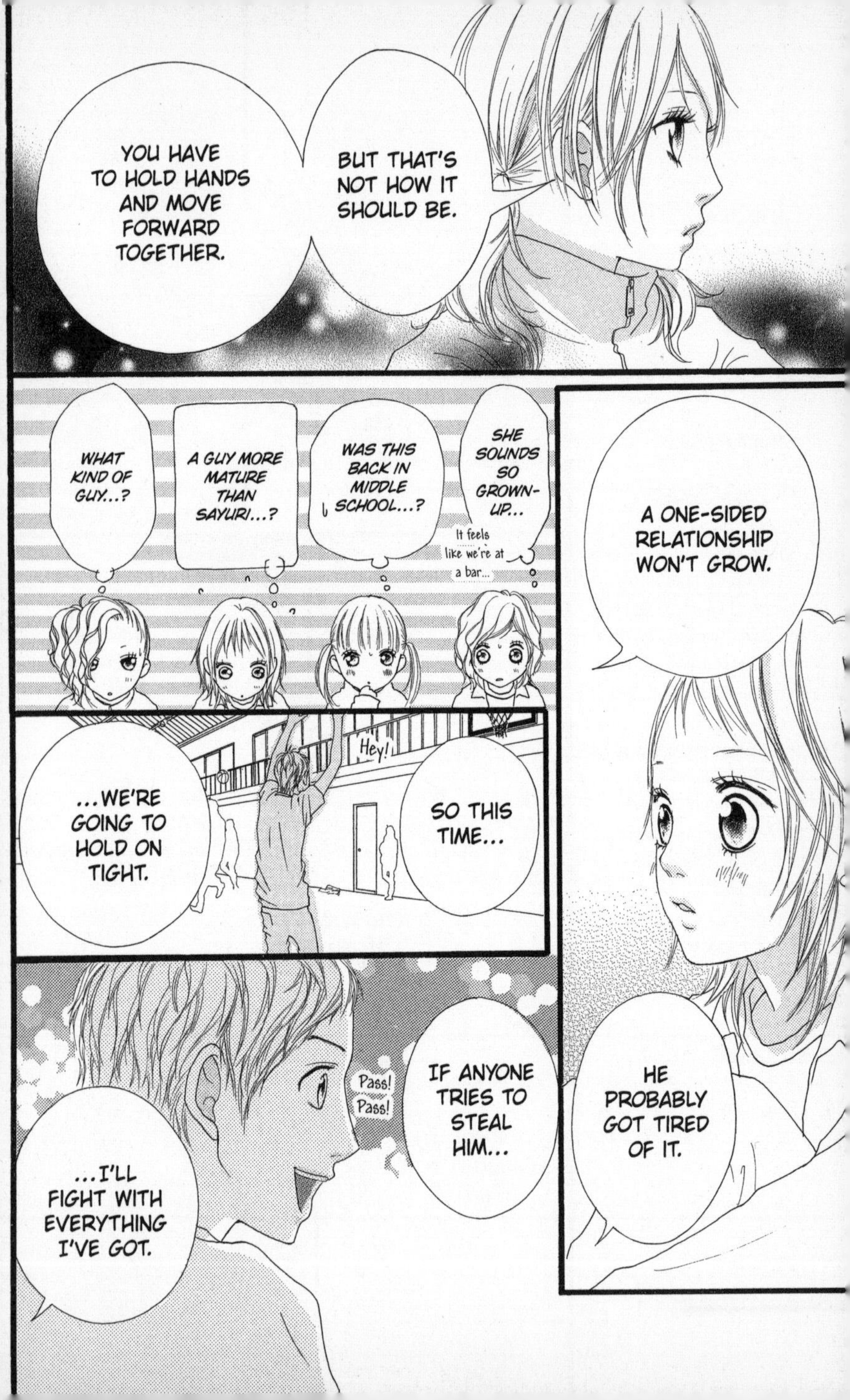
BUT THAT'S NOT HOW IT SHOULD BE.
YOU HAVE TO HOLD HANDS AND MOVE FORWARD TOGETHER.
A ONE-SIDED RELATIONSHIP WON'T GROW.
HE PROBABLY GOT TIRED OF IT.
SHE SOUNDS SO GROWN-UP...
It feels like we're at a bar...
WAS THIS BACK IN MIDDLE SCHOOL...?
A GUY MORE MATURE THAN SAYURI...?
WHAT KIND OF GUY...?
Hey!
SO THIS TIME...
...WE'RE GOING TO HOLD ON TIGHT.
Pass! Pass!
IF ANYONE TRIES TO STEAL HIM...
...I'LL FIGHT WITH EVERYTHING I'VE GOT.

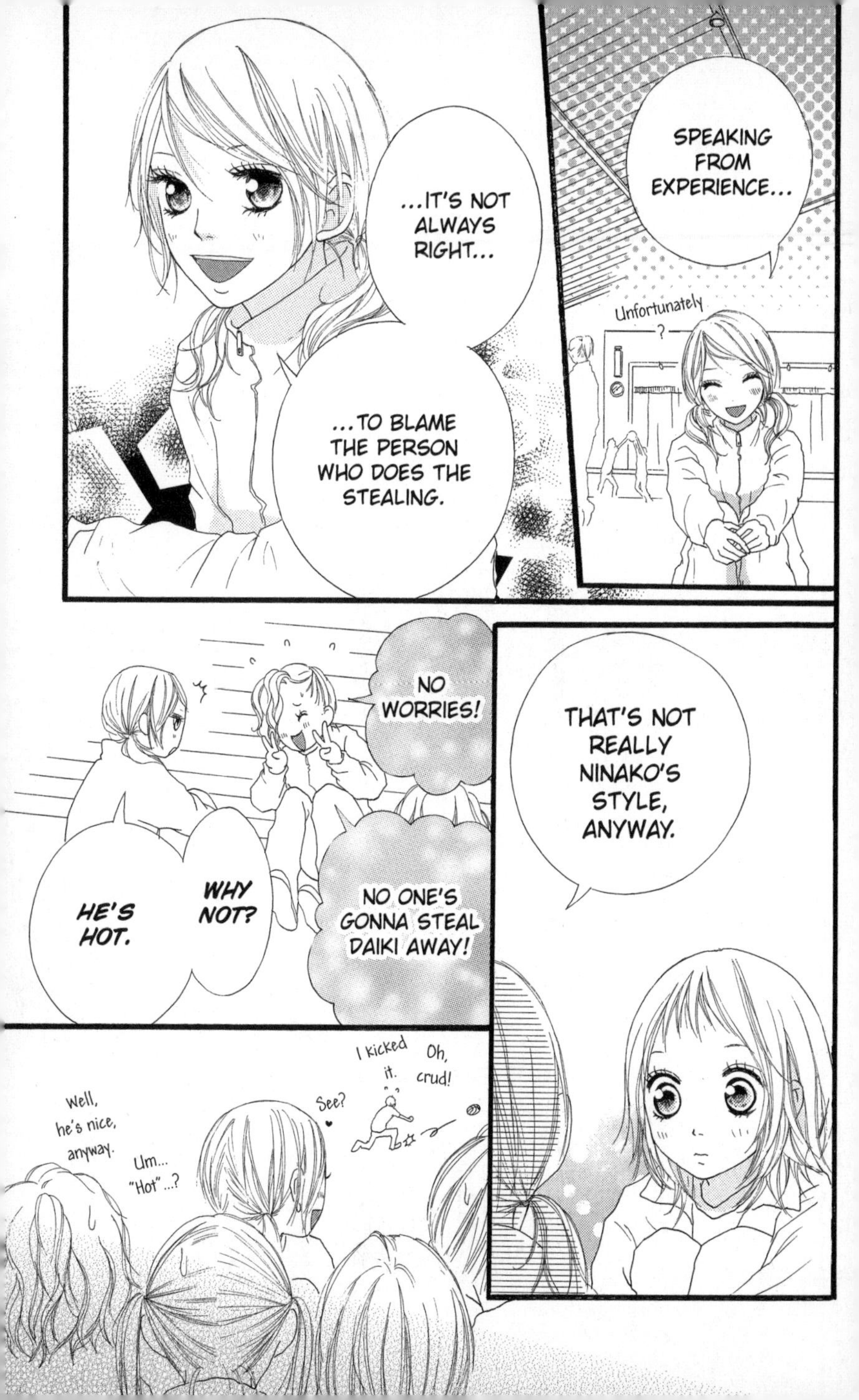
SPEAKING FROM EXPERIENCE...
Unfortunately
?
...IT'S NOT ALWAYS RIGHT...
...TO BLAME THE PERSON WHO DOES THE STEALING.
THAT'S NOT REALLY NINAKO'S STYLE, ANYWAY.
NO WORRIES!
NO ONE'S GONNA STEAL DAIKI AWAY!
WHY NOT?
HE'S HOT.
Oh, crud!
I kicked it.
See?
Um... "Hot"...?
Well, he's nice, anyway.

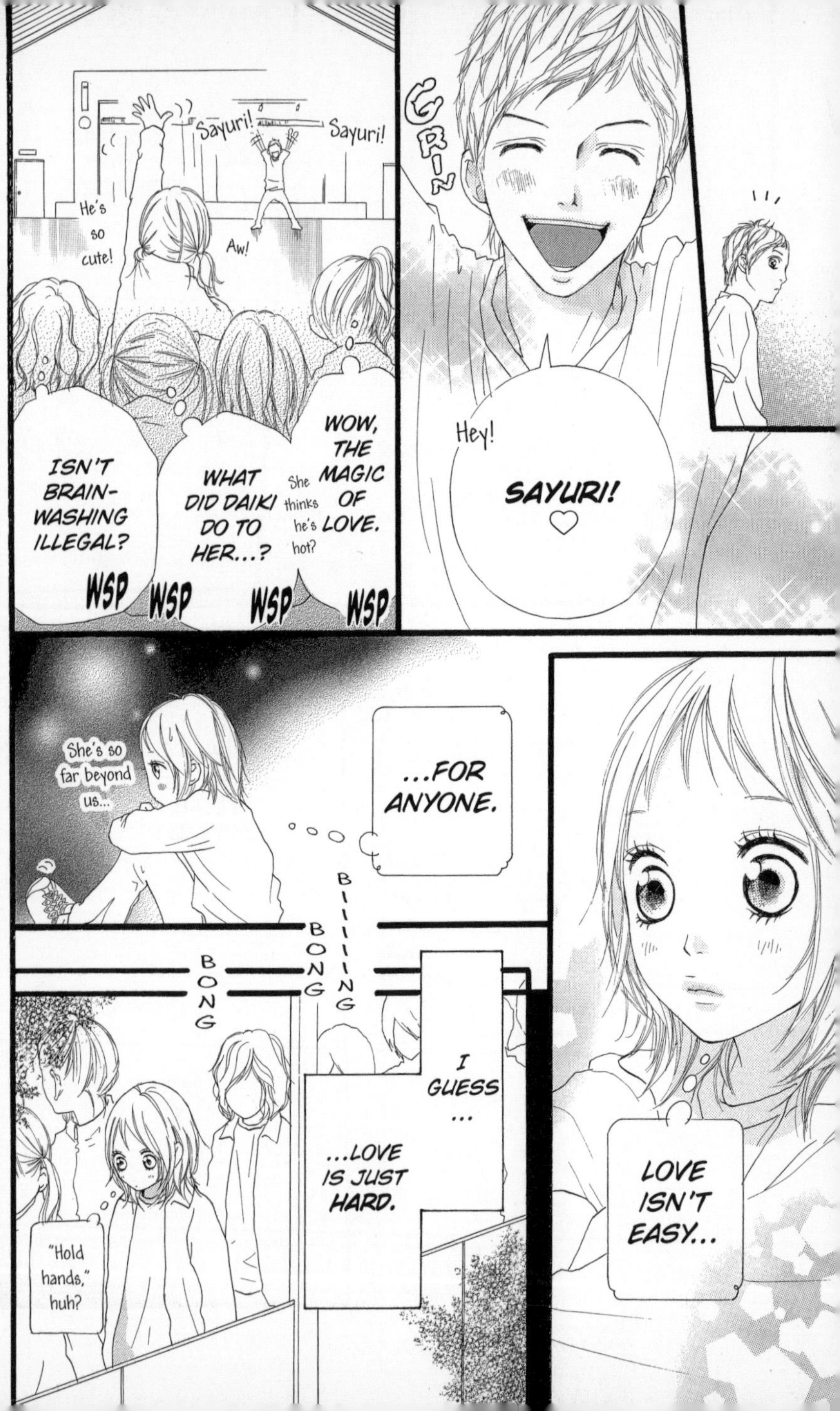
GRIN
Hey!
SAYURI! ♡
Sayuri!
Sayuri!
He's so cute!
Aw!
WOW, THE MAGIC OF LOVE.
She thinks he's hot?
WHAT DID DAIKI DO TO HER...?
ISN'T BRAIN-WASHING ILLEGAL?
WSP
WSP
WSP
WSP
LOVE ISN'T EASY...
...FOR ANYONE.
She's so far beyond us...
BIIIING
BONG
BONG
I GUESS...
...LOVE IS JUST HARD.
"Hold hands," huh?

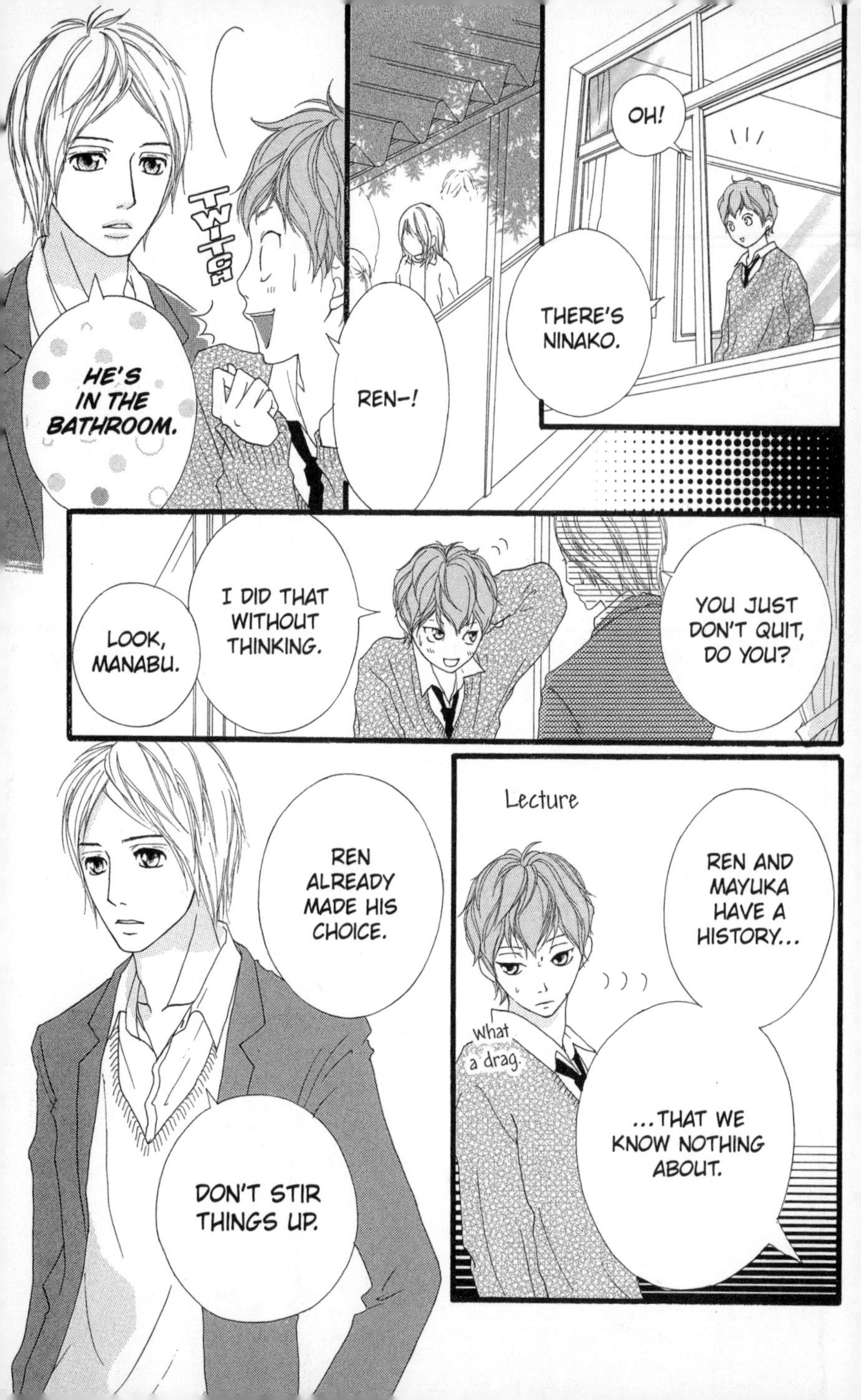
OH!
THERE'S NINAKO.
REN-!
TWITCH
HE'S IN THE BATHROOM.
YOU JUST DON'T QUIT, DO YOU?
I DID THAT WITHOUT THINKING.
LOOK, MANABU.
Lecture
REN AND MAYUKA HAVE A HISTORY...
...THAT WE KNOW NOTHING ABOUT.
What a drag.
REN ALREADY MADE HIS CHOICE.
DON'T STIR THINGS UP.

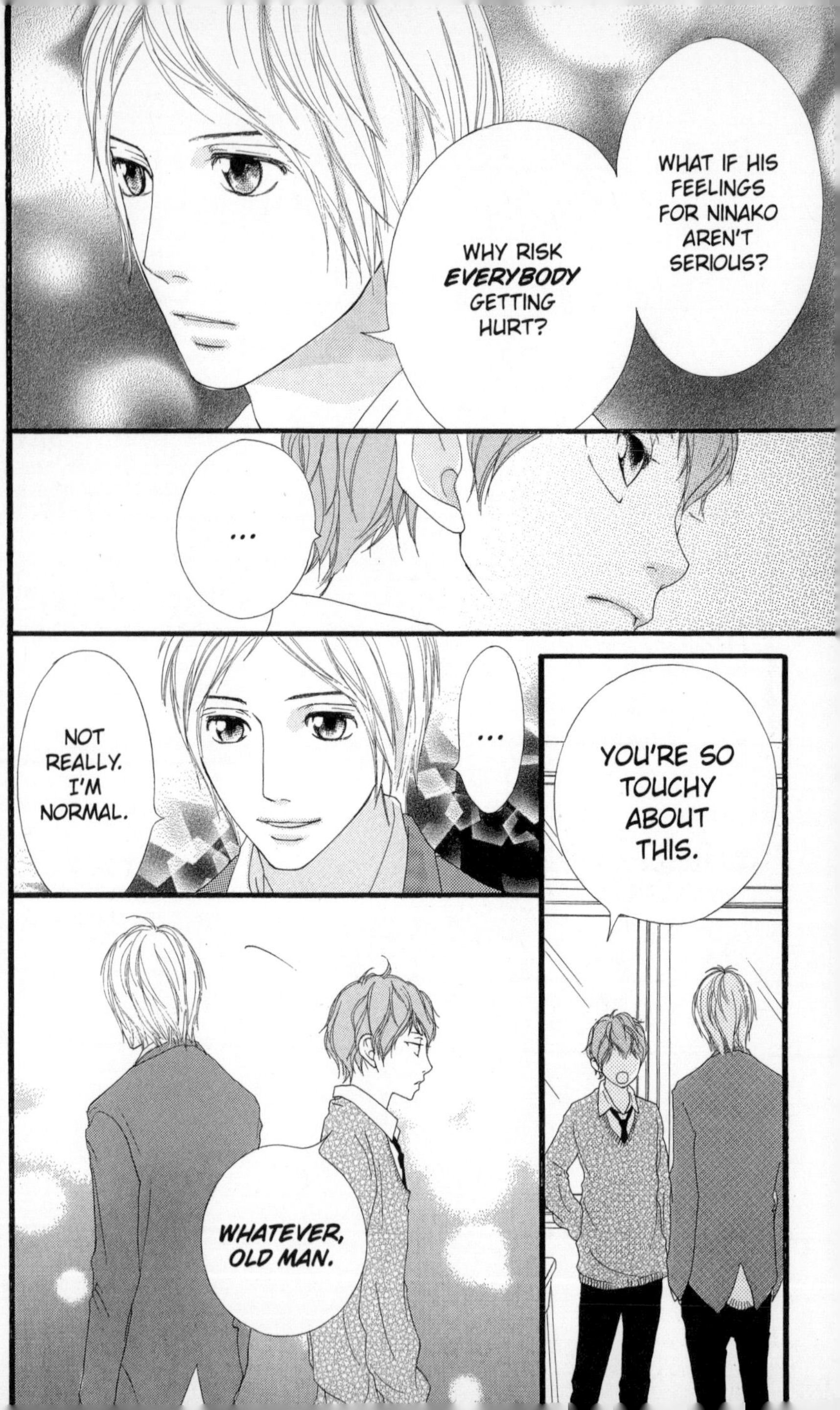
WHAT IF HIS FEELINGS FOR NINAKO AREN'T SERIOUS?
WHY RISK ***EVERYBODY*** GETTING HURT?
...
YOU'RE SO TOUCHY ABOUT THIS.
...
NOT REALLY. I'M NORMAL.
WHATEVER, OLD MAN.

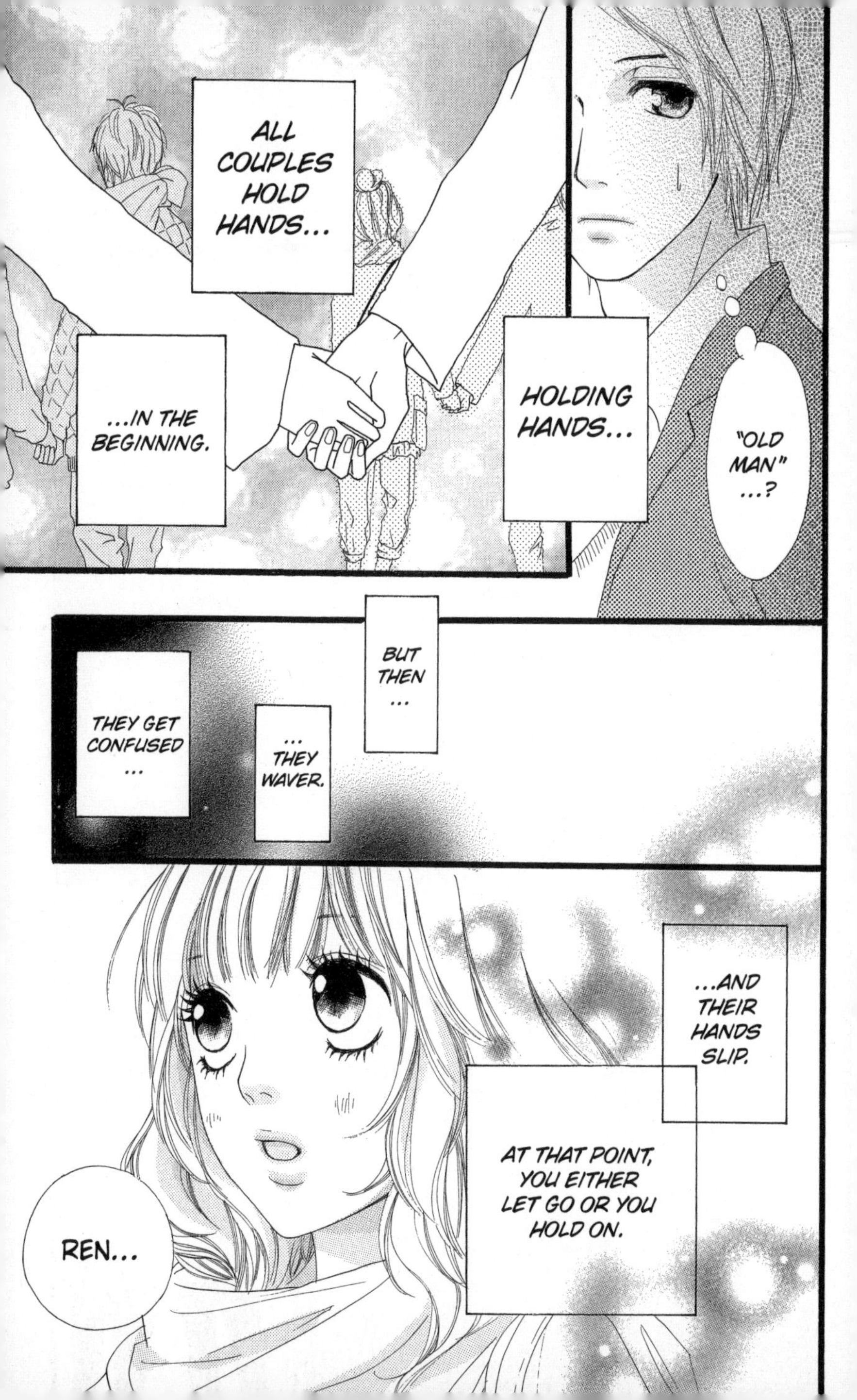
"OLD MAN" ...?
HOLDING HANDS...
ALL COUPLES HOLD HANDS...
...IN THE BEGINNING.
BUT THEN ...
... THEY WAVER.
THEY GET CONFUSED ...
...AND THEIR HANDS SLIP.
AT THAT POINT, YOU EITHER LET GO OR YOU HOLD ON.
REN...

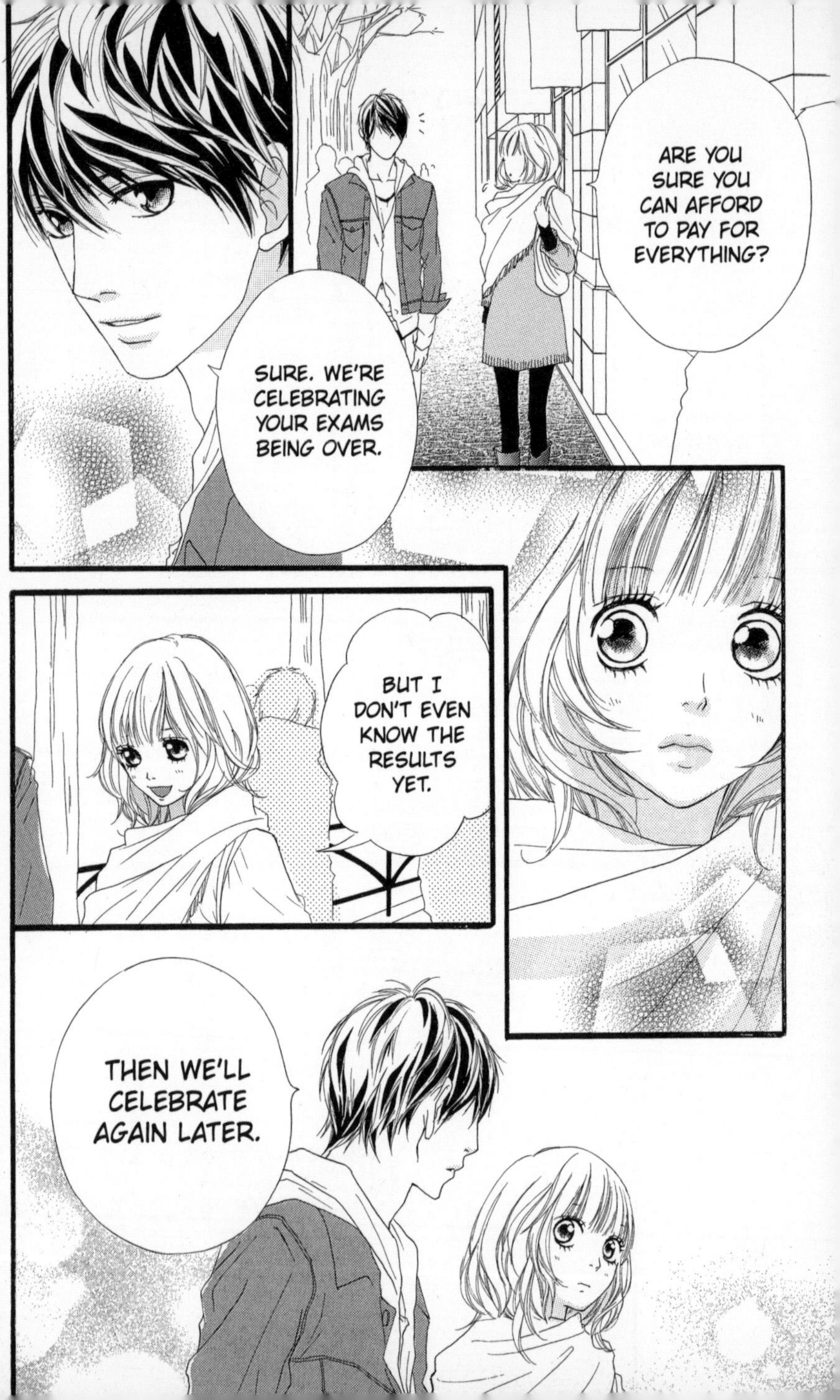
ARE YOU SURE YOU CAN AFFORD TO PAY FOR EVERYTHING?
SURE. WE'RE CELEBRATING YOUR EXAMS BEING OVER.
BUT I DON'T EVEN KNOW THE RESULTS YET.
THEN WE'LL CELEBRATE AGAIN LATER.

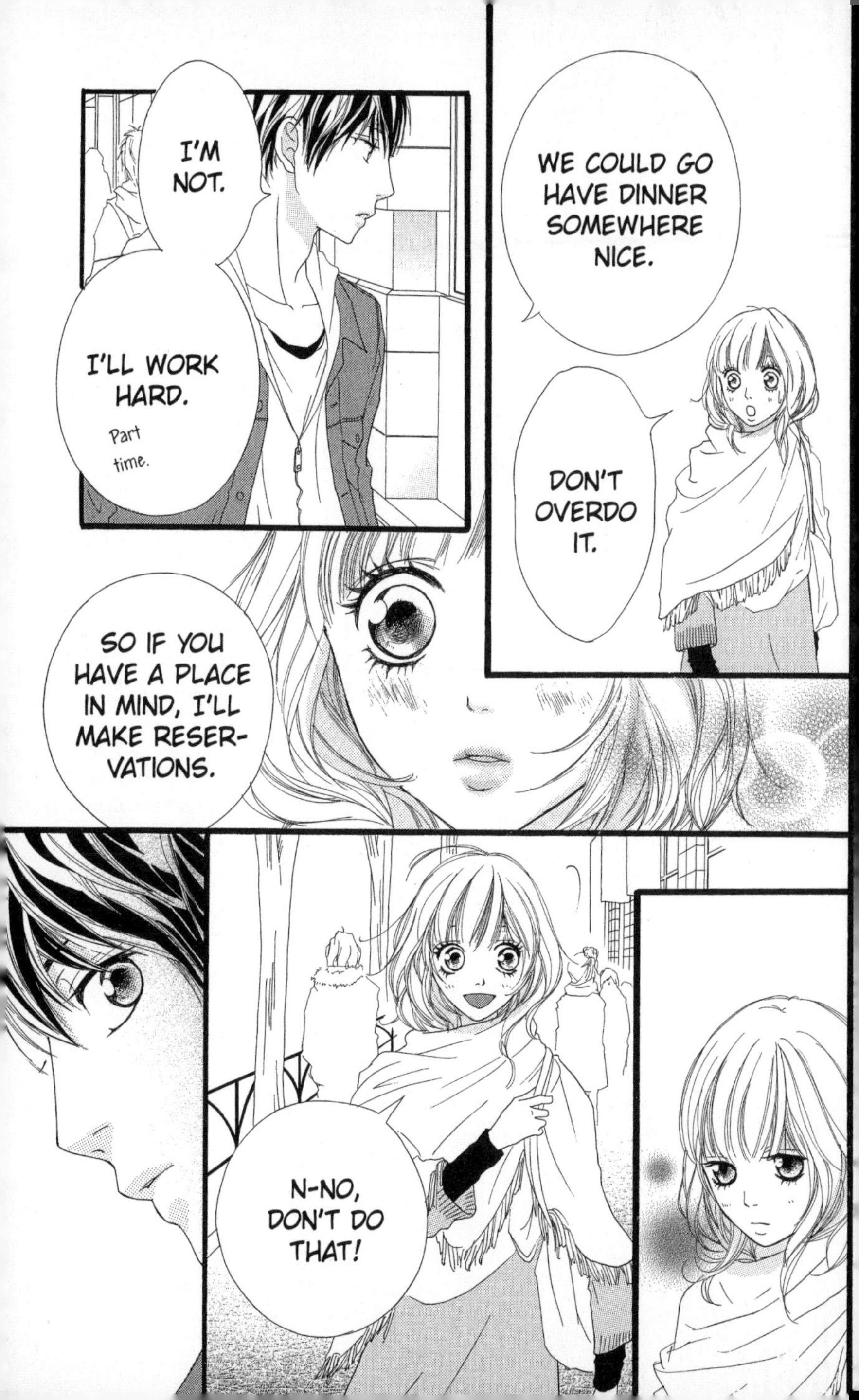
WE COULD GO HAVE DINNER SOMEWHERE NICE.
DON'T OVERDO IT.
I'M NOT.
I'LL WORK HARD.
Part time.
SO IF YOU HAVE A PLACE IN MIND, I'LL MAKE RESER-VATIONS.
N-NO, DON'T DO THAT!

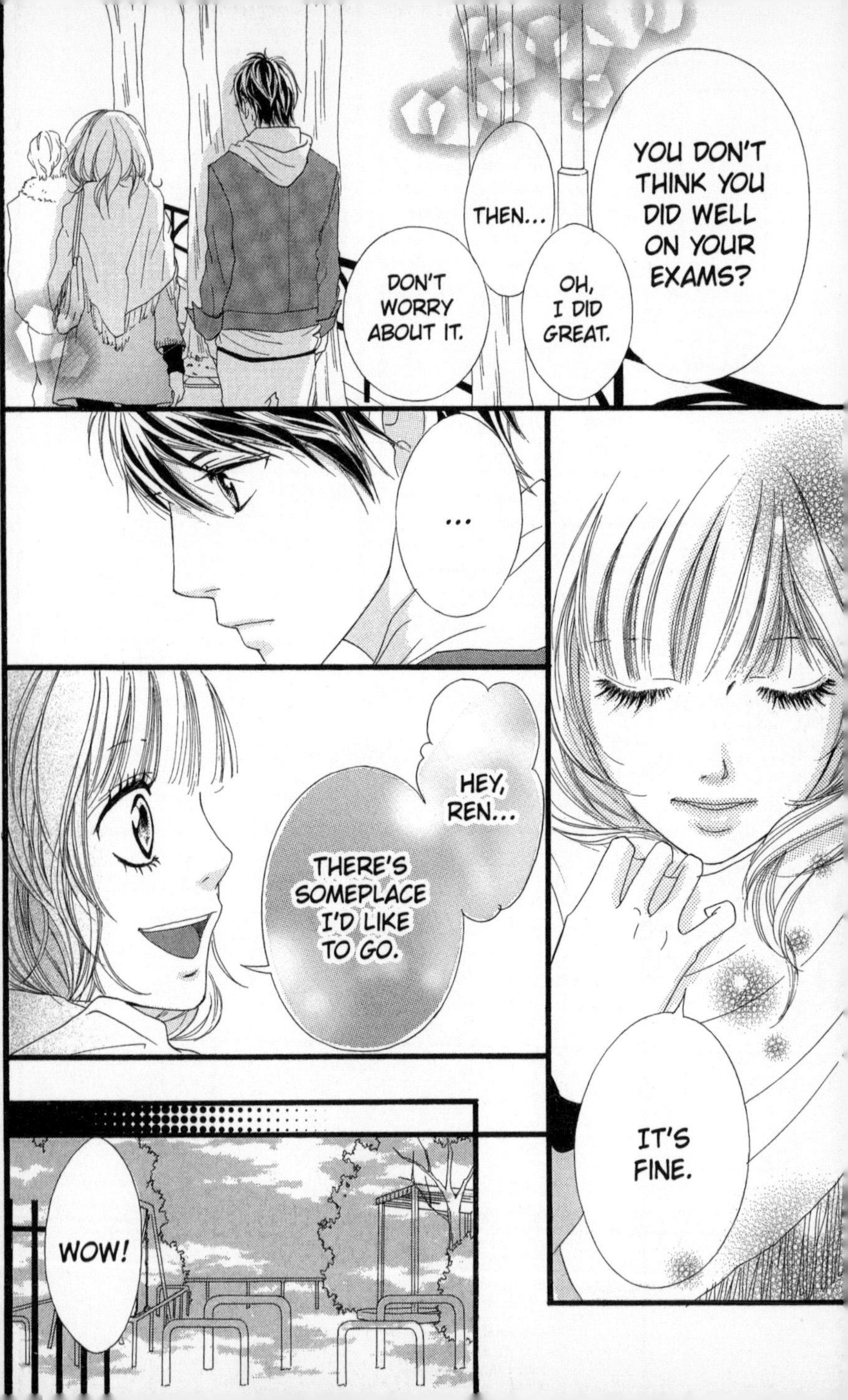
YOU DON'T THINK YOU DID WELL ON YOUR EXAMS?
OH, I DID GREAT.
THEN...
DON'T WORRY ABOUT IT.
IT'S FINE.
...
HEY, REN...
THERE'S SOMEPLACE I'D LIKE TO GO.
WOW!

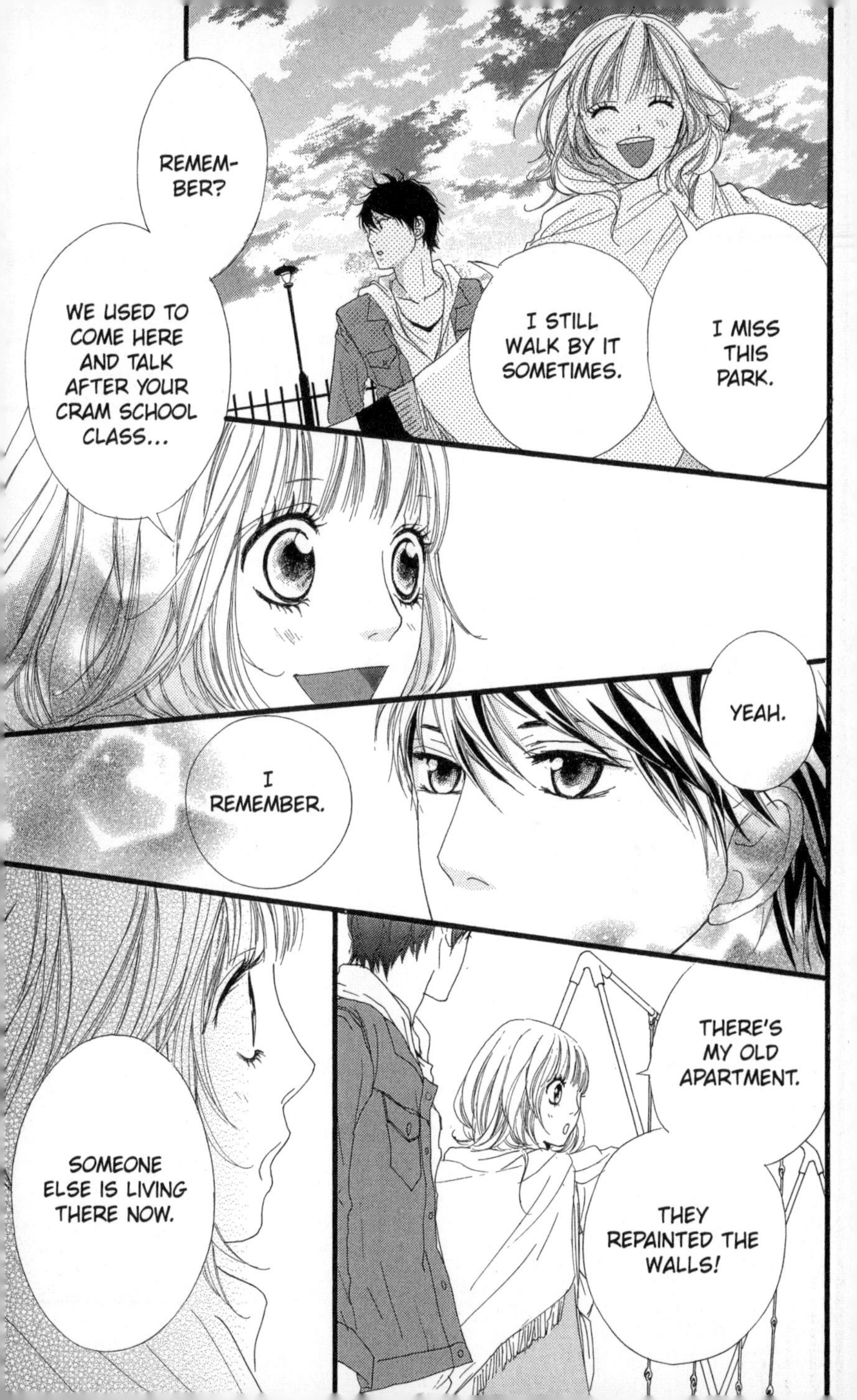
I MISS THIS PARK.
I STILL WALK BY IT SOMETIMES.
REMEMBER?
WE USED TO COME HERE AND TALK AFTER YOUR CRAM SCHOOL CLASS...
YEAH.
I REMEMBER.
THERE'S MY OLD APARTMENT.
THEY REPAINTED THE WALLS!
SOMEONE ELSE IS LIVING THERE NOW.

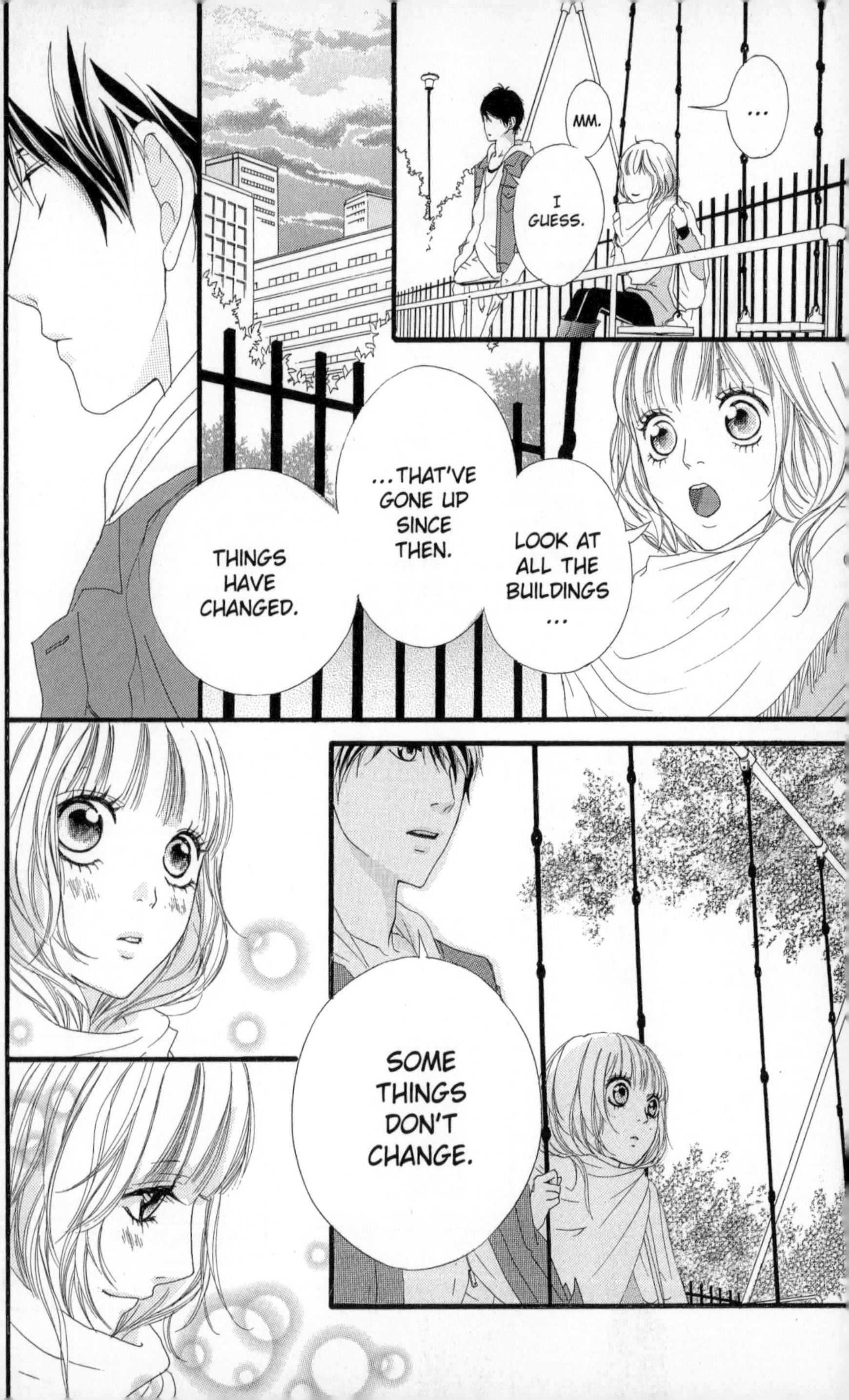
...
MM.
I GUESS.
LOOK AT ALL THE BUILDINGS ...
...THAT'VE GONE UP SINCE THEN.
THINGS HAVE CHANGED.
SOME THINGS DON'T CHANGE.

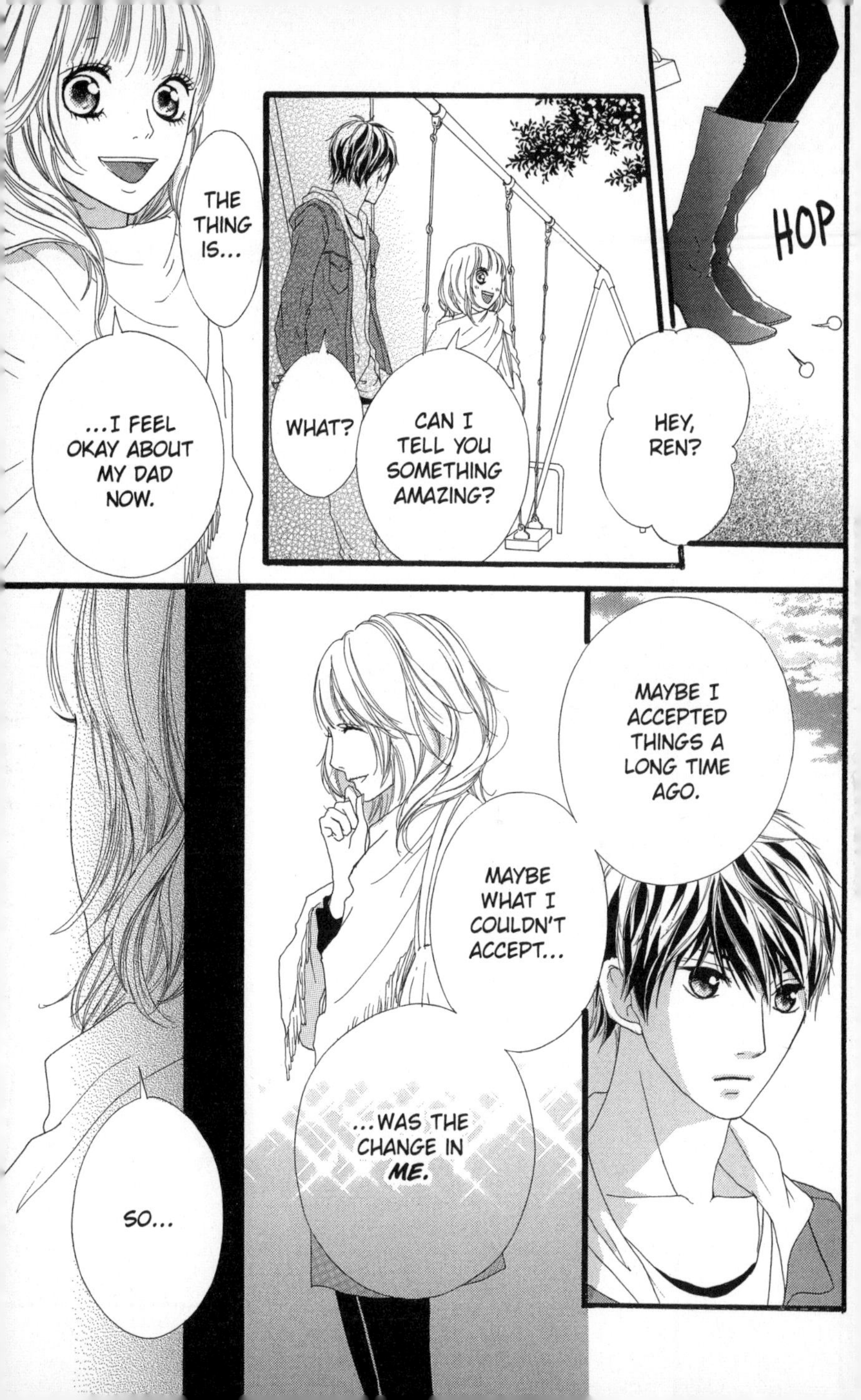
HOP
HEY, REN?
CAN I TELL YOU SOMETHING AMAZING?
WHAT?
THE THING IS...
...I FEEL OKAY ABOUT MY DAD NOW.
MAYBE I ACCEPTED THINGS A LONG TIME AGO.
MAYBE WHAT I COULDN'T ACCEPT...
...WAS THE CHANGE IN *ME.*
SO...

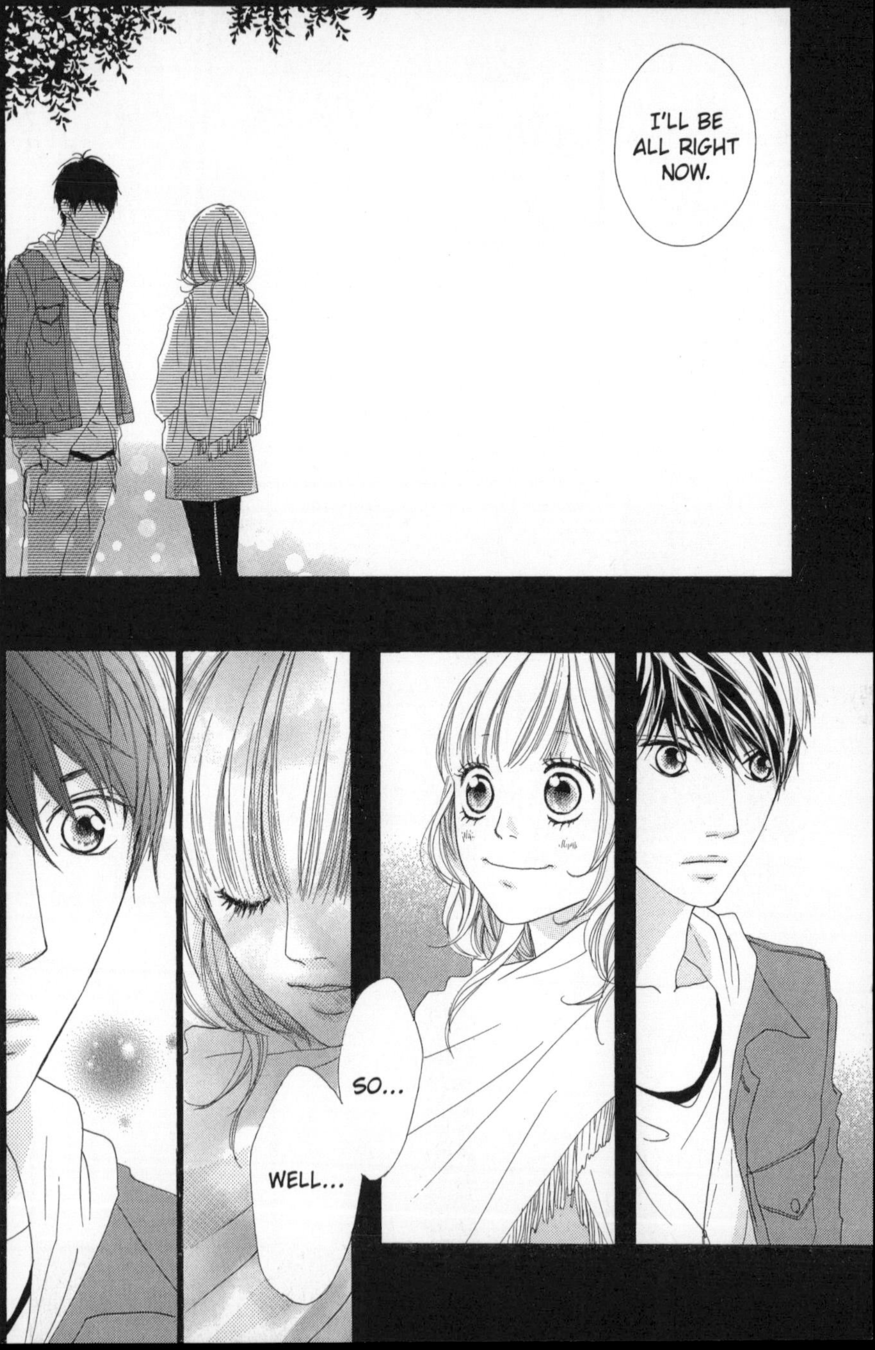
I'LL BE ALL RIGHT NOW.
SO...
WELL...

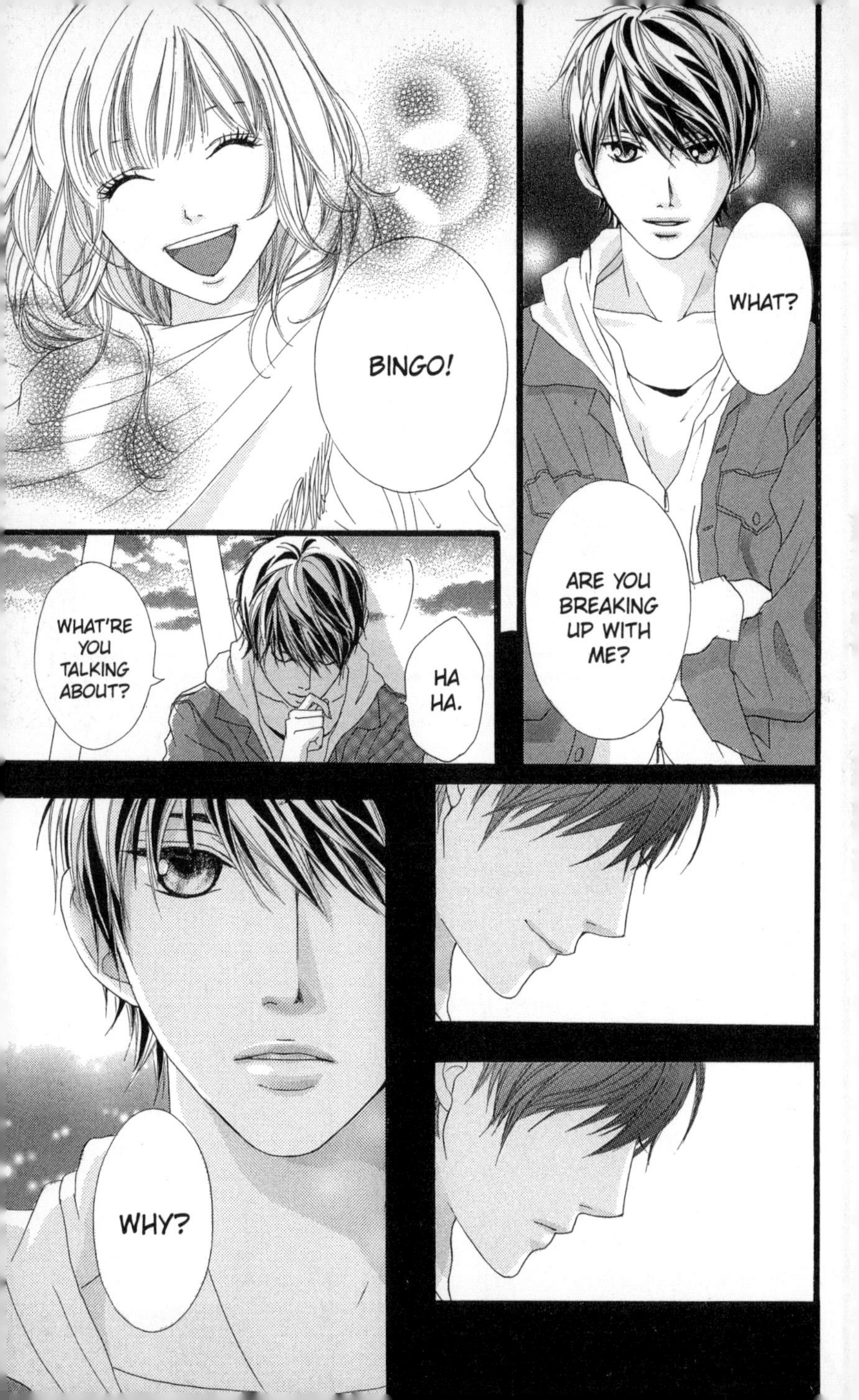
WHAT?
ARE YOU BREAKING UP WITH ME?
BINGO!
HA HA.
WHAT'RE YOU TALKING ABOUT?
WHY?

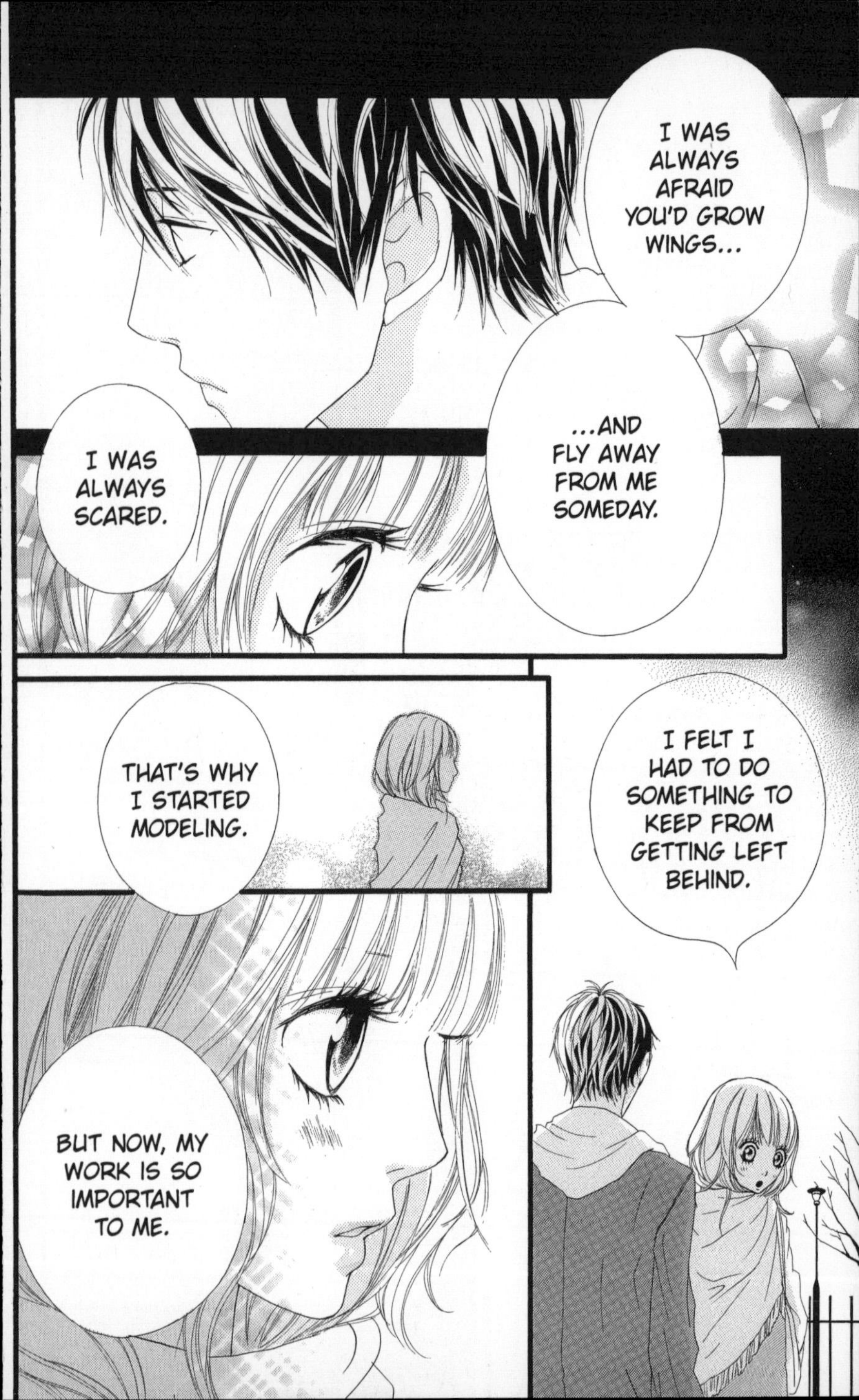
I WAS ALWAYS AFRAID YOU'D GROW WINGS...
...AND FLY AWAY FROM ME SOMEDAY.
I WAS ALWAYS SCARED.
I FELT I HAD TO DO SOMETHING TO KEEP FROM GETTING LEFT BEHIND.
THAT'S WHY I STARTED MODELING.
BUT NOW, MY WORK IS SO IMPORTANT TO ME.

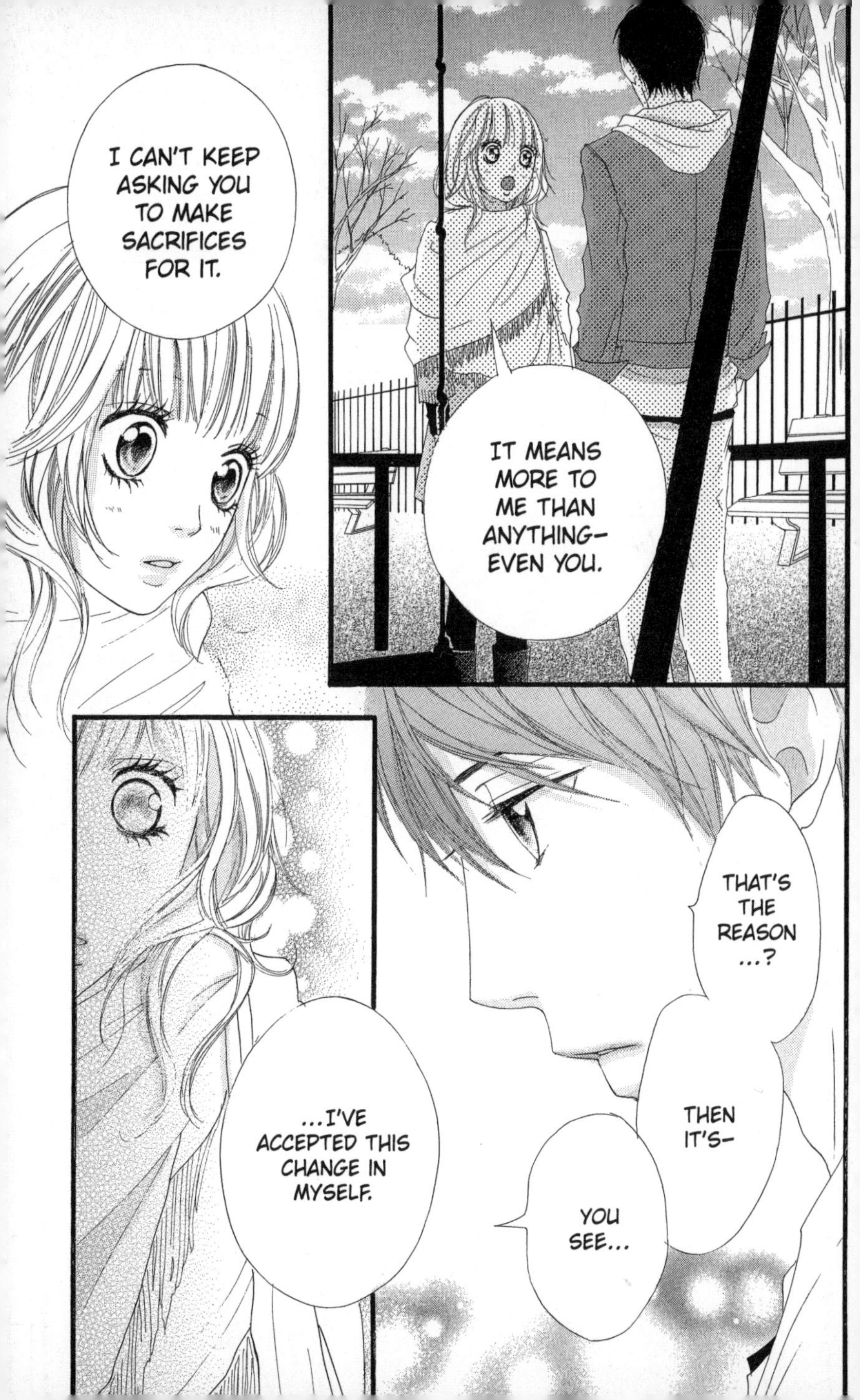
IT MEANS MORE TO ME THAN ANYTHING— EVEN YOU.
I CAN'T KEEP ASKING YOU TO MAKE SACRIFICES FOR IT.
THAT'S THE REASON ...?
THEN IT'S—
YOU SEE...
...I'VE ACCEPTED THIS CHANGE IN MYSELF.

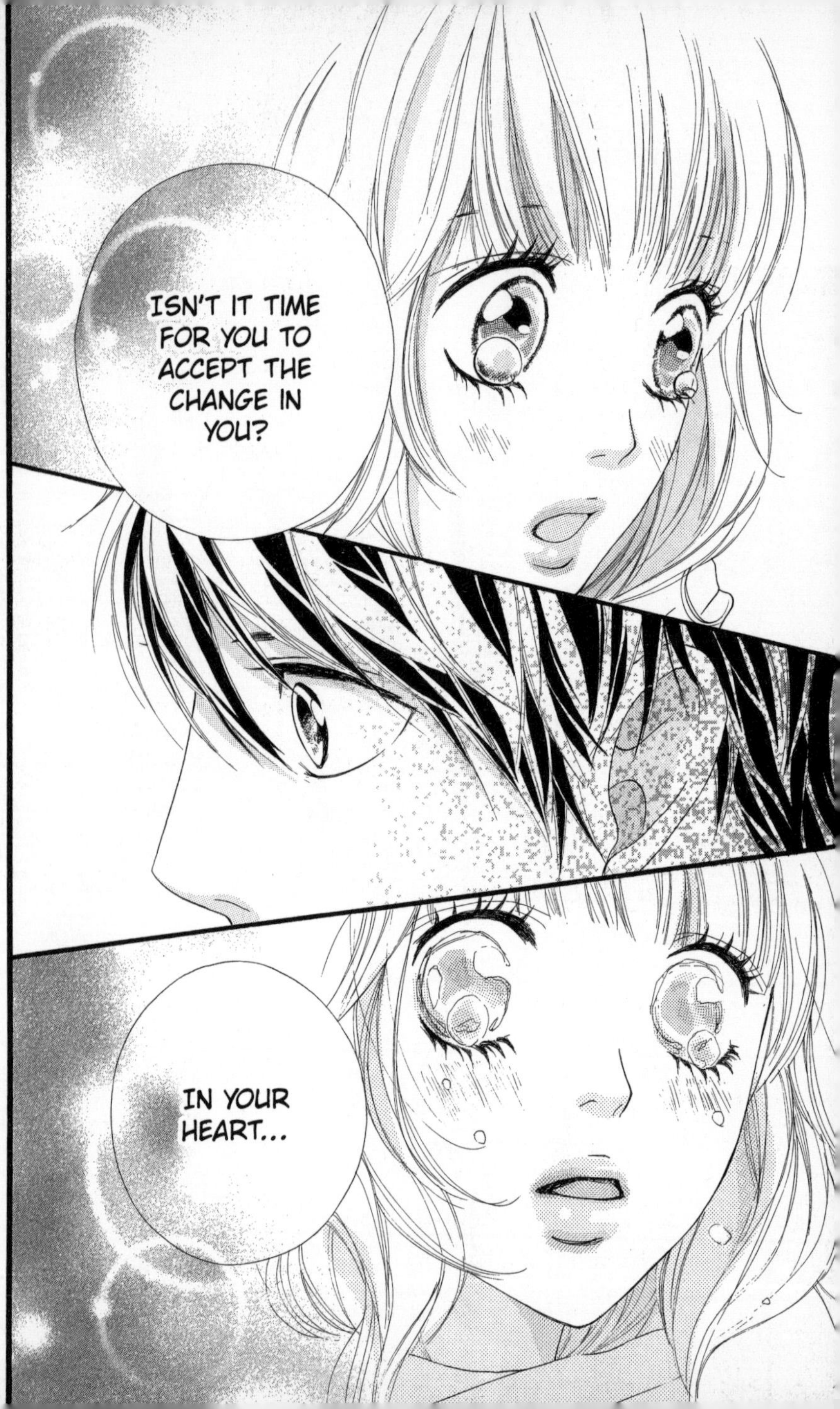
ISN'T IT TIME FOR YOU TO ACCEPT THE CHANGE IN YOU?
IN YOUR HEART...

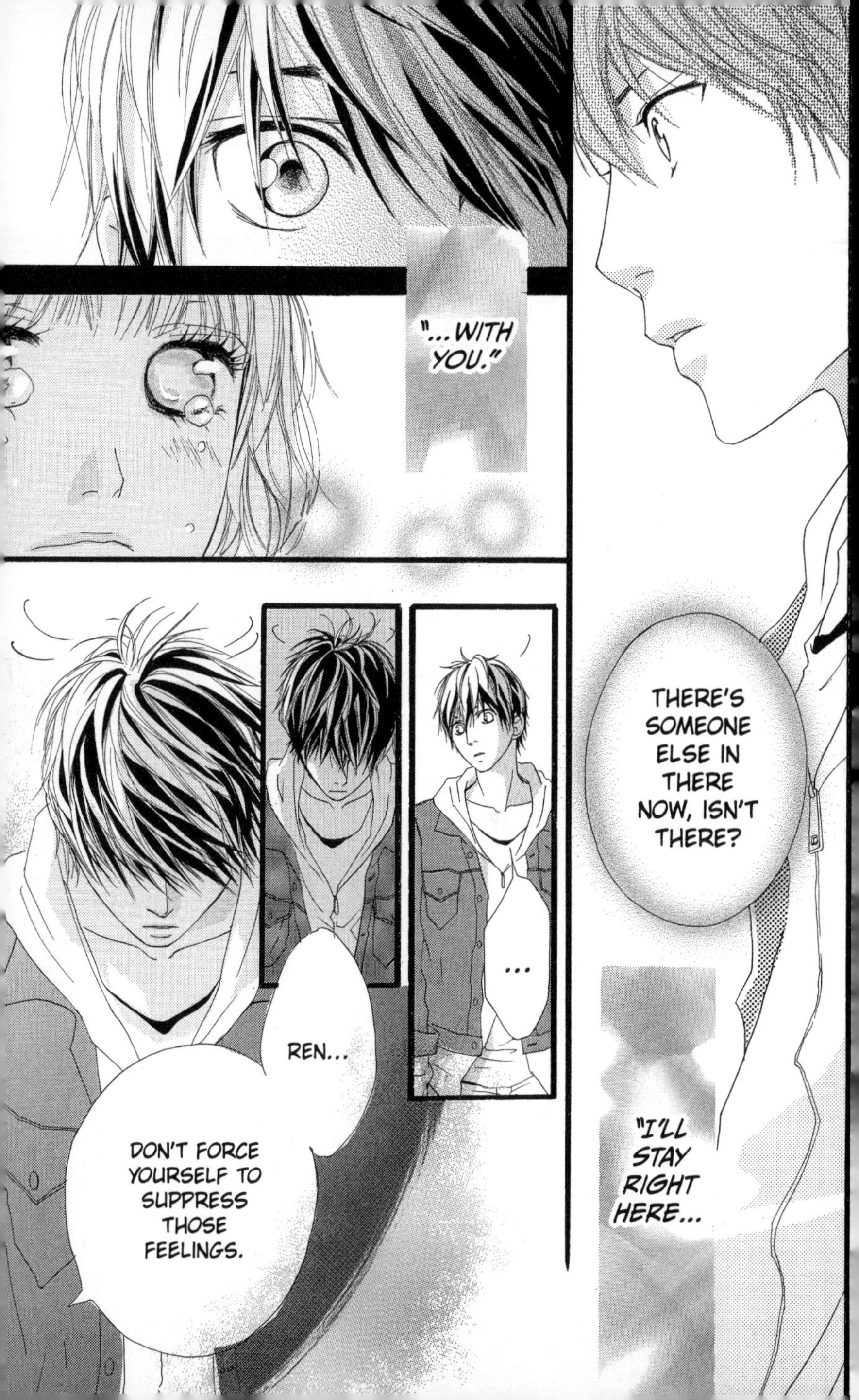
THERE'S SOMEONE ELSE IN THERE NOW, ISN'T THERE?
"I'LL STAY RIGHT HERE...
"...WITH YOU."
...
REN...
DON'T FORCE YOURSELF TO SUPPRESS THOSE FEELINGS.

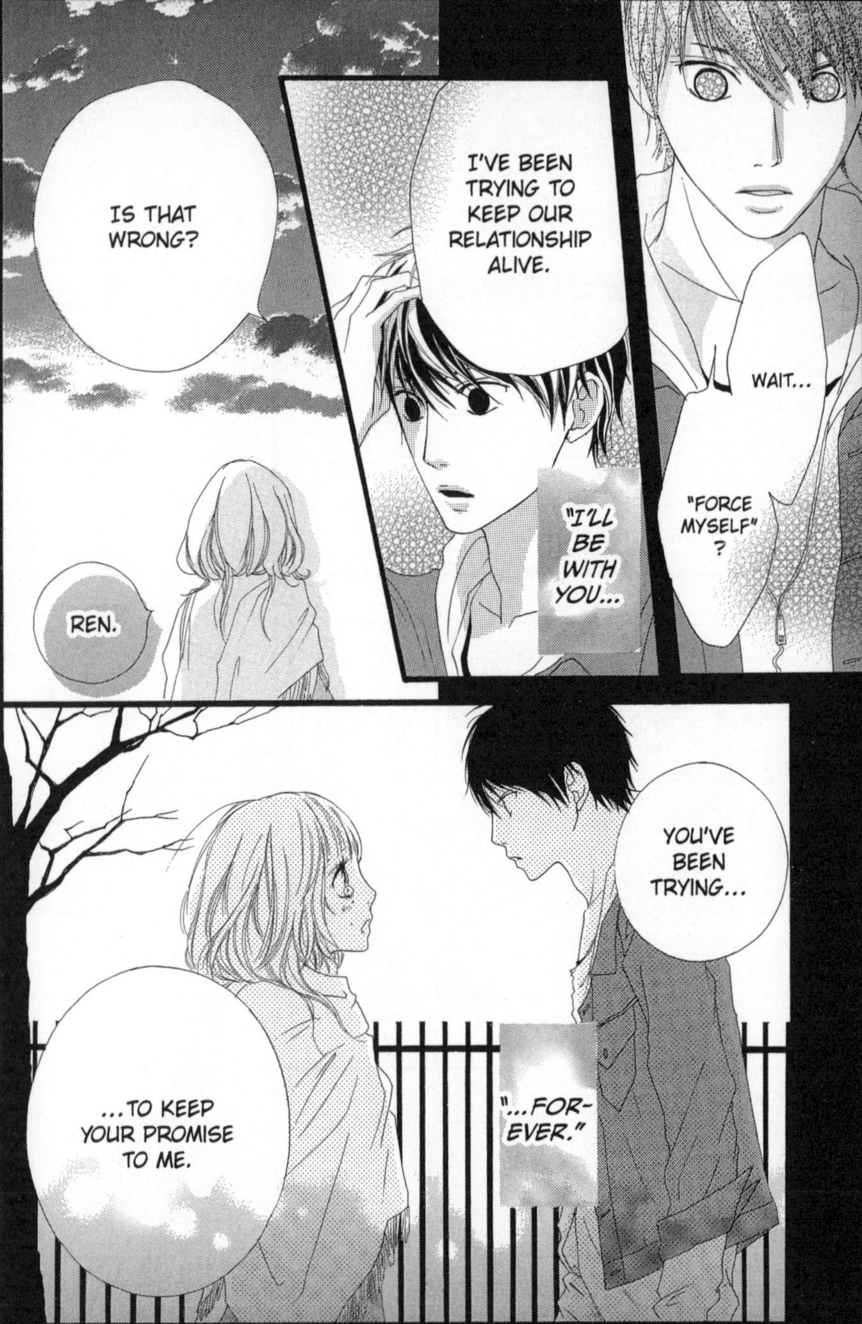
WAIT...
"FORCE MYSELF"?
I'VE BEEN TRYING TO KEEP OUR RELATIONSHIP ALIVE.
"I'LL BE WITH YOU...
IS THAT WRONG?
REN.
YOU'VE BEEN TRYING...
"...FOR-EVER."
...TO KEEP YOUR PROMISE TO ME.

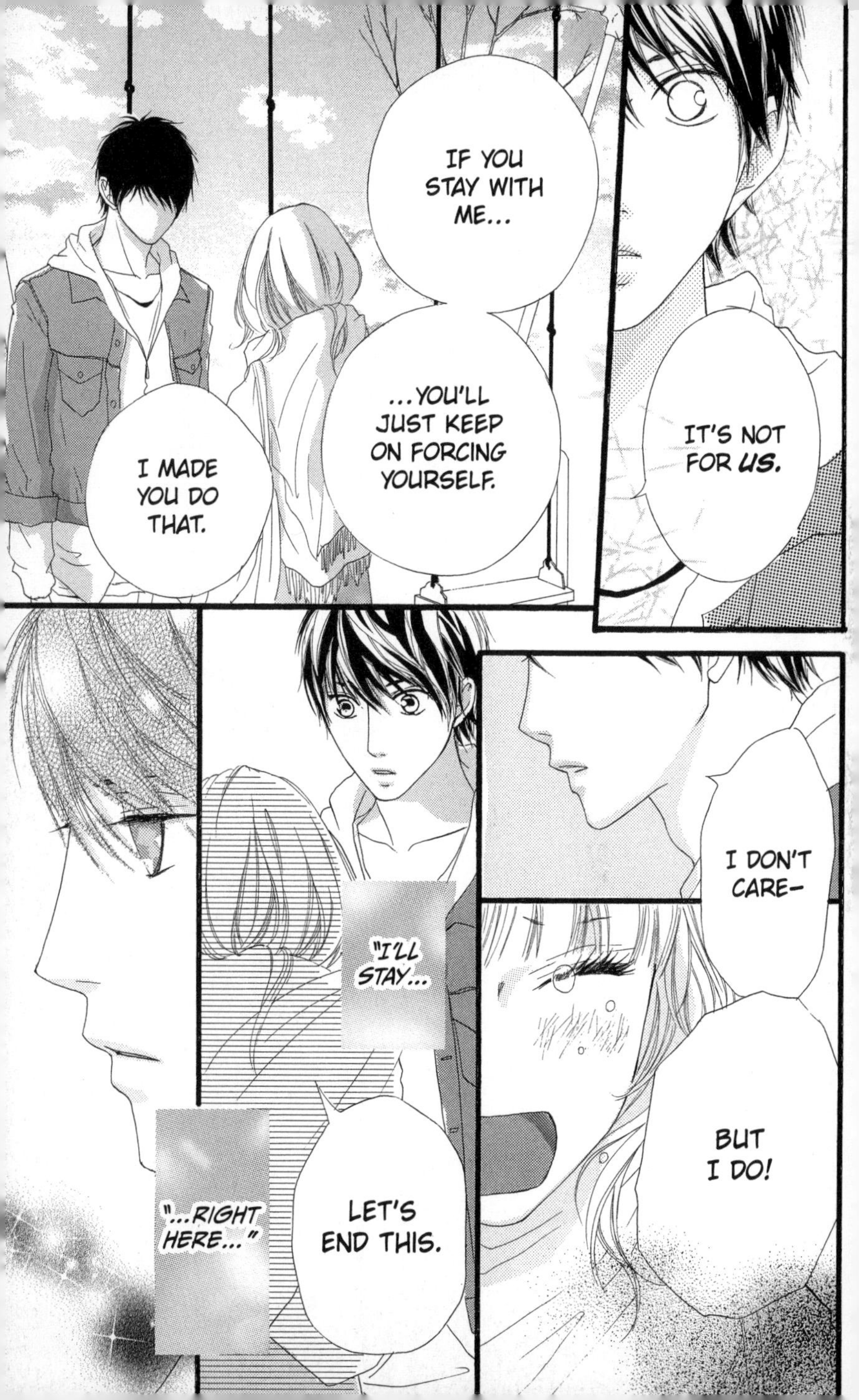
IT'S NOT FOR *US.*
IF YOU STAY WITH ME...
...YOU'LL JUST KEEP ON FORCING YOURSELF.
I MADE YOU DO THAT.
I DON'T CARE-
BUT I DO!
"I'LL STAY...
LET'S END THIS.
"...RIGHT HERE..."

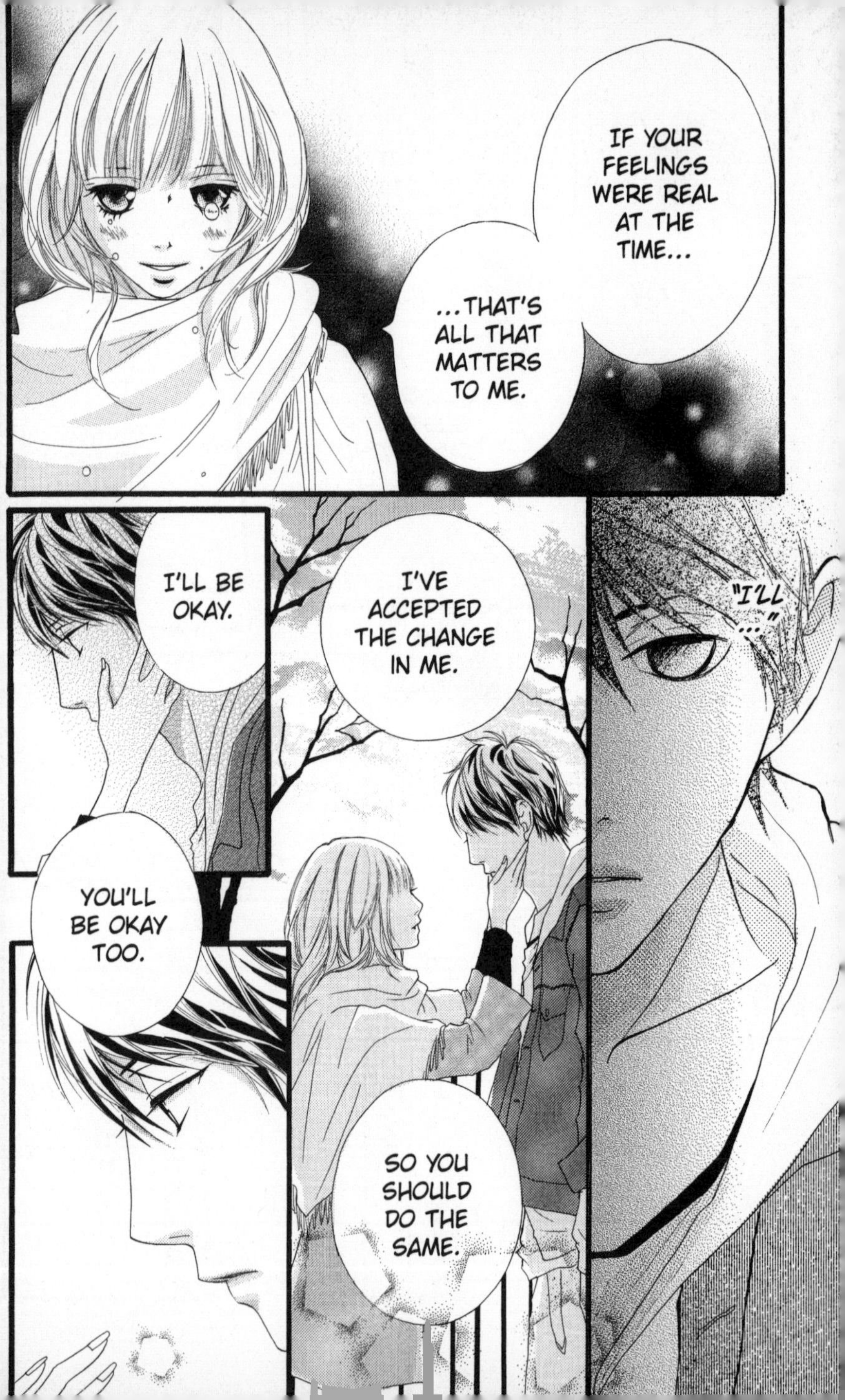
IF YOUR FEELINGS WERE REAL AT THE TIME...
...THAT'S ALL THAT MATTERS TO ME.
"I'LL ..."
I'VE ACCEPTED THE CHANGE IN ME.
SO YOU SHOULD DO THE SAME.
I'LL BE OKAY.
YOU'LL BE OKAY TOO.

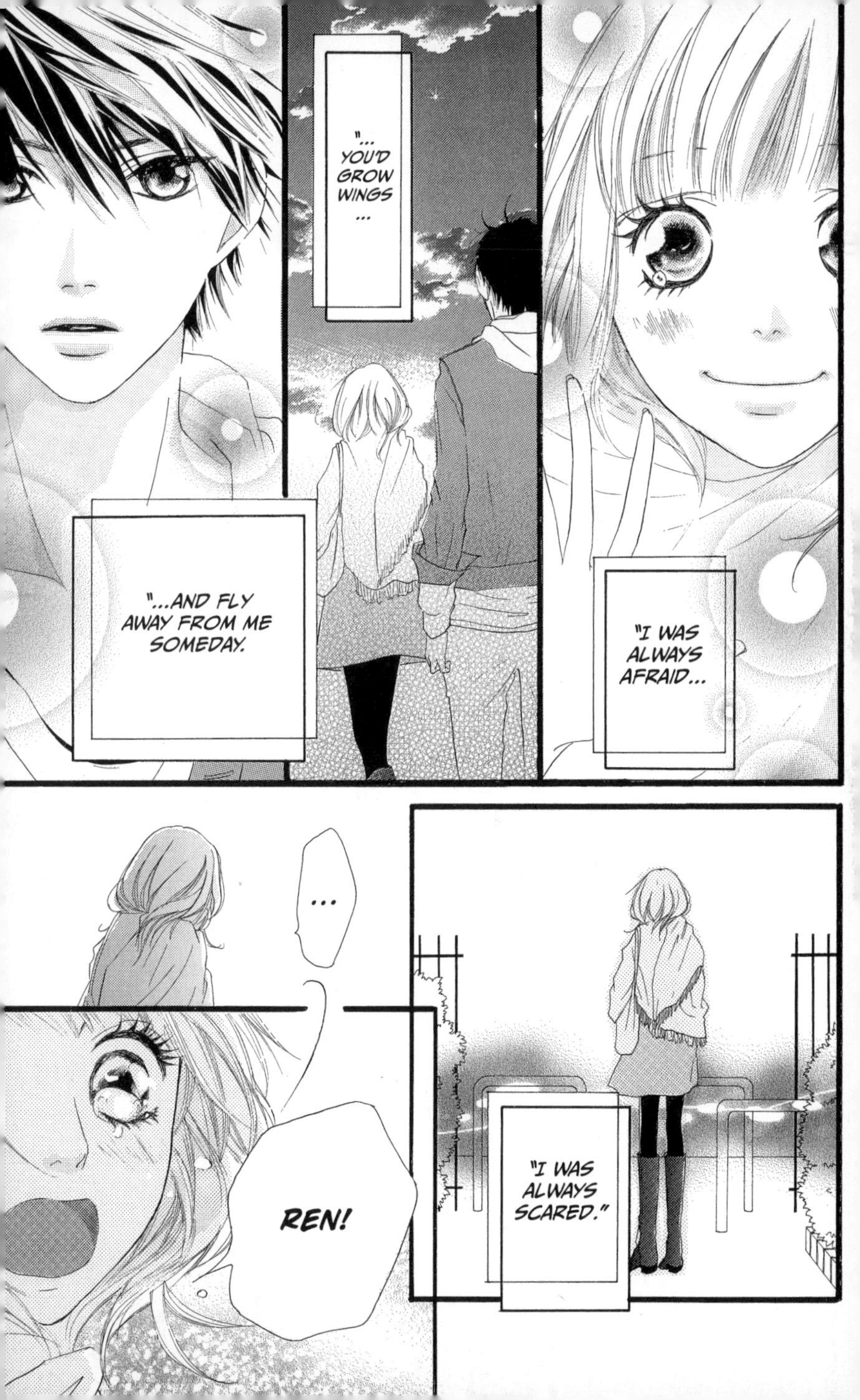
"I WAS ALWAYS AFRAID...
"... YOU'D GROW WINGS ...
"...AND FLY AWAY FROM ME SOMEDAY.
"I WAS ALWAYS SCARED."
...
REN!

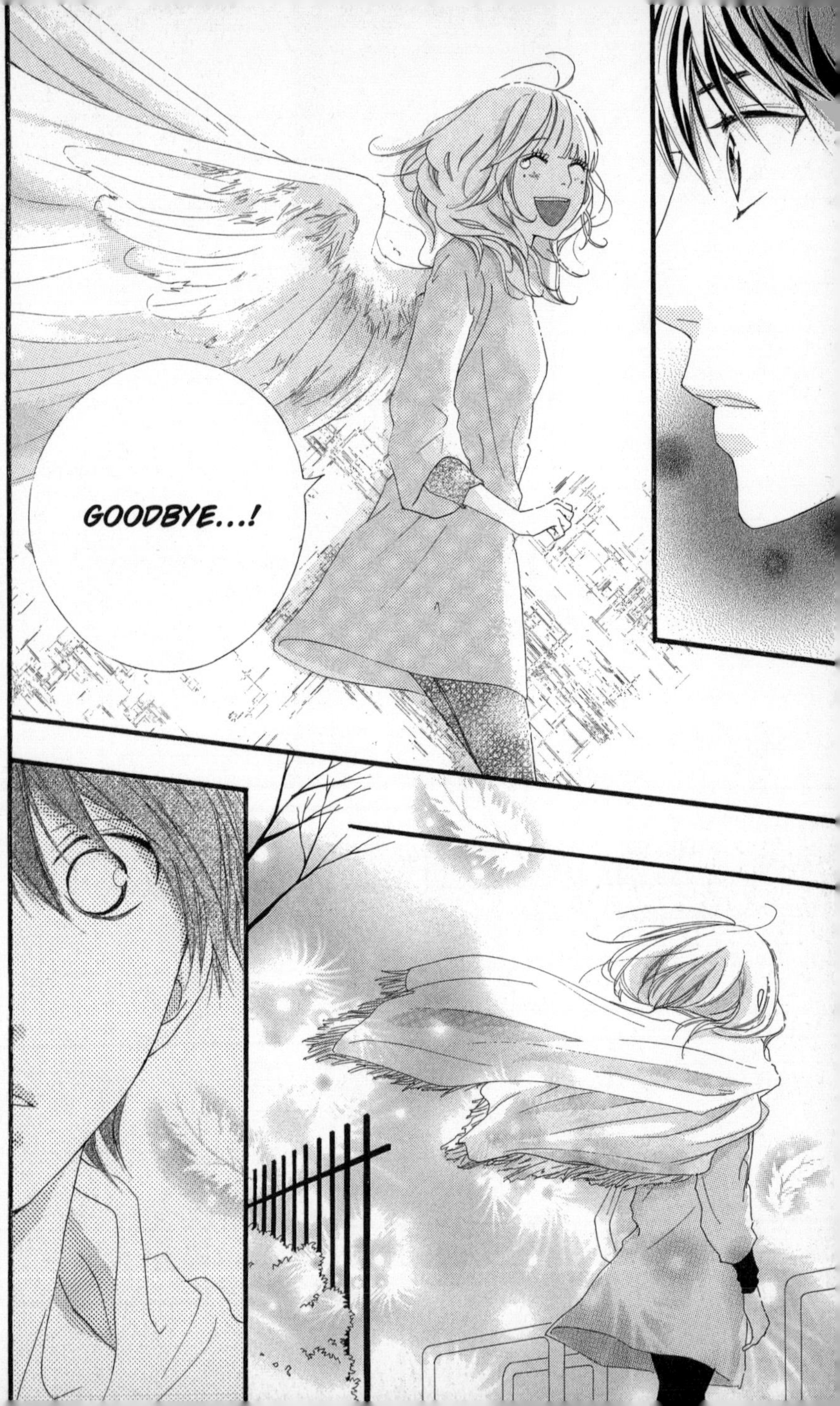
GOODBYE...!

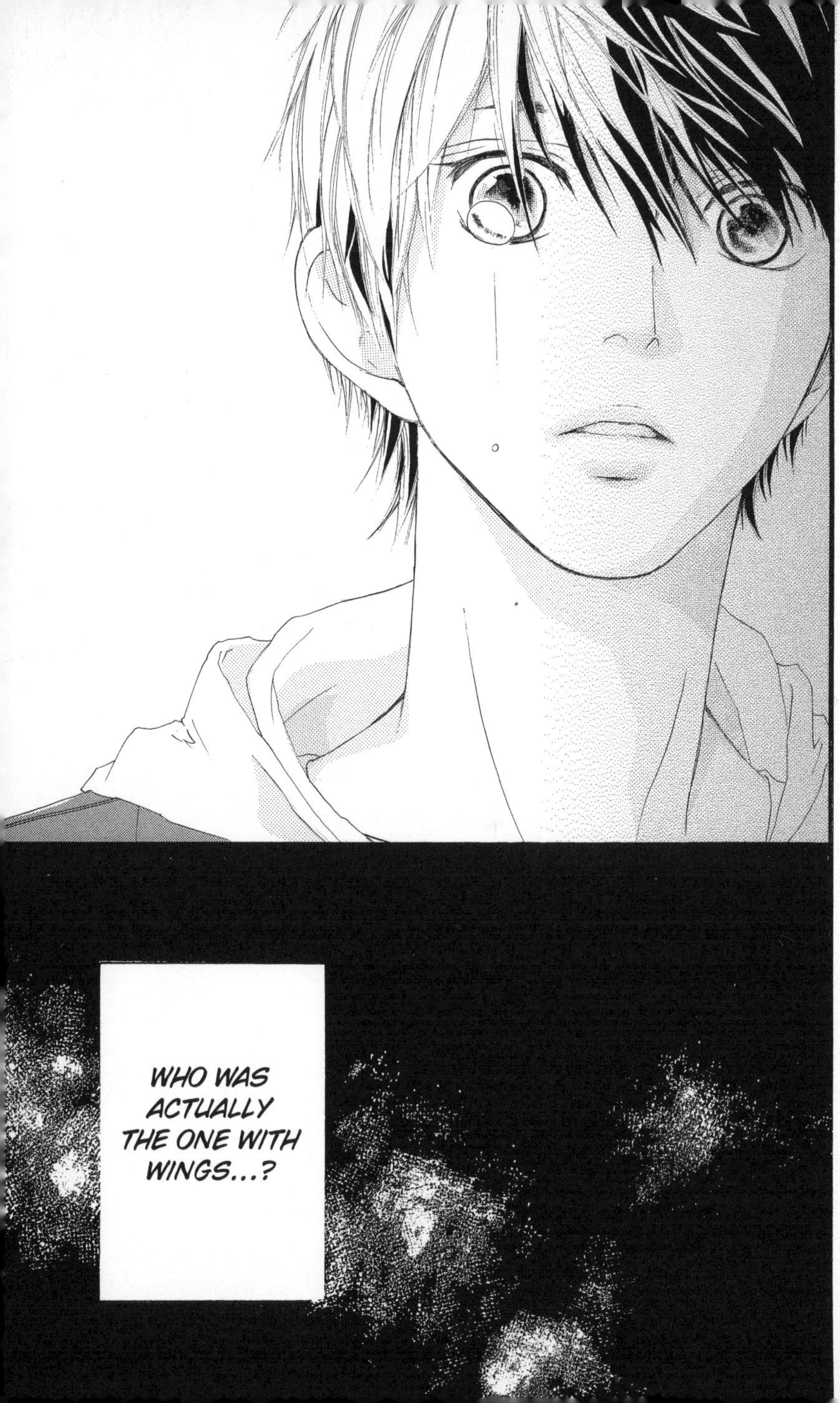
WHO WAS ACTUALLY THE ONE WITH WINGS...?

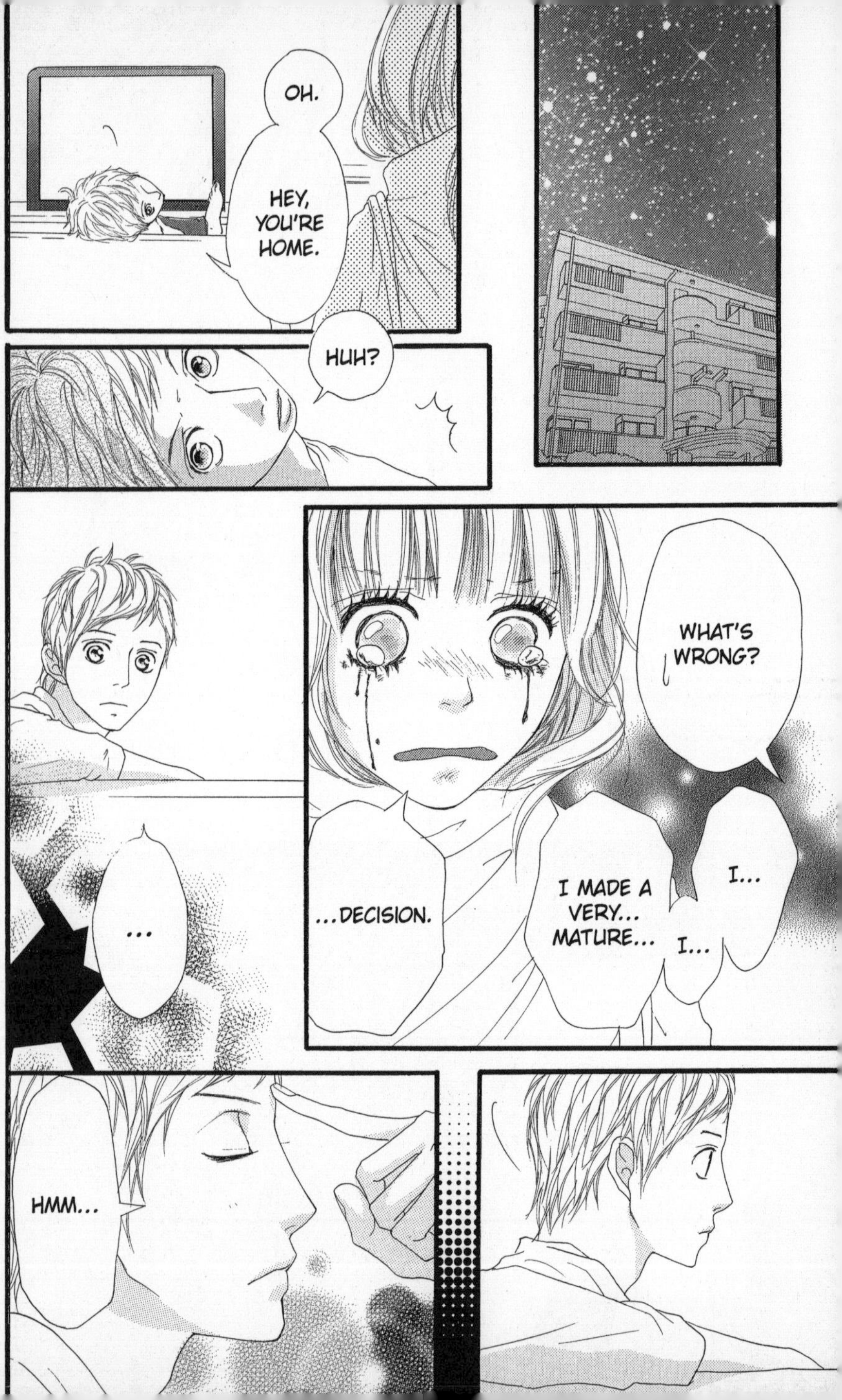

OH.
HEY, YOU'RE HOME.
HUH?
WHAT'S WRONG?
I...
I...
I MADE A VERY... MATURE...
...DECISION.
...
HMM...

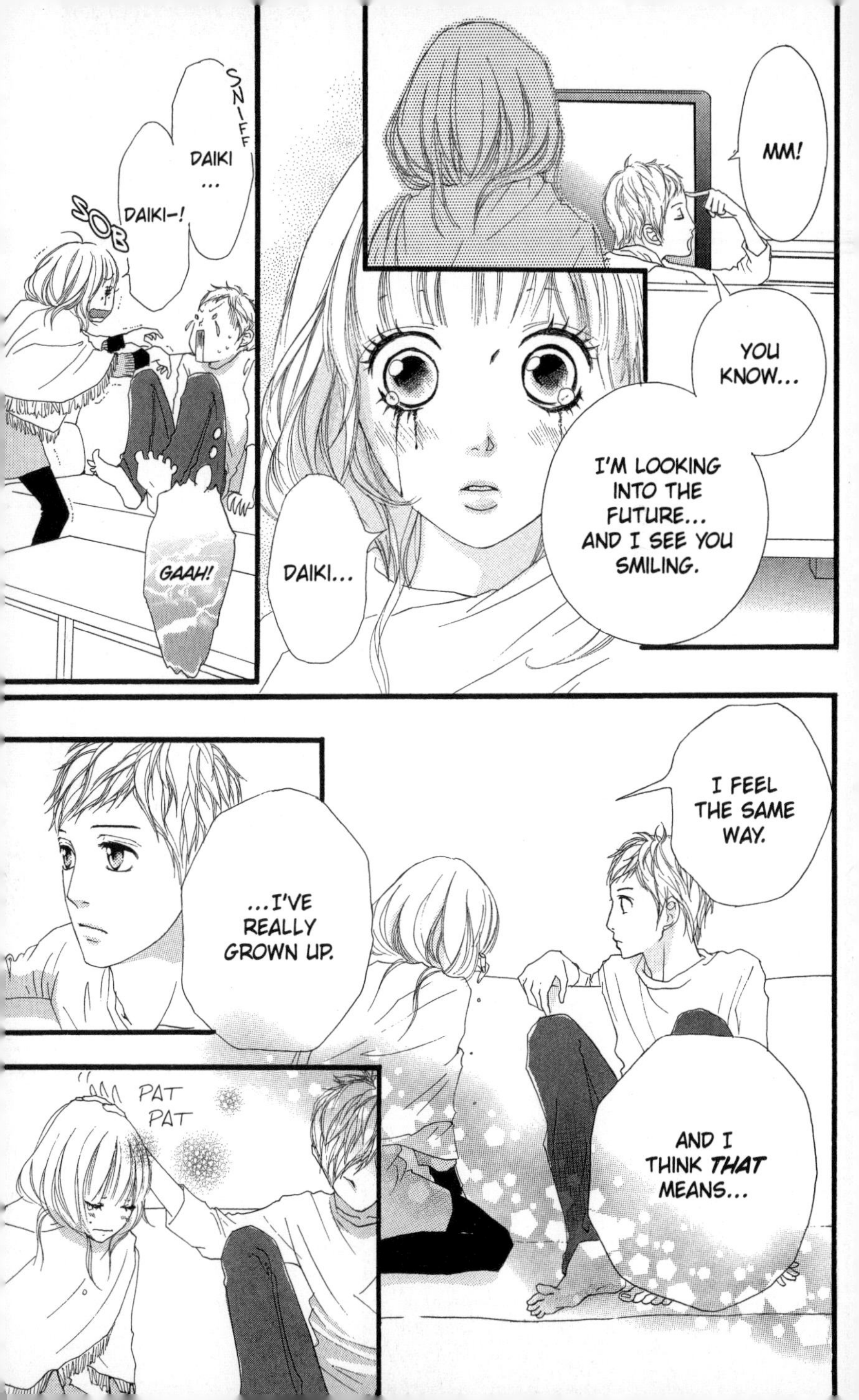
MM!
YOU KNOW...
I'M LOOKING INTO THE FUTURE... AND I SEE YOU SMILING.
DAIKI...
SNIFF
DAIKI ...
DAIKI-!
SOB
GAAH!
I FEEL THE SAME WAY.
AND I THINK *THAT* MEANS...
...I'VE REALLY GROWN UP.
PAT PAT

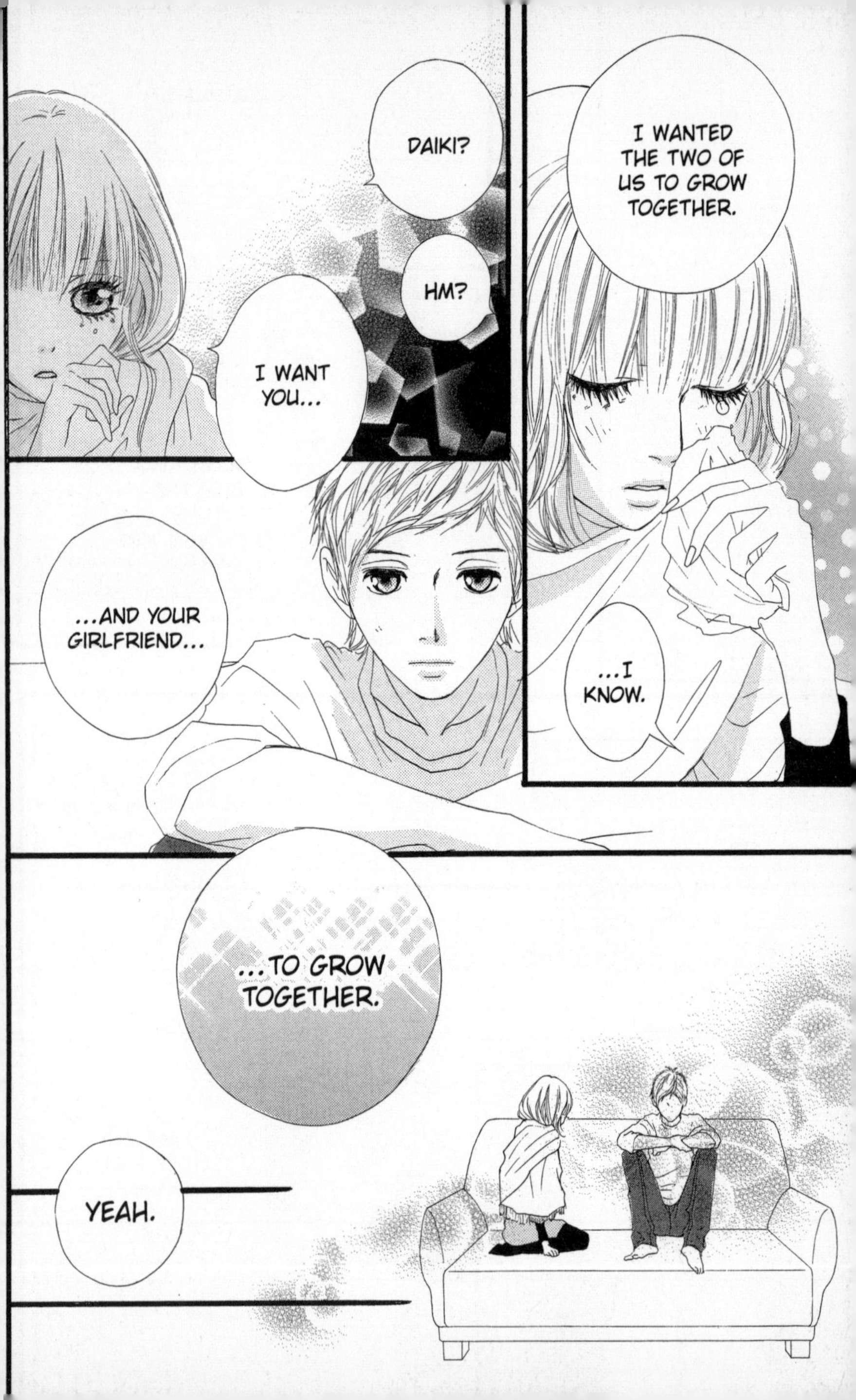
I WANTED THE TWO OF US TO GROW TOGETHER.
...I KNOW.
DAIKI?
HM?
I WANT YOU...
...AND YOUR GIRLFRIEND...
...TO GROW TOGETHER.
YEAH.

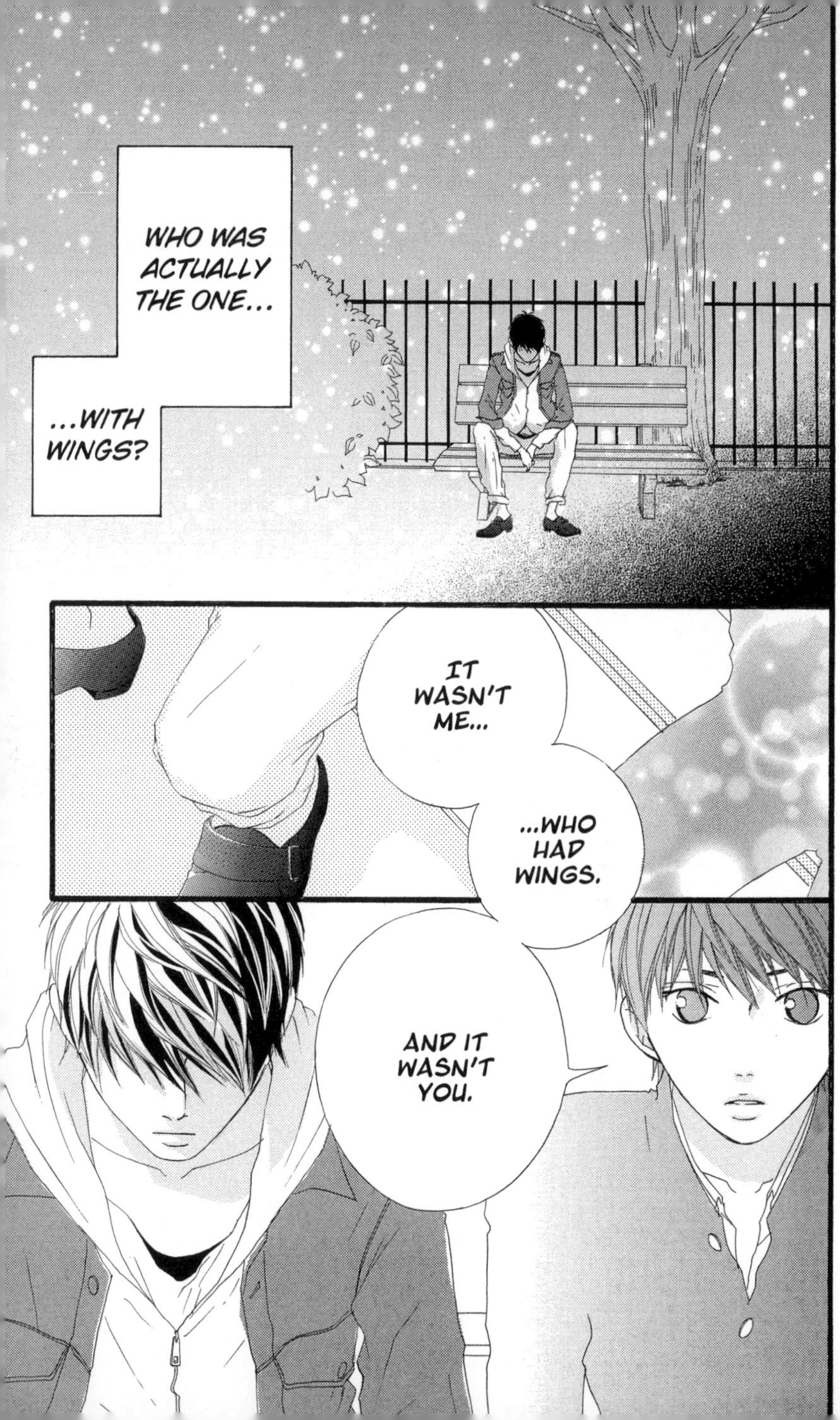
WHO WAS ACTUALLY THE ONE...
...WITH WINGS?
IT WASN'T ME...
...WHO HAD WINGS.
AND IT WASN'T YOU.

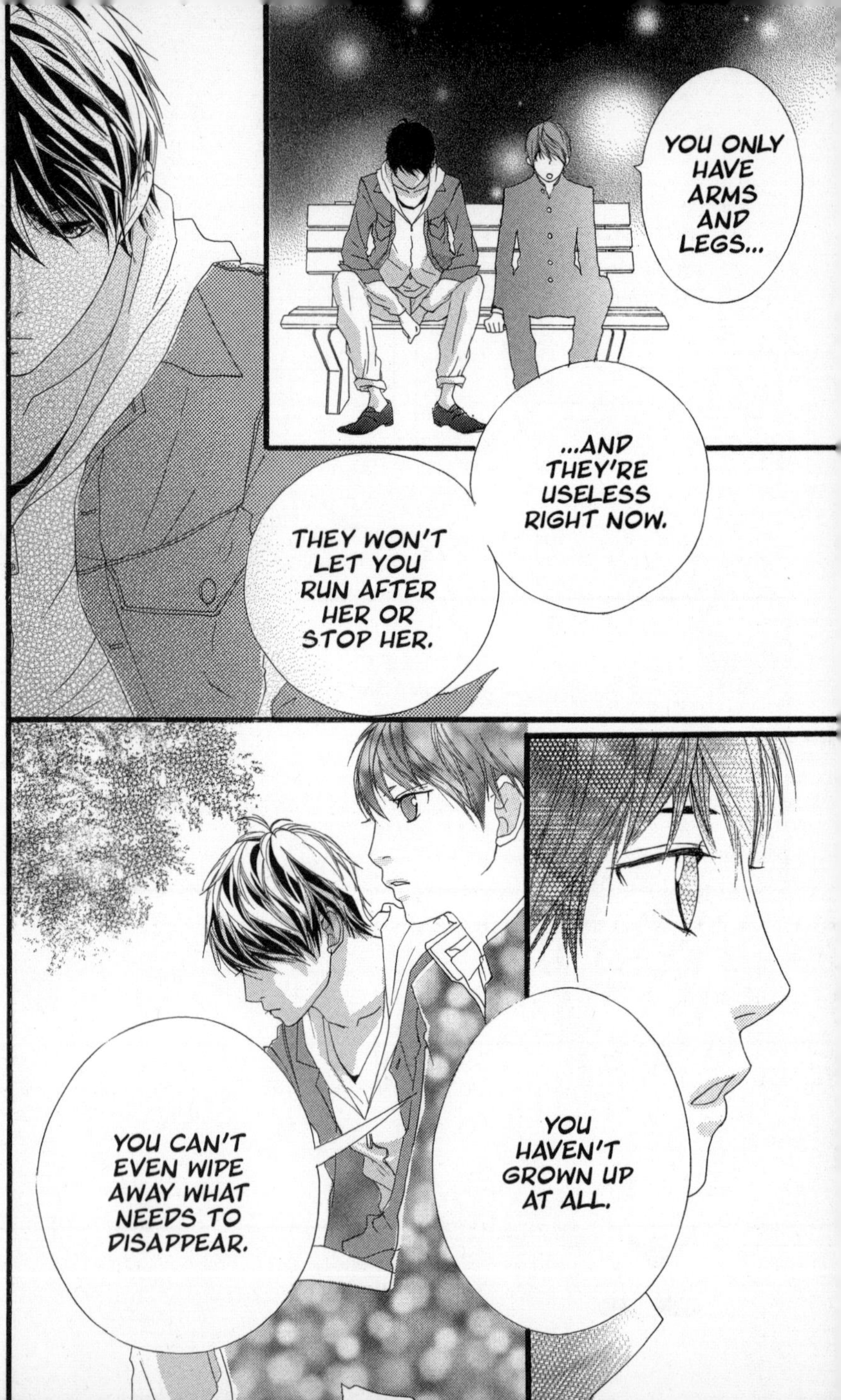
YOU ONLY HAVE ARMS AND LEGS...
...AND THEY'RE USELESS RIGHT NOW.
THEY WON'T LET YOU RUN AFTER HER OR STOP HER.
YOU HAVEN'T GROWN UP AT ALL.
YOU CAN'T EVEN WIPE AWAY WHAT NEEDS TO DISAPPEAR.

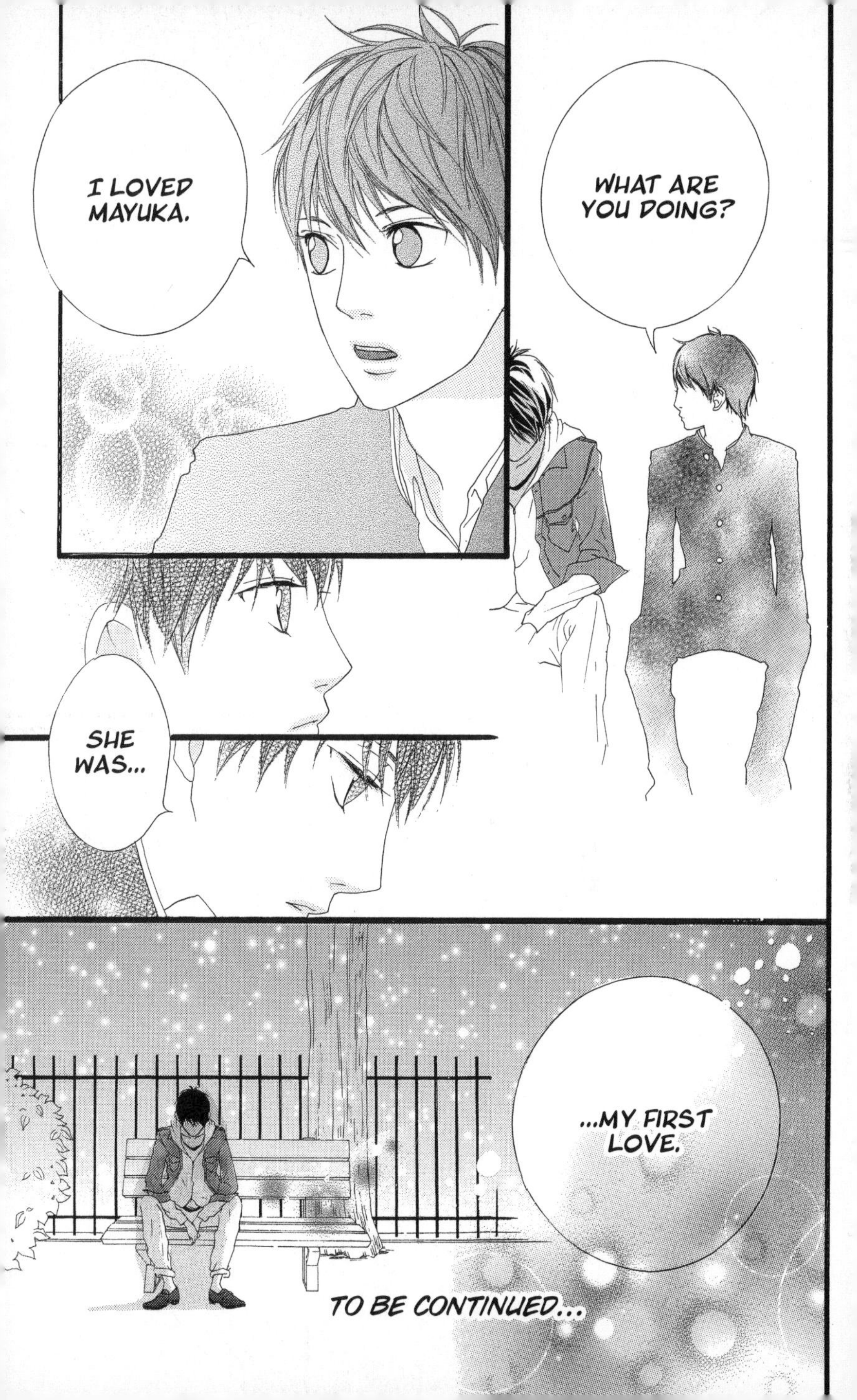
WHAT ARE YOU DOING?
I LOVED MAYUKA.
SHE WAS...
...MY FIRST LOVE.
TO BE CONTINUED...

ONE LAST STEP BEFORE THE AFTERWORD!

Lately, I've been feeling truly blessed for being surrounded by such good people. My editor, my fellow artists, my neighborhood friends—they're all beautiful, well-rounded people. Isn't that amazing?

Because I get to do my work while surrounded by these people, I haven't had to deal with work-related stress. Sometimes it's physically taxing (including some personal issues), but it's nothing I can't overcome. It's because the goodness of the people around me has a healing effect. (Including your letters!) (Energy drinks help too!)

I'm surrounded by hard workers who serve as my role models. They're so inspiring! Even an irresponsible person like me gets motivated: Do your best or don't do it at all!

I wish I'd learned that sooner...

BE WELL-ROUNDED AND DO YOUR BEST!

That will be my motto as I continue with my endeavors. Please continue to give me your support!

★ Io Sakisaka ★

Lately, I'm also shocked at how "well-rounded" my body has become.

Round

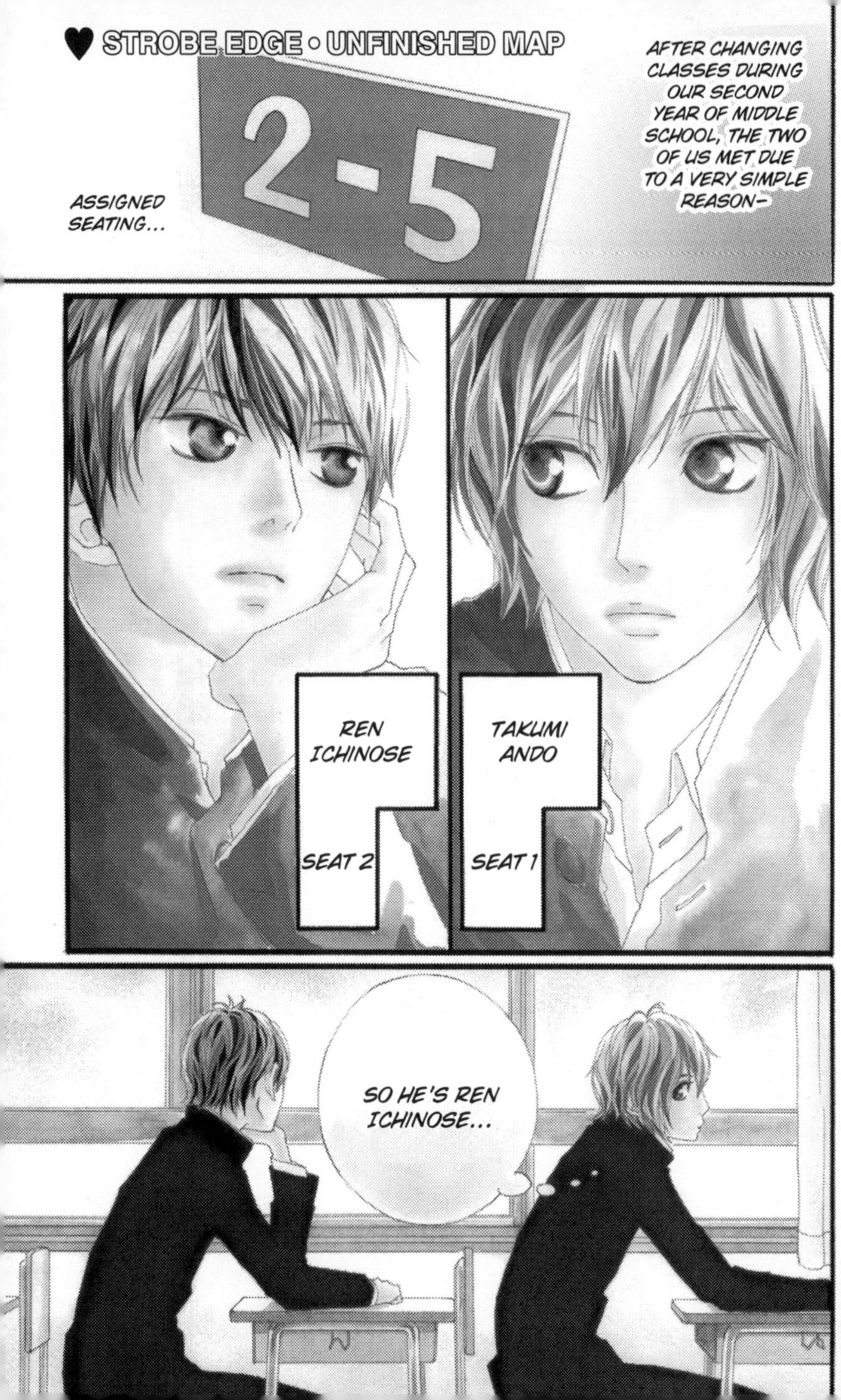
AFTER CHANGING CLASSES DURING OUR SECOND YEAR OF MIDDLE SCHOOL, THE TWO OF US MET DUE TO A VERY SIMPLE REASON–
2-5
ASSIGNED SEATING...
TAKUMI ANDO
SEAT 1
REN ICHINOSE
SEAT 2
SO HE'S REN ICHINOSE...

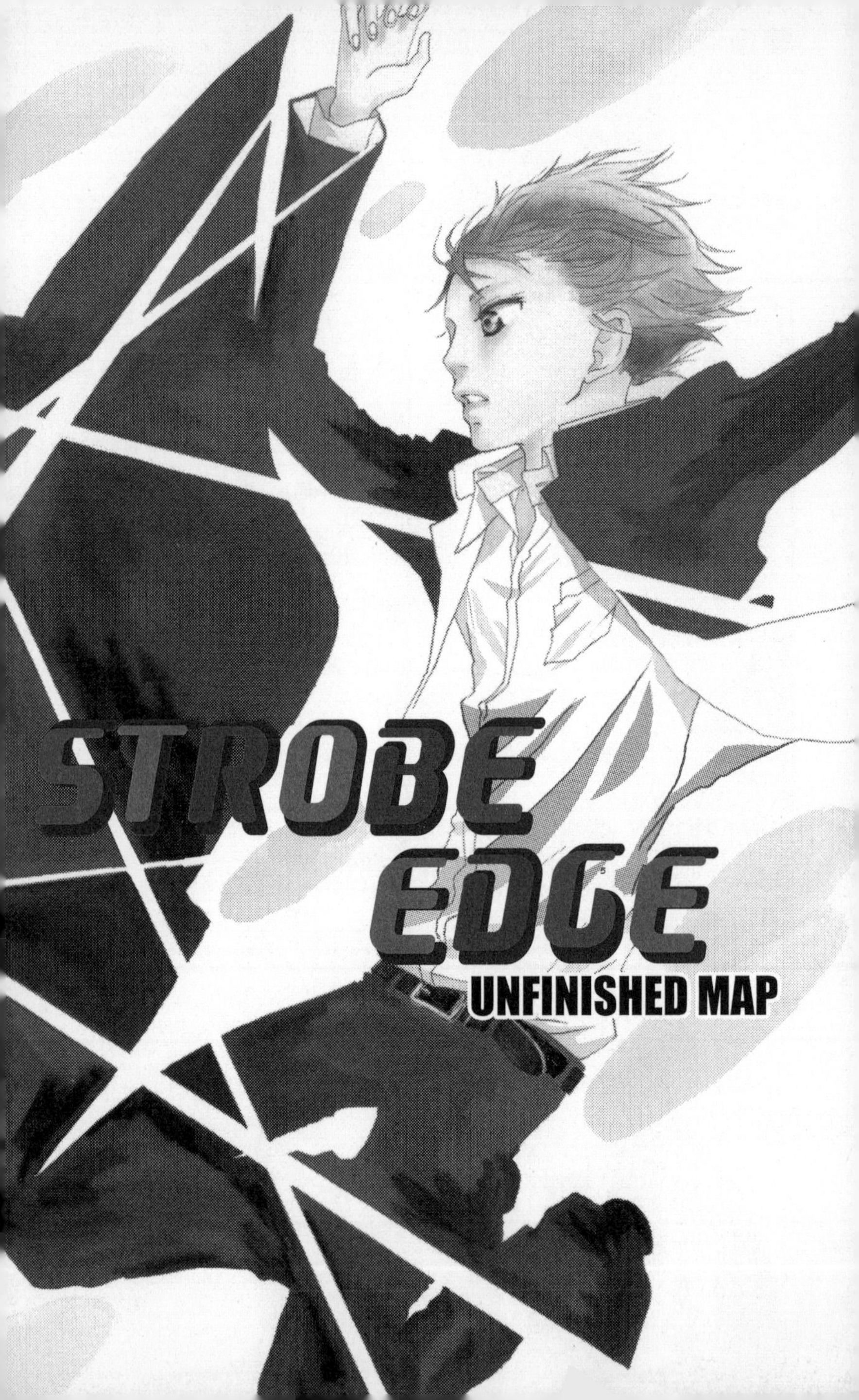
STROBE EDGE
UNFINISHED MAP

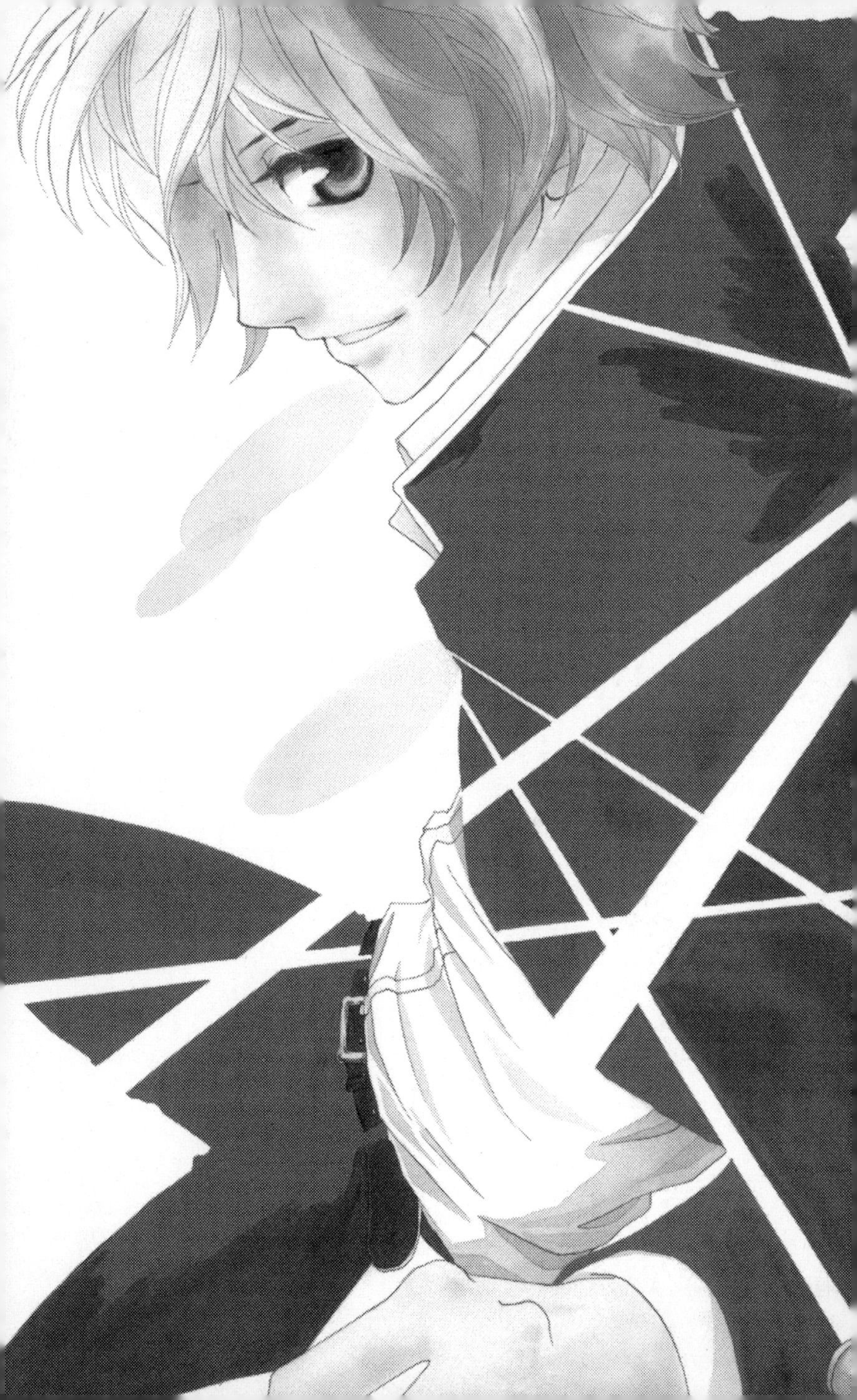

STROBE EDGE BONUS CHAPTER
ABOUT "UNFINISHED MAP"

Ando and Ren are in middle school at this point, and Ando is the main character in this story.

I've always wanted to touch on Ando and Ren's past in *Strobe Edge*, so when I was asked if I wanted to do a bonus chapter, I immediately said, "Yes! About Ando and Ren!"

I've been dying to write about them, so my vision grew and grew and grew... I was afraid 30 pages wouldn't be enough.

I was hoping to capture the tenderness and heartache of adolescence. Who cares if you lose your way, as long as you try your best? I wanted to return to my own middle school years and get another chance to study hard. Waaah! Robot cat Doraemon! Lend me your pocket time machine! That's all I want from you! I'm getting off topic... (On purpose! ☆)

Please enjoy this *Strobe Edge* bonus chapter, "Unfinished Map"!

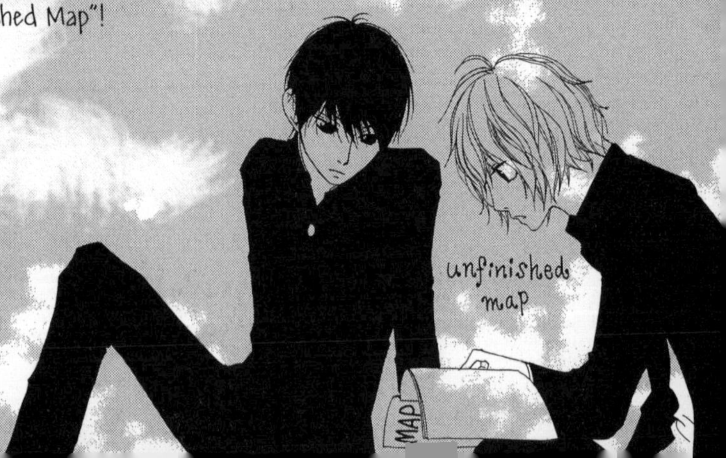
unfinished
map
MAP

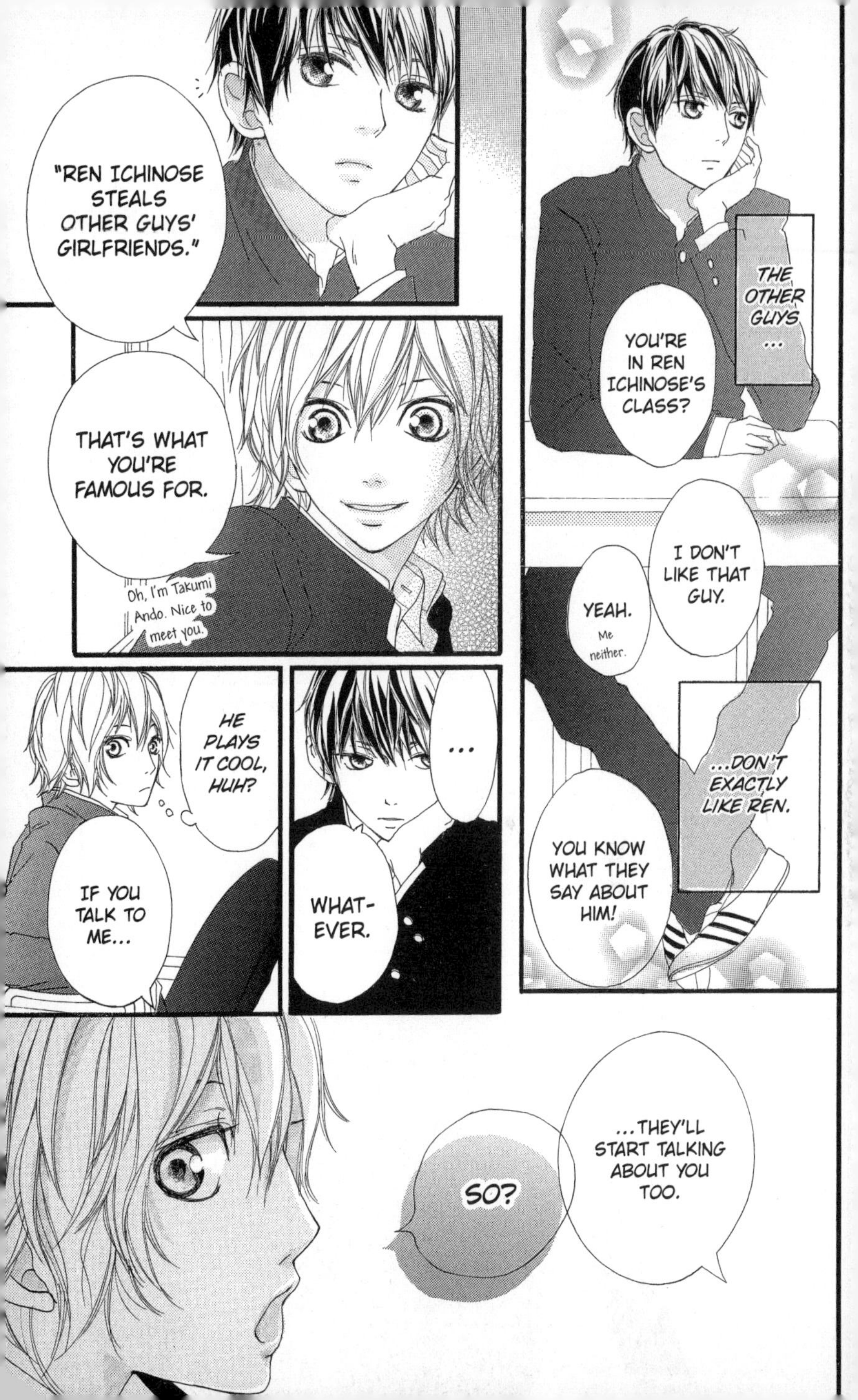
THE OTHER GUYS...
YOU'RE IN REN ICHINOSE'S CLASS?
I DON'T LIKE THAT GUY.
YEAH.
Me neither.
...DON'T EXACTLY LIKE REN.
YOU KNOW WHAT THEY SAY ABOUT HIM!
"REN ICHINOSE STEALS OTHER GUYS' GIRLFRIENDS."
THAT'S WHAT YOU'RE FAMOUS FOR.
Oh, I'm Takumi Ando. Nice to meet you.
...
WHAT-EVER.
HE PLAYS IT COOL, HUH?
IF YOU TALK TO ME...
...THEY'LL START TALKING ABOUT YOU TOO.
SO?

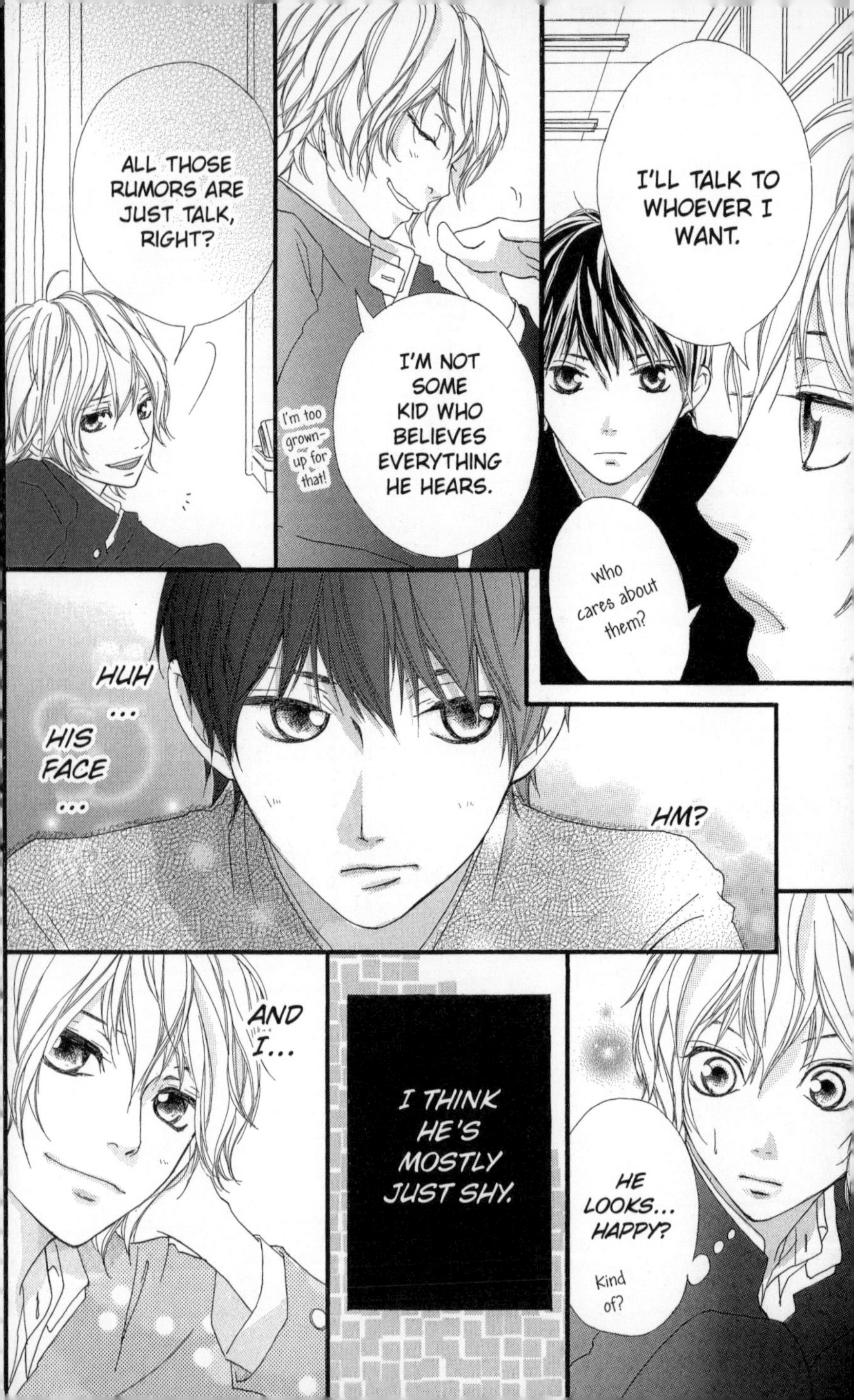
I'LL TALK TO WHOEVER I WANT.
Who cares about them?
I'M NOT SOME KID WHO BELIEVES EVERYTHING HE HEARS.
I'm too grown-up for that!
ALL THOSE RUMORS ARE JUST TALK, RIGHT?
HUH ... HIS FACE ...
HM?
HE LOOKS... HAPPY?
Kind of?
I THINK HE'S MOSTLY JUST SHY.
AND I...

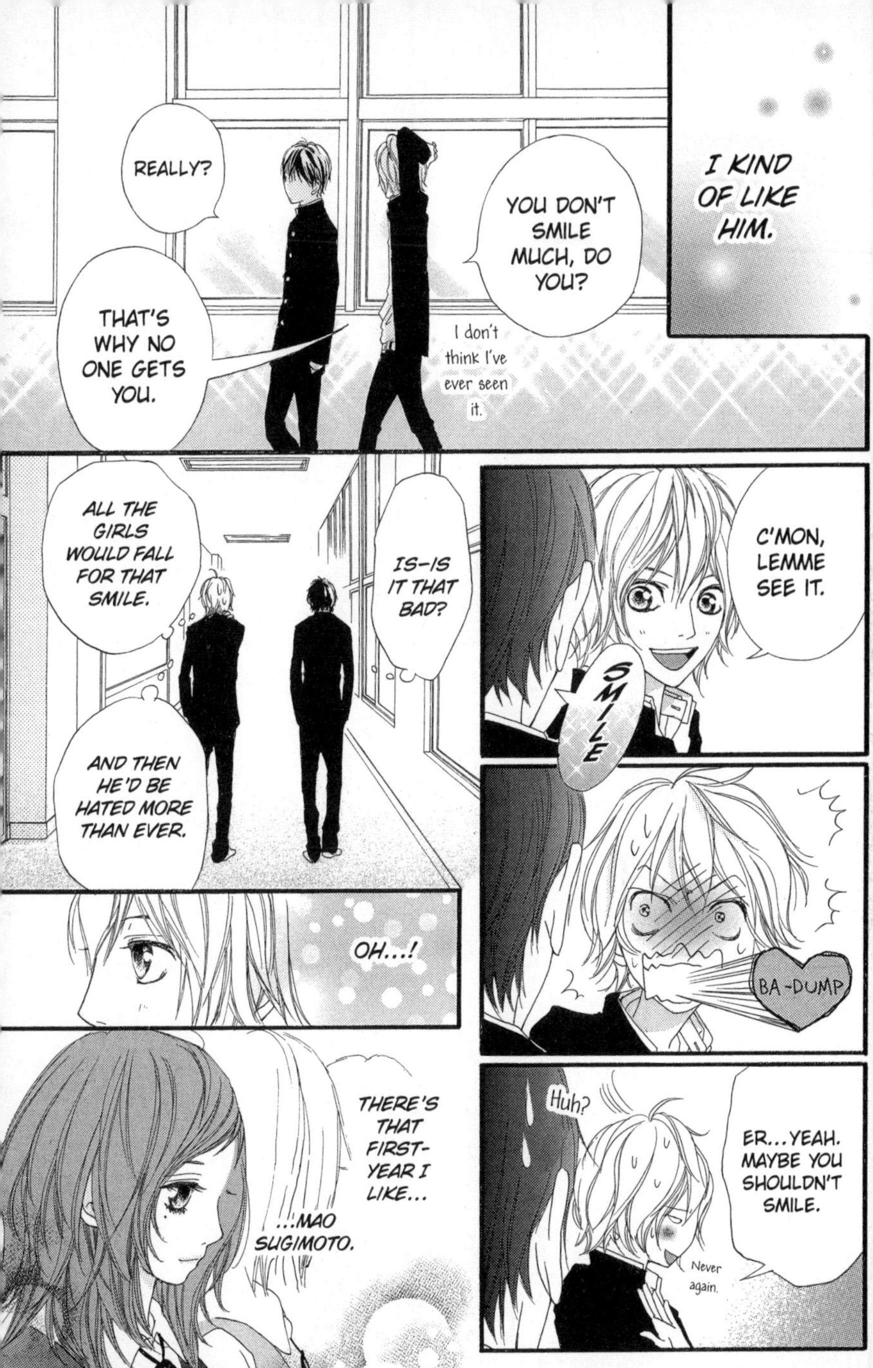
I KIND OF LIKE HIM.
YOU DON'T SMILE MUCH, DO YOU?
I don't think I've ever seen it.
REALLY?
THAT'S WHY NO ONE GETS YOU.
C'MON, LEMME SEE IT.
SMILE
BA-DUMP
Huh?
ER...YEAH. MAYBE YOU SHOULDN'T SMILE.
Never again.
IS-IS IT THAT BAD?
ALL THE GIRLS WOULD FALL FOR THAT SMILE.
AND THEN HE'D BE HATED MORE THAN EVER.
OH...!
THERE'S THAT FIRST-YEAR I LIKE...
...MAO SUGIMOTO.

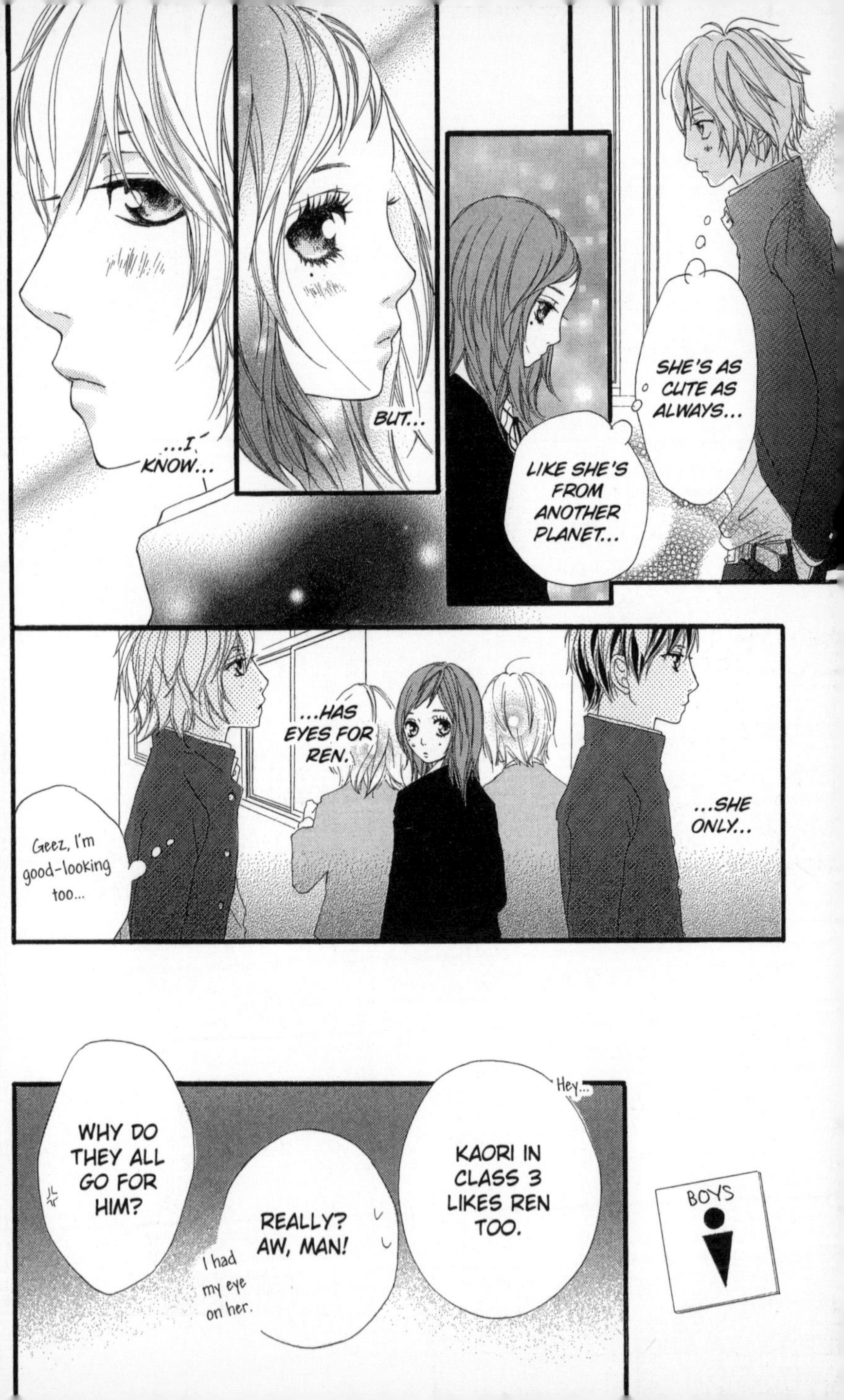
SHE'S AS CUTE AS ALWAYS...
LIKE SHE'S FROM ANOTHER PLANET...
BUT...
...I KNOW...
...SHE ONLY...
...HAS EYES FOR REN.
Geez, I'm good-looking too...
BOYS
Hey...
KAORI IN CLASS 3 LIKES REN TOO.
REALLY? AW, MAN!
I had my eye on her.
WHY DO THEY ALL GO FOR HIM?

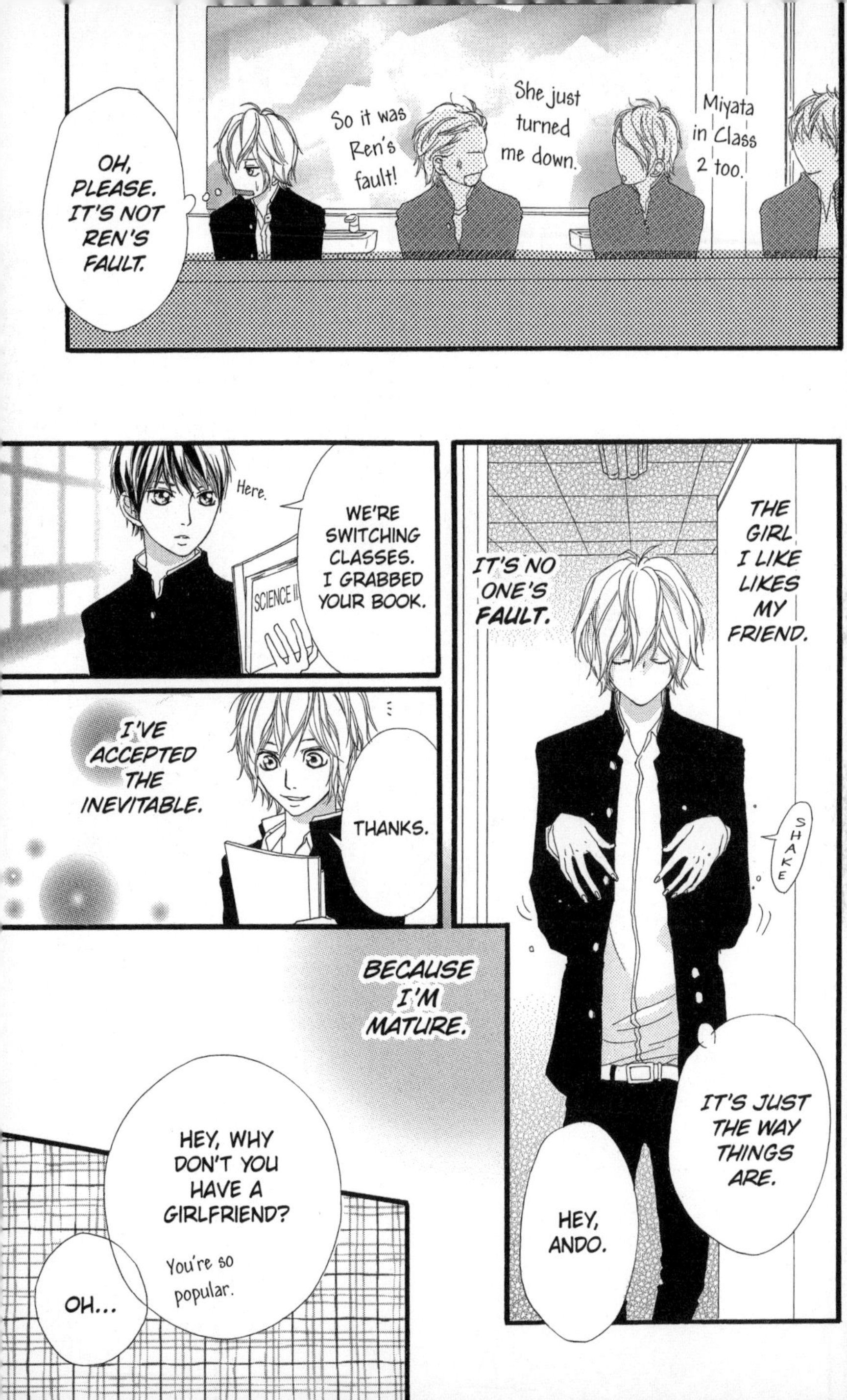
Miyata in Class 2 too.
She just turned me down.
So it was Ren's fault!
OH, PLEASE. IT'S NOT REN'S FAULT.
THE GIRL I LIKE LIKES MY FRIEND.
IT'S NO ONE'S FAULT.
SHAKE
IT'S JUST THE WAY THINGS ARE.
HEY, ANDO.
WE'RE SWITCHING CLASSES. I GRABBED YOUR BOOK.
Here.
SCIENCE II
THANKS.
I'VE ACCEPTED THE INEVITABLE.
BECAUSE I'M MATURE.
HEY, WHY DON'T YOU HAVE A GIRLFRIEND?
You're so popular.
OH...

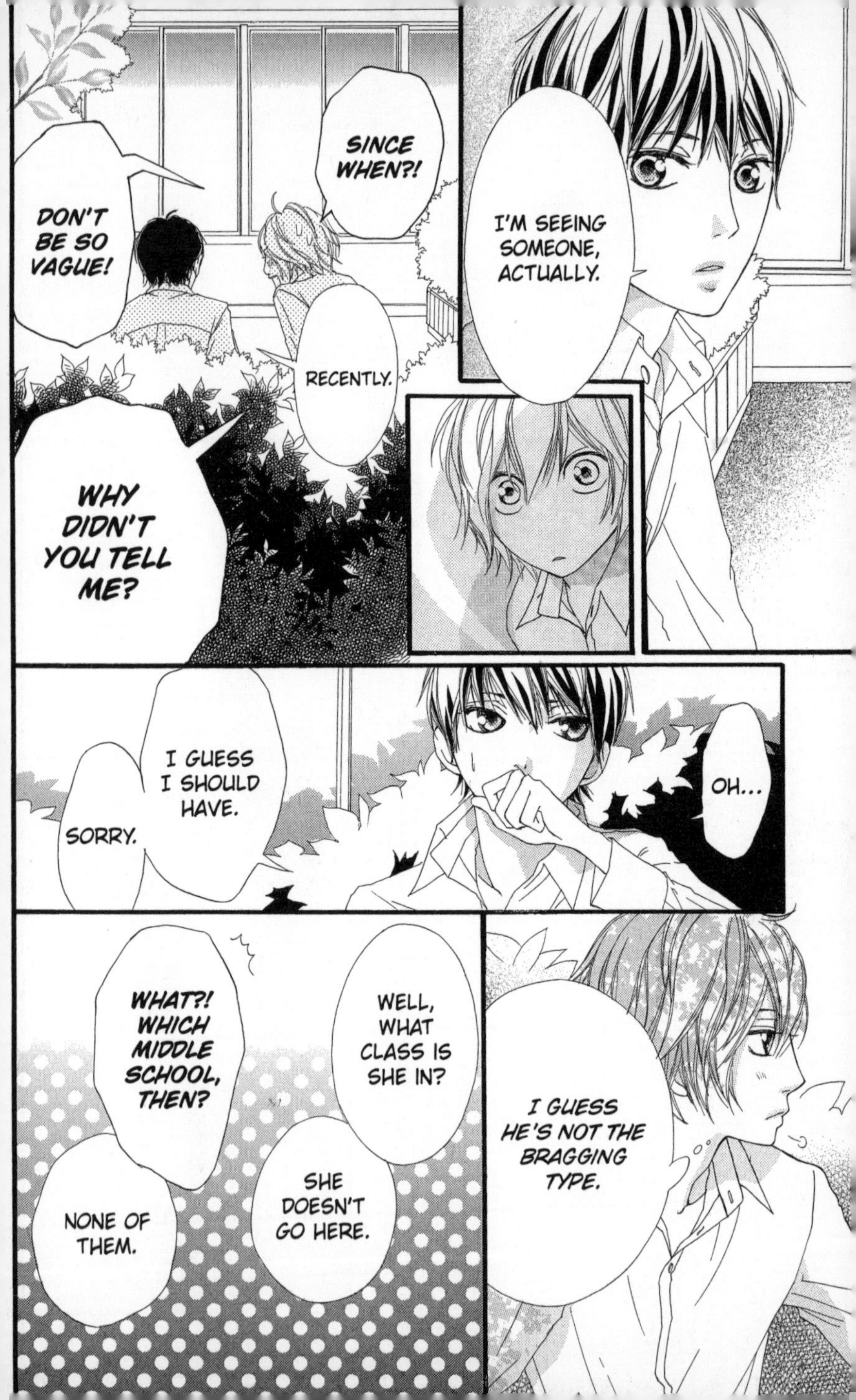
I'M SEEING SOMEONE, ACTUALLY.
SINCE WHEN?!
RECENTLY.
DON'T BE SO VAGUE!
WHY DIDN'T YOU TELL ME?
OH...
I GUESS I SHOULD HAVE.
SORRY.
I GUESS HE'S NOT THE BRAGGING TYPE.
WELL, WHAT CLASS IS SHE IN?
SHE DOESN'T GO HERE.
WHAT?! WHICH MIDDLE SCHOOL, THEN?
NONE OF THEM.

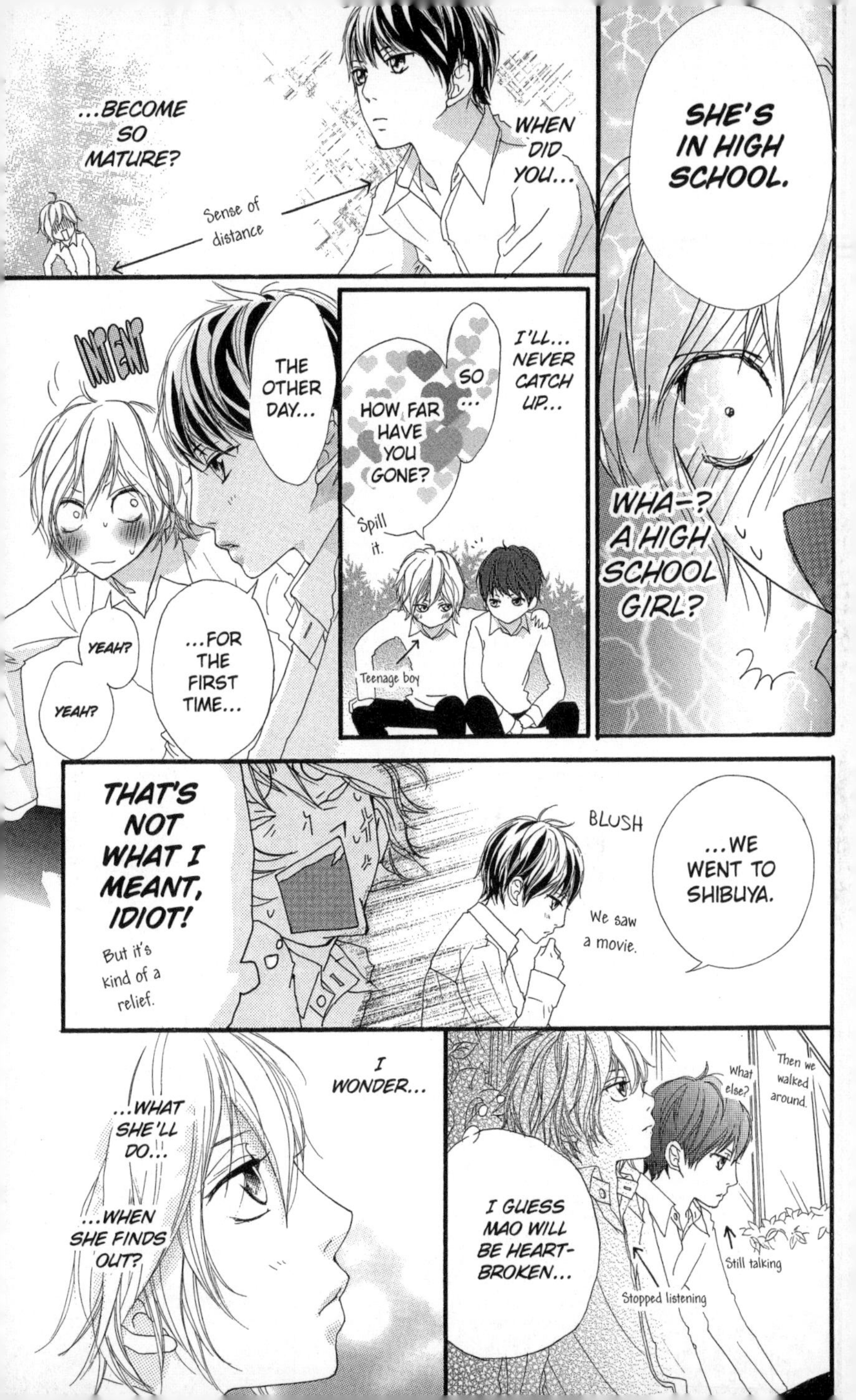
SHE'S IN HIGH SCHOOL.
WHA-? A HIGH SCHOOL GIRL?
WHEN DID YOU...
...BECOME SO MATURE?
Sense of distance
I'LL... NEVER CATCH UP...
SO... HOW FAR HAVE YOU GONE?
Spill it.
Teenage boy
INTENT
THE OTHER DAY...
...FOR THE FIRST TIME...
YEAH?
YEAH?
...WE WENT TO SHIBUYA.
BLUSH
We saw a movie.
THAT'S NOT WHAT I MEANT, IDIOT!
But it's kind of a relief.
Then we walked around.
What else?
I GUESS MAO WILL BE HEART-BROKEN...
Still talking
Stopped listening
I WONDER...
...WHAT SHE'LL DO...
...WHEN SHE FINDS OUT?

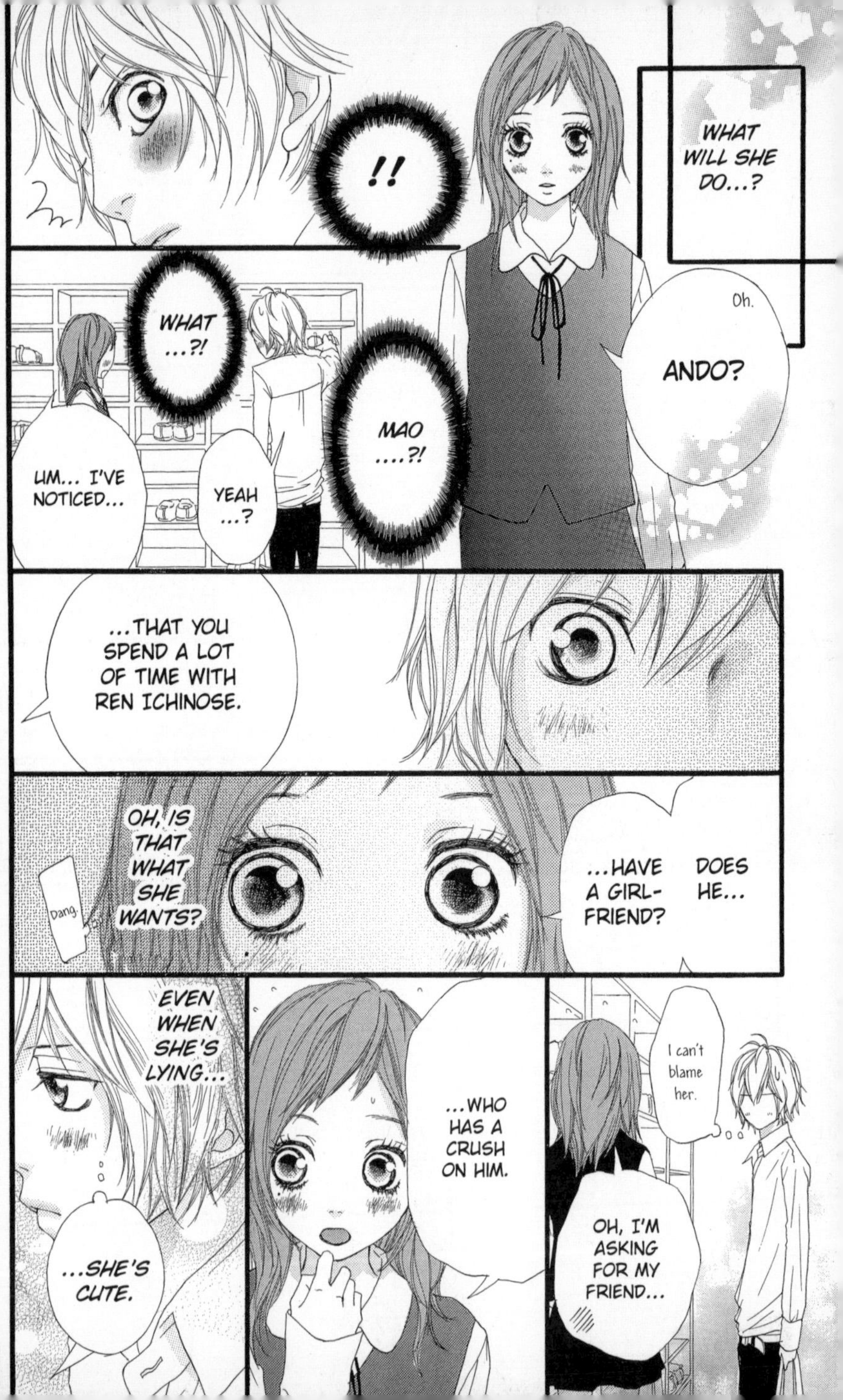
WHAT WILL SHE DO...?
Oh.
ANDO?
!!
MAO ....?!
WHAT ...?!
YEAH ...?
UM... I'VE NOTICED...
...THAT YOU SPEND A LOT OF TIME WITH REN ICHINOSE.
DOES HE...
...HAVE A GIRL-FRIEND?
OH, IS THAT WHAT SHE WANTS?
Dang.
I can't blame her.
OH, I'M ASKING FOR MY FRIEND...
...WHO HAS A CRUSH ON HIM.
EVEN WHEN SHE'S LYING...
...SHE'S CUTE.

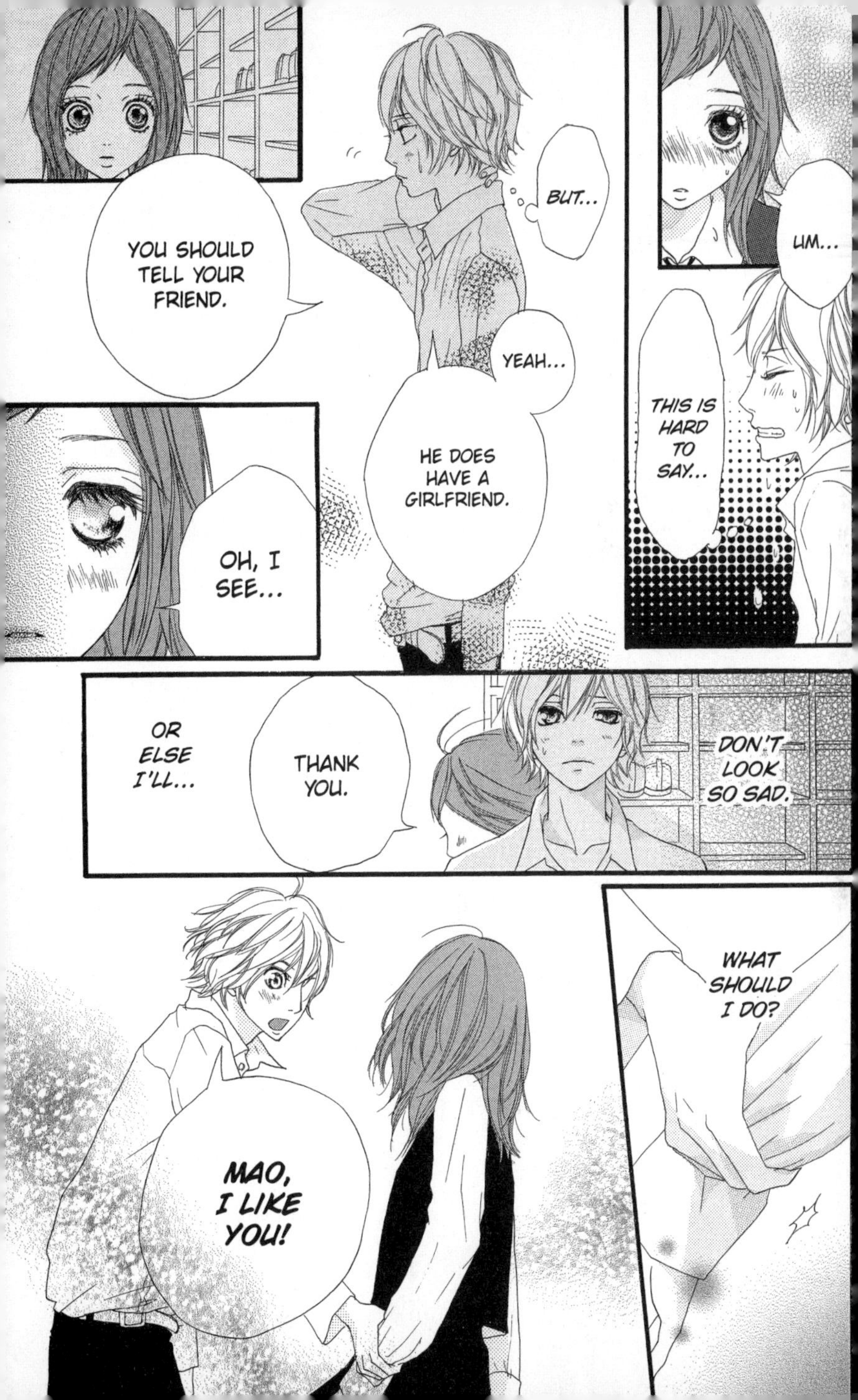
UM...
THIS IS HARD TO SAY...
BUT...
YEAH...
HE DOES HAVE A GIRLFRIEND.
YOU SHOULD TELL YOUR FRIEND.
OH, I SEE...
DON'T LOOK SO SAD.
THANK YOU.
OR ELSE I'LL...
WHAT SHOULD I DO?
MAO, I LIKE YOU!

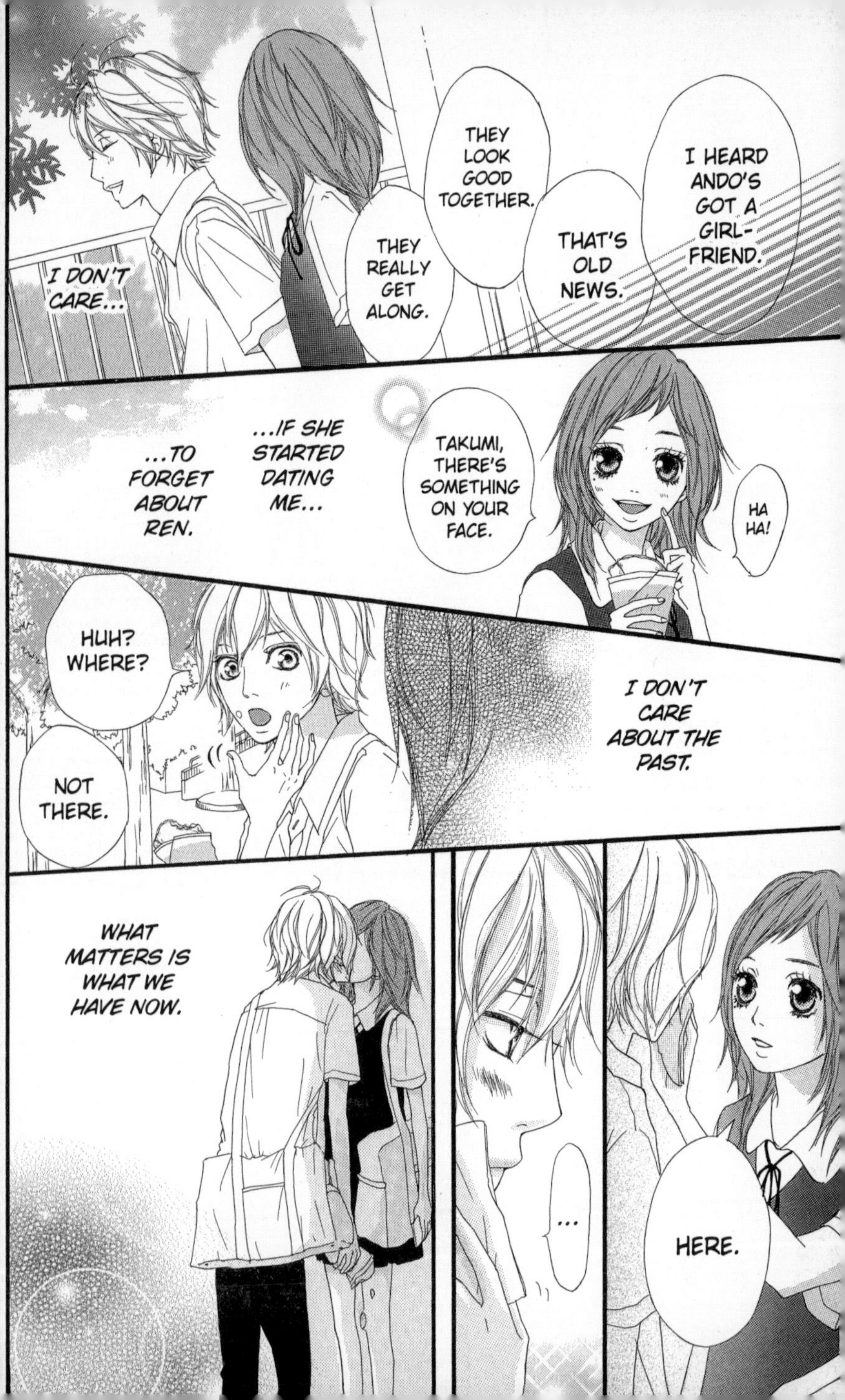
I HEARD ANDO'S GOT A GIRL-FRIEND.
THAT'S OLD NEWS.
THEY LOOK GOOD TOGETHER.
THEY REALLY GET ALONG.
I DON'T CARE...
HA HA!
TAKUMI, THERE'S SOMETHING ON YOUR FACE.
...IF SHE STARTED DATING ME...
...TO FORGET ABOUT REN.
I DON'T CARE ABOUT THE PAST.
HUH? WHERE?
NOT THERE.
HERE.
...
WHAT MATTERS IS WHAT WE HAVE NOW.

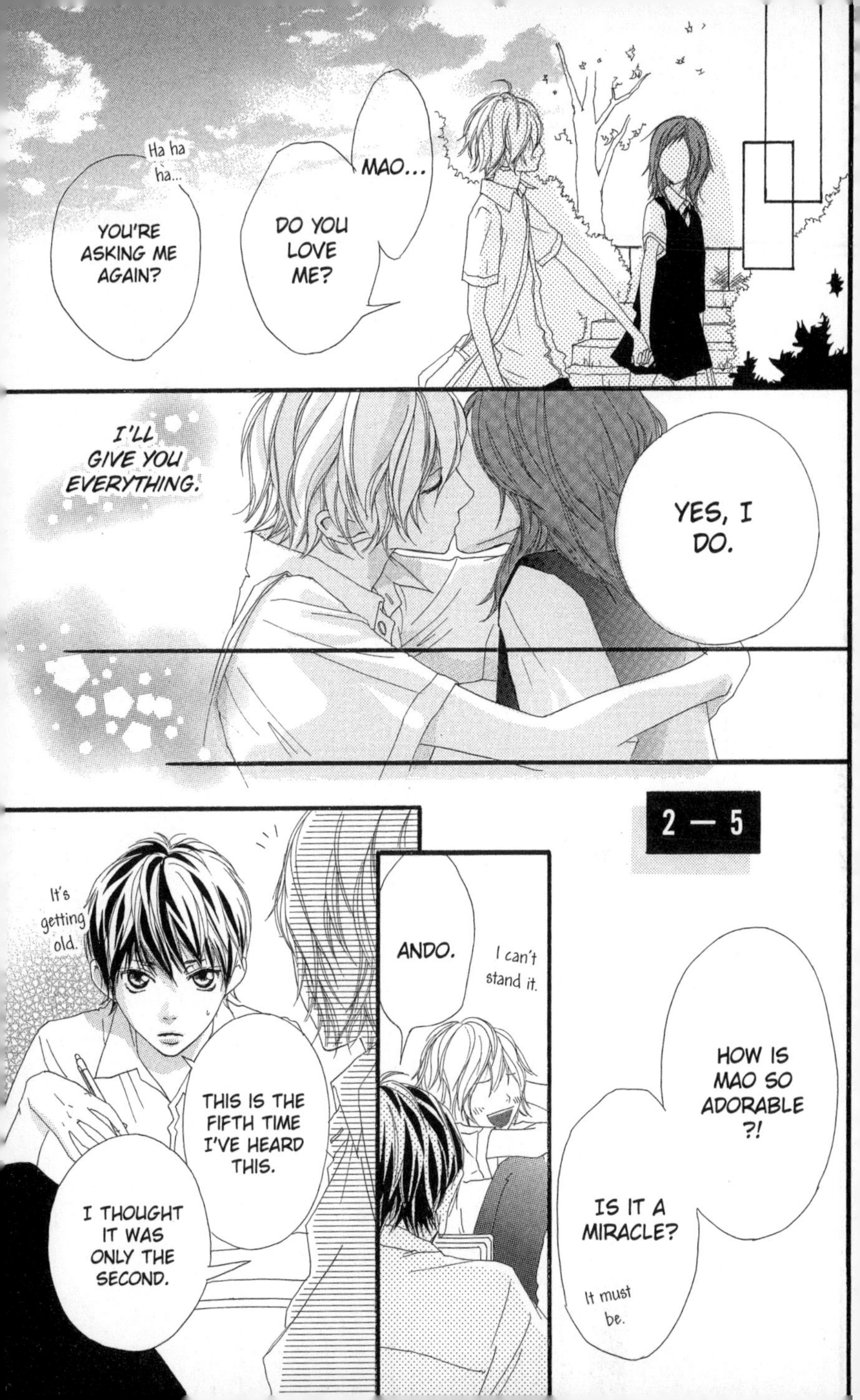
MAO...
DO YOU LOVE ME?
Ha ha ha...
YOU'RE ASKING ME AGAIN?
YES, I DO.
I'LL GIVE YOU EVERYTHING.
2 — 5
HOW IS MAO SO ADORABLE ?!
IS IT A MIRACLE?
It must be.
ANDO.
I can't stand it.
It's getting old.
THIS IS THE FIFTH TIME I'VE HEARD THIS.
I THOUGHT IT WAS ONLY THE SECOND.

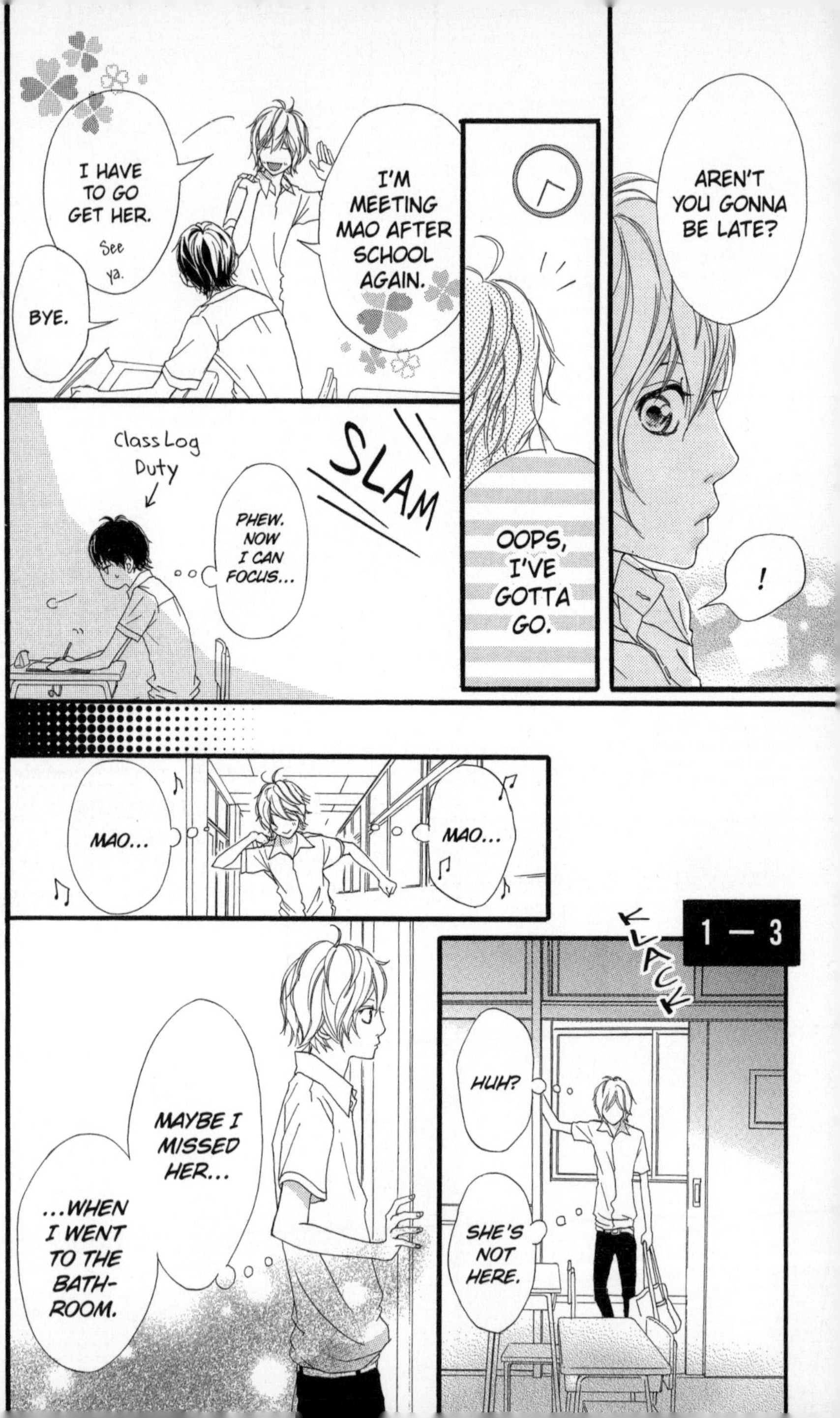
AREN'T YOU GONNA BE LATE?
!
OOPS, I'VE GOTTA GO.
I'M MEETING MAO AFTER SCHOOL AGAIN.
I HAVE TO GO GET HER.
See ya.
BYE.
SLAM
PHEW. NOW I CAN FOCUS...
Class Log Duty
MAO...
MAO...
1—3
KLACK
HUH?
SHE'S NOT HERE.
MAYBE I MISSED HER...
...WHEN I WENT TO THE BATHROOM.

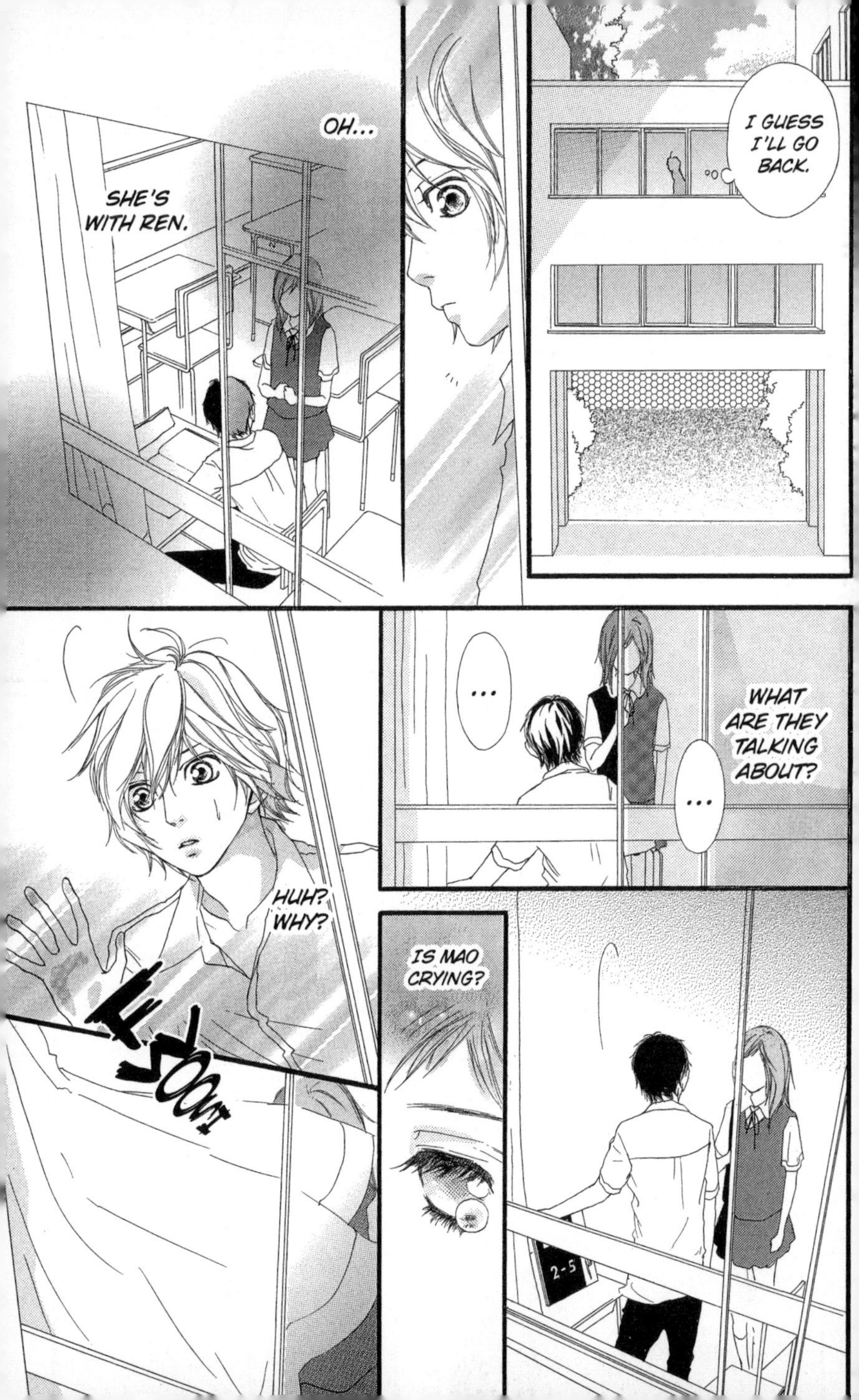
I GUESS I'LL GO BACK.
OH...
SHE'S WITH REN.
WHAT ARE THEY TALKING ABOUT?
...
...
IS MAO CRYING?
HUH? WHY?
FSOOM!

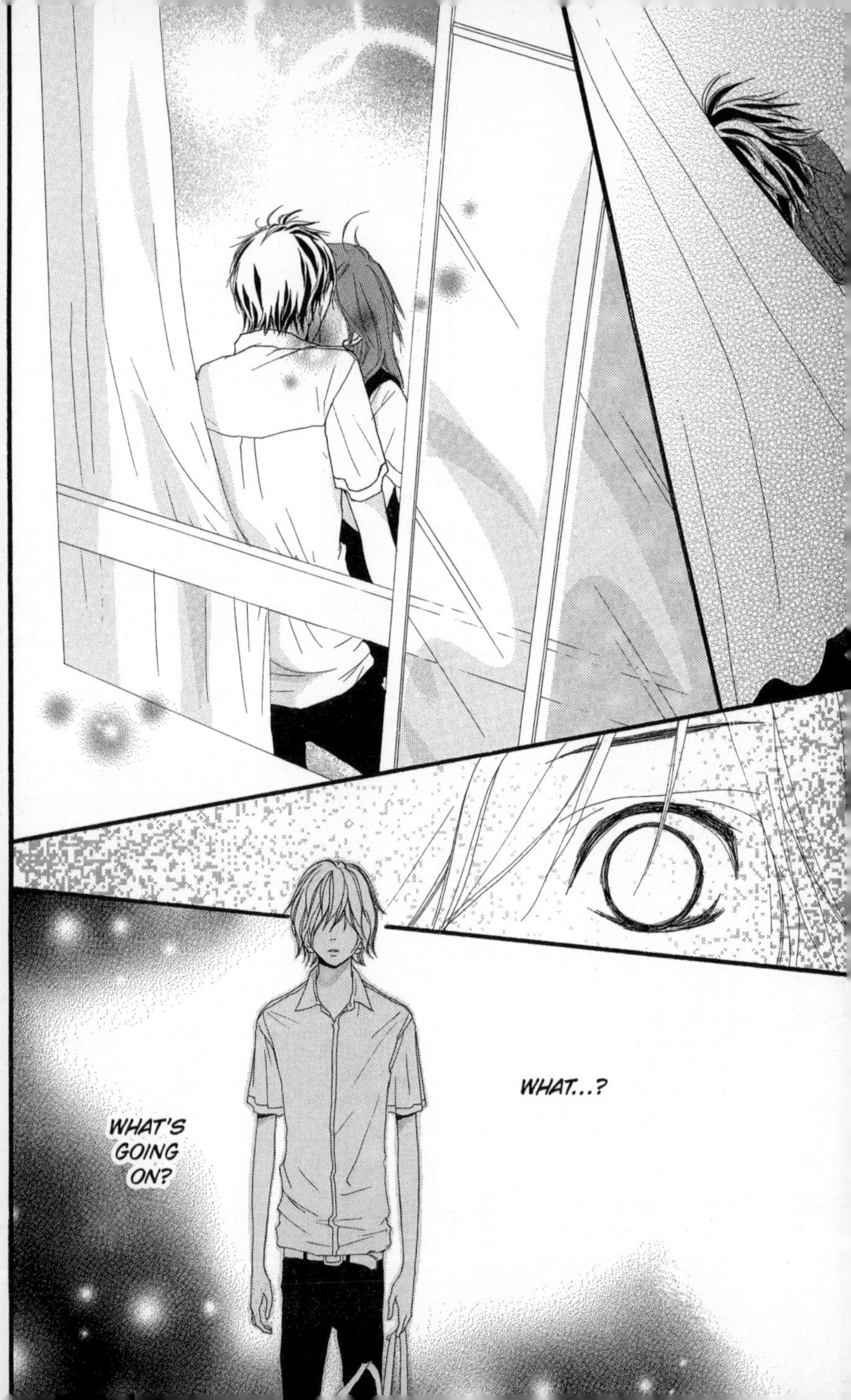
WHAT...?
WHAT'S GOING ON?

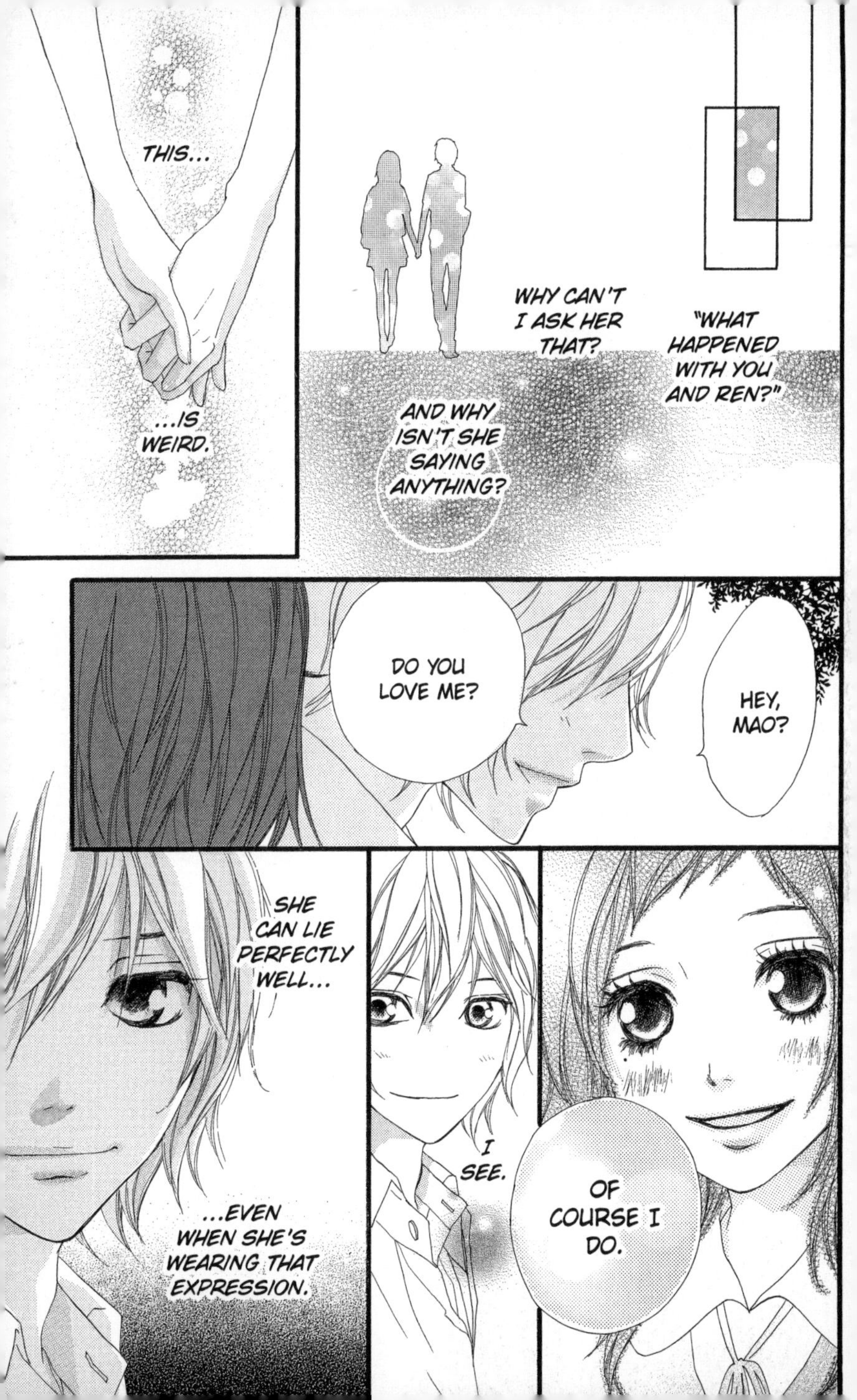
"WHAT HAPPENED WITH YOU AND REN?"
WHY CAN'T I ASK HER THAT?
AND WHY ISN'T SHE SAYING ANYTHING?
THIS...
...IS WEIRD.
HEY, MAO?
DO YOU LOVE ME?
OF COURSE I DO.
I SEE.
SHE CAN LIE PERFECTLY WELL...
...EVEN WHEN SHE'S WEARING THAT EXPRESSION.

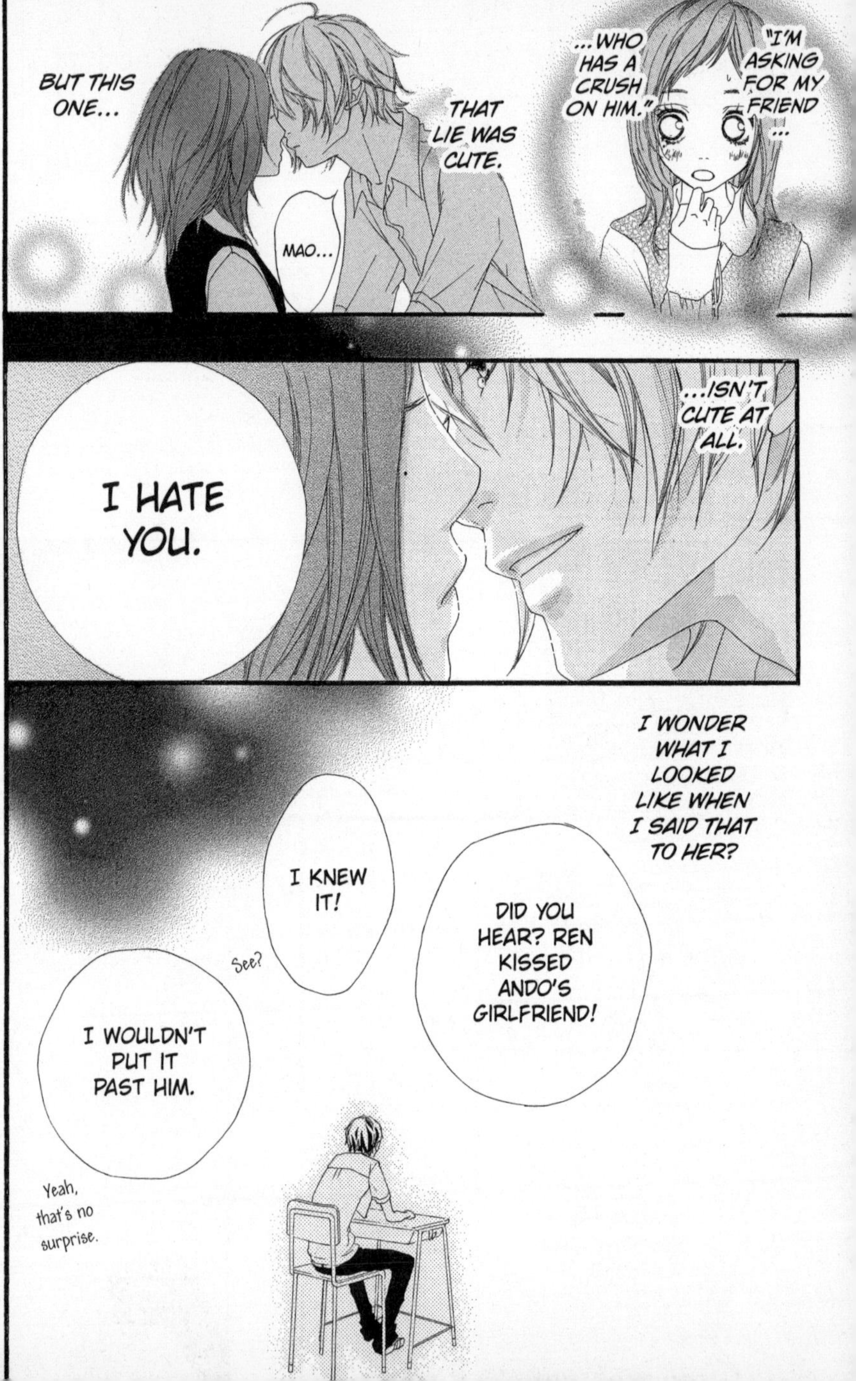
"I'M ASKING FOR MY FRIEND ...
...WHO HAS A CRUSH ON HIM."
THAT LIE WAS CUTE.
MAO...
BUT THIS ONE...
...ISN'T CUTE AT ALL.
I HATE YOU.
I WONDER WHAT I LOOKED LIKE WHEN I SAID THAT TO HER?
DID YOU HEAR? REN KISSED ANDO'S GIRLFRIEND!
I KNEW IT!
See?
I WOULDN'T PUT IT PAST HIM.
Yeah, that's no surprise.

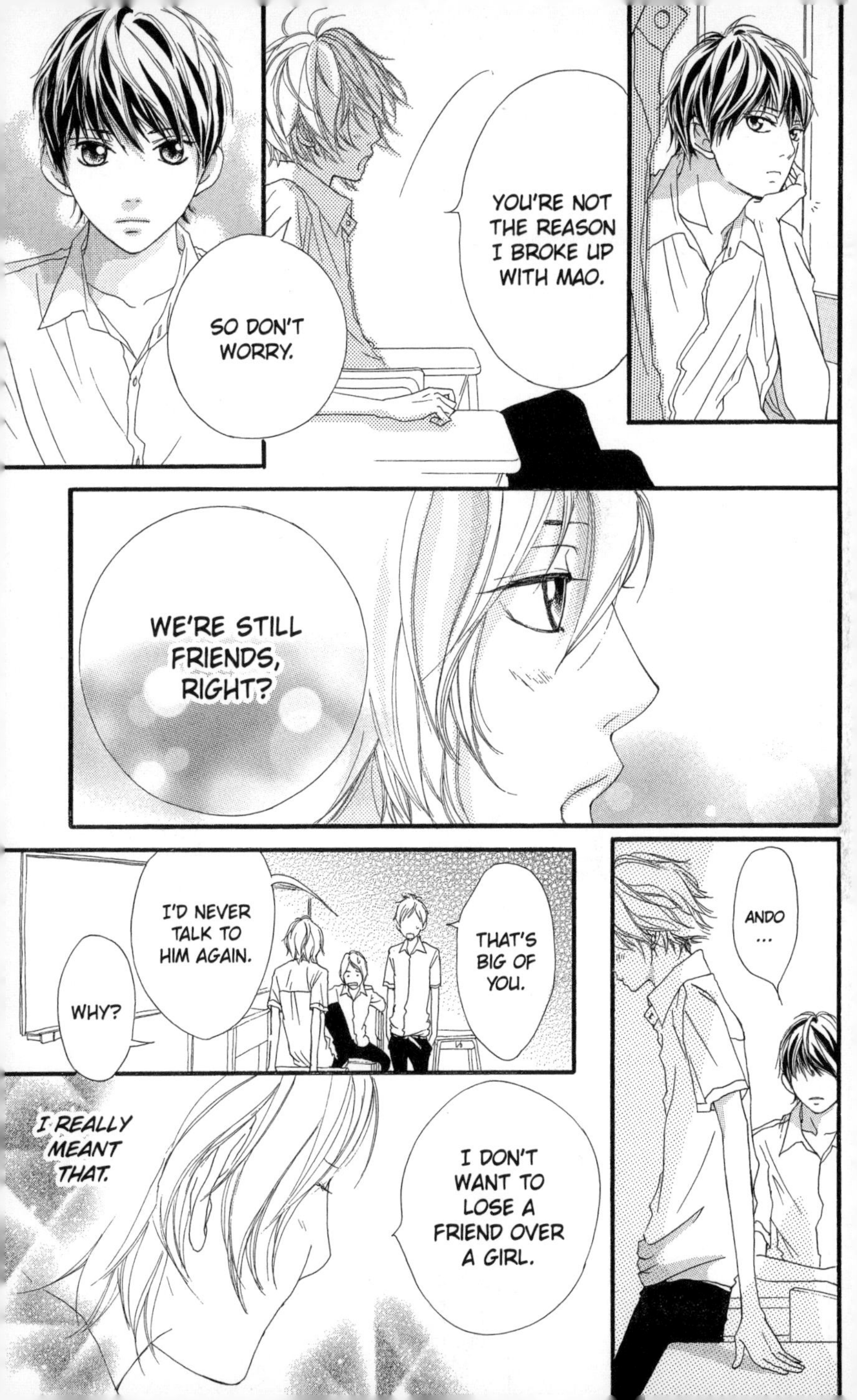
YOU'RE NOT THE REASON I BROKE UP WITH MAO.
SO DON'T WORRY.
WE'RE STILL FRIENDS, RIGHT?
ANDO...
THAT'S BIG OF YOU.
I'D NEVER TALK TO HIM AGAIN.
WHY?
I DON'T WANT TO LOSE A FRIEND OVER A GIRL.
I REALLY MEANT THAT.

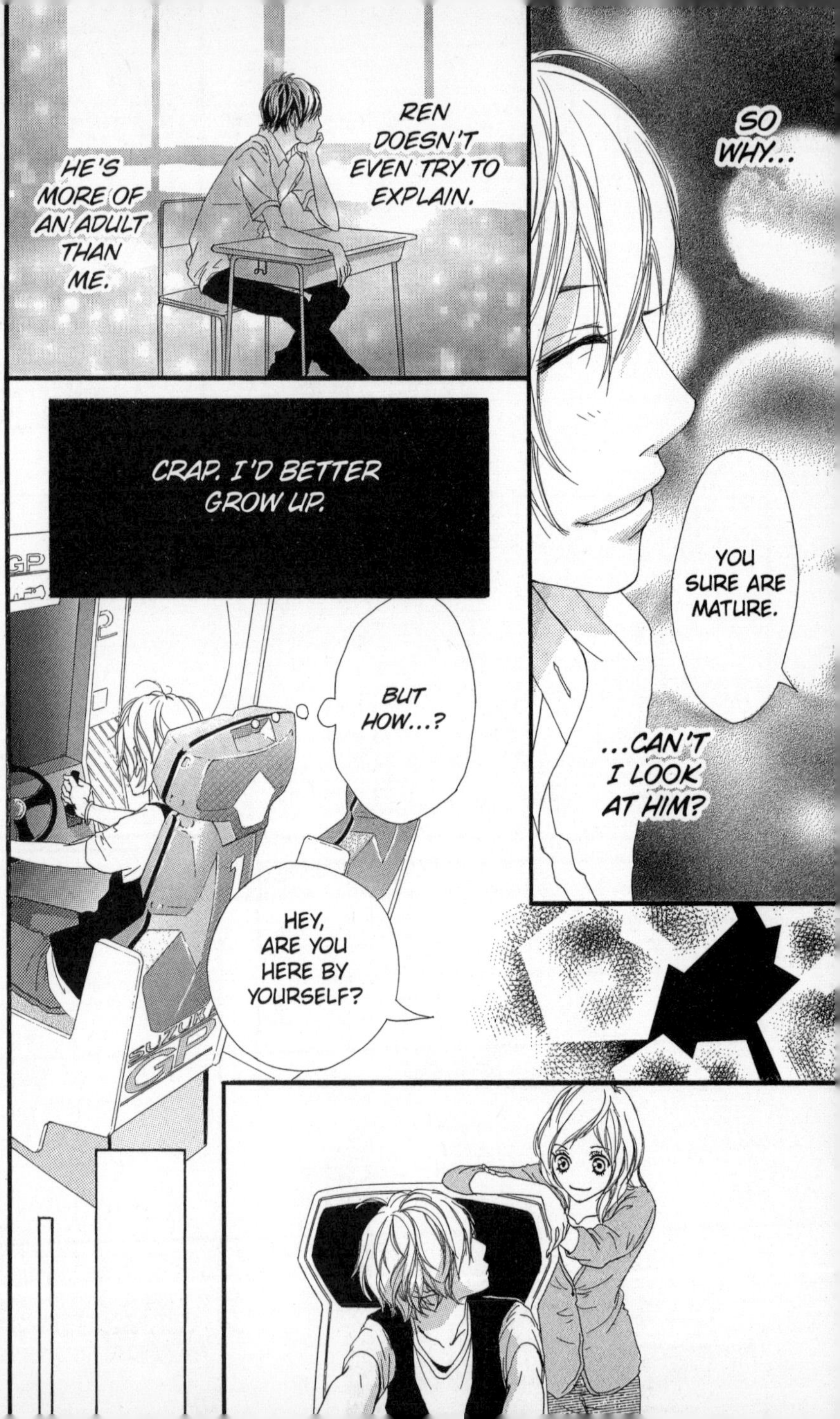
SO WHY...
YOU SURE ARE MATURE.
...CAN'T I LOOK AT HIM?
REN DOESN'T EVEN TRY TO EXPLAIN.
HE'S MORE OF AN ADULT THAN ME.
CRAP. I'D BETTER GROW UP.
BUT HOW...?
HEY, ARE YOU HERE BY YOURSELF?

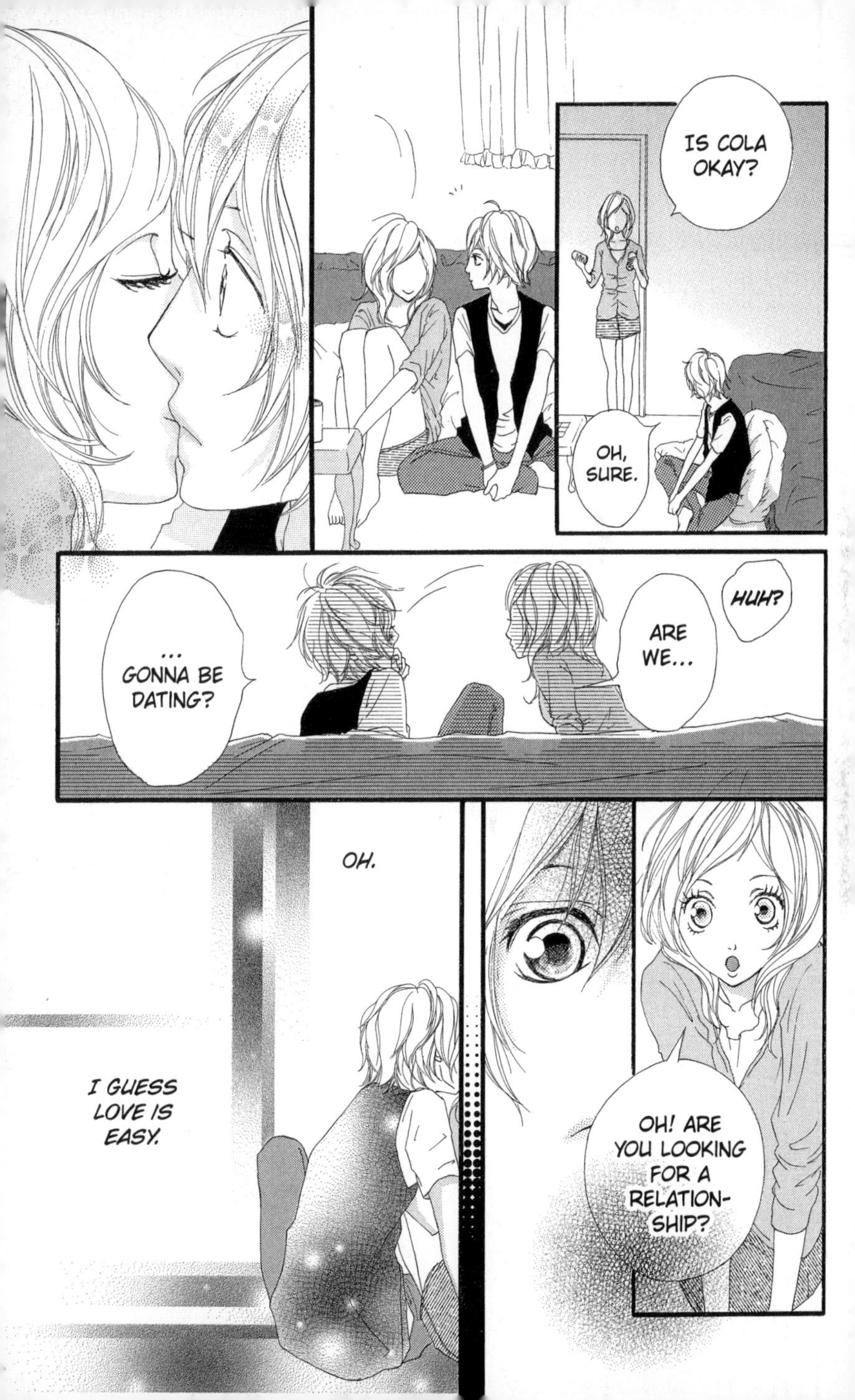
IS COLA OKAY?
OH, SURE.
HUH?
ARE WE...
... GONNA BE DATING?
OH! ARE YOU LOOKING FOR A RELATION-SHIP?
OH.
I GUESS LOVE IS EASY.

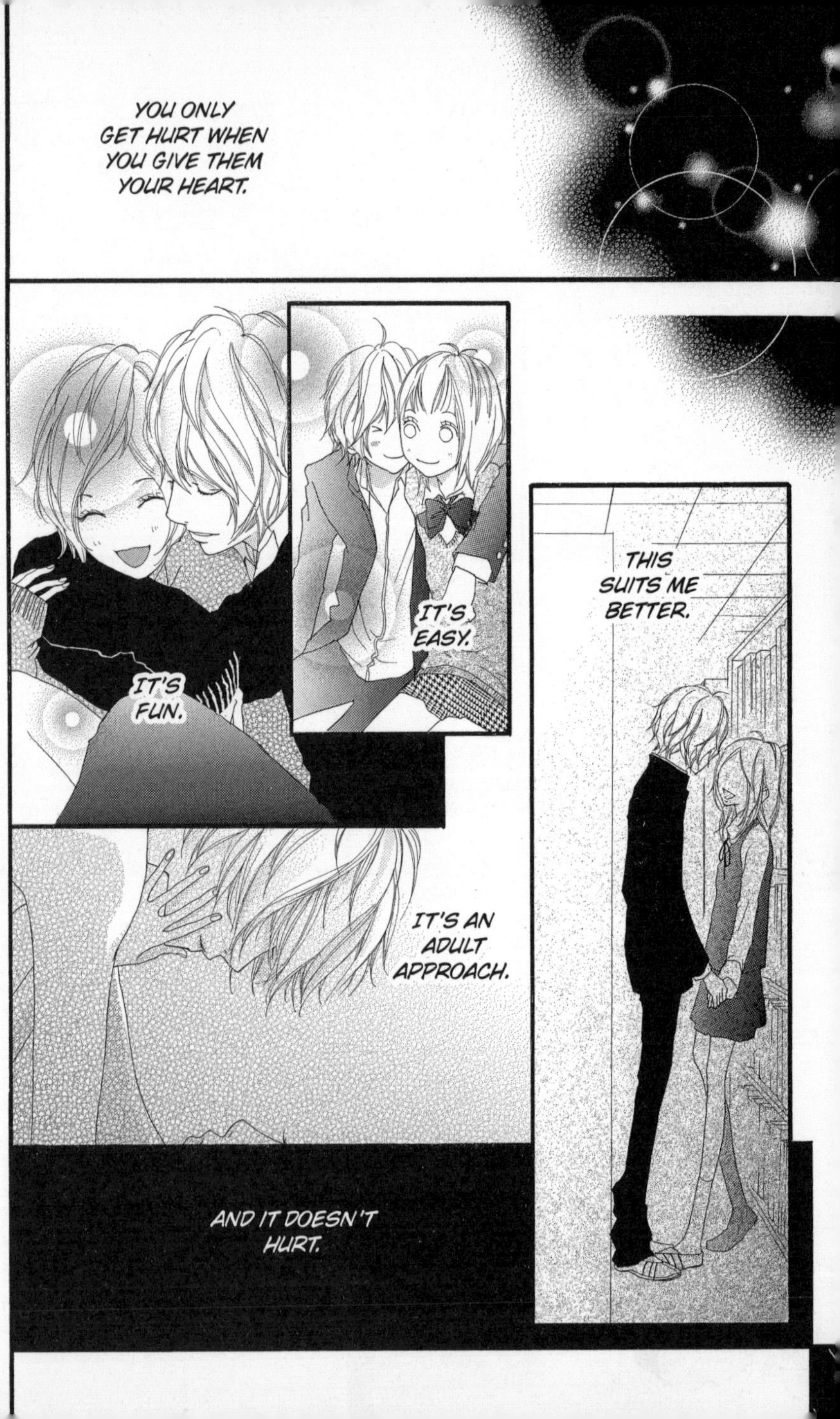
YOU ONLY GET HURT WHEN YOU GIVE THEM YOUR HEART.
IT'S EASY.
IT'S FUN.
THIS SUITS ME BETTER.
IT'S AN ADULT APPROACH.
AND IT DOESN'T HURT.

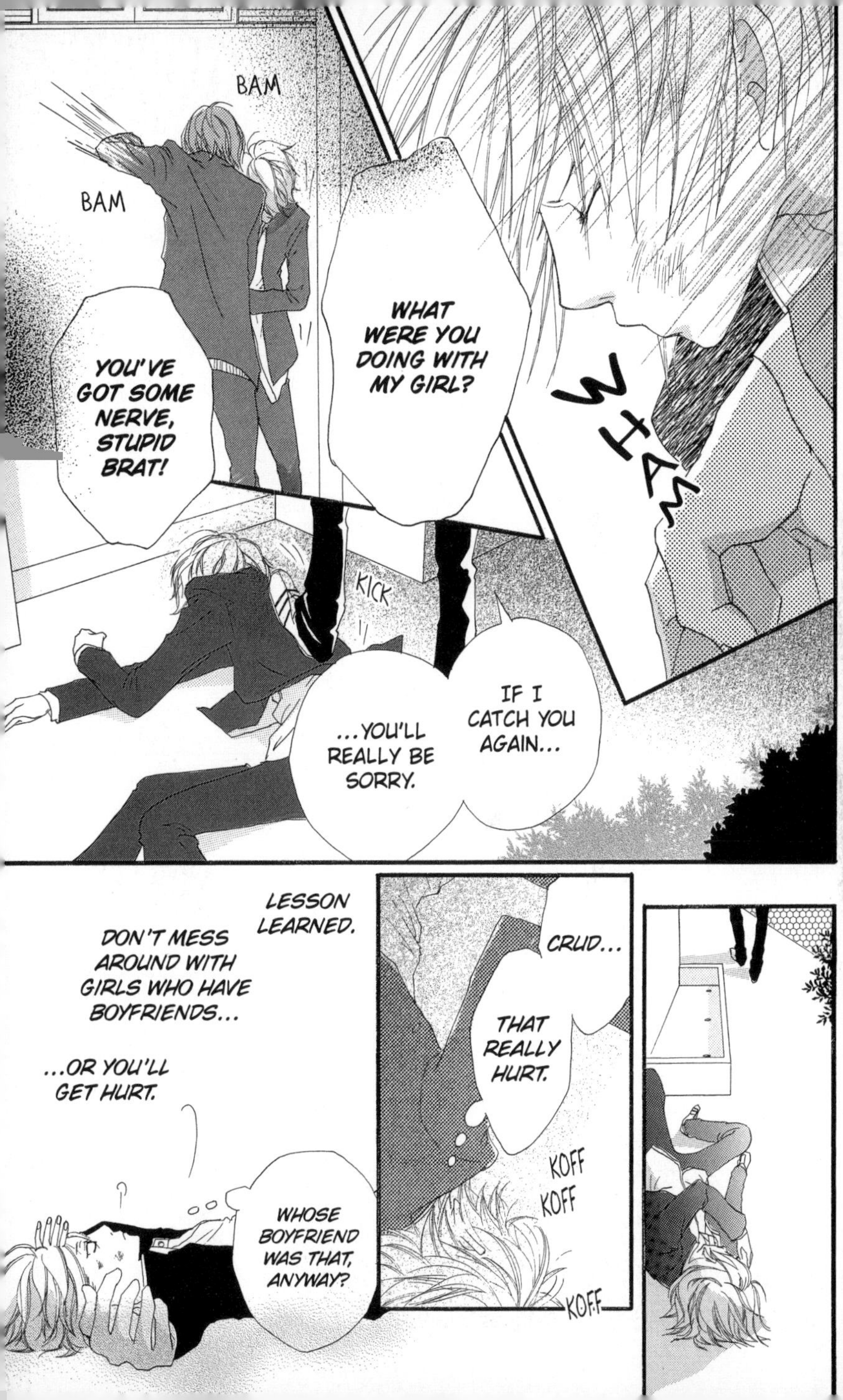
WHAM
BAM
BAM
WHAT WERE YOU DOING WITH MY GIRL?
YOU'VE GOT SOME NERVE, STUPID BRAT!
KICK
IF I CATCH YOU AGAIN...
...YOU'LL REALLY BE SORRY.
CRUD...
THAT REALLY HURT.
KOFF
KOFF
KOFF
LESSON LEARNED.
DON'T MESS AROUND WITH GIRLS WHO HAVE BOYFRIENDS...
...OR YOU'LL GET HURT.
WHOSE BOYFRIEND WAS THAT, ANYWAY?

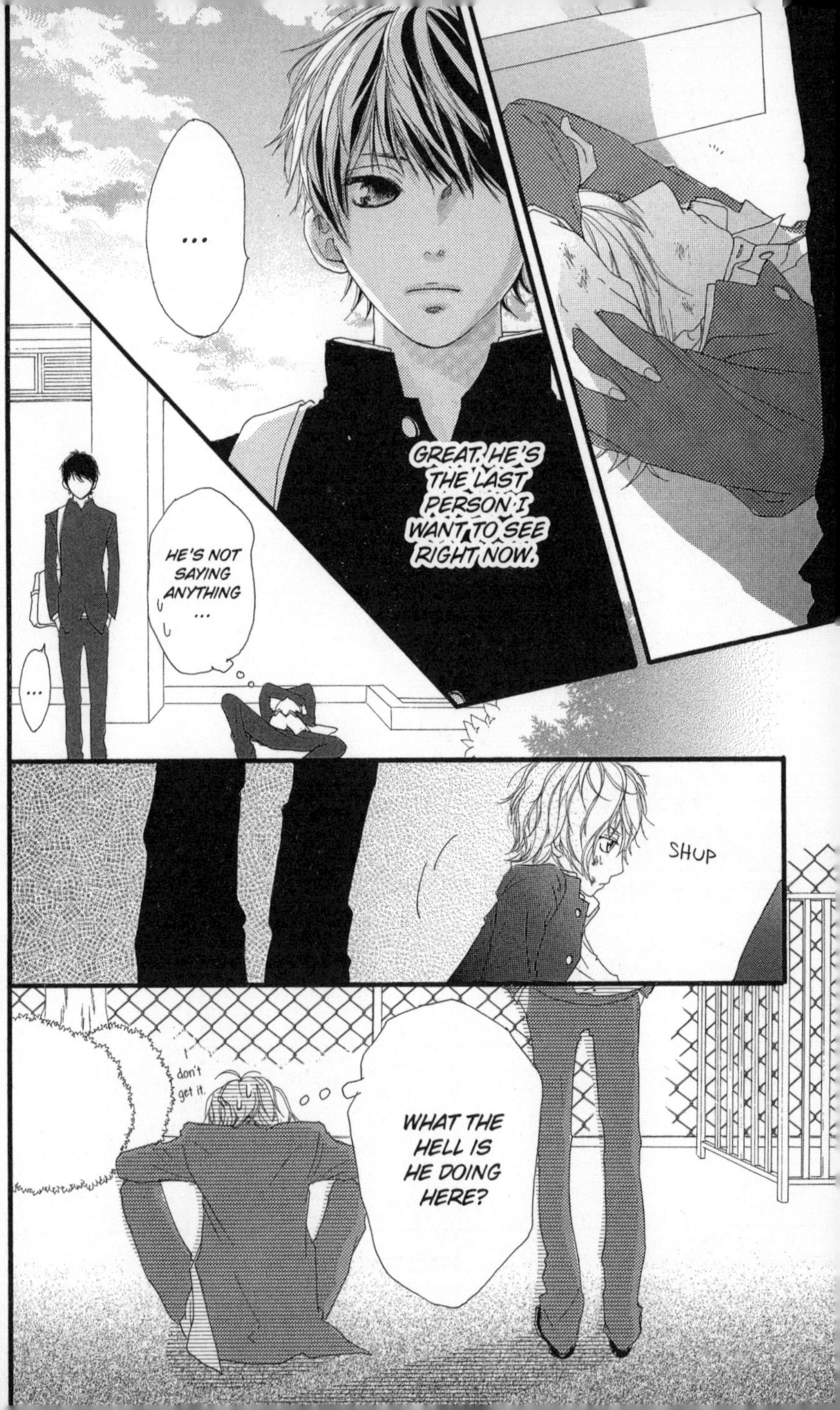
...
GREAT. HE'S THE LAST PERSON I WANT TO SEE RIGHT NOW.
HE'S NOT SAYING ANYTHING ...
...
SHUP
I don't get it.
WHAT THE HELL IS HE DOING HERE?

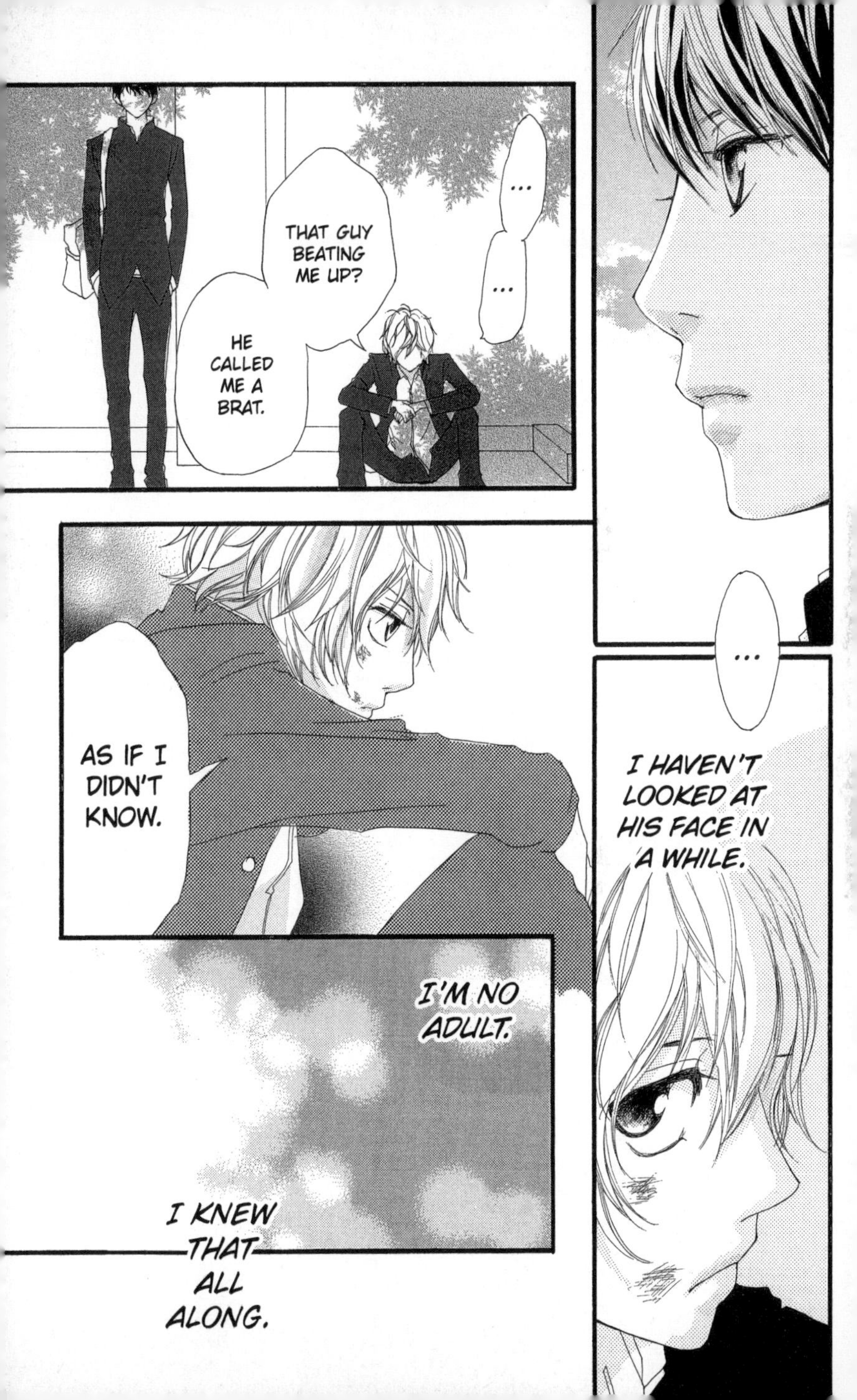
...
...
THAT GUY BEATING ME UP?
HE CALLED ME A BRAT.
AS IF I DIDN'T KNOW.
...
I HAVEN'T LOOKED AT HIS FACE IN A WHILE.
I'M NO ADULT.
I KNEW THAT ALL ALONG.

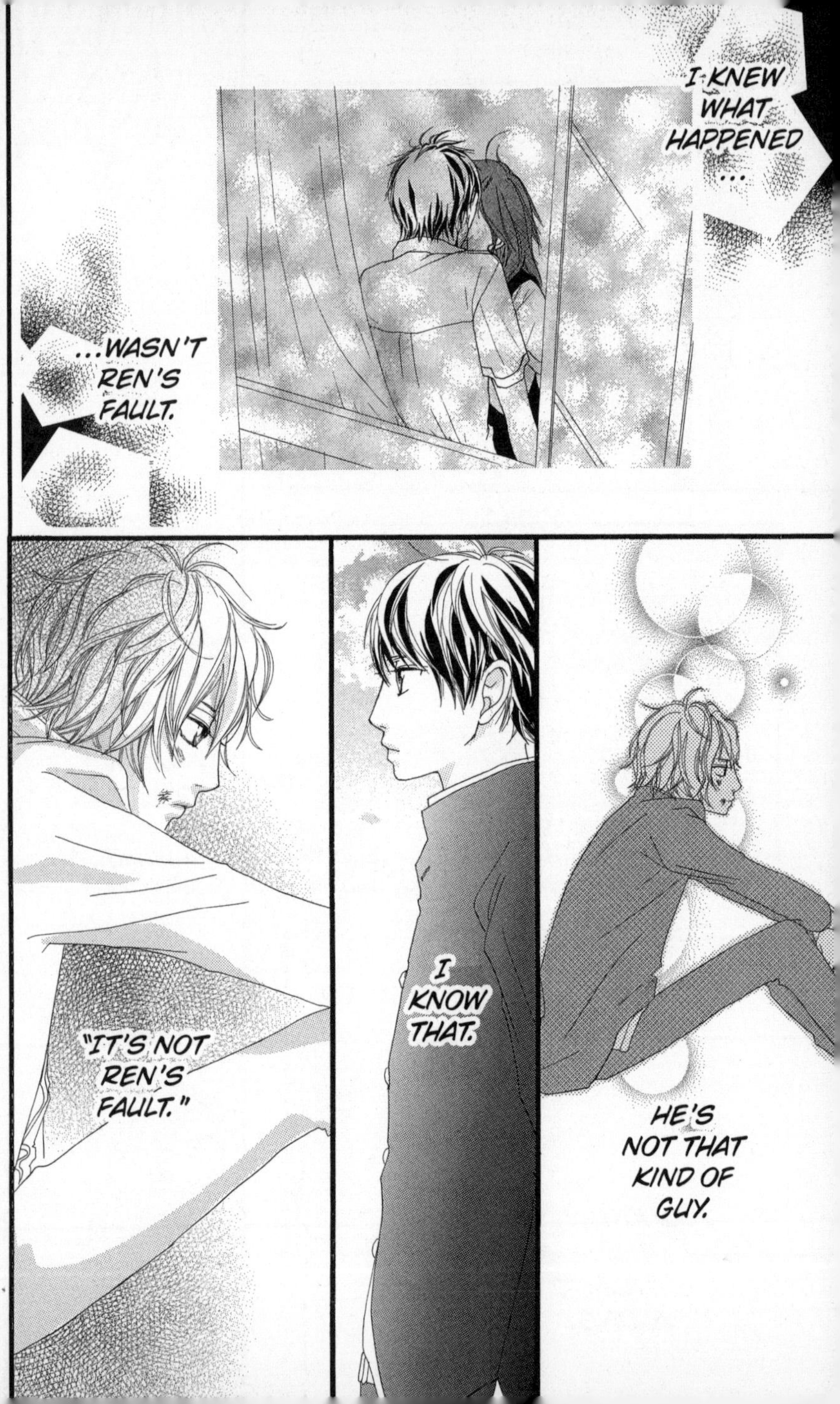
I KNEW WHAT HAPPENED...
...WASN'T REN'S FAULT.
HE'S NOT THAT KIND OF GUY.
I KNOW THAT.
"IT'S NOT REN'S FAULT."

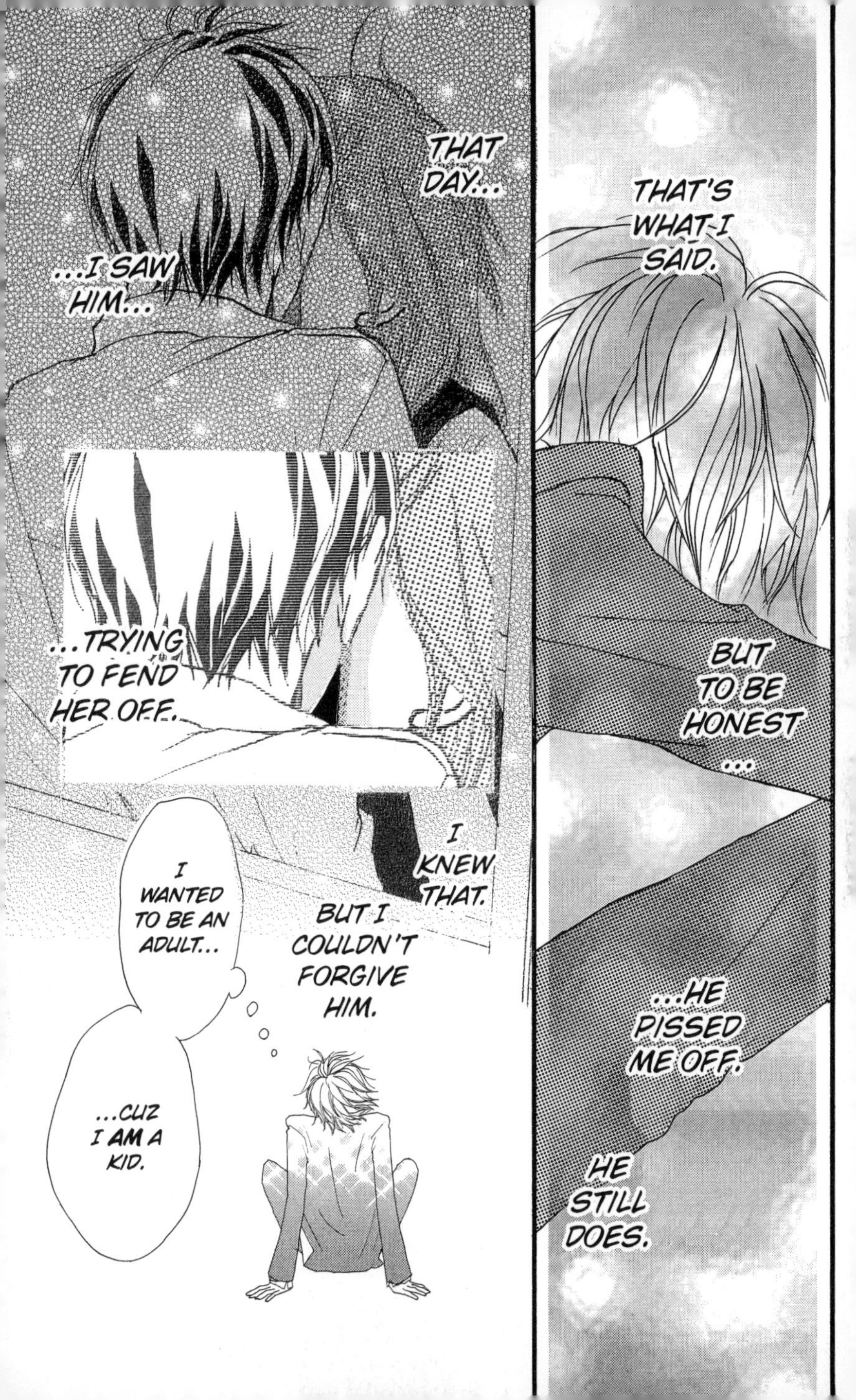
THAT'S WHAT I SAID.
BUT TO BE HONEST...
...HE PISSED ME OFF.
HE STILL DOES.
THAT DAY...
...I SAW HIM...
...TRYING TO FEND HER OFF.
I KNEW THAT.
BUT I COULDN'T FORGIVE HIM.
I WANTED TO BE AN ADULT...
...CUZ I AM A KID.

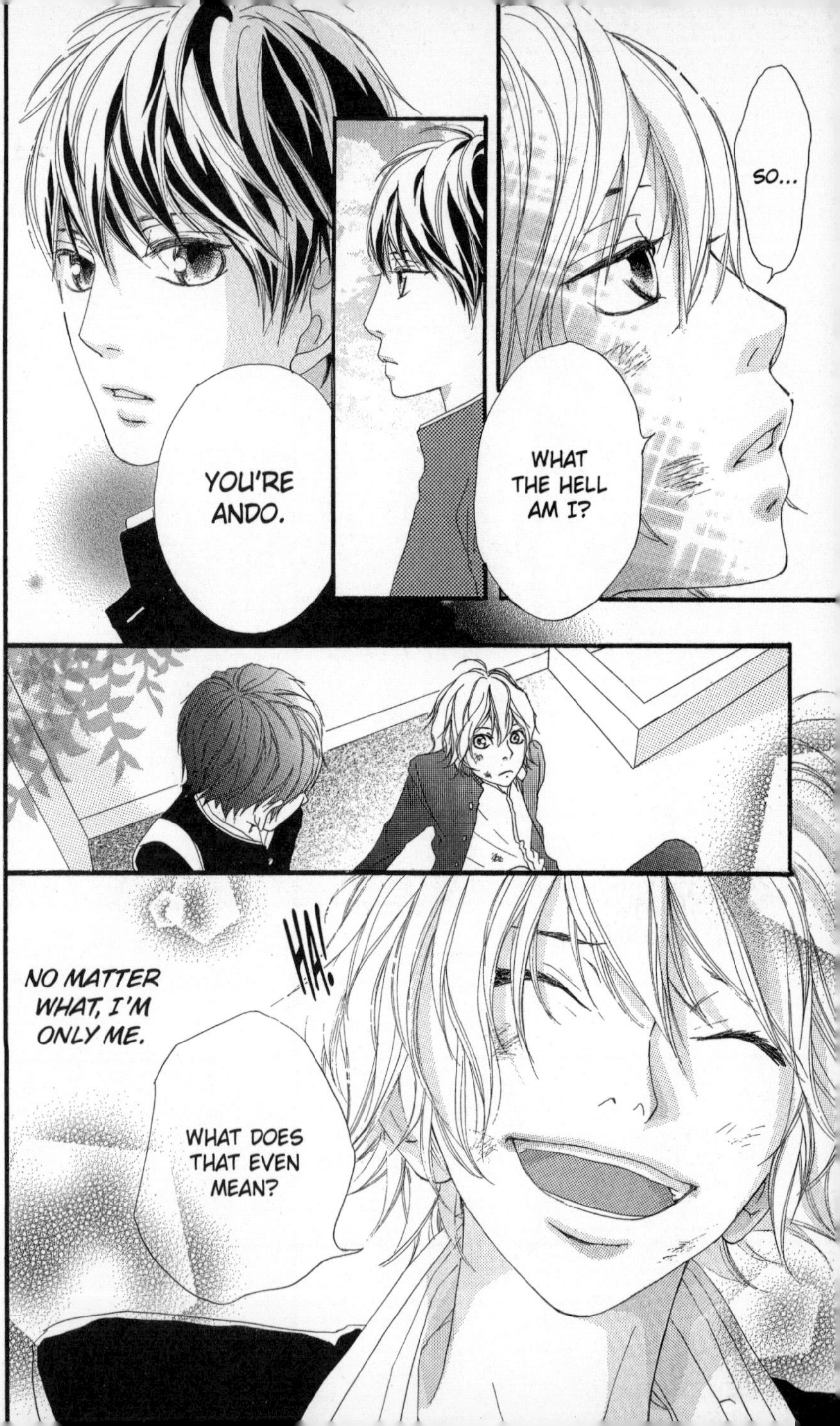
SO...
WHAT THE HELL AM I?
YOU'RE ANDO.
HA!
NO MATTER WHAT, I'M ONLY ME.
WHAT DOES THAT EVEN MEAN?

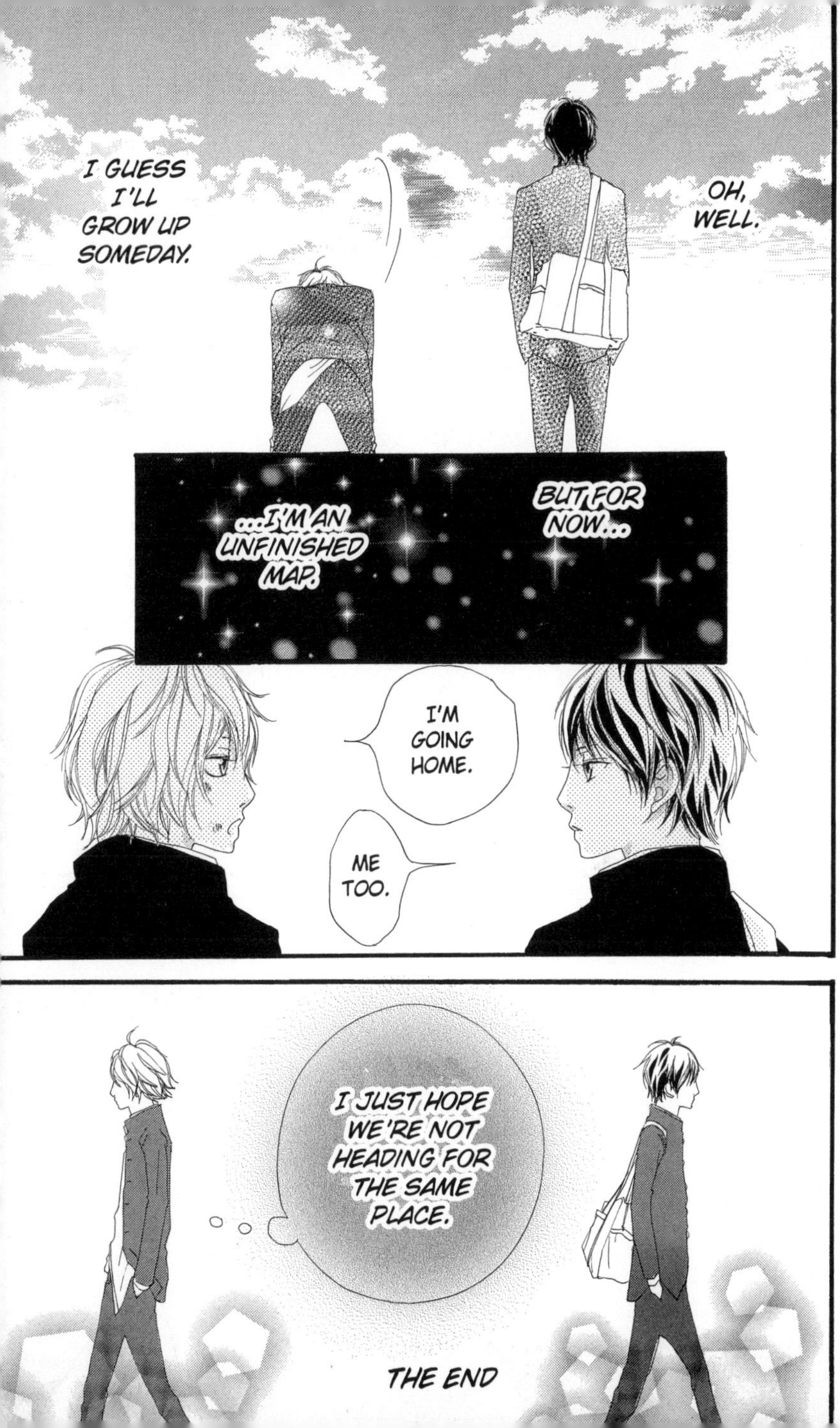
OH, WELL.
I GUESS I'LL GROW UP SOMEDAY.
BUT FOR NOW...
...I'M AN UNFINISHED MAP.
I'M GOING HOME.
ME TOO.
I JUST HOPE WE'RE NOT HEADING FOR THE SAME PLACE.
THE END

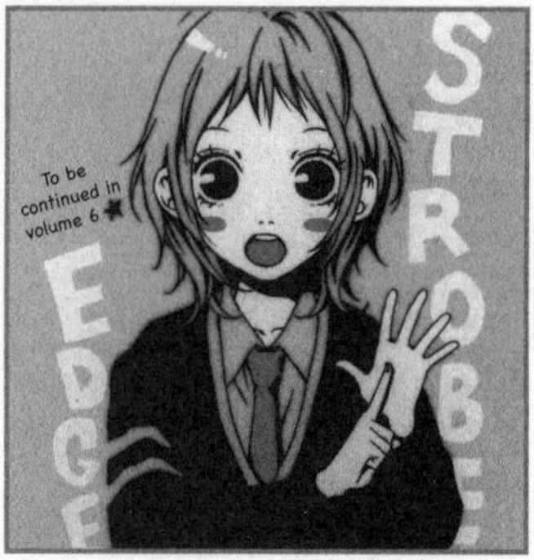
To be continued in volume 6
STROBE EDGE

It's spring.
Spring is my favorite season. I love the feeling of new beginnings. Things begin anew at other times too, but I feel like this sensation is heightened during springtime. To those of you moving up to a new grade, going off to college, starting to work, and everyone else (like myself), I hope something wonderful and new comes your way!

–Io Sakisaka

Born on June 8, Io Sakisaka made her debut as a manga creator with *Sakura, Chiru*. Her works include *Call My Name*, *Gate of Planet*, and *Blue*. Her current series, *Ao Haru Ride*, is currently running in *Bessatsu Margaret* magazine. In her spare time, Sakisaka likes to paint things and sleep.

STROBE EDGE
Vol. 5
Shojo Beat Edition

STORY AND ART BY
IO SAKISAKA

English Adaptation/Ysabet MacFarlane
Translation/JN Productions
Touch-up Art & Lettering/John Hunt
Cover Design/Shawn Carrico
Interior Design/Yukiko Whitley
Editor/Amy Yu

STROBE EDGE © 2007 by Io Sakisaka
All rights reserved.
First published in Japan in 2007 by SHUEISHA Inc., Tokyo.
English translation rights arranged by SHUEISHA Inc.

The rights of the author(s) of the work(s) in this publication to be so identified
have been asserted in accordance with the Copyright, Designs and Patents Act 1988.
A CIP catalogue record for this book is available from the British Library.

The stories, characters and incidents mentioned in this publication are
entirely fictional.

Printed in the U.S.A.

Published by VIZ Media, LLC
P.O. Box 77010
San Francisco, CA 94107

10 9 8 7 6 5 4 3 2 1
First printing, July 2013

www.viz.com   www.shojobeat.com

 PARENTAL ADVISORY
STROBE EDGE is rated T for Teen and is
recommended for ages 13 and up. This
volume contains suggestive themes.
ratings.viz.com

Surprise!

You may be reading the wrong way!

It's true: In keeping with the original Japanese comic format, this book reads from right to left—so action, sound effects, and word balloons are completely reversed. This preserves the orientation of the original artwork—plus, it's fun! Check out the diagram shown here to get the hang of things, and then turn to the other side of the book to get started!

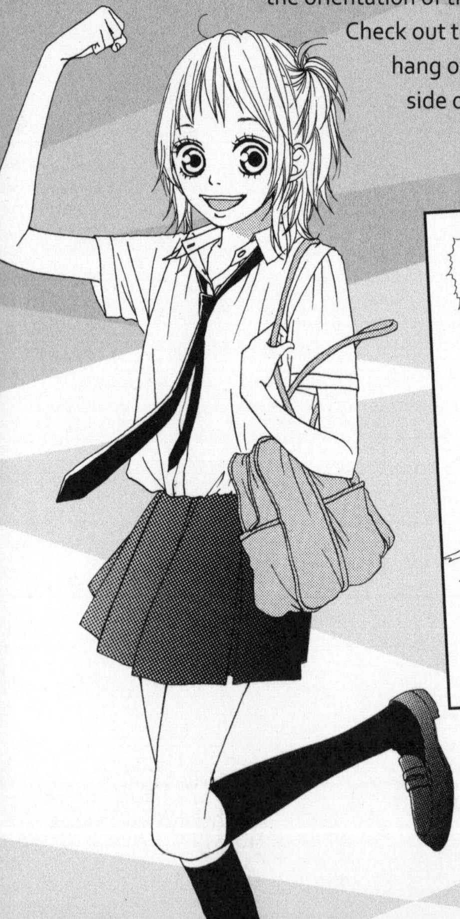

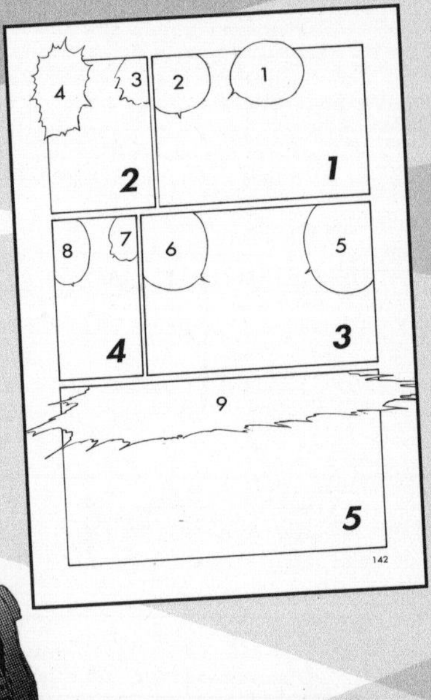
1
2
3
4
1
2
5
6
7
8
3
4
9
5
142